Politics in India

Providing a comprehensive analysis of the broad spectrum of India's politics, this introductory text explains the key features of politics in India in a comparative and accessible narrative, illustrated with relevant maps, life stories, visuals, statistics and public opinion. Familiar concepts of comparative politics are used to highlight the policy process, with a focus on anti-poverty measures, liberalization of the economy, nuclearization, and relations with the United States and Asian neighbours such as Pakistan and China.

The author raises several key questions relevant to Indian politics, including:

* Why has India succeeded in making a relatively peaceful transition from colonial rule to a resilient, multi-party democracy in contrast to her neighbours?
* How has the interaction of modern politics and traditional society contributed to the resilience of post-colonial democracy?
* How did India's economy – moribund for several decades following Independence – make a breakthrough into rapid growth and can India sustain it?
* And finally, why have collective identity and nationhood emerged as the core issues for India in the twenty-first century?

Introducing the novice to India, this accessible, genuinely comparative account of India's political evolution also engages the expert in a deep contemplation of the nature of strategic manoeuvring within India's domestic and international context. In addition to pedagogical features such as text boxes, a set of further readings is provided as a guide to readers who wish to go beyond the remit of this text.

Subrata K. Mitra is Professor of Political Science at the South Asia Institute, Heidelberg University, Germany, and a Visiting Fellow at the Centre for the Study of Developing Societies, Delhi. His publications include *The Puzzle of India's Governance* (2005), (co-author) *A Political and Economic Dictionary of South Asia* (2006), *Modern Politics of South Asia* (5 volumes, 2008), and *Power, Protest and Participation* (1992), all published by Routledge, and he is the series editor of the Routledge *Advances in South Asian Studies* series. He is currently engaged in a comparative study of marginality, empowerment and citizenship. Subrata Mitra is the coordinator of 'Governance and Administration', one of the four research areas of the 'Cluster of Excellence', 'Asia and Europe in a Global Context: Shifting Asymmetries in Cultural Flows' at Heidelberg University, and supported by the German Research Council (DFG).

Politics in India

Structure, process and policy

Subrata K. Mitra

Routledge
Taylor & Francis Group

LONDON AND NEW YORK

First published 2011
by Routledge
2 Park Square, Milton Park, Abingdon, Oxon OX14 4RN

Simultaneously published in the USA and Canada
by Routledge
270 Madison Ave, New York, NY 10016

Routledge is an imprint of the Taylor & Francis Group, an informa business

Typeset in Times New Roman by
Florence Production Ltd, Stoodleigh, Devon
Printed and bound in Great Britain by
TJ International Ltd, Padstow, Cornwall

British Library Cataloguing in Publication Data
A catalogue record for this book is available from the British Library

Library of Congress Cataloging in Publication Data
Mitra, Subrata Kumar, 1949–.
  Politics in India: structure, process and policy/Subrata K. Mitra.
      p. cm.
    Includes bibliographical references and index.
  1. India – Politics and government.   2. Democracy – India.
  3. Postcolonialism – India.   4. Comparative government.
  5. India – Social conditions.   6. India – Economic conditions.
  I. Title.
  JQ231.M56 2011
  320.954 – dc22   2010003328

ISBN 978-0-415-58588-0 (hbk)
ISBN 978-0-415-58589-7 (pbk)
ISBN 978-0-203-84686-5 (ebk)

Contents

Figures

Diagrams

Tables

Maps

Boxes

Preface

India gained Independence from British colonial rule on 15 August, 1947. The status of a free-standing actor in international politics came a little later, on 26 January, 1950, when the country became a republic. The new Republic of India chose, nevertheless, to remain a member of the British Commonwealth. The path that this ancient civilization took to Independence was different from many other non-western countries which became free in the twentieth century. India was liberated from colonial rule not through a violent overthrow of the colonial power, but on the basis of prolonged, mostly non-violent agitation and negotiation, leading to the transfer of power by the British rulers to their Indian successors. The process of the Transfer of Power through which Independence came has deeply affected the state, society, economy and the international profile of India.

When it came, Independence was marked by excitement and jubilation, but sorrow and anxiety as well. Unprecedented civil strife resulting from the partition of British India on the basis of religion marked the coming of Independence. Millions of Hindu, Muslim and Sikh refugees fled across the new frontier that divided British India into Pakistan and India – the successor states – which immediately locked into a lingering war over Kashmir. The memory of these events continues to affect domestic politics in India and Pakistan, embitters Hindu–Muslim relations, severely affects security in the subcontinent, and continues to poison relations between the two neighbours.

With the story of Independence in the background, this book raises several key questions. Why has India succeeded in making a relatively peaceful transition from colonial rule to a resilient, multi-party democracy in contrast to her neighbours, which also emerged from colonial rule at the same time as India? How has the interaction of modern politics and traditional society contributed to the resilience of post-colonial democracy? How have India's local, regional and national leaders, straddling the modern state and traditional society, sustained First World institutions in the setting of a Third World society and economy? How did India's economy – moribund for several decades following Independence – make a breakthrough into rapid growth, and can India sustain it? Why has India, long an advocate of peace and non-alignment, acquired the nuclear bomb, and what implication does this have for global order? And finally, why have collective identity and nationhood emerged as the core issues of India in the twenty-first century? The book formulates answers to these questions through facts, figures and narratives, leavened with a flavour of everyday life in India's towns and villages. A set of further readings to guide readers who wish to go beyond the remit of this text is provided in Chapter 10.

The book targets several groups of readers. First and foremost are those who wish to know something about the distinct style of India's politics. It is designed to ease the access of these readers to India's modern institutions, the political process, and the robust but noisy democracy. For readers who might view India's political process merely as extensions of castes and religions, the book sheds light on the hard political negotiations that take place behind the scene. Another group I wish to reach comprises students of comparative politics and political theory, keen to learn the results of the Indian 'experiment' in transplanting liberal democracy onto alien political soil. The analysis of India's record would help them compare the legacy of the anti-colonial movement and political innovations that have been made since Independence. Yet another group of readers that interests me is made up of men and women of action, committed to global issues like democracy, poverty, development, human rights, identity and environment. I hope they will find some new insights into how India has attempted to cope with these complex challenges of our times. Finally, I would like this book to bring to Indians abroad – the 'Indian Diaspora' – knowledge of the country's politics and economy, and of the unique identity and emerging opportunities of contemporary India, the result of the conflation of indigenous tradition and western modernity.

Many in the western world had seen the coming of India's Independence as an experiment in orderly decolonization and transition to democracy. Indians, like people in other newly emerging Afro-Asian post-colonial states, aspired to the same modern institutions, standard of living and dignity as their former western rulers. After six decades of Independence, the Indian case is ripe for a stock taking in terms of the widespread sense of agency, institutional arrangement and innovation, and most of all, the transition to democratic governance. That adds a comparative dimension to this study.

In writing this book, I have benefited very much from my teaching and research over the past three decades in India, the United States, France, the United Kingdom and Germany. The students, readers, colleagues, critics and teachers who have helped shape my approach to politics are far too numerous for me to be able to thank them personally. I can only hope that they will recognize themselves in the text. At Routledge, my editor Dorothea Schaefter has alternated in her double role of policing the time-line and nurturing the spirit. I would like to thank the members of the Cluster of Excellence 'Asia and Europe in a Global Context: Shifting Asymmetries in Cultural Flows', funded by the German Research Council (DFG) for academic support, criticism and friendship. As always, Professor G. Bingham Powell of the Department of Political Science, University of Rochester, and Professor Bruce Bueno de Mesquita of New York University have remained a source of advice and inspiration. Finally, I would like to thank Professor Harihar Bhattacharayya and Ivo Bielitz; Radu Carciumaru, Dominik Frommherz, Anja Kluge, Lion Koenig and Markus Pauli for their critical reading of the manuscript in its final stage; Nils Harm for drawing the maps; and Sarah Enticknap for her meticulous attention to the proofs.

As an undergraduate in the 1990s, my daughter Emilie had asked for a text on Indian politics that would 'say it as it is'. The idea had appealed to me then. Sadly, in writing as in life, the urgent takes precedence over the essential. In the end, the project took longer than I had intended. But, now that the book is finally there, I would still like to offer it to Emilie, with the hope that she will find in it something of the India of her childhood and plenty of the India of now.

Heidelberg, September 2010

Abbreviations

ABVP	Akhil Bharatiya Vidyarthi Parishad
ADMK	Anna Dravida Munetra Kazagam
AICC	All India Congress Committee
AIDMK	All India Dravida Munetra Kazhgam
AISSF	All India Sikh Students' Federation
BJP	Bharatiya Janata Party
BKS	Bharatiya Kisan Sangh
BSP	Bahujan Samaj Party
CBI	Central Bureau of Investigation
CPI	Communist Party of India
CPI (M-L)	Communist Party of India (Marxist-Leninist)
CPI(M), CPM	Communist Party of India (Marxist)
CrPC	Criminal Procedure Code
CWC	Congress Working Committee
CSDS	Centre for the Study of Developing Societies, Delhi
DK	Dravida Kazhagam
DMK	Dravida Munnetra Kazhagam
DRDA	District Rural Development Agency
FBL	All-India Forward Bloc
GNP	Gross National Product
IAS	Indian Administrative Service
IFDP	Indian Federal Democratic Party
INC	Indian National Congress. A breakaway faction of the Congress, founded in 1978 by Devaraj Urs, renamed in 1981 as Indian Congress (Socialist)
IPC	Indian Penal Code
JD	Janata Dal
JNP	Janata Party
LF	Left Front (in West Bengal)
LJNS	Lok Jan Shakti Party
MDMK	Marumalarchi Dravida Munnetra Kazhagam
MLA	Member of the Legislative Assembly
MP	Member of Parliament (of either the Lok Sabha or the Rajya Sabha)
NCP	Nationalist Congress Party
NDA	National Democratic Alliance

NES	National Election Study (of the CSDS)
NF	National Front (the Janta Dal and its allies)
NTC	National Trinamool Congress
OBC	Other Backward Classes
PDS	Party for Democratic Socialism
PMK	Pattali Makkal Katchi
RJD	Rashtriya Janata Dal
RPI	Republican Party of India
RSP	Revolutionary Socialist Party
RSS	Rashtriya Swayamsevak Sangh
SGPC	Shiromani Gurudwara Prabandhak Committee
SP	Samajwadi Party
SRC	States' Reorganization Commission, 1957
TDP	Teluga Desam Party
UPA	United Progressive Alliance
WTO	World Trade Organization

Glossary

Adivasi	Forest-dwelling aboriginal tribes
Ahimsa	Sanskrit for non-violence, an important element of the politics of Mahatma Gandhi
Bandh	Collective cessation of public activities
Bhadralok	Upper strata of society in Eastern India
Bhukh	Hindi for 'hunger', is used in particular forms of strike, e.g. *bhukh hartal*, meaning 'hunger strike'
Booth Capturing	Forcible take-over of a polling booth by criminal elements with the intention of appropriating the votes
Boycott	A form of strike action where all contact is broken off
Brahmin	Member of the first *varna*; the priestly class
Dak bungalow	Outposts of the British Raj in the country, temporary home to civilian officers on tour, still in use all over India
Dalal	Commission agent
Dalit	Literally, oppressed; often refers to the Scheduled Castes
Dharma	Universal cosmic law, specific to Hindu scriptures and social practice
Dharna	A form of sit-in strike
Devaswam Boards	Set up during British rule to administer religious property in South India. Similar administrative bodies were set up in other parts of the colony as well. Their successor institutions are still responsible for the administration of religious property.
Durbar	A royal court in a traditional set-up. The practice was taken over by British rulers and was organized on occasions of great imperial significance.
Emerging Markets	Less developed countries where new markets for global trade and servces are emerging
Gherao	To surround a decision-maker
Harijan	Literally, children of God; coined by Mahatma Gandhi to give respectability to the former Untouchables
Hartal	Strike action
Jail Bharo	To fill the jails in a form of radical protest
Jajmani	Traditional system of patron–client relationship
Jati	Localized caste
Joint Venture	Private corporations with Indian and foreign partners

Karma	Accumulated result of past actions
Kharif	Monsoon crop
Kisan	Literally, peasant
Kshatriya	Member of the second *varna*; the warrior, governing or princely class
Mixed Economy	A core principle of India's developmental model based on public private partnership
Moksha	Salvation; ultimate liberation from the nexus of rebirth
Neta	A vernacular term for 'leader'
Morcha	A demonstration intended as a show of force
Panchayat	Village council
Panchayati Raj	Local self-government at the village, sub-district and the district level (literally, the rule of the five)
Panchayat Samiti	Area council, consisting of village *panchayats*
Partition	The territorial division of British India in 1947 into the independent states of India and Pakistan
President's Rule	Direct rule by the central govrnment in a federal state (under Article 356 of the Indian constitution)
Quota Permit Raj	Literally, a regime based on the grant of quotas, permits and licences – an expression used to indicate patronage as a part of the politics of the INC
Rabi	Winter crops
Raj	Literally, rule; hence, British Raj or *Panchayati Raj*
Rasta Roko	Hindi for stopping vehicular traffic as a part of a protest movement
Reservation Policy	The policy of setting aside a quota of jobs in public services and places in educational institutions for underpriviledged social groups
Riots	Criminal uprising of five or more people
Sadhu	Hindu holy man
Sanskritization	A traditional method of upward social mobility practised by lower Hindu castes, consisting of imitating rituals and dress of the upper castes
Sarkar	Hindi for 'government'
Sarpanch	Leader of a *panchayat*
Satyagraha	In Sanskrit 'holding on to truth', employed most famously by Mahatma Gandhi against British colonial rule
Scheduled Castes	Formerly untouchable communities grouped together by the government under Article 341 of the Indian constitution which entitles them to special privileges under the policy of reservation
Scheduled Tribes	Forest-dwelling tribes grouped together by the government under Article 342 of the Indian constitution which entitles them to special privileges under the policy of reservation
Sudras	The lowest stratum (*varna*) of the Hindu caste system
Swadeshi	A term popularized by Mahatma Gandhi to refer to the consumption of only home-made goods
Swaraj	Hindi for 'self-rule' or 'self-determination', popularized by Mahatma Gandhi

Untouchables	Lower orders of the Hindu caste system who are considered ritually polluted
Vaisyas	Literally, 'commoners', members of the third *varna*; traditionally the economically productive classes, such as farmers, merchants, bookkeepers and money lenders
Varna	The four-fold division of Hindu society as referred to in classical texts
Vote Bank	A group of voters whose votes are controlled by a local leader
Zamindari	From the Hindi *zamindar* (landlord); *zamindari* denotes a pratice introduced by the British colonial government
Zilla Parishad	District council, comprising all *Sarpanchs* and other directly elected members

1 Introduction

Modern politics and traditional society in the making of Indian democracy

Men make their history upon the basis of prior conditions.

> Hazel Barnes, paraphrasing Marx, Engels and Sartre, in
> *Search for a Method* (1963) translated by Hazel Barnes
> (1968), p. xviii.

. . . Democracy breaks the chain and severs every link of it.

> Alexis de Tocqueville, quoted in Dumont (1970), p. 1.

Some puzzles of India's politics

Politics in contemporary India can come across as exotic and confusing to those who are unfamiliar with its distinct style. Though in most senses a modern state with an emerging market, India still retains some features of a Third World country. Modern politicians in ethnic garb, mass poverty, urban squalor, traditional rituals and subsistence agriculture co-existing next to state-of-the-art technology mark the landscape of the vast country. With her continental dimensions, ancient traditions, living religions, huge ethnic and linguistic diversity (Box 1.1), expanding market, steady economic growth and an effective but noisy democracy, modern India is a bundle of contradictions. Even for visitors who come equipped with prior knowledge of the country, surprises abound.

A country that still cherishes the non-violent legacies of Gautama Buddha and Mahatma Gandhi, India is nonetheless a proud possessor of the atom bomb. But the bickering within India's political establishment and ambiguity of the nuclear doctrine lead to confusion about the real objectives of India's nuclear policy. India's general elections, the largest in the world in scale, are mostly free and fair but armed troops need to be deployed for safe conduct of the poll. Power changes hands peacefully through democratic elections, but an alarming number of legislators at local and regional levels carry criminal records. Beyond politics, one comes across the same welter of images that are at once baffling and contradictory. Internet cafes, slums and beggars jostle for space in crowded cities; vicious inter-community riots and terrorist attacks come and go, and yet life continues at an even pace, apparently undisturbed. A deeper cultural unity and political consensus appear to underpin the conflict and strife at the surface of the political landscape. The combination of diversity and inequality, the bane of many developing societies, does not appear to disturb the stability of India's democratic political system.[1]

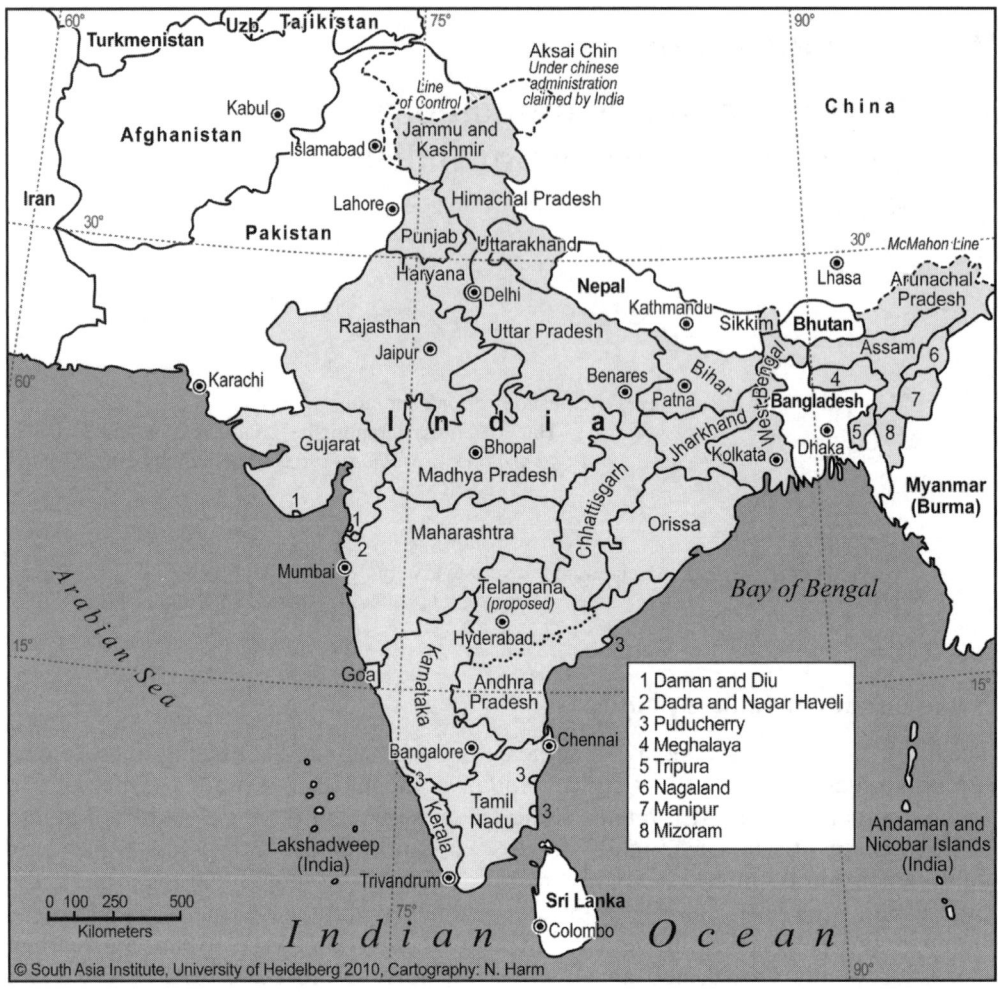

Map 1.1 Political map of India

Compared to the state of affairs in 1947 when India emerged from a century and a half of British colonial rule with a truncated territory and a stagnant economy, the country today offers a picture of remarkable achievements across a number of fields. Most of all, in contrast to the majority of post-colonial states, India has achieved *both* democracy and social change. Seen in cross-national comparison,[2] India belongs to the middle level of developing countries such as Mexico and Iran in terms of health, education and welfare. With regard to scale, China, which has an edge on India in terms of quality of life, is a better point of comparison.[3] However, India's overall ability to sustain democratic governance *and* social change marks her out as exceptional in comparison both to the middle-level developing countries, and to China, calling for detailed investigation.

India's emergence as a major player in the global economy and its growing nuclear and missile delivery capacity constitute yet another case for a detailed study of the country's politics. The economy, torpid under long years of British colonial rule, gathered momentum after independence, but grew only at a pace that many referred to derisively as the 'Hindu rate of growth'[4] during the four decades following Independence, and in consequence, was outpaced by India's competitors, big and small. The breakthrough came in the 1990s with the 'liberalization' of the economy in 1991 that started dismantling the legal and administrative barriers to free trade and industry. The past decade and a half have seen both a respectable rate of growth at about 6 per cent and a significant reduction of mass poverty.[5] Though, like the rest of the world, India's economy has been hit by the economic crisis of 2008–9, the impact has been less severe and might even produce an opportunity for the country to tackle the problem of its infrastructure.[6]

Still, these shining stories of success are framed by a penumbra of a darker hue. Every violent outbreak of conflict between castes, classes, ethnic groups, religious communities or police and demonstrators makes one ask if the relative calm of India is merely a façade, superimposed on mass discontent, seething just under the surface. But in India, a country of apparent contradictions, the opposite argument is equally plausible. Raucous manifestations and unruly crowds often turn out to be in practice a part of political theatre – a quintessentially Indian form of political participation – where the characters are manipulated from behind the scenes by leaders who have themselves risen from the ranks of the discontented, and subsequently have developed a taste for office and a deep stake in the system.[7]

These puzzling facts of Indian politics can be formulated in terms of five inter-related questions aimed at the country's sophisticated political system. Firstly, why did India, in contrast to the majority of post-colonial states, succeed in making a relatively peaceful transition from colonial rule to a resilient, multi-party democracy? Secondly, how did India, long a synonym for mass poverty and low growth, change into a fast-growing economy, with a burgeoning middle class, global networks and

---

Box 1.1 'Unity in diversity'

Population	1,156,897 billion (2009)
Territory	1,269,338 square miles

28 Federal States

7 Union Territories

Official Languages:
English, Hindi (primary tongue of 30 per cent of the population), Bengali, Telugu, Marathi, Tamil, Urdu, Gujarati, Malayalam, Kannada, Oriya, Punjabi, Assamese, Kashmiri, Sindhi, Sanskrit

Religion:
Hindu (80.5 per cent), Muslim (13.5 per cent), Christian (2.3 per cent), Sikh (1.9 per cent), Buddhist (0.8 per cent), Jain (0.4 per cent), others (0.6 per cent)

GDP per capita	$3,700 (2007)
Scheduled Castes	16.2 per cent of the population
Scheduled Tribes	8.2 per cent of the population

ambitions, without curtailing democratic institutions and rights? Thirdly, what is the impact of high growth and integration with the international market economy on the capacity of the economy to tackle mass poverty? Fourthly, how successful has India been in turning her hierarchic society into equal *citizens*, with a moral and political stake in the system?[8] Finally, with regard to global ranking in terms of national security and power, is India still a country that is 'constantly emerging but never quite emerging'?[9]

These questions, important in the context of India, are of general and comparative significance. The book responds to them by drawing on India's complex and diverse culture, economic heritage, political attitudes, the vitality of her social and political processes, the strategies and rhetoric of the political elites, particularly from the lower social classes, and the expanding democratic system that directly affects India's 600,000 villages.[10] The book pitches the analysis of India's politics at three levels of the *system*.[11] The first, *structure*, refers to the main institutional arrangements of the state such as the federation (referred to as the Union in India's constitution), the executive, legislative and judicial organs of the state and the separation of powers, the implementing and quasi-rule-making bodies such as the bureaucracy and national commissions, and the bodies responsible for articulating and aggregating political demands of the electorate such as political parties, interest groups and non-governmental organizations.[12] The second, *process*, refers to the two-way routes that connect the government and the people. These are defined by Almond *et al.* as 'interest articulation, interest aggregation, policymaking, policy implementation and policy adjudication'.[13] The third, *public policy*, broadly refers to what India's federal, regional and local governments do in their day-to-day activities. Grouped under four headings by Mitra (2008b),[14] these functions have implications for the economy, security, social solidarity, identity and foreign affairs, broadly referring to India's standing in the international arena.[15]

Democracy and elite agency: the 'room to manoeuvre in the middle'

The search for answers to these questions points towards a bewildering variety of sources and methods. India has been a subject of fascination for visitors – from ancient Greece onwards – just as it continues to be, for authors of a wide range of modern travelogues.[16] The reference list has been further enriched thanks to the vast post-war literature on democracy, development and modernization, where India features as an interesting, and sometimes deviant, case in point.[17] The liberal, evolutionary, developmental approach that casts the Indian case as part of a general process of democratization is still the most popular among specialists.[18] The opposite genre that focuses on the unique and exceptional character of India goes by the name of Orientalism.[19] A third approach finds the best entry point to India in the caste system, which many see as a unique attribute of the country. One of its best-known exponents is Louis Dumont, whose *homo hierarchicus* presents Indian society in terms of the cohesive bond of caste – an inter-dependent social network based on complementary status and function – which has held Indian society together through millennia, despite foreign invasion and other forms of political dislocation.[20] At the other extreme are various shades of Marxist analysts who cast Indian society in terms of a state of disequilibrium, caused by the main contradiction between the owners of capital and land on the one hand, and the emerging classes of peasants and workers on the other.[21]

The main approach to Indian politics in this book[22] combines elements of several schools of thought. While retaining the structural-functional core of the liberal modernization approach, the analysis undertaken here brings on board conflict – of classes, castes, ethnic groups, regions and religions – as an integral part of India's political process and not merely as its aberration. Culturally embedded categories of affinity, loyalty, kin solidarity, identity or religion are seen as important phenomena in their own right and not necessarily as the sublimation of some deeper value, such as class or the Indian 'way of life'. My approach puts the main burden of explanation on the role of the state as *both* neutral and partisan, and the capacity of the political elites – both those in power and those contesting it – dispersed over the system, mobilizing supporters comprising men and women acting in their own interest or according to their own beliefs. These leaders and followers are *rational* actors in the sense that they consciously pursue their goals and combine all the resources – material, symbolic and moral – at their command to bring influence to bear on the decision-maker, hoping for an outcome favourable to them.[23]

These decision-makers – *netas* in Hindi – or leaders are located at the crucial nodes of the political system such as the federal government, regional States, district headquarters and local government. They are ubiquitous, ensconced in public commissions, departments of the government and semi-official bodies, political parties and movements and other arenas of public and sometimes private life. Socially, they are a heterogeneous body, comprising both men and women (though fewer women than men), the old and young, people from upper social classes just as those from the middle and lower castes (some of whom are recruited through India's functioning quota system), and people of different religions and ethnic origins. What distinguishes them from their fellow citizens is a shared sense of authority; and accountability, both horizontal and vertical. Their ability to act as intermediaries between the traditional society and the modern state – to pass legislation and implement it, to arbitrate, and to innovate new institutional arrangements – without being exclusively identified with either modernity or tradition, explains the success of India's democracy and governance in large measure.[24]

The existence of the room to manoeuvre for political elites in a Third World democracy is by no means automatic, universal or self-evident. Nor is elite capacity, which is crucial to our analysis, only a matter of political will. It is influenced by an ensemble of factors, such as the political context and culture in which the decision-making body is ensconced, the institutional arrangement, the vertical and horizontal accountability of the elites, and the method of their recruitment.[25] Compared to Marxist models of politics in India, which see conflict as natural and necessary, society as bi-polar and choice as preordained, the model in Figure 1.1 introduces the additional parameters of choice on the part of the decision-makers and policy responsiveness (including strategic reform) as a tool of intervention. The perception of elites by ordinary people as responsive and effective can lower the incentive for breaking the law and taking things into their own hands.

The model provides the key argument to the analysis of the structure and process of the Indian political system and the consolidation of Indian democracy. The country's significant achievement in the area of positive discrimination, discussed at length in

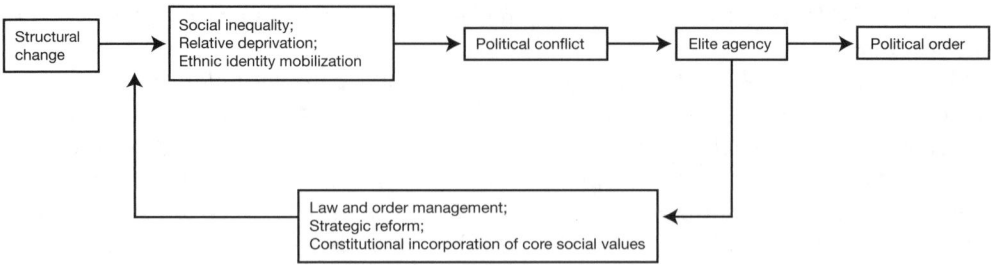

Figure 1.1 Structure, process and policy: the dynamics of India's governance
Source: Drawn by author.

Chapter 3, provides an illustration of how the country has successfully severed the cultural and economic links between caste and occupation, and transformed rebels into stakeholders.[26] Legislative reform and administrative measures have whittled away social privilege, and introduced punitive measures against discrimination. The institution of quotas in education, legislatures and government jobs has permitted former *Untouchables*,[27] who have suffered from centuries of discrimination, to climb the social and political ladder.[28] When elite initiatives result in redistributive policies and constitutional change, they lead to the reduction of perceived inequality and accommodation of normative issues such as that of collective identity. Once abstract issues like values and identity are incorporated into the constitution through appropriate changes in the rules of the game and creation of new arenas, political conflict on values and symbols reverts back to the everyday politics of conflict over material interests.

The account of Indian politics offered in this book is based crucially on the premise that orderly social and economic change is possible when the decision-making elite are able to maintain law and order, undertake the social and economic reform that is strategically important to key political groups and understand and respect core values of society. The process of democratic social change has acquired a steady character in India because, despite occasional lapses, the country's leadership has succeeded in carrying out this task most of the time, and in most places of the vast landscape. The functioning of India's elections, judiciary and the media has ensured that elites remain politically accountable. The fact that most of India's elites, rather than being social notables born to power and privilege, are professional politicians who have risen from the ranks makes them a crucial intermediary between the modern state and traditional society.

The availability of this room to manoeuvre in the middle sets India sharply apart from other post-colonial societies. Political stability in the locality and region in post-Independence India, as in most post-colonial societies, was sharply challenged by socially marginal groups empowered by competitive electoral mobilization. However, the response of the decision-making elites to crises through law and order management, strategic reform and redistributive policies, and constitutional change in order to give legitimacy to contested, embedded values, acted as a corrective measure that contributed to the resilience of the democratic political system.

Democratic legitimacy and current policy challenges

Public policy – the selective and strategic allocation of resources, rather than the threat of violence or manipulation of kin networks – is the main mode of politics in

India. In this, India is not alone, because most political systems, regardless of the level of their affluence, ideological orientation of their leaders and the political assertiveness of their population, need to meet some minimum criteria of performance in order to retain their legitimacy. However, India is different from other developing societies in the sense that though the country lacks the resources and organized interest groups of affluent Western democracies, India's level of participation, using the criterion of electoral participation, is still very impressive. The engagement of elites with policy making in the four areas, namely distribution, extraction, regulation and symbolic outputs, remains generally high, though there is considerable variation over the issues involved. The interplay of federalism, elections and party competition, the impartial and socially engaged Indian judiciary and the watchful eye of Indian and international human rights movements have combined to produce a political environment which has helped sustain democracy and development. Each chapter of this book tells the story of the evolution of appropriate institutions, State–society interaction and the making of effective public policy such as scholarships and educational quotas for the children of the underprivileged, midday meal schemes in schools, and loan waivers for farmers in response to specific problems.

In consequence, following sustained governance in the past six decades, today the stock image of India as a Third World country caught in the grooves of persistent poverty and under-development no longer corresponds to reality. The opening up of India's economy to internal and international competition over the past two decades is one of the most important aspects of the environment that influences the making of public policy in India. As India's economy gets gradually integrated with the international market economy, the political institutions, designed during the tumultuous days of the *Transfer of Power* and the violence of the *Partition* – discussed at length in Chapter 2 – are called upon to face new, unforeseen challenges. The emerging markets, joint ventures and the availability of skilled, low-cost professionals adept with new information technologies are a challenge as well as an opportunity for Western business and industry.

As macro-economic decisions taken by elites at the national level cascade down the levels of government of the vast country, their reverberations affect lives and political processes in the federal States, districts and villages, calling for counter-mobilization by the disaffected. The international visibility of India's successful IT sector and the outsourcing of routine, clerical functions by many of the world's major companies to India to take advantage of lower wages and the rate of economic growth at about 8 per cent may have temporarily shifted attention away from India's mass poverty. But the issue of poverty returns to haunt the politicians and bureaucrats at the time of elections. Even by India's modestly defined poverty rate, about 29 per cent of the population continues to be classified as poor.[29] The reduction in numbers, which used to be as high as 50 per cent of the population in 1995, gives some scope for optimism. But the gains of economic growth have not trickled down to the hard core poor, trapped in inaccessible parts of the country which are beyond the pale of the market and the competitive political process.[30] To the list of the deprived one has to add the 'new poor' – deeply indebted farmers whose sad fate has come to the attention of the world through spectacular cases of suicide.

India's infrastructure is yet another challenge to the policy maker. It is basically a remnant from the colonial days when roads and railway lines served security more than commercial interests. In the new global economy of which India aspires to be a part, this has emerged as a major obstacle to sustained growth. Now that the economy has shifted gear, the slow, clumsy roads, the airports and the handling of freight by rail and sea ports are utterly inadequate to the needs of the competitive twenty-first-century world. The same holds for mass literacy, in which India still lags behind the industrial nations as well as China and most of the 'tiger' economies of East Asia. The intellectual back-up for India's prowess in IT, biotechnology and medical research is provided by a few elite institutions such as the world-famous IIT (Indian Institution of Technology), IIM (Indian Institute of Management) and the major metropolitan universities. Beyond these institutions, which cater to the educational needs of a small section of the population, the infrastructure for mass literacy and the kind of technical training that a growing economy demands is sorely lacking. Under the federal division of powers, education is the responsibility of India's regional governments which makes coordination for mass education difficult to achieve at the national level. There are some indications that the government at the federal and regional levels is responding to this challenge. The current project to build a system of highways that would link India's major cities, started under the previous NDA government and continued by the UPA coalition which has ruled India from 2004, indicates the salience that the government attaches to this issue.

The protection of life, liberty and property of individuals from external and internal threats is an essential function of government. The threat to internal security has emerged as a major source of challenge to public policy making in India. A corollary to this is the entanglement of Indo-Pakistan rivalry with internal security, and its potential for nuclear war, which remains a source of great anxiety. These security concerns affect the flow of capital, investment and trade. The leaders of both India and Pakistan have shown great concern about the effects of terrorism for the growth of trade, communication and development, and opened multiple channels of diplomatic negotiation. The international media geared up for an arms race and the intensification of conflict in South Asia, following the nuclear tests of 1998. But contrary to such apprehensions, soon after the tests, India and Pakistan started a series of negotiations and set up confidence-building measures (CBMs). The hope that the introduction of nuclear deterrence would lower tensions along the Kashmir border was short lived. The outbreak of armed conflict in the Kargil district of Kashmir in 1999, and the build-up of more than a million Indian and Pakistani troops along the Line of Control (LoC) in Kashmir following the terrorist attack on Taj Mahal Palace Hotel, Mumbai (see Figure 1.2), the Trident Oberoi Hotel, the Jewish Chabad Center/Nariman House and the Chhatrapati Shivaji Terminus, again heightened international fears of yet another Indo-Pakistani confrontation, this time with the possible use of nuclear weapons. However, the subsequent resumption of dialogue between India and Pakistan belied this pessimistic prognosis.

The political message one gets from Figure 1.2 is of the two faces of India. Democracy prevails, but terror lurks in the background. Terrorists (who describe themselves as freedom fighters or Mujahiddin) are supported by their sympathizers in Pakistan and Afghanistan, and gain significant local support in India. This cross-border terrorist linkage has emerged as an additional irritant to Indo-Pak relations. Contrary to Indian arguments, Pakistan, for reasons of both solidarity and tactical

Figure 1.2 Taj Mahal Palace Hotel, Mumbai, site of the terrorist attack on 26 November, 2008
Source: *Frontline*, 25 (25), 6–19 December, 2008.

advantage, claims that the terrorists are freedom fighters, seeking to liberate Kashmir from Indian rule. Kashmir, deeply evocative of the memory of India's Partition and the contradictory ideologies about the role of religion espoused by India and Pakistan, is thus a complex issue that needs to be understood in its historical context.[31]

India's Kashmir policy, indicative of the incomplete character of India's national and territorial integration, has a complex genealogy and is a subject of endless debates in the press and in scholarly accounts. However, some of these challenges have helped quicken the pace of national integration and democratic consolidation. The state of Emergency of 1975–77 (see Chapter 4), during which India's democratic process was held in abeyance, has become a distant memory but still serves to unite people in the defence of democratic rights when things appear to get out of hand. Hindu nationalism, which came into prominence as a major political force in the 1980s, has now acquired a legitimate presence within the political spectrum. The venerable Indian National Congress, no longer the hegemonic party which it once was, has learnt to play the game of coalition building and maintenance, creating a reasonably stable political environment with two broad-based centre-left and centre-right coalitions competing against one another (Chapter 6). The label of regionalism no longer evokes the fear of Balkanization that was so characteristic of the politics of the 1950s and 1960s. Instead, one finds large, well-organized regional parties comfortably coalescing with all-India parties at the national level and competing against them in the regional arena.[32]

The distinctiveness of Indian politics: resilience of democracy and governance

The policy challenges discussed above, involving governments at the federal, regional and local levels, against the backdrop of India's democratic political system, free media and politically assertive citizenry, create a dense political field. Compared to the process of interest articulation and aggregation in developed countries, or the middle-level developing countries cohort of which India is a part in terms of some of her social and economic features, however, the manner in which India copes with this challenge has some distinctive features.

Resilient political institutions and orderly rule have long made India an exception in the turbulent political world of changing societies. This record of high governance registered a sharp decline in the 1980s. But this decline did not become terminal, and was reversed steadily after reaching the peak in 1985 (see Diagram 1.1). The level of orderly rule varies widely across regional States; but even there, democratic governance and accountability have been achieved nation-wide, and no part of India has seceded from the country since Independence. India's political resilience has consistently drawn wide interest and generated a lengthy debate.[33] Selig Harrison's early warning of impending chaos in India, *The Most Dangerous Decades* (1965), found a contrast in Rajni Kothari's *Politics in India* (1970) and Morris-Jones's *Government and Politics in India* (1987), both of which have provided succinct explanations of the resilience of India's political institutions.[34]

The resilience of the Indian state and its attempts to generate a level playing field have accelerated the pace and durability of India's democracy.[35] In contrast to the spate of recent travelogues that dwell on factors that make India exceptional,[36] this book focuses on the state and the political process that underpins it. It explains the intricacies of India's multiple political arenas by focusing on the political choices and strategies of India's elites and the vast electorate as they cope with factors such as caste, religious conflict and natural catastrophe that are symbolic of India's presumed uniqueness. Crucial to this story are India's new political elites emerging from the lower social orders who, unlike old-style social notables whom they have increasingly replaced, act as binding factors between tradition and modernity.

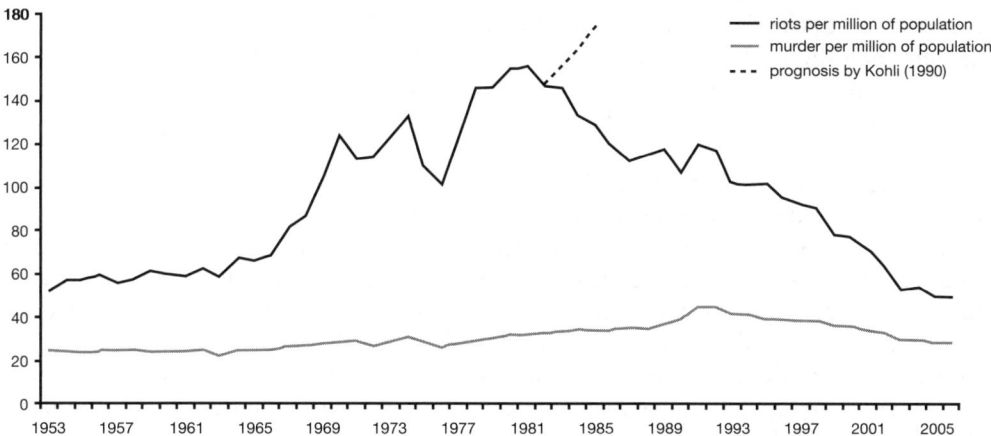

Diagram 1.1 Riots in India (1950–2005)
Source: Adapted from Mitra (2005), p. 8.

They link the diverse and continental dimensions of India's political system together into a functional and cohesive whole.

Level playing fields: the multiple roles of the state in India

Though enthusiasm for bureaucratic planning has considerably waned since 1991 and the state no longer has exclusive control over the 'commanding heights of the economy',[37] the influential role of the government continues to be a part of everyday life all over India.[38] The ubiquitous *sarkar* – government as traditionally referred to in rural India – represents the power of the state, symbolized by towering public buildings, spacious colonial bungalows where ministers and high civil servants reside, and dusty offices in small towns and villages. Civil servants are still required to preside over prize-giving ceremonies in village schools, allocate agricultural subsidies, maintain the safe conduct of the polls, and keep order in religious festivals. Many of the outer symbols of their authority that are colonial in origin remain intact. The omnipresent peon wearing the uniform designed by the *British Raj* is still in evidence in some district towns. The crucial difference between the colonial world and India today, however, lies in the perception of authority by the public. Whereas the British civil servant on horseback was the symbol of the distant, incorruptible, neutral Raj, their post-Independence descendants are seen as part of the outer fringe of India's politics, charged with the task of delivering the goods and open to manipulation by political leaders. This realization, even as it contradicts the norms of rational administration, has immensely contributed to the agency of ordinary people. The survey findings discussed in Chapter 3 show a growing sense of efficacy and entitlement on the part of the citizens of this vast, multi-national country.

The state in India comes across simultaneously as neutral and partisan between competing social interests, and, in practice, can take many different forms. At the centre of its institutional structure one can find a constant evocation of the traditional paternalism of the pre-modern Indian state. Beyond that is the usual paraphernalia of the liberal state, committed to the dignity of man, and more recently, to the freedom of individual enterprise from bureaucratic meddling. The core institutions of the state also embody the tradition of European social democracy in terms of a commitment to social justice. Finally, there is also the spectre of the occasional breakdown of the liberal superstructure, and the abuse of the authority of the state for personal benefit.[39]

Creating a level playing field is the quintessence of the ideology of the post-colonial state in India. In their characterization of the state in India, Lloyd and Susanne Rudolph show how it has successfully incorporated some apparently contradictory values in order to create a space where different social groups can enhance their status by periodically renegotiating the priorities for the politics of the day.[40] The 'negotiation' itself takes many different forms – stretching from participating in elections to mass uprisings and political violence. These political transactions take place under the watchful eyes of the public, the media, politicians and civil servants. In their inimitable metaphor, the Rudolphs describe the Indian state in terms of 'Hindu conceptions of the divine', 'polymorphous', and 'a creature of manifold forms and orientations'. The state shuttles between contradictory roles of being a neutral referee between competing social groups, and occasionally becomes partisan – leaning in favour of political groups in the name of positive discrimination, secularism, democratic rights, or dominant local or regional power.[41] In extreme cases of conflict or secessionist movements, the state takes an active and forceful initiative, and responds to challenges with a mixed strategy that combines both repression and accommodation.[42] In their attempts to get the best deal, both leaders and followers mobilize their social networks, transform traditional customs and innovate new political norms. The consequent musings, tactics, anger, anxiety – or spells of sullen silence from leaders and followers – are significant for the understanding of politics and governance in India.

Eternal, enduring and changing: India's non-linear modernity

Over the recent past, particularly since the nuclear tests of 1998 and the emergence of India as the world's back office thanks to outsourcing, the international perception of India has changed significantly. The new image of India as the country of 'the bomb and Bangalore' – synonymous with India's brand recognition as a rising power in information technology – has begun to challenge the stock representation of India as the epitome of backwardness, a poor country of holy cows competing for road space with the latest brands of motor cars, popularly elected *sadhus* in the parliament, mutilated beggars outside car windows in the crowded, clogged streets of the national capital, and ramshackle infrastructure. In stark contrast to India's earlier obsession with *swadeshi* – the politics of import substitution and diplomatic isolation – contemporary India is an avid buyer of fuel, weapons, foreign firms, brand-named goods and luxury products. To the leaders of western business and industry, and to the movers and shakers of world politics, India is a lucrative market and a powerful and ambivalent presence, holding up a basket of assets such as her vast, trained, cost-effective, manpower skilled at business processing, top Indian companies specializing in capital-intensive manufacture and information technology. In view of India's 'Third World society' and democratic institutions comparable to the 'First World' liberal democratic states of the West, and the living presence of religion in the public sphere, many see India as unique and attribute the success of democratic institutions to her 'exceptionalism'.

Instead, the book argues that while the cluster of factors that explain the stability of India's modern political institutions is quite atypical,[43] the factors themselves are not. The book analyses these culturally specific and historically contingent factors that have made this remarkable phenomenon possible. They are understood as the consequence of both competition for power and social mobility under the aegis of the modern, liberal state.

Competition for power as the cutting edge of India's political culture

The competition for power under the aegis of a democratic state, supported by the check and balance of *countervailing forces* – where power meets counter-power – has led to the remaking of a traditional society to a modern design. The approach taken in this book juxtaposes India's political dynamism with the image of a traditional, essential, hierarchical and static world view that has long held sway in the European imagination of India. I argue in this book that India is no more unique or special than any other major country with a long historical tradition and religious beliefs deeply anchored in society. If India has succeeded in establishing a sustainable democratic process, it is because an unusual set of factors has come together to create a political environment that has made stakeholders out of ordinary people.[44] The competition for power – an ineluctable fact of organized life – has neatly dovetailed into the interstices of Indian society. Keeping in tune with the changing social structure is the political system whose outer reaches occasionally spill over from conventional politics into anti-system behaviour. But the manner of its happening actually reinforces the strength and efficacy of the political process. Incredible as it may sound, the legitimacy of the post-colonial state in India issues from the struggle for power in the everyday life of Indian politics.[45] The point is crucial and needs to be laboured because it can be missed easily.[46]

For those unfamiliar with the country, the proposition that competition for power is the key to understanding Indian society might sit uncomfortably with the 'idea of India' as imagined by generations of European philosophers, writers and painters. The country of Buddha, Gandhi and Nehru, India has long enjoyed international recognition as an abode of peace, spirituality, harmony and the abnegation of material riches. The single-minded focus on political power that underpins this book is quite likely to raise doubts, particularly in the minds of those who are unfamiliar with the vibrancy of India's local politics.[47] Popular images of India as a spiritual society rather than one based on material interests and power has been formed by the dominance of cultural and religious motifs.[48] A steady stream of new writing on Indian politics questions this 'otherworldly image' of India[49] and argues that competition for power is the constant refrain of India's political life. The assertion, distribution and contestation of power and India's characteristic mix of institutional participation and rational protest give Indian politics its typical élan and explain the many paradoxes that underpin it. The great achievement of the post-Independence state has been to contain the struggle for power within limits defined by Indian politics and the constitution.

The competition for power has helped integrate new norms, radically affecting the equilibrium of power, that were introduced by the British in the course of their efforts to keep the colony orderly and profitable (Chapter 2). These norms of individual rights, equality before the law and representation were introduced into India to meet specific needs.[50] In retrospect, their side-effects have been enduring, making the secondary effect even more significant than the primary intentions. This 'cunning' of imperial reason,[51] for example, made minority politics, built into separate electorates introduced as early as 1909, an integral part of India's electoral rules (see Chapter 2) and, judging by the impact of the political mobilization surrounding positive discrimination, a key factor in contemporary Indian politics.

Multiple modes of politics

As we have seen earlier in this chapter, despite its outwardly naive appearance India's *style* of politics, which draws on symbols from culture and religion on the one hand, and modern political institutions and the market on the other, is both complex and sophisticated. After more than six decades of post-Independence politics based on democratic participation, protest movements, and accommodation within the framework of modern institutions, this mode of politics has come to characterize virtually all the arenas of the state. There are numerous examples of this. Most ethno-nationalist movements attract media attention when they first appear with their customary fury, mass insurgency and military action, but eventually they find an institutional solution within the Indian political system (Chapter 5). And though continued political unrest in Kashmir continues to challenge this thesis, the case of Punjab in the 1990s and Tamil Nadu in the 1960s, both of which, after a spate of political turbulence, have settled down to normal parliamentary politics, illustrate this mode of successful conflict resolution in India.

The strategic manoeuvres of India's politicians range between the peculiarly Indian, like *gherao, dharna, rasta roko, bhukh hartal* – various forms of individual and collective protest – and familiar forms of modern politics like electoral campaigns, lobbying and petitions.[52] The book builds on these makers of modern India – civil servants, captains of business and industry, political leaders and their networks of agents, and rebels – located in different regional and local contexts, for whom involvement with everyday politics has become a method of survival and an essential part of life. Very much in the tradition of the 'two-track politics' of Mahatma Gandhi in which he sought to combine institutional participation with political protest, India's political actors combine both modern institutions and traditional forms of politics based on social networks. One consequence is the emergence of the state, both as the quintessential mediator between competing social forces, but crucially, the mentor of specific, underprivileged groups, promoting them from subject-hood to citizenship of the Indian Republic. Turbulent political 'activists', in the long run, become catalysts of social change.

The scheme of chapters

The chapters have been arranged around issues that will be of interest to the students of both comparative and Indian area studies. The first chapter analyses how, and with what success, the post-colonial state – a top-down system par excellence – has tried to live with borrowed categories. These had evolved, incrementally, in course of the conflict and collaboration of the British Raj and Indian resistance to it. India's democratic system has a dark side to it in terms of its propensity to break off into short-term and localized violence, and long-standing secessionist movements. However, such conflicts, often reinforce the countervailing forces of region, caste, class and ideology that underpin the system. The introductory chapter makes a list of current policy challenges, emphasizing what the system must deliver in order to keep itself in business, i.e. replenish its political capital and legitimacy. The structure, process and policy are part of the *distinctive* character of Indian politics – a political system in dynamic equilibrium – whose democratic character is the result of the ability of its political leaders of all ideological hues to conflate modern and traditional forms of politics and produce a uniquely Indian *style* of politics.

Chapter 2 analyses the multiple pasts of modern Indian politics, focusing in particular on how the embryonic 'modern' state – a British colonial outpost locked in uneasy coexistence with India's indigenous rulers – eventually gained exclusive control over the entire Indian land mass and her coastal waters in a series of wars against Indian rulers and European rivals. The colonial state established order through a complex process of dominance and collaboration with its subjects and native princes, and prolonged its rule through spasms of incremental devolution of power to the Indian population.[53] When Independence came, as a final act of the Transfer of Power into Indian hands, the departing British left behind the bitter legacy of the Partition that has led to a series of inconclusive wars between India and Pakistan.

The diversity and complexity of the Indian population and its political culture, dominated by the modernity of tradition and multiple modes of politics, are the main theme of Chapter 3. The chapter, following the method of other chapters in this book, lists the key events and legislations that have altered the composition of the political community and deeply affected the nature of political transaction. The main components of Indian society, the castes and social classes, tribes, religions, gender, languages, the geography and political culture, are analysed later in the book on the basis of the key facts and narratives.

India's institutional arrangement which has introduced an effective and characteristic form of checks and balances, combining strength with democracy, is the core theme of Chapter 4. The main components of the government, namely, the executive, legislative and judicial wings, are introduced, and discussed on the basis of their constitutional organization and political evolution. The structure and function of the bureaucracy, some key national commissions, non-governmental organizations, urban and rural governance and the police and the military – the main organs of internal and external security – are discussed here. Another key feature is the National Emergency of 1975, and its disputed legacy in terms of the 42nd and the 44th amendments. This is discussed in terms of the analysis of the resilience of India's democracy, in subsequent chapters of the book.

Federalism, or rather, Union–State relations, as they are called in India, comes in for a detailed discussion in Chapter 5. The 73rd amendment of the Indian constitution (1993), recognizing the village as an arena in its own right, and *panchayats* as the third tier of the Indian federation, is introduced in this chapter. The chapter highlights some key events and major legislative acts such as the States Reorganisation Act. The resilience of the federal division of powers is discussed in terms of its ability to balance self-rule and shared rule, and to ensure both the unity of the nation and diversity of the society in India. The federal levels such as the States, Sub-states, Union territories, special districts, local administration and special features such as Article 371a for Nagaland, the anomalous status of Kashmir (Art. 370), are brought in to emphasize the distinct character of India's federalism. Other distinguishing features such as finance federalism, the impact of liberalization and globalization on the federal division of powers, and the new trend of political interlocking, inter-jurisdictional rather than inter-state interactions, are also introduced here.

The process aspects of Indian politics, namely, the articulation, aggregation and marginalization of interests, are discussed in Chapter 6. Key events and legislations like the Representation of People Act, and reservations that have changed the course of politics, are introduced here. The main structural components of the political process, such as elections – to central, regional, local bodies – and public bodies of a semi-official character, recruitment of civil servants – the twin principles of merit and representation through India's modified quota system, are discussed. The party system and major political parties – Congress, BJP, regional parties – trade unions, social and political 'protest' movements, pressure groups, and lobbies are analysed. Finally, 'communalism', the violent politics of inter-community conflict that simultaneously quickens the pace of the political process and registers its breakdown, concludes this chapter.

Chapter 7 discusses the economy, welfare and the politics of poverty reduction in India. Key events and legislations, such as the two industrial acts from the 1950s, and liberalization legislation from the 1990s, are introduced. The main ethos of India's political economy, namely the politics of incremental growth and redistribution, planning the mixed economy, the green revolution, poverty and peasant radicalism, liberalization, the IT industry, globalization and *swadeshi* economics are analysed to show the complexity of India's political economy.

India's propensity to simultaneously engage the world while appearing to stay aloof from international politics – a typical feature of Nehru's non-alignment – and the ambiguities of recent Indian foreign policy with regard to nuclear weapons constitute the core elements of Chapter 8. Its key focus is the discussion of foreign policy as an integral element of nation-building in India. Key events, such as the three Kashmir wars, the Indo-China border war and the Indian 'peaceful' intervention in Sri Lanka (1987), are introduced to illustrate the distinct character of India's foreign policy as it oscillates between national interest and national ideals. Current Indian manoeuvres in the WTO, the tactical engagement with China and the spate of strategic 'partnerships' that India has embarked on are analysed to indicate India's transition from non-alignment to engagement. The growing links of trade and foreign policy between India and the European Union (EU) are highlighted to indicate a steady shift of Indian policy, from protectionism to wider, international commitments. Finally, the domestic roots of India's foreign policy, as seen in the fissures that the Indo-US Framework Agreement produced between the ruling coalition and its communist allies, are discussed in order to explain the apparently contradictory features of India's foreign policy.

Finally, the concluding chapter focuses on India in the twenty-first century and the challenges the country faces, and opportunities that it might miss. The chapter also provides a brief résumé of the state of Indian democracy, still solid but fraying at the edges, and explains why the myth of territorial integrity is so vital for India. The economy – how to sustain growth, and redistribute money to the poor without eroding the incentive to work and earn profits – is presented as part of the world-wide problem that neo-liberal reforms face in developing countries at the threshold of breakthrough into self-sustaining growth. Other specific problems of the Indian economy such as energy – balancing need and capacity through exploration, alliance and the price mechanism – and the environment, where India has to acquire the necessary skills to cope with the regular wear and tear of a fast-growing economy and with natural catastrophes. The problems of infrastructure, transport, communication, education and health are highlighted as those where urgent and sustained attention is indispensable to maintain the pace of development. Main political challenges such as citizenship – making subjects and 'minorities' into citizens – and violent challenges to order, such as cross-border terrorism, and the Naxalites are discussed as necessary adjuncts to India's political economy. The challenges and promises of globalization, the Indian 'Diaspora', corruption, crime and other aspects of governance and the question of identity are analysed as integral parts of Indian modernity and secularism. The chapter concludes with an invocation of the limitations to the Indian model and some policy recommendations such as enhancing political capital and trust, institution-building, reinforcing India's countervailing forces, indigenous modernity and taking popular categories seriously as being crucial to India's continued growth and legitimacy in the twenty-first century.

Conclusion

With over a billion inhabitants – a sixth of the population of the globe – the story of India is significant in its own right. Of even greater significance is the fact that the Indian case helps us take stock of conventional theories of democratic social change. The Indian case brings new perspectives into cross-national comparison of citizenship, governance, development and its transition to democracy. These larger questions underpin the specific issues and events discussed in this book. What is the student of comparative politics to infer from the conflicting images of contemporary India with regard to transition to democracy? How comprehensive and enduring are these changes? Are the symbols of modernity and the display of high-tech affluence in the new shopping malls merely the latest addition to the multilayered diversity of India's tradition, or is this the much awaited beginning of a take-off into sustained growth? Can India sustain growth, keep inflation down, build up her infrastructure, invest in public services, and still remain democratic? With the majority of the Indian population classified by the census as Hindus, will Indian democracy steadily acquire a 'saffron tinge' – the internationally recognized colour coding of Hindu extremism – of religious intolerance, as argued by some observers?[54] Will a nuclear-powered India, an international outlaw for some, be a danger to herself and to international stability, or a balancing factor, a fulcrum of a multi-polar world?

There are no simple answers to these complex questions, and I do not offer any in this book. Instead, my intention in this text is to give the reader a ring-side view of how these issues are debated in India's universities – a vast, inchoate mass of teachers, students and politicians – in the free-wheeling and prolific Indian media, in the vast, dusty corridors of power in Delhi and capital cities of the regional States, inside political parties, movements, the chambers of legislatures, public inquiry commissions and the judiciary, and more recently, in the ubiquitous non-governmental organizations.

Keeping to the character of the book as a text meant for those making their first serious foray into Indian politics, the analysis keeps to the well-lit main street of the complex politics of the country, leaving out the darker alleys so dear to the specialist. However, these enticing detours into theoretical and comparative issues are signposted, and, wherever possible, are illustrated with images of real life, and facts from India's vibrant print media, village studies and survey research. Additional supplementary reading for those wishing to delve deeper into the more intricate and cutting-edge issues is provided separately at the end of the book.

Instead of looking towards the uniqueness of India's culture and religion to search for an explanation to the puzzles of Indian politics, the book builds on the agency of India's political leaders and their followers as the key to understanding the structure and evolution of the complex political system. In this respect, the antics of India's political leaders at all levels of the system, which are avidly reported in India's largely free media, can be misleading. In fact, they combine modern and indigenous forms of participation, and contribute to the dynamism of Indian politics. The subsequent chapters present a fragment of this rich discourse in response to the questions addressed to the puzzling resilience of democracy, buoyancy of the economy, persistence of poverty and the endemic ambiguity of India's foreign policy.

Notes

1 In fact, India combines one of the lowest levels of per capita income with one of the lowest levels of murder. India has a murder rate of 3.4 per 100,000 inhabitants compared to 3.2 for Germany. However, with regard to other indicators of crime, India has 5.8 sexual offences, 25.2 serious assault, 35.1 theft, 5.75 fraud, 0.1 counterfeit currency and 2.4 drug offences, compared to, respectively, 65.3, 154.0, 3819.8, 1124.3, 7.0 and 304.4 for similar crimes in Germany. See National Crime Records Bureau, Ministry of Home Affairs (2004), p. 21.

2 See Almond *et al.* (2008), p. XIV, p. 19, and p. 129 for details of comparative data on India and a selection of developed and developing countries.

3 The Freedom House (Berlin) rankings put India at 2 and China at 7 on political rights, India at 3 and China at 6 on social rights (1 is the highest), and India at 6.7 and China at 5.7 on economic freedom (10 is highest). See Almond *et al.* (2008), p. 137. Many consider the future of the Chinese political system uncertain in contrast to the long-term stability of the Indian political system.

4 The concept, often used in Indian politics, indicates the glacial pace at which Hinduism changes. This expression was meant to imply the slow and incremental rate of the annual net growth of about 1.5 per cent during the first four decades after Independence.

5 The exact extent of poverty reduction remains a matter of controversy. See Chapter 7.

6 The combination of deft macroeconomic management by the Reserve Bank of India, a stimulus package consisting of a long-awaited pay hike for India's civil servants, and the construction boom have helped cushion the impact of the world financial crisis on India. *The Economist* reports: 'Now that India's economy is slowing and competition for men, materials and moneny is slackening, India's public infrastructure may have a chance to catch up. In Gurgaon the Delhi Metro Rail Corporation is building an elevated railway that will connect the upstart city to the capital. It is a public project backed up by the governments of India, Delhi and the neighbouring state. It is also the busiest construction site in the city' ('India's Economy: Bridges to Somewhere', *The Economist*, 7 March, 2009, p. 71).

7 The pitched battles between the police, hoodlums and peasants in Nandigram, West Bengal, during most of the year 2008 is one such incident where, beyond the actual breakdown of law and order, one can see the long-term strategic calculations of the ruling Left Front coalition and the parties opposed to it, as well as competition among coalition partners themselves, with the dominant CPM struggling to defend its political base and the partners trying to expand theirs, at the cost of their ally. This has not, however, prevented the holding of parliamentary elections. For the general argument regarding how Indian politics accommodates discontent, see Mitra and Singh (2009).

8 Stakeholders are people who consider themselves efficacious and who hold the system to be legitimate. See Chapter 3, 'Political socialization and political culture', for a discussion of survey findings about these variables. For a measurement of citizenship in India, see Mitra 2010.

9 Cohen (2001), p. 2. See Chapter 8.

10 The 73rd amendment of the constitution, undertaken in 1993, transferred some financial and legislative power to the *panchayats* – directly elected village councils – and requires that one-third of the seats be reserved for women.

11 The book subscribes to the following definition of a system. 'The political system is a set of institutions and agencies concerned with formulating and implementing the collective goals of a society or of groups within it' (Almond *et al.* 2008, p. 28).

12 This definition is more inclusive than the definition of structure in Almond *et al.* (2008) who see it merely as 'specialised agencies of the government' such as 'parliament, bureaucracies, administrative agencies and courts' (ibid, p. 31). In India, structures, as Almond *et al.* suggest,

perform functions which enable the government to formulate, implement and enforce its policies. However, some structures which do not formally belong to the government – such as national commissions, some members of the media, and exceptionally, members of the parliament not belonging to the ruling party or coalition – might also influence policy.

13 Almond *et al.* (2008) pp. 32–3.

14 These are: (1) distribution – of money, goods, and services – to citizens, residents and clients of the state; (2) extraction of resources – money, goods, persons and services – from the domestic and international environments; (3) regulation of human behaviour – the use of compulsion and inducement to bring about desired behaviour; and (4) symbolic outputs – political speeches, holidays, rites, public monuments and statues, and the like – used to exhort citizens to engage in desired forms of behaviour, build community, or celebrate exemplary conduct' Mitra (2008b), p. 128.

15 Those interested in theories of political resilience and discontinuities should refer to North (1991), March and Olsen (1996), Bates *et al.* (1998), who supplement the functionalist concepts of structure and function with other variables such as risk, chance and institutional memory. For an application of these factors to an analysis of democracy and governance in India see Mitra (2005).

16 Das (2000), Luce (2006), Tharoor (1997),Varma (2004) are exemplary of this genre.

17 See in Mitra (1999) 'Flawed paradigms'.

18 Austin (1966), Brown (1985), Hardgrave and Kochanek (2008), Ganguly and de Votta (2003), Thakur (1995) are some leading titles.

19 Though often the staple of journalists in search of a coup, the 'otherness' of India has a respecable scholarly genealogy. The complexity and diversity of India's politics, the dexterity of her politicians, the seeming timelessness of the myths underpinning political rhetoric and in some cases, practice, have given rise to this genre that Edward Said has described as 'Orientalism'. For those using this line of reasoning, India defies the precise categories of historical and political analysis.

20 See Dumont (1970). Quigly (1993) provides a résumé of the debate around Dumont's contribution.

21 Palme, Dutt and Bettelheim were representative of the earlier generation; Frankel and Rao (1989/90), Brass (1992), Moore (1966), Vanaik (1990) provide shades of the more recent contributions to this field.

22 I have called this the 'neo-institutional rational choice' approach in my *Puzzle of India's Governance* (Mitra 2005).

23 Rationality is used to imply both 'instrumental' and 'value' rationality as defined by Max Weber.

24 For an illustration of the structure, functions and social origin of such elites at the local level – the *gaon ka neta* – see Mitra (1991).

25 The availability of free, fair and effective elections based on universal adult franchise is crucial for this.

26 See Mitra and Singh (2009).

27 See Mitra *et al.* (2006), p. 397. For a definition of this key term and others used in this book, the glossary at the beginning of this book is a source of further information.

28 Quotas produce clienteles and vested interests that seek to freeze social justice at a particular level. The dynamics of Indian politics can be seen in the fact that the process of challenging the system of reservations – of jobs, seats in legislatures and admission to educational institutions for Scheduled Castes, Scheduled Tribes and Backward Classes – has already set in. See Krishna Kumar, 'Fine-tune positive discrimination regimes', in *The Hindu*, 14 March 2009.

29 According to World Bank data derived on the basis of the Indian national poverty line (2006).

30 Measured in terms of population below $2 per day (2000), India's 80.6 per cent compares unfavourably to Brazil's 22.4 per cent, China's 46.7 per cent, Iran's 7.3 per cent, Mexico's 26.3 per cent and Russia's 7.5 per cent. India's dismal record is surpassed only by Nigeria's 90.8 per cent. World Bank, *World Development Indicators*, 2005. Cited in Almond *et al.* (2008), p. 139.

31 See Mitra (2001a), pp. 361–79.

32 Thus, the Communist Party of India (CPM) has been a supporter of the United Progressive Alliance-led government in Delhi (2004–9) but that did not prevent the CPM and the Congress being rivals in West Bengal.

In terms of the sophisticated political bargaining that this form of cohabitation involves, Indian politics is comparable to similar support-splitting in French and German politics. See Chapters 4 and 6 for details of how competition and collaboration take place at the regional and national arenas between political parties.

33 In the voluminous literature that has grown around governance, one notices more a pendulum-like mood swing between optimism and pessimism with regard to the state of governance, reflecting the political reality of the day, than the cumulating of analytical rigour and methodological precision. The tendency in some recent studies is to lean towards a pessimistic prognosis (Brass 2003). In contrast to his earlier prognosis (Kohli 1990), his *The Success of India's Democracy* (2001) endorses the achievements of India's institutional arrangements.

34 The impression of impending chaos that one gets from Kohli's early work on the crisis of governability in India had the turbulent 1980s in its background. Kohli referred to this period as 'deinstitutionalisation' which saw the rise of terrorism in Punjab, insurgency in Kashmir and Assam and challenges to the modern secular state from religious fanatics. This trend found an echo in his forecast of increasing disorder. However, the predictions have not come true, as seen in Diagram 1.1. In contrast to prediction (indicated by the broken lines), the real incidences of riots in India have, on the average, actually come down after the peak of the mid-1980s.

35 Rudolph and Rudolph (1987) refer to this as 'state dominated pluralism.'

36 Luce (2006).

37 An epithet applied to the pyramidal structure of planning where the state, located at the peak, had the overview of the whole society and the economy. See Chapter 7.

38 For the levelling role of the state which seeks to equalize opportunities, see Mitra (2008).

39 Tilly (1985) has described this generally as 'organised criminality'.

40 Rudolph and Rudolph (1987), pp. 400–1.

41 See Kohli (1990, 2001) and Mitra (2005) for an analysis of loss and recovery of order. The role of the state as a dispenser of social justice is discussed in greater detail in Chapter 6.

42 Stephen Cohen, an American specialist of India's defence and security policy, quotes a senior member of the Indian Police Service (IPS) to explain Indian strategy with regard to secessionist movements as 'hit them hard over the head with a hammer and then teach them how to play the piano!' Cohen (2001, p. 112).

43 See Luce (2006).

44 Mitra and Singh (2009).

45 See the tables on efficacy and legitimacy in Chapter 3.

46 Mitra (1988). Also see Luce (2006) on the BJP and Varma (2004).

47 For those who do not see the quest for power as a central fact of Indian life, the unabashed quest for power that underpins classic works of political theory such as the *Arthasastra* or the *Mahabharata* might come across as a surprise. Contemporary India may very well be on the way to becoming a global player, an economic giant, and an aspirant for membership of the atomic club, but many in India, and abroad, expect India to be different!

48 Max Weber, one of the leading exponents of this view, held caste as the 'transmission belt' between the 'speculative ideas of the intellectual elite, and the mundane orientation of religious observance among the people at large. By its traditionalism, the caste system retards economic development, and conversely, inter-caste barriers become attenuated wherever economic activities attain an increased momentum. Thus, *the spirit of the caste system militated against an indigenous development of capitalism*' (Bendix 1960, emphasis added).

49 Bailey (1970), Varma (2004) and Krishna (2002).

50 The 'Breast cloth controversy' in Hardgrave (1979), p. 153.

51 The Cunning of Reason consists in the 'hidden dynamic or dialectic which sums the consequences of actions in ways unforeseen by the actors' (Hollis 1987, p. 5). India's complex system of 'reservation', intended to benefit redressive action (former Untouchables), Scheduled Tribes (tribals) and Backward Classes that have been systematically discriminated against for centuries. These are examples of pro-democratic forces arising from policies adopted by India's colonial rulers which gradually took an institutional form.

52 The genealogy of these unconventional forms of political participation in a modern context can be traced to India's Freedom Movement under the leadership of Mahatma Gandhi. I have analysed the origin of this two-track strategy which combines participation in conventional politics and protest in 'The room to maneuver in the middle: Local elites, political action and the state in India' (1991a).

53 Morris-Jones (1987), Brown (1985).

54 Brass (2003), Wilkinson (2000).

2 Pre-modern pasts of modern politics

The legacies of British colonial rule

... in a sense it was by doing things properly – more often at least than most Indians – that the British had established themselves in India and that so few ruled so many with so slight a use of overt force. There was a subconscious awareness of this that involved us in a continual effort and expressed itself in all kinds of ways – from insisting on absolute precision in military drill to the punctilious observance of outdated etiquette, or a meticulous insistence on a knife-edge crease to khaki shorts.

Allen (1976), p. 18.

Like Hindu conceptions of the divine, the state in India is polymorphous, a creature of manifold forms and orientations. One is the third actor whose scale and power contribute to the marginality of class politics. Another is a liberal or citizens' state, a juridical body whose legislative reach is limited by a written constitution, judicial review, and fundamental rights. Still another is a capitalist state that guards the boundaries of the mixed economy by protecting the rights and promoting the interests of property in agriculture, commerce, and industry. Finally, a socialist state is concerned to use public power to eradicate poverty and privilege and tame private power. Which combination prevails in a particular historical setting is a matter for inquiry.

Rudolph and Rudolph (1987), pp. 400–1.

Introduction

From Alexander the Great (third century BC) to the terrorist attack on Mumbai in 2008, India has been no stranger to foreign invasion and occupation. But British colonial rule of a century and a half which ended in 1947 had a unique quality to it. It left India poor in wealth but rich in democratic potential. The story of this 'loss and recovery of self under colonial rule' in the words of Ashis Nandy,[1] and its implication for the post-colonial state, is the main theme of this chapter. The chapter, focused on the history of British rule in India, draws on the specific form of British–Indian interaction, in order to analyse the significance of colonial rule for the resilience of the post-colonial political system.[2] Starting with a few trading posts located in some port cities, the British built the huge British Indian Empire over a span of about two centuries. The chapter analyses the factors that made this possible. It also sheds light on the singularity of the Indian context which explains why democracy and governance have had very different careers in the states – India, Pakistan and Bangladesh – which emerged out of the British colony.

Why the British encounter that ended with Independence in 1947 should be singled out for special attention in a book primarily on modern India calls for a brief explanation. The British were not the only external invaders to have ruled India. But the impact of British colonization has had a significance that differentiates it radically from all other rulers of external provenance. There are two crucial reasons for this. First, even though India's British rulers did not think of colonial rule as a permanent condition, they still regarded their contribution to Indian civilization as permanent.[3] The consequent investments of time, effort and talent in designing institutions that the British thought appropriate for Indian conditions were enormous. One needs only to look below the surface of most modern institutions in India to discover the British imprint. Modern institutions of India, nationalist sentiments notwithstanding, are a true British legacy. In the second place, a critical analysis of British rule and Indian resistance to it helps explain why democratic institutions have worked more effectively in India as compared to her neighbours. The synthesis of British constitutional norms and political forms with India's indigenous political tradition led to a different outcome from the path that other successor states took. This ensues from India's tradition of 're-use', where the past often continues within the present by deliberate design. In the hands of British architects and designers of political institutions, the British tradition of re-use met its Indian equivalent, leading to the creation of new capital cities and an array of legislation.[4] Avid re-users, post-independent India's leaders have appropriated many of the symbols and institutions of their predecessors, and cloaked them in Indian garb. This blending of indigenous tradition and imported institutions explains both the ability of the British to rule for so long with little recourse to overt force, and the smooth transition from colonial rule to multi-party democracy.

India's living pasts

That the past influences the present is commonplace. Even revolutionaries, for whom wiping out the vestiges of the *ancien régime* is part of their legitimating myth, end up by re-admitting elements of the past into the present.[5] The constitution of India admits the pre-modern origins of the modern Republic squarely by stating in the first article, 'India, that is Bharat' – the reference is to the country of a mythical king – 'shall be a Union of States'. Choices made in the past influence the political framework of the present, consisting of the institutions, issues and mentality within which the present generation of leaders has to choose between the different alternatives. In India, as we shall see in this chapter, there have been no great political ruptures with the past comparable to the October revolution of 1917 in Russia or the peasant revolution that led to the setting up of the People's Democratic Republic of China in 1949. Nor has any historical phenomenon, equivalent to the European Industrial Revolution, the Enlightenment or the Inquisition, drawn a sharp line between the natural and the supernatural.[6] In India, in contrast to China, Pakistan or European liberal democratic states, continuity with the distant past rather than rupture is the rule.

Reading history backwards, one can see how closely India's pasts have influenced the evolving present. The salient events that connect Indian antiquity with the post-Independence republic help understand the tortuous path that the evolution of the modern state has taken (see Box 2.1). The declaration of India's Independence by the British Parliament in 1947 had been facilitated by the fact that there was a government-in-waiting, led by Jawaharlal Nehru and his colleagues from the Indian National Congress, some with considerable administrative experience, to whom power could be ceded. The successors to the British, both in India and Pakistan, were parties that emerged victorious out of elections held in 1945–46. However, quite fortuitously for India, the Congress party was much better placed to act as the vehicle for the transfer of power from colonial rule to multi-party democracy. After Partition, it stayed put on its own political soil, with its links to its constituents intact. The leaders of the Muslim League, on the other hand, left India for West and East Pakistan, where they were soon embroiled in a power conflict with the local leaders, and eventually, the army. Despite great efforts to keep British India intact as one inde-pendent country, the project had foundered on the issue of the creation of a separate homeland for Muslims – as demanded by the Lahore resolution of the League in 1940. The Pakistan Resolution of 1940 was itself the outcome of elite competition for the spoils of office, and distrust between the two main protagonists – the Congress Party and the Muslim League – resulting from the refusal of the former to share power on an equitable basis after the elections of 1937. This critical election was held under the Government of India Act, 1935, passed by the British Parliament which introduced a measure of self-government in India. One can keep tracing the political transition backwards until recorded history shades off into the mythical past.[7]

The process of devolution of power by the British that started with the 1909 Morley–Minto Reforms, leading up to the 1935 Government of India Act, will be discussed below as part of the analysis of the institutional arrangement of colonial rule. These reforms, in turn, were possible because of strategic *re-use* of pre-British institutions and practices – both of India's Muslim rulers and their Hindu predecessors – by the victorious colonial power. The process of institutional evolution accounts for the continuities of Indian politics, and as part of the same process, the memory of past conflicts and collaboration have continued in the form of the rituals, customs and traditions which are an integral part of the present institutional structure and political process.[8] Reading history backwards, as one can see below (Box 2.1), has an important advantage for comparative political analysis. It helps appreciate the *political* basis of many phenomena that come across as essentially cultural.[9] The section that follows will draw on India's past to illuminate the present.

'Arrested decay': colonial representations of the Indian past

At first glance, one notices few vestiges of British colonial rule that are still recogniz-ably British on the political landscape of contemporary India. A period of sixty years of competitive politics has whittled down institutions and practices of foreign proven-ance and recast them to fit local moulds and local political environments. India's traditional institutions have generated the requisite space to accommodate foreign bodies in their midst. The memory of colonial rule has gradually faded and re-emerged in a new form; the examples of such re-use of colonial institutions in post-Independence politics are plentiful. Though not always so clearly visible to those who are unfamiliar with India's colonial interlude, specialists recognize the British derivation of the rules, procedures and rituals of the Indian Parliament.[10] The *Devaswam Boards* in South India and their equivalents in other parts of the vast country – departments of religious property, also set up during the British rule – are in charge of administration of old temples as of the new. Government ministers of democratic India hold court – much

Box 2.1 Reading history backwards: re-use of the past in the making of the present

1947	Independence of India Act, Partition and the Transfer of Power.
1945–46	Elections held to name members to the central and provincial legislatures.
1940	The Muslim League passes the Pakistan resolution in Lahore.
1935	The Government of India Act established a federal government; turned over provincial governments completely to Indian ministers, with Governors retaining emergency powers.
1919	Montagu–Chelmsford Act introduced the constitutional principle of dyarchy which separated 'reserved' subjects, controlled by British officials, from 'transferred' subjects, to be controlled by non-officials.
1909	Morley–Minto Reforms, undertaken by the colonial government, expanded central and provincial legislatures, made non-official majorities in provincial legislatures possible, and provided for separate electorates to give minorities additional weight.
1906	Founding of the Muslim League.
1885	Founding of the Indian National Congress.
1861	Indian Councils Act created the office of the Secretary of State for India, and made the Governor General of India the Viceroy – representative of the Crown in India.
1858	The British Crown abolished the East India Company and assumed direct control of India
1857	Indian Mutiny – the 'First War of Independence'.
1837	Macaulay drafts the Indian Penal Code.
1833	The Charter Renewal Act explicitly recognized the East India Company as the Government of India and gave it the power to issue acts.
1793	Lord Cornwallis establishes the *zamindari system* through the Permanent Settlement of Bengal.
1784	The British Parliament passes the India Act which sets up the Board of Control to supervise the Company's affairs in India.
1773	The British Parliament passes the Regulating Act to define the commercial and political functions of the East India Company.
1757	Battle of Plassey. Clive defeats Nawab Siraj-ud-Daulah.

1600	The grant of Charter to the British East India Company by Queen Elizabeth I.
1556–1605	Reign of Akbar the Great Mughal.
1398	Tamerlane wins the battle of Panipat and reduces Delhi to 'rubble'.
998 AD	First raid by Mahmud of Ghazni, followed by 16 further raids.
711 AD	Landing of Mohammed-bin-Kasin in Sind, the first Islamic invasion of India.
4th century AD	Organization of the Gupta Empire.
321 BC	Formation of the Maurya Empire by Chandragupta Maurya.
326 BC	The invasion of northern India by Alexander the Great.
BC	Writing of the *Ramayana* and *Mahabharata*, India's two greatest epics.

like their colonial and pre-colonial predecessors held *durbar* – and transact state business with a motley crowd of visitors, with the same display of power, privilege and pomp. Independent India has clearly moved on and shown, once again, the country's capacity to achieve change without revolution.

The British strategy of domination, which took into account the enormous gain in legitimacy through the re-use of the institutions and sacred symbols of those defeated by it, consisted of selected incorporation of some elements of the Indian past and conspicuous rejection of the rest. Imperial design and utilitarian ideology converged in the *Anglo-Indian style* in architectural – as much as institutional – design. The sole opportunity for colonized Indians to advance, as they saw it, consisted in the acceptance of modern (i.e. European) science, technology and values. The coming of Gandhi, and subsequently, India's Independence, challenged it, opening up, in the process, the flood-gates into India's pre-modern past for those fighting for freedom from colonial rule.

While India has been no stranger to invasions through the north-west mountain passes in the high Himalayas, British rule was special in terms of its representation of the Indian past. Up to the arrival of the British, in India, the past and the present had lived in a complex and dynamic symbiosis. But, under the British, the past really became the *past*.[11] The point is made by Metcalf (1998) in a seminal article on aesthetics and power under colonial rule. While the British continued the tradition of 'appropriating the politically charged forms of their predecessors as a way of legitimizing their own regime' (ibid., p. 14), their method of depicting the past differed radically from that of their predecessors. Previous rulers of India had added their visions and symbols to existing designs so that the past and present could appear as part of a continuous flow. However, in British public buildings and political institutions, the past was depicted definitely as the 'past' whose only function was to serve as a foil, on which the British present could shine brighter, while staying aloof and distant. In a memorable passage, Metcalf recounts how the British *durbar* was traditional in form but thoroughly modern in content.

> In his 1903 *durbar* . . . Curzon sought to utilize the 'familiar' and even sacred form of 'the East'. As he proudly proclaimed, the entire arena was 'built and decorated exclusively in the Mogul, or Indo-Saracenic style'. Yet Curzon refused to sanction an exchange of presents, or *nazrs* which had formed the central binding element of pre-colonial durbars. Instead, he had each prince in their turn mount the dais and offer a message of congratulation to the King-Emperor. Curzon then simply shook hands with the chief as he passed by. Incorporation and inclusion, so powerfully symbolized by *khillat* and *nazr*, had given way, despite the Mughal scenery and pretence, to a wholly colonial ritual.[12]

In aesthetics as in politics, the colonial strategy consisted of the incorporation of the past – Indian tradition in this case – within the present in a subsidiary capacity. The past, as Metcalf points out, could be a figment of colonial imagination and representation. Nandy adds in the same vein, 'Modern colonialism won its great victories not so much through its military and technological prowess as through its ability to create secular hierarchies incompatible with the traditional order.'[13]

Colonial aesthetic and colonial politics were of one piece. The architecture of colonial rule worked to one common purpose – of selective incorporation, de-linking traditional elites from their ancestral moorings, and justifying their power in terms of the common purpose of Progress, of which colonial rule was but an instrument.[14] The Archaeological Survey of India preserved India's monuments – both sacred and administrative – in a state of 'arrested decay',[15] isolated and distanced from the community of which they used to be an integral part. So did the new British-established political and administrative institutions, which presented the Indian past as inferior to the British present, and by the same analogy, the modernity symbolized by colonial rule as the superior future.

Colonial rule thus affected Indian society much more widely and radically than any previous invasion of India. The combination of Utilitarian logic – of using the power of science, technology and politics for 'the greatest good of the greatest number' – and the British solicitude to build alliances based on short-term interests, a policy that eventually came to be known as 'divide and rule', generated enthusiastic support for British rule from some corners of Indian society. There were winners, and new stakeholders, on the Indian side too. Nandy comments, 'These hierarchies [modern as opposed to traditional] opened up new vistas for many, particularly for those exploited or cornered within the traditional order.'[16]

The result of these artistic and political innovations was the most profound social change that India had experienced until then – a process that transformed a race of British subjects of 1858 into a politically charged society, ready to assume power and exercise it democratically by 1947. Politics rather than industry, religion or war was the prime mover of social change, and the state and its bureaucracy, rather than captains of industry, generals or the church, were the main agents of change in Indian society. That became the basis of the centrality of the state and bureaucratic politics in the political landscape of British India under colonial rule and subsequently in the post-colonial state.

Never before in history had so few decided the fate of so many in such important ways as the British conquerors of India. At the height of their power, the British thought of themselves as charged with the responsibility of re-casting Indian tradition in the design of modernity, much like the Utilitarian plans for the spread of enlightenment. In this mission, the British government and the technicians of the Empire made progress their common cause. Subsequently, the post-colonial government under the leadership of Jawaharlal Nehru and the Indian planners continued this legacy in their Five Year Plans – an image evocatively described by the metaphor of the Indian state as 'avatars of Vishnu' (Rudolph and Rudolph 1987) – incarnations of the Hindu god – indicating thereby the capacity of the state to draw on the cumulative political capital of the past and pour it into a new form.

Institutional innovation under colonial rule: re-use of the Indian pasts

By 15 August, 1947, with the famous 'Freedom at Midnight' speech behind him (see Figure 2.1 and Box 2.2), Jawaharlal Nehru was firmly ensconced in office as the first Prime Minister of independent India. The administrative and political challenges that the new government faced were enormous. Independence entailed both the departure of substantial numbers of British civil servants and the division of assets, establishments and personnel of all wings of the government and, crucially, the armed forces and foreign services between India and Pakistan. Added to these normal demands of everyday administration there was a war in Kashmir against Pakistan, the closing of the Indian mission in Lhasa, in Tibet, and the responsibility of caring for millions of refugees pouring into India from West and East Pakistan, crowding every available corner in Delhi and Calcutta. The fact that the new government was able to cope with the stress successfully and still hold the first General Election to the Indian Parliament and provincial assemblies is to be attributed to the

---

Box 2.2 Freedom at midnight

Long years ago we made a tryst with destiny, and now the time comes when we shall redeem our pledge, not wholly or in full measure, but very substantially. At the stroke of the midnight hour, when the world sleeps, India will awake to life and freedom. A moment comes, which comes but rarely in history, when we step out from the old to the new, when an age ends, and when the soul of a nation, long suppressed, finds utterance. It is fitting that at this solemn moment we take the pledge of dedication to the service of India and her people and to the still larger cause of humanity.

At the dawn of history India started on her unending quest, and trackless centuries are filled with her striving and the grandeur of her success and her failures. Through good and ill fortune alike she has never lost sight of that quest or forgotten the ideals which gave her strength. We end today a period of ill fortune and India discovers herself again. The achievement we celebrate today is but a step, an opening of opportunity, to the greater triumphs and achievements that await us. Are we brave enough and wise enough to grasp this opportunity and accept the challenge of the future?

Source: Jawaharlal Nehru, *Tryst with Destiny*, in Rushdie and West (1997), pp. 1–2.

fortuitous presence of a talented team of Indian leaders and administrators (discussed later in this chapter) and to the special circumstances under which the Transfer of Power to Indian hands took place.

Going by the discourse of the British Parliament, India's Independence was a story foretold. Already, as far back as 1833 (Box 2.1), the Charter Renewal Act had put on record a commitment in favour of 'greater measure of Indian participation in the governing of the country'.[17] The terms under which the British Parliament recognized the East India Company set up in 1600 under a licence from the British Crown to trade with India as the lawful government of India under the authority of the British Crown, stated explicitly that '. . . no native of India, nor any natural born subject of His Majesty, should be disabled from holding any place, office or employment by reason of his religion, place of birth, descent or colour.'[18] Nor did the British express any explicit intention to stay in India in perpetuity. Unlike Australia, Canada or Rhodesia, India was never 'home' for the British. It was a colony, a market, a career opportunity, the Jewel in the Crown, but distant and, in the last analysis, dispensable. When the time was ripe, the reins to India's governance were to be bequeathed to Indians.

During the eventful century that connected the Charter Renewal Act (1833) and the Government of India Act (1935), British dominance of India reached its zenith. A series of Governors General, each committed to reform and the maintenance of colonial hegemony, though in different measures, stood by the ultimate goals of

Figure 2.1 Freedom at midnight
Source: www.thehindu.com/.../images/2004081500530301.jpg

sustaining orderly rule, and profitability of the colony to the British Treasury. Both objectives required the recruitment of vast numbers of Indians to the lower ranks in the revenue administration, police and army, judiciary, health and other colonial services and in the burgeoning Indian schools and universities. The numbers of educated Indians who poured out of the new universities but could not get gainful employment grew. In the absence of industrial growth, the stagnant economy (see Table 2.1) could not absorb this growing army of job seekers. This contributed to the pressure on the colonial government for more jobs in Indian hands, and seats in the legislatures to be allocated to Indian leaders.

After Macaulay's Minutes of 1835 which stated the case firmly for introducing modern English education in India, there was no turning back. The growing Indian middle class – whom the new educational system and media could wean away from the traditional, vernacular set-up – became a bastion of the Indian 'renaissance', civic and political activity and, under the leadership of Raja Rammohan Roy, support for social and political reform.

Colonial support for the social agenda got a setback after the 1857 Mutiny against British rule, led by an assortment of Muslim and Hindu notables made destitute by British rule. In the end, despite the successes, the rebellion was ruthlessly put down by the British who controlled intelligence, transport and the techniques of modern warfare. The British Crown assumed direct control of India in 1858 once the mutineers were decisively defeated, and a comprehensive legal structure called the Indian Councils Act was drawn up in 1861. It provided for a Secretary of State for India with cabinet rank, with sole responsibility for India. The Governor General and Viceroy was to represent the Crown in India. The founding of the Indian National Congress (INC) in 1885 gave an institutional focus to the articulation of Indian demands. Thus, towards the end of the nineteenth century, the full spectrum of forces was in place – the INC to press for reform, the Viceroy and the Secretary of State for India to defend imperial interests while trying to process Indian demands for the consideration of the British Parliament. These pulls and counter-pulls led to the incremental devolution of power to Indian hands through the reform acts of 1909, 1919 and finally the Government of India Act of 1935.

The exact nature of state formation in India is a subject of wide debate.[19] The British colonial rule was the most recent of foreign incursions on the Indian land mass but it was not the only enduring legacy of exogenous provenance. While the legacy of British colonial rule and Indian resistance to it is easy to detect, one can

Table 2.1 India's GDP as a share of the world economy (1–2001 AD) in per cent

	1	1000	1500	1600	1700	1820	1870	1913	1950	1973	2001
Western Europe	10.8	8.7	17.8	19.8	21.9	23.0	33.0	33.0	26.2	25.6	20.3
Former USSR	1.5	2.4	3.4	3.5	4.4	5.4	7.5	8.5	9.6	9.4	3.6
United States	–	–	0.3	0.2	0.1	1.8	8.8	18.9	27.3	22.1	21.4
Japan	1.2	2.7	3.1	2.9	4.1	3.0	2.3	2.6	3.0	7.8	7.1
China	26.1	22.7	24.9	29.0	22.3	32.9	17.1	8.8	4.5	4.6	12.3
India	32.9	28.9	24.4	22.4	24.4	16.0	12.1	7.5	4.2	3.1	5.4

Source: Maddison (2003), p. 261 (table 8b).

see the survival of pre-British India just under the surface. The Greek invasion of India[20] was followed by the Mongols, Mughals, the Portuguese, the Dutch and the French. Each invasion left behind a residue that in the course of time became a part of the antecedent culture and state tradition of India (see Box 2.1).

The expansion of the British Empire

The expansion of British rule in India has many explanations, of which the most popular attributes it to the European rivalry for overseas markets in the seventeenth century. The key events in Box 2.1 identify the turning points in the expansion of British influence and, subsequently, imperial domination of India. The exact reasons for the apparent ease with which it spread (see Box 2.3) are subject to controversy.[21] How did the East India Company come to dominate India's political economy? Was this a function of inherent racial or social superiority, or a more complex causation, linked to international political economy of the time, and the nature of state formation in India? Pitched against the institutional and military strength of the modern state, India – a *segmentary* state[22] – was not in a position to offer collective resistance. This is the common narrative thread that connects the defeat of Siraj-ud-Daula in the *Battle of Plassey* (1775) with the heroic and futile battles of the Hindu and Muslim leaders of the *Sepoy Mutiny* (1857), which England won because of her superior sense of organization. Ultimately, it is not so much the Enfield gun as modern book-keeping and the telegraph that won the empire for the British.

Once the British established their rule, they succeeded in bringing the various local and regional units under a central government, which nevertheless drew heavily on indirect rule through quasi-autonomous intermediaries such as native princes, landholders and *zamindars*.[23] Taken as a whole, these three functions – wars of conquest, alliances and plunder – describe the dynamic behind the expansion of colonial rule in India. Rothermund explains this remarkable phenomenon in terms of *parasitism* and *paralysis*.[24] Further support for Rothermund's explanation with regard to the interlocking of the economy and politics, and the superior–subordinate development of England and India, comes from Eric Stokes.[25] Several shades of belief in racial supremacy ultimately came to characterize the nature of the colonial mission.[26] Chris Bayly explains the momentum behind the British expansion in terms of *tax-farming*, *extraction of surplus*, and ultimately, the investment of the

---

Box 2.3 Phases of British colonial rule in India

1600–1757	Competing European powers as a mercantile presence in India.
1757–1857	Expansion of the British Empire.
1857	Sepoy Mutiny. British victory over the rebels leads to the 'High Noon' of the Empire.
1858–1947	Consolidation and decline of British rule, and the Transfer of Power leading to Independence.

wealth of India by Company servants through private trade. What initiative Indians could come up with was often discouraged by the colonial authorities. *Zamindari* and the system of indirect rule,[27] accompanied by the annexation of native princely states, marked the steady expansion of British rule. Map 2.1 shows all these factors at work.

As conquerors of India, the British were not any more benign than their Muslim predecessors, but the vast changes in technology and international political economy had transformed the nature of political domination. Plunder of precious metal and stones got transformed into the mode of colonial exploitation.[28] The consequences are best seen in terms of the decline of India's share of world GDP from 24.4 per cent at the start of colonial rule (c. 1700) to 4.2 per cent in 1950 when it formally came to an end (see Table 2.1).

The British Raj and Indian resistance

The Indian National Congress was the main political party in the Constituent Assembly that produced the Indian constitution and subsequently formed the government, having won the first General Election. Its origin and development are yet more evidence of India's useful pasts with regard to the structure and content of its modern politics.

For over half a century, between its formation in 1885 and the final coming of Independence in 1947, the Congress remained the focus of the national struggle for the end of British rule. It followed a strategy that combined political objectives with those of social reform and national administration. This complex repertoire of competition and collaboration with the foreign rulers became the hallmark of Congress politics. It steadily expanded the political agenda to include virtually all aspects of national life, exerting pressure on the British to concede more power to Indian hands. It used the power and resources thus gained to strengthen the organizational and political network. When the British thought that they had conceded enough and the negotiations came to a standstill, the Congress took to direct action and mass struggle, imposing pressure until the British returned to the negotiations. This legacy of direct action, mass movement, and transactional politics based on patronage became an important ingredient of the political culture that sustained democratic rule in India after Independence. The Gandhian blend of British parliamentary methods and indigenous techniques made direct political action such as *satyagraha* an integral part of political culture and tradition in post-Independence India.[29]

The Gandhian synthesis of modernity and tradition

The Congress party became the vehicle of the synthesis of the two main strands of Indian nationalism – the liberal constitutionalists like the 'moderate' Gopal Krishna Gokhale and the radical 'extremists' led by Bal Gangadhar Tilak. Following its foundation in 1885 by a retired British civil servant – Sir Alan Octavian Hume – the Indian National Congress gradually acquired a complex character of collaborator and competitor with colonial rule, combining participation and protest action as a two-track strategy of power[30] (see Box 2.4). After Independence, when its rival Muslim League left India for Pakistan, the Congress, complete with its party organization,

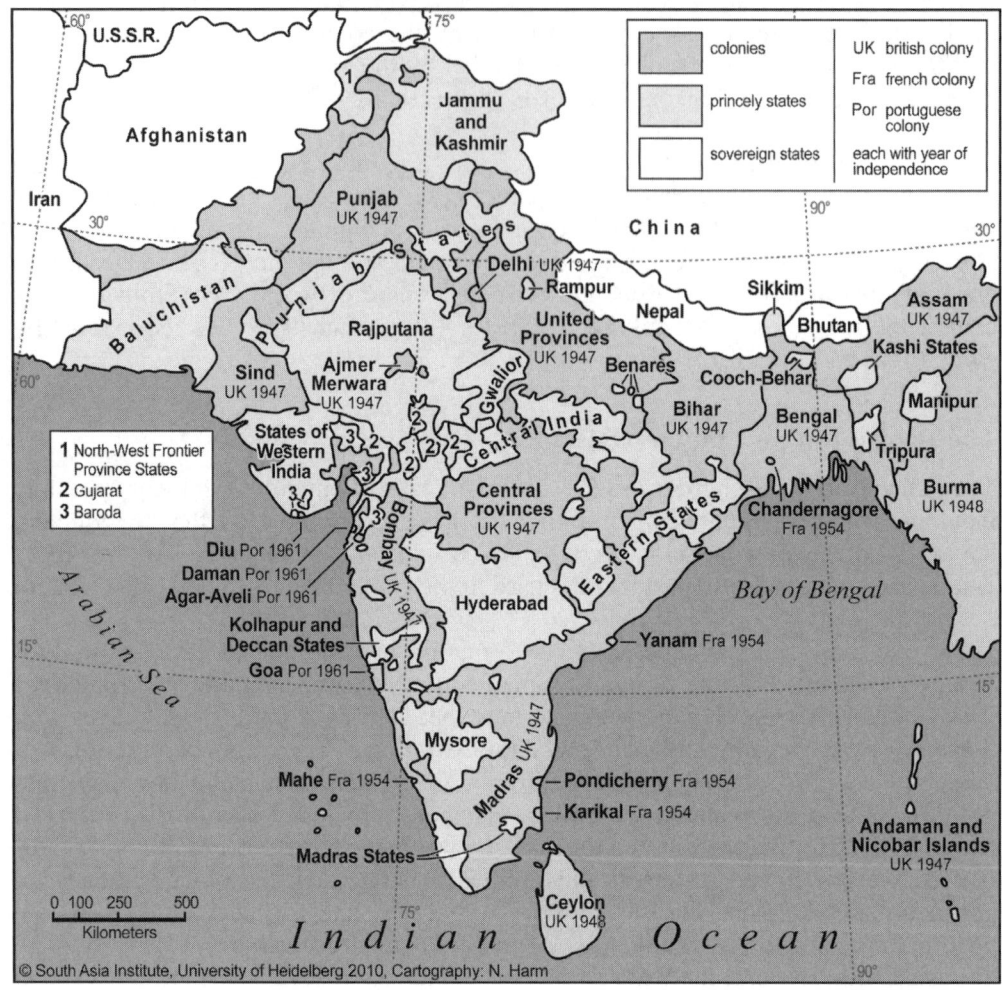

Map 2.1 Political map of British India

Nehru as Prime Minister-in-waiting, its core ideas about planning, foreign policy and nation-building already shaped, was more than ready for succession to power.

Mahatma Gandhi, the most outstanding leader of India's struggle for independence and a continuing source of moral inspiration, was trained as a barrister in England. He developed the method of *satyagraha* – non-violent resistance – while he was in South Africa working for an Indian law firm. The South African experience also taught Gandhi the importance of cross-community coalitions, a theme that he subsequently transformed into 'Hindu–Muslim unity'. This became a salient feature of Gandhi's politics upon his return to India in 1915, and a hallmark of the politics of the Congress party which found it useful as a political instrument to fend off its challengers – the Hindu Right, the Muslim League and their British patrons. Under his leadership, the Indian National Congress became increasingly sensitive to

Box 2.4 Phases of India's struggle for Independence

- Moderate
- Extremist
- The Gandhian synthesis

the gap between the predominantly urban middle-class Congress party and the Indian masses, and shifted its attention to the Indian peasantry.

Under Gandhi's leadership, the Indian National Congress steadily broadened its reach in terms of both social class and geography. In 1918, while introducing *satyagraha* in India, Gandhi courted arrest in support of the indigo plantation workers of Bihar. There were similar movements in Punjab, Gujarat and other parts of India. To mobilize mass support, Gandhi also introduced a number of indigenous political practices like fasting and general strikes or *hartal* (a form of boycott accompanied by a work stoppage). In choosing civil disobedience to resist the Salt Tax imposed by the British, Gandhi showed his brilliance as a strategist. When the British rulers responded with repressive measures, their efforts to contain the unrest only contributed to the intensification of the struggle. This became a model for subsequent civil disobedience movements through which Gandhi mobilized peasantry and workers as well as the urban middle classes. He combined the techniques of political negotiation with more coercive direct action (such as *hartal*, *satyagraha*, etc.) and derived both the political resources and the methods from within Indian culture and history.

The British responded to increasingly vocal demands for political participation with the Government of India Act of 1935 and its predecessors – the Montagu–Chelmsford Act of 1919 and the Morley–Minto Reforms of 1909 (Box 2.1). These became the legal basis of India's constitutional development and, subsequently, an important blueprint for the constitution of independent India. The voting franchise continued to carry a property qualification, but the electorate was nevertheless expanded from 6 million to 30 million. Provincial elections held under restricted franchise gave the Congress party valuable experience in electoral campaigns and governance. Both became crucial assets for the establishment of an orderly political process after Independence.

While the political and constitutional developments that took place under British rule are important legacies on their own, the effect of British rule itself on Indian society was also very important in terms of the psychological impact on Indian identity and selfhood.[31] The first social reformers, whose agenda included some of the programmes advocated by the British Utilitarian movement, looked up to the British colonial government as allies in a joint struggle. The Congress, which brought the reformist and radical strands of Indian nationalism together, acquired a new social base as the movement, under Gandhi's leadership, mobilized the peasantry, labour and other occupational groups in rural and urban areas. The Congress as an office-seeking and anti-colonial movement became the instigator and beneficiary of reform. The constitutional reforms of 1909 had conceded limited Indian representation. But the extent of the franchise and the power and functions of elected members were severely circumscribed.

The reforms of 1919 provided for a relatively large measure of responsibility at the local and provincial levels in areas such as education, health and public works that were not 'reserved' or deemed crucial for colonial control. The Congress took advantage of these reforms to participate in the local and municipal elections, which greatly enhanced the strength and vigour of the democratic government after Independence. By making common cause with middle-class aspirations, it earned the trust and loyalty of the middle class while challenging the authority and legitimacy of British rule. These same social groups were among its more important social bases of support. In addition, the Congress developed the ability for the aggregation of interests, a talent for sustained and coordinated political action, and the skills of administration through vigorous participation in elections, particularly in those to the provincial legislature under the 1935 Government of India Act. The leaders of the Congress party also gained what few anti-colonial movements had – namely, a taste of genuine political competition and the experience of patronage as a tool of political transactions.

'Divide and quit': Independence and the bitter aftermath of Partition

The approach of the Second World War saw India's politics organized around two intersecting dimensions. On the one hand, there was an anti-imperial dimension which aligned the Indian National Congress, the Muslim League and other groups against the British colonial government. On the other hand, the demand for Pakistan – a territorial state that could act as a homeland for the Muslims of South Asia – was increasingly voiced by the League. It saw itself as the champion of Muslim demands, which led to a different alignment of forces, with the Congress party opposed to the demand for Partition, and the British government and some sections of India's non-Congress opinion either supportive of it or equivocal towards it.

In the event, following the Lahore Resolution of 1940 in which the League categorically asked for Pakistan as a homeland for the Muslims of South Asia, the polarization of opinion between it and the Congress on the issue of Partition was complete. The Congress party, in its Quit India Resolution of 1942, rejected the British demand for cooperation with the war effort, and chose, instead, to court mass arrest as a protest against British rule. This accelerated the Congress–League divide on the one hand and British sympathy towards the League on the other. The large-scale arrest of Congress leaders in 1942 temporarily removed the Congress party from the arena as an active player, enabling the Muslim League and the Communist Party of India to increase their strength. Jinnah's call for Pakistan gave the Muslim League a political slogan of great mass appeal among the Muslims of India. In 1944, Chakravarti Rajgopalachari – a Congress leader from South India – voiced his support for partition of the subcontinent on religious lines as a better alternative to violence and bloodshed if the Pakistan issue had to be settled by force. His proposal was vehemently opposed by the Congress leadership, which led to his withdrawal from leadership of the party. But British government opinion was steadily moving in the direction of Partition. In 1945, the Labour Party won the election in England and expressed its keen desire to end colonial rule in India. In 1945–46, elections were held in India to appoint members of the central and provincial legislatures. In these elections, the Congress and the Muslim League emerged as winners – the former winning almost all the Hindu-dominated constituencies and the latter doing likewise in Muslim-dominated constituencies. Clearly, the League could demonstrate its strong presence in all the Muslim-dominated parts of the country except the North West Frontier Province.

The British Prime Minister Clement Attlee sent the Cabinet Mission in 1946 which proposed a federal Union for India which would have dominion status and be fully free to secede from the British Empire. A Constituent Assembly was to be elected by the provincial legislative assemblies, and a constitution was to be formed, with limited functions held by the Union (foreign affairs, defence, and communications) and with the residual powers to be held by the provinces. The interim government was to carry on until the constitution was devised; provinces with a Muslim majority could meet together to consider forming an intermediary government between the Union and the provinces to safeguard the interests of Muslims.

Although there was some opposition to the terms of the Cabinet Mission plan, it became increasingly clear that the idea had the implicit support of most of the groups active in Indian politics of the time. Elections were held for the Constituent Assembly in July 1946. The Congress won 205 of the British Indian seats and the Muslim League won 73. The Constituent Assembly held its first meeting on 9 December, 1946, but Muslim League members did not participate then or at any time later. Ultimately, the Viceroy invited the Congress Party under the leadership of Jawaharlal Nehru to constitute the government which took the oath of office on 6 August, 1946. Seats were reserved for the Muslim League which took them up in October 1946; but the chasm between the two parties had by then become almost unbridgeable. Finally, following the great Calcutta killings, triggered by Jinnah's call for 'direct action' to secure Pakistan, the Congress agreed to the Partition. The Indian Independence Act of 1947 passed by the British Parliament included the terms of the Transfer of Power, which saw Jinnah become the Governor General of Pakistan and Lord Mountbatten that of India.

After 150 years of British colonial rule, often referred to as the British Raj, India became independent on 15 August, 1947. Jawaharlal Nehru, India's first Prime Minister, a leading figure in the anti-colonial campaign and a proponent of non-alignment for India, soon became one of the leaders of the newly emerging Third World. Unlike the post-revolutionary elite of China and the USSR, Nehru and his associates were a national leadership constituted through a process of consensus building, of inclusion rather than elimination of challengers, and accommodation of a broad political spectrum. The character of the new political system was shaped by the legacies of Indian history and social diversity, but most of all by the nature of the local and regional resistance to colonial rule. The middle class, which included many of these leaders, had an ambiguous relationship with the British presence in India. Some of this class fought for the Raj and some against it, but the class as a whole became a political link between British rule and Indian society. This served a critical function in the evolution of an authentic Indian form of politics that drew as much on British institutions as on Indian tradition.

Some legacies of colonial rule

Though India has been subjected to foreign aggression since the beginning of recorded history, the British impact was the most penetrating, and remains paramount. During the struggle for independence, many found it convenient to blame colonial rule for many of India's ills.[32] This tendency of blame-shifting appears to have given way to a more sophisticated and nuanced evaluation.[33] India's current prowess in IT and outsourcing are attributed to her skilled manpower, well versed in English, an obvious legacy of colonial rule. If India has succeeded in achieving a generally peaceful and orderly transition from colonial rule to Independence, and subsequently to a stable multi-party democracy with slow but steady economic growth, as some argue,[34] then British colonial rule must bear part of the responsibility both for its main achievements and for its failings.

The distinct character of Indian politics derives in no small measure from the trickling down of the norms of British constitutionalism, and the 'trickling up' of Indian custom, as a consequence of the British solicitude to rule with the minimum necessary use of force. Honouring local custom, accommodating local rulers and transforming local and regional power into props of imperial rule were all a part of this grand strategy. The legacies continue to affect politics in contemporary India.

The most important of the legacies consist of the modern political institutions – which will be discussed in detail in Chapter 4 – and the process of parties and interest groups as well as the quintessential Indian political strategy that combines institutional participation and political protest (Chapter 6). The main legacy of pre-Independence politics to post-Independence practice is the effort on all sides to bring political competition into the ambit of the rule of law, moderate politics and political institutions. When rules appear too restrictive or not sufficiently legitimate and the game threatens to get out of hand, the state intervenes with its own mixed strategy of suppression and accommodation, in a manner akin to that of its British predecessor. With some exceptions such as the continuing conflict in Kashmir, and the North-east, this strategy has worked successfully, adding layers of new elites and political arenas into the political system. The modest origin of decentralization has matured into a fully fledged federal system, comparable to the now defunct Soviet federal system in its institutional complexity but endowed with far more vitality, as one can see from its resilience.

The strength of India's institutional arrangement derives in part from the Indian bureaucracy which is yet another legacy of British rule. The Indian Civil Service (ICS) which was considered the steel frame of the Empire at its peak, was renamed the IAS, standing for the Indian Administrative Service, following Independence. It became the long arm of the post-colonial state and started reaching out to the periphery of society. Thanks to the bold endeavour to extend representation through India's complex quota system, unlike its colonial predecessor, the IAS and other similar services soon began to resemble Indian society in terms of social composition. The Indian police and army, after the traumatic event of the Partition, which saw them split into the security wings of two hostile neighbours, have nevertheless emerged as professional bodies.

The legacy is more mixed in the economic arena. The decline of India's economy, particularly in manufacturing, was a direct consequence of British protectionism. But even more important was the isolation of India from the two-way transfer of knowledge – a process that revolutionized European industry in a matter of a few decades – because of the colonial boundaries over international trade.[35] A more basic problem for India's economy was the colonial form of trade which transformed India into an importer of British manufactured goods. True, taking advantage of the disruption of the inter-war years, some industry had grown in areas such as textiles, but even these developed their own pathologies of limited growth, militant trade unionism, and a culture of dependence on the government. These attitudes carried over into the immediate post-war years and produced the same dependent mentality (Chapter 7).

The tradition of planning to meet wartime scarcity also carried over to independent India, and made bureaucratic control a higher priority than productivity. Finally, in agriculture, the residual legacy of the *zamindari* system and its deeply exploitative 'rack-renting' made subsistence farming an enduring phenomenon.[36] Though the Green Revolution has helped parts of India to move away from this low-risk, low-yield method of cultivation, large parts of the country are still in the grip of this form of cultivation and its consequences in terms of poverty and violent class conflict.

In the social sphere, though the British withdrew from large-scale reform after the Mutiny of 1857, the seeds of reform planted in the period that preceded it took root and generated a dynamic of their own. The result was the emergence of movements of emancipation on the part of the untouchable castes,[37] the slow politicization of Muslims, leading to Islamic separatism, and the slow but steady emancipation of *tribals* and *untouchables* – situated at the lower levels of Hindu society – and women.

Yet another British legacy that continues to affect Indian politics is the moral attitude to power. Colonial rule generated loyalty as well as resistance, both violent and non-violent. But most of all, Indians could relate to power only as subjects – willing or unwilling – but not as citizens. As such, trust in those organs of the government with which people come into contact on an everyday basis – the police, bureaucrats and politicians – continues to be low, whereas trust in those institutions that had helped subjects stand up to superior power, such as the judiciary, continues to be high. This creates a hiatus between trust in parties and the government, but not in politicians and the police, which makes legitimacy a difficult proposition, and elections very much an opportunity to 'throw the rascals out' rather than the meticulous weighing up of the options being offered by the competing parties.[38]

Finally, the structure and process of India's political system (Figure 1.1) should be considered the most important of British legacies. As we have already seen in the Introduction, this institutional framework offers a method of State–society interaction where the new social elites, themselves the outcome of a process of fair and efficient political recruitment, play a two-track strategy and institute processes of law and order management, strategic social and economic reform and accommodation of identity as an operationally testable model. India's regional diversity is thus at least partly explained by the variation in the length and depth of colonial rule, state formation and integration of the local economy with the wider world.

Conclusion

With the passage of the Independence of India Act in 1947, political power came into Indian hands, through negotiation and contingency. British dependence on Indian collaboration[39] and the threat of the withdrawal of consent through the counter-hegemonic politics of Mahatma Gandhi led to the creation and transfer of constitutional power to localities and regions, introducing a process of slow and incremental state formation.[40] In the end, when Independence came, India's British-schooled leaders were able and willing to continue a mission of modernity and state formation that had been on course already for a century.

The first modern political institutions introduced by the British such as the telegraph, rail and the police were part of an elaborate system that sustained colonial rule.[41] Those that came later – such as the civil service, elections under restricted franchise, the media, the judiciary and the legal profession, the universities and modern educational system – soon became the social base of the Indian middle classes. Each of these institutions had a pyramidal structure with the British elites at the top.[42] However, the lower levels of these institutions were almost exclusively staffed with native Indians. Suspended uneasily between the ruler and the ruled, the new, vernacular-educated Indians – scribes, journalists, teachers, petty officials – were recruited from those sections of Indian society whom the British Raj considered loyal. After Independence, under the pressure of competitive politics, vote-hungry politicians inducted the excluded groups – the Hindu right, backward classes, some sections of the former untouchables and subjects of the former princely states which were not directly affected by colonial rule – into mainstream politics. These newly mobilized groups, as we shall see in Chapter 6, started questioning not only the policies of the generation of leaders who came to power immediately after Independence, but in some cases also the institutions that were closely tied to their power and prominence in society. During the eventful six decades following Independence, the deepening of democracy has led to the questioning of some aspects of the British legacy.[43] Thanks to the manner of its ending – through a Transfer of Power to Indian leaders cast very much in the British mould (though with vital links to Indian society) rather than through a revolutionary party as in neighbouring China – the British legacy lived on, even after the formal end to colonial rule.

The British legacy of constitutionalism – quickened through its adaptation to Indian conditions and the cultural context by a series of exceptionally gifted leaders – has had a better run in India than in its neighbouring countries. The chapter has analysed some of the reasons, focused particularly on the tradition of re-use of the past for the reinforcement of modern institutions that the British perfected for their own imperial purposes, and in departing, bequeathed to the leaders of the Indian National Congress. These leaders were deeply schooled in British ways, partly through their own experience of the British educational system and partly through their resistance to colonial rule which obliged them to look for power and legitimacy through a deeper bonding with their own society. That was more or less the case also with the leaders of Pakistan, but unlike the Muslim League which left India for the new homeland in Pakistan, the Congress party retained its deep roots in India's political soil, and quickly developed an effective political and electoral machine following Independence (Chapter 4). Short of a similar vital bond in its new political arena, the Muslim League gradually atrophied, yielding place to military rule.

The analysis undertaken in this chapter also helps us understand how the British Raj achieved a masterful economy of force through the strategic accommodation of a part of the Indian population as their collaborators and intermediaries between the natives and their foreign rulers. Sections of Indian society which opposed the British were excluded from office, and not permitted to engage in political participation. Competitive political mobilization in the course of six decades of vigorous party competition has now ushered the excluded groups such as Hindu nationalists, *backward castes* and *dalits* into the political arena. For some of these previously excluded groups, the pre-modern past is not merely a museum piece, ensconced within the structure of modernity in a state of 'arrested decay', but a vital link to their identity and culture which needs to be restored to its legitimate place in the public sphere. This argument has, in many instances, revived the pre-British political tradition and pre-modern political culture. In consequence, some of India's institutions that are part of the legacy of British rule stand questioned. The induction of pre-modern practices and symbols into an institutional arrangement based primarily on modern politics has raised basic questions about the core values that underpin the political institutions which formed the basis of India's political system following the Transfer of Power. The exegesis of British rule and the manner of Indian resistance to it are crucial to the understanding of the stability of India's political system and the residual uncertainty that underlies it.

Scholarship on contemporary India with a typical starting point at Independence does not take the epochal character of the consequences of this double transition – into and out of colonial rule – sufficiently on board.[44] The interaction of the British rulers with their Indian subjects, and how this interaction helped in preparing India's elites to take over the reins of power, which facilitated the Transfer of Power to native hands and in the long run paved India's path towards electoral competition, provide valuable insights into the functioning of multi-party democracy in contemporary India.

While the chapter has made references to India's many pasts as far as recorded history permits, it mainly focuses on the complex legacies of British rule with reference to the main events that characterize the colonial period.[45] It has concentrated on how British institutions have affected the origin and evolution of modern institutions and India's distinct political style. The subsequent chapters delve into the question of how modern parliamentary politics and individual interests – the cutting edge of modern politics – got enmeshed with indigenous values and forms of politics rooted in Hinduism and the caste system. British rule had taken over many administrative practices from antecedent rulers of India. The chapter has formulated answers to these key questions through an analysis of the fusion of Indian and British norms of politics, particularly under the leadership of Mahatma Gandhi and Jawaharlal Nehru. This is responsible in large measure for the post-Independence coexistence of modernity and tradition.

The distinct character of India's politics and salient features of India's constitution carry the imprint of her complex cultural and historical heritage. Continuity between India's pre-modern history and modern institutions is important in explaining the resilience of India's political system, as well as the diversity of levels of governance in different regions of India's continental expanse, and most crucially, the periodic outbreak of intense inter-community violence.[46]

The evolution of India's institutional arrangement, which will be discussed in more detail in the next chapter, has been nurtured by a strategic re-use of the past. Conquerors have systematically plundered the best ideas and assets of the losers, and claimed the appropriated tradition set to new specifications as uniquely their own.[47] In turn, they have fallen by the wayside, overtaken by new arrivals who have continued the same tradition of appropriation and re-use. In its own way, this has become an acceptable norm of Indian politics. If one marvels at the continuity of policy in spite of governmental change,[48] then the deep roots of this practice are to be found several years before Independence when British colonial officers and elected Indian politicians learnt to share office and exercise power. The modern institutions of India, emerging from this process of long evolution, bear recognizable traces of the past and historical memories of loss that carry their urge for revenge and create anxiety on the part of the potential victims. These themes of institution-building and the hidden reservoirs of anxiety that blight them sometimes will be analysed in detail in the subsequent chapters on institutional arrangements and the process of India's politics.

Notes

1 *The Intimate Enemy: Loss and Recovery of Self under Colonial Rule* (Nandy 1983) is an evocative narrative of this foundational phase of modern India.
2 See Rudolph and Rudolph (1967) for a theoretical insight into why and how Indian tradition carries itself over into the framing of India's modern institutions.
3 Thus, for example, the system of land tenure known as the Permanent Settlement was worked out as an optimal solution for India's agrarian problems, taking into account Indian conditions and the British experience.
4 See Hegewald and Mitra, eds. (forthcoming) *Re-use: The Art and Politics of Integration and Anxiety* for several applications of the concept.
5 Schama (1989) makes this point with reference to the continuation of pre-revolutionary practices and symbols in post-revolutionary France.
6 There has been no equivalent of the European witch hunt in Indian history, nor of the long battle to establish the superiority of scientific knowledge over custom and religion.
7 The past is kept alive in the Indian Sub-continent through ancestor worship which forms an important part of religious ritual. The governments have followed suit – by naming their missiles after mythical and historical figures (see Chapter 8).
8 For examples of the re-use – the incorporation of antecedent norms and structures into the structure of subsequent forms of art, sculpture and political institutions – see Hegewald and Mitra (2008).
9 By tracing the historical origin of deep conflicts one can comprehend the role that past political choices have played in the origin of present conflicts, even as they appear to be timeless and traditional. Political analysis, leavened with the requisite knowledge of the path dependency of the present, affected by seminal events of the past, can help gather insights towards the making of appropriate institutional designs for the future.
10 The signs of the lingering British presence – Sunday as the official holiday of the week, left-hand drive vehicles, and the ubiquitous Ambassador car, a hybrid British Austin Rover adapted to Indian roads which has become the sturdy emblem of Indian officialdom, are everywhere. The Dak Bungalows, outposts of the British Raj in the country, temporary homes for the British civilian officers on tour, are tended with the same attention to detail by the PWD – the Public Works Department, also of British vintage – just as are the post-Independence guest houses of the national and State governments.
11 Metcalf (1998) makes this point in his interpretation of the decorative role of past artefacts in the modern architecture of Lutyens.
12 Metcalf (1998) sums up the reciprocal relation of Orientalism and Empire in the following passage:

> Perhaps Curzon's lamp [which he got designed in Egypt and arranged to be placed on the grave of Mumtaz in the Taj Mahal] might be taken to represent the colonial aesthetic. It is an aesthetic of difference, of distance, of substantiation, of control – an aesthetic in which the Taj Mahal, the mosque of Cairo, even the *Arabian Nights*, all merge and become indistinguishable, and hence are avaiable for use however the colonial ruler chooses. It is an aesthetic in which the past, though ordered with scrupulous attention to detail, stays firmly in the past. It is an aesthetic Shah Jahan [the Mughal emperor who built the Taj Mahal as a memorium to Mumtaz Mahal, his deceased Queen] could never have comprehended.
>
> p. 24

13 Nandy (1983), p. IX.
14 See Allen (1976).
15 Metcalf (1998), p. 18.
16 Nandy (1983), p. IX.
17 Park and Bueno de Mesquita (1979), p. 21.
18 Ibid.

19 See Rudolph (1987). Also, 'Introduction' in Mitra (1990).

20 This is the subject of the feature film *Alexander*, directed by Oliver Stone in 2004, which breaks with tradition in terms of giving the Indian side the power and authority of a worthy and equal adversary to the all-conquering Greeks.

21 The logic of imperial expansion is best described by Tilly (1985). Tilly begins with a 'warning' about the nature of states. 'If *protection rackets* represent crime at its smoothest, then war making and state making – quintessential protection rackets with the added advantage of legitimacy – qualify as our largest example of organized crime' (p. 169). Tilly then goes on to define the functions of states in terms of the following: '[1] *War making*: Eliminating or neutralizing their own rivals outside the territories in which they have clear and continuous priority as wielders of force; [2] *State making*: Eliminating or neutralizing their rivals inside those territories; [3] *Protection*: Eliminating or neutralizing the enemies of their *clients*; [4] *Extraction*: Acquiring the means of carrying out the first three activities – war making, state making, and protection' (p. 181, emphasis added).

22 See Stein (1982) for the definition of segmentary states.

23 See Brown (1985).

24   The East India Company as a modern capitalist corporation of an advanced bourgeois nation entrenched itself, like a parasite in the agrarian state dominated by a decaying military feudal regime. The parasite adjusted to the system of its host and benefited from it without changing it very much. The company was well geared to function in this way. It had developed a modern bureaucracy in the course of its trading operations. This bureaucracy had all the characteristics of a modern civil service: a structured hierarchy and definite career patterns, free transferability, regular accounts and files regarding all administrative transactions, etc. Moreover, the company had a corporate memory. It could learn and correct mistakes; even a mediocre member of its service could contribute efficiently to this process – perhaps even more so than the brilliant exception to general rule.

Rothermund (1988, reprinted in 1993), p. 16.

25   British power in India came to be regarded after 1800 as . . . an instrument for ensuring the necessary conditions of law and order by which the potentially vast Indian market could be conquered for British industry. This transformation of economic purpose carried with it a new, expansive, and aggressive attitude, which the French, who were its later masters, termed that of *la mission civilisatrice*. The missionaries of English civilization in India stood openly for a policy of 'assimilation'. Britain was to stamp her image upon India. The physical and mental distance separating East and West was to be annihilated by the discoveries of science, by commercial intercourse, and by transplanting the genius of English laws and English education. It was the attitude of English liberalism in its clear, untroubled dawn, and its most representative in both England and in India was Macaulay.

Stokes (1959), pp. xii–xiv.

Also see Said (1993), pp. xiii–xiv.

26 Said quotes the French advocate of colonialism, Jules Harmand, who said in 1910:

It is necessary, then, to accept as a principle and point of departure the fact that there is a hierarchy of races and civilizations, and that we belong to the superior races and civilizations, still recognizing that, while superiority confers rights, it imposes strict obligations in return. The basic legitimation of conquest over native peoples is the conviction of our superiority, not merely our mechanical, economic, and military superiority, but our moral superiority. Our dignity rests on that quality, and it underlies our right to direct the rest of humanity. Material power is nothing but a means to that end.

Said (1993), p. 16.

27 Bayly (1983). Also see Brown (1985).

28 India's nationalist historians have described this phenomenon as 'de-industrialization'.

29 See Mitra (1991).

30 Rudolph and Rudolph (1987) and Parekh (1989).

31 See Nandy (1983).

32 Naoroji's 'drain theory' – which argued that British rule caused India's riches to be drained away to Britain – was one of the earliest formulations of this line of thinking.

33 Post-Independence formulations of the psychological and economic impacts of British rule have been more nuanced. See Nandy (1983) for the former and Moore (1966), Chapter 6 on 'Democracy in Asia: India and the Price of Peaceful Change', for the latter.

34 See Brown (1985).

35 British manufactured textiles decimated the market for homemade cloth in India because of their competitive price. For the historical evidence of how it happened see the 'Indian Textile Exhibition' in the Whitworth Gallery, Manchester. Personal communication, Julia Hegewald, 25 October, 2008.

36 The *zamindari* system vested permanent rights of tax collection on designated landlords. However, instead of investing in agricultural development, the system encouraged exploitation of peasants by intermediaries between the zamindar and the peasant because of the growing pressure of population in a stagnant economy.

37 Hardgrave (1968).

38 See Chapter 3 for the paradox of high trust in institutions but low trust of politicians.

39 Brown (1985) and Bayly (1988).

40 Fox (1971) and Mitra (1990).

41 Bayly (1996).

42 Misra (1961).

43 But even the forms of political protest such as *satyagraha* had their origin in Indian resistance to the British Raj. That, as we shall see in Chapter 6, explains why protest in India does not necessarily turn into anti-system behaviour.

44 Nandy (1983) has pointedly referred to it as the 'loss and recovery of self under colonial rule'.

45 The Subaltern School of Indian historians argues that mainstream colonial and nationalist history leaves out the regional arenas as well as the struggles of groups marginal to British colonial power. In a series of analytical works, these authors have shed light on themes such as peasant revolts, tribal movements and the growth of the Hindu–Muslim divide.

46 Chakrabarty *et al.* (2007) provides a succinct explanation of this puzzle by reaching back into colonial rule and beyond it to the pre-modern roots of modern politics.

47 See Hegewald and Mitra (2008).

48 Thus the policy of liberalization, introduced by a Congress government in 1991, was continued by the Hindu nationalist Bharatiya Janata Party which succeeded it in power. In turn, the Congress party, upon assuming power in 2004 after defeating the BJP-led NDA coalition, has continued both nuclearization and rapprochement with Pakistan – policies that were started by their predecessors (see Chapter 8).

3 From *homo hierarchicus* to plural society

Politics and social change in India

> Mr. Gandhi is never so much disgusted as he is when he is confronted with the question of Majority versus Minority. He would like to forget it and ignore it. But circumstances will not let him do either and he is often forced to deal with the issue.
>
> Ambedkar (1945), p. 268.

> The memory of Muli's humiliation stayed with me. I recalled similar incidents in my own country, and I wondered if the responses of untouchables to discrimination paralleled those of minorities in other countries. Was Muli indifferent to the insults he bore in silence? I hardly thought so; but I wondered how an ordinary untouchable like Muli survived economically, socially, and psychologically as a member of a despised group at the bottom of society. What were his joys, aspirations, and triumphs, as well as his humiliations? What would provoke someone like him to question the treatment he received from upper-caste people, to fight back?
>
> Freeman (1979), p. 5.

Introduction

The chapter analyses the interaction of the main components of Indian society with India's modern political institutions and the democratic political process. It draws on the process of social mobility which, in a relatively brief period and with little overt conflict compared to similar transformations in Europe, has radically transformed the hierarchical structure of India's social system. It explains why *caste* survives as a part of social life and ritual and why *caste networks* are still very much in evidence in electoral campaigns, housing and allocation of developmental resources, but the *caste system* – once the epitome of social, economic and political dominance – is no longer what it used to be. Its functional basis – the hierarchy of status, power and wealth (see below) – has been steadily challenged by the egalitarian logic of democracy and the market. The chapter illustrates the interaction of social hierarchy and electoral democracy through the changes induced by legislation and administrative action, and selected indicators from survey data.

From hierarchy to plurality

Box 1.1 in the introductory chapter has already provided a snapshot of India's diverse society. This heterogeneity is to be found in the social origin of the Indian elite as well. The diversity in the social background of the holders of public office in India, no longer a monopoly of those born to power and privilege, is testimony to social mobility in post-Independence India. Over the past six decades, the democratic process, the growing economy, and legislative and administrative measures aimed at positive discrimination have brought in people with skills and ambition from social groups that were previously excluded from public office and social prominence. Social transformation has established a direct link between the state and the citizen, which, in turn, has enhanced the legitimacy of modern political institutions. Such an assertion, however, must take into consideration rural India – beyond the pale of the media – where the bulk of the Indian population lives, and, as some would argue, steeped in age-old tradition, living out their lives within the small kin categories of caste, tribe and family, still tied together within an unequal social system that the French sociologist Louis Dumont had famously described as *homo hierarchicus*.[1]

Indian sociologists describe the traditional social system in terms of a concept called the *Jajmani* system. It is based on the reciprocal relationship between the Hindu householder (*Jajman*), his ritual superior and a cluster of occupational groups (see Figure 3.1). At the centre of this exchange network are the landholding groups who share their products with service castes in exchange for their skills and labour. The services cover the entire spectrum of life – from priestly functions to agrarian production and the rituals associated with death. In terms of power, the *Jajmani*-based social system can be conceptualized as a pyramid (Figure 3.2) where the components are arranged in terms of their status, with the upper social classes at the peak of the pyramid. The broad, popular base is inhabited by lower social groups.

The spread of political consciousness, electoral mobility, legislation and administrative action and social mobility brought about by economic change have combined to challenge the legitimacy of social dominance based on caste status alone. Stripped of the traditional belief in the superiority of the upper castes over the lower, the structure of social dominance has increasingly acquired the character of a glass ceiling, through which the dominated groups can see the top but from which they feel unjustly excluded (Figure 3.2). In many cases, this has led to considerable social

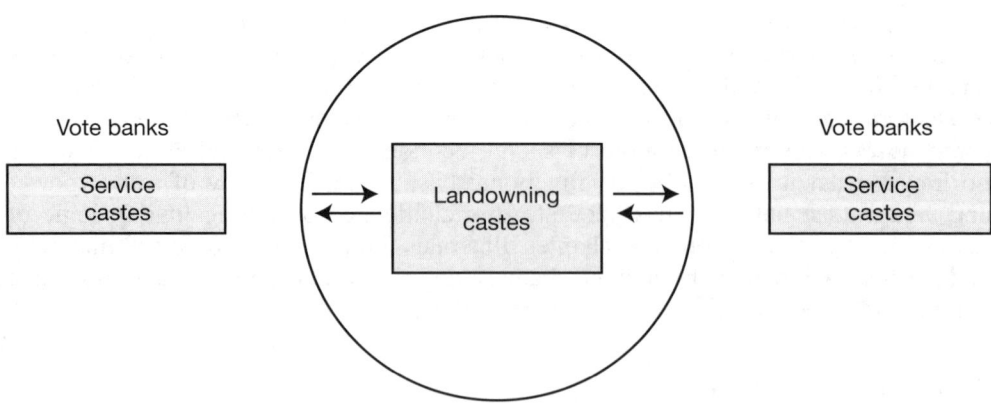

Figure 3.1 Jajmani system
Source: Drawn by author.

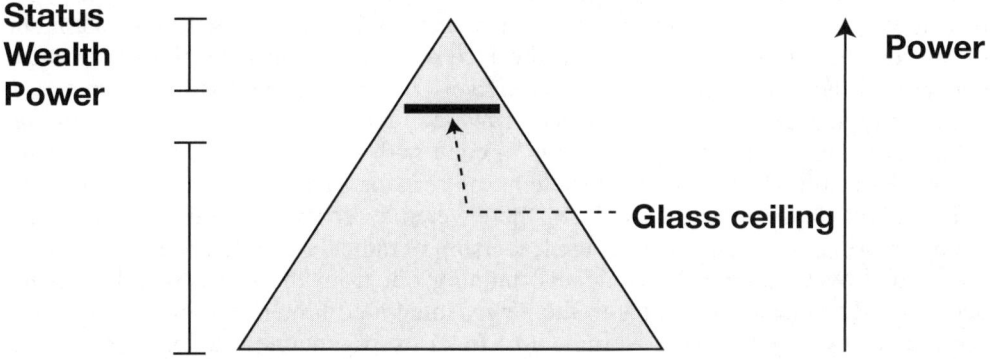

Figure 3.2 The social pyramid
Source: Drawn by author.

strife. More often than not, the challenge to the social pyramid has come from within the local caste system, causing it to implode.[2]

The collapse of the traditional social pyramid, written into fundamental rights to equality and freedom and the prohibition of discrimination based on social origin in the constitution and ardently advocated by Nehru, has become a reality in six decades since Independence. Transactional politics added to entrepreneurship produces the political depth and complexity that have the potential to transform constitutional intent to political reality.

The political agenda which underpins the process of social change in India took shape in the final years of colonial rule, with several social visions competing for attention. The Gandhian vision, for instance, argued in favour of a national political community based on social harmony. This was contested by those who saw in class consciousness and class conflict the only effective method of transition from hierarchy to an egalitarian society. Nehru sought to reconcile these two social philosophies in a liberal, socialist and democratic state, committed to progress through legislation, positive discrimination and social mobilization. The result has been an unprecedented measure of social transformation without the massive costs in human lives incurred in eighteenth-century Europe, post-revolutionary China or contemporary Africa.

India's Independence, as we have already seen in the previous chapter, coincided with the division of the country into Pakistan and India. The Partition of British India on religious grounds, inadequately administered by the departing British, was violent and chaotic. Bitter inter-community riots marked the refugee trails that criss-crossed the new borders in the East and the West. Another political change that was to have deep and enduring social implications was brought about by the integration of princely states, roughly six hundred in all (see Map 2.1), which, with the transfer of paramountcy, acquired the right to choose their future political affiliation. The great majority, with the notable exception of Kashmir and Hyderabad, decided to merge with India or Pakistan. The merger was seen as an opportunity by some residents of the princely states who had chafed under the feudal customs and lack of social and economic opportunities. However, it was a trauma for others who felt threatened by competition from the residents of erstwhile British India who were better placed to take advantage of the new political and economic opportunities. In either case, residents of the former princely states were suddenly catapulted into a new world – of new weights and measures, political rights and opportunities, and anxiety born out of the likelihood of the loss of status and privilege in the face of competition from the lower social classes and the new arrivals from the relatively more developed British India.

The first decade after Independence (1947–57) was marked by efforts at refugee settlement, and administrative attempts to cope with the massive dislocation caused by the Partition. Added to the problems of refugee settlements, inter-community strife and the merger of princely states, there were new forms of political mobilization led by land-hungry peasants under the leadership of radical Marxists. A new dimension was added by vote-hungry politicians, fanning out from the parts of India already accustomed to electoral politics to the newly integrated hinterland, in search of new constituencies. Finally, the government of India itself generated radical expectations through a slew of egalitarian legislation aimed at reinforcing the rights of industrial workers and peasants, and the abolition of *zamindaris* and untouchability (Box 3.1). Policies of rural development, planning and positive discrimination – administered by new bureaucracies specially commissioned for the purpose – reinforced the atmosphere of action and radicalism.

Indian society was deeply affected by British rule, which unleashed change in many key areas of life across the country. First, though the British became weary of direct intervention in Indian life after the Mutiny of 1857, reform initiatives like the ban on Sati and widow remarriage affected the hard core of Hindu orthodoxy. In the second place, the rule of law – and legal codes such as the Indian Penal Code (IPC) and Criminal Procedure Code (CrPC) insisted on equality before the law – posed a direct challenge to social hierarchy. The third measure that shook the foundations of Indian tradition was the most important and complex. In order to enhance the efficiency of civil administration, the British government had required a lot of statistical information on the subject of population. Thus was born the decennial census of India, which, starting in 1881, required Indians to identify themselves in terms of categories, such as family seen as a unit, property and religion. These concepts were Western in provenance and soon initiated a dynamic of their own. Categories

---

Box 3.1 Key social legislations (in chronological order)

- Industrial Disputes Act, 1947
- Untouchability Offences Act, 1955
- Hindu Code Act, 1956
- Muslim Women (Protection of Rights on Divorce) Act, 1986
- The Scheduled Castes and Scheduled Tribes (Prevention of Atrocities) Act, 1989
- The 73rd Amendment of the Constitution, 1992
- National Commission for Minorities Act, 1992
- The National Commission for Backward Classes Act, 1993
- National Rural Employment Guarantee Act, 2005
- Maintenance and Welfare of Parents and Senior Citizens Act, 2007

such as caste and language that were specially innovated to suit the Indian context, once enumerated, induced a static character to a dynamic social process. In other words, the sheer fact of enumeration injected a measure of rigid categories into the fluid Indian social process. Whereas the traditional methods of social mobility, which M.N. Srinivas, one of the most important sociologists of modern India, has conceptualized as *sanskritization*, had permitted a degree of upward social mobility, albeit over several generations, the census-inspired castes and tribes became rigid, static categories connected to one another within the caste system. Lower social groups who were on the way up economically tried to have themselves categorized under new names, thinking that would give them higher social status. Though this form of status enhancement was not always a successful strategy, it nevertheless introduced a new political process with regard to status-seeking in colonial India.[3]

The Anti-Brahmin movement of South India in the 1920s brought together many such local challenges to social hierarchy. Following Independence and the enactment of social legislation aimed at combating social hierarchy, political challenges to upper-caste hegemony spread to North India. The new administrative and juridical bodies such as the Commission for Scheduled Castes and Tribals and the Minorities Commission gave the necessary political and moral impetus to these early stirrings of resentment against social inequality. Thanks to these early developments, Indian society, seen in terms of status ranking, resembles a mosaic in motion, where one can distinguish different mobile pieces, without a central pattern to it. The variation in this overall picture becomes intelligible when one takes the local and regional diversity in social history and political conditions into account.

The Indian mosaic

The key to many of the issues arising out of India's politics is to be found in the interaction of India's traditional institutions and social diversity on the one hand, and the modern democratic political process on the other. A brief perusal of a national newspaper on any given day is likely to yield a rich harvest of social conflict, assertion of regional autonomy and communal conflagration. However, these conflicts take place in the context of a national community that both reinforces and questions the sense of regional separateness. These contradictory and converging pictures help explain why, despite a culture traditionally based on social hierarchy and patriarchy, steeped in mass poverty and high illiteracy, India has so resolutely moved towards a resilient democratic political order.

Caste and politics

Castes are endogamous status groups, traditionally based on hereditary occupations. The word entered Indian usage from its origin in the Portuguese word *casta* – which is how the early Portuguese traders referred to *jatis* – the generic term – to describe social stratification in India. Though *jatis* are derivatives of Hindu social practice, they are not exclusive to Hinduism. There are caste-like groupings among Muslims, Christians, Sikhs and Jains as well.

Castes are organized into caste systems in which they are ranked and tied together in a complex reciprocal relationship, based on the core idea of purity and pollution. The British codification of the caste system was based on the reading of holy texts written by Brahmins, glorifying their own role and power. Once codified, castes became fixed, rigid categories, for the purpose of the decennial census and administration. The ground reality was something else. Indian society was different from feudal Europe in terms of the flexibility of social differentiation. In pre-modern India, manufacture and agriculture were differentiated, and tradesmen thrived. That an indigenous capitalist class did not emerge came across to the early theorists of class as puzzling. Weber explains this puzzling coexistence of entrepreneurship and failure of a capitalist class to rise in terms of the role of the caste system as a transmission belt which transformed surplus wealth not into investment in productivity but into spirituality. From Bendix we learn:

'The people of Asia are notorious all over the world for their unlimited and unequalled greed. . . . But the point is that this "acquisitive drive" is pursued by all the tricks of the trade and with the aid of that cure-all: magic. In Asia the element was lacking which was decisive for the economy of the Occident, namely *the sublimation and rational utilization of this emotional drive which is endemic in the pursuit of gain.* . . .' (emphasis added).[4] As Weber saw it, popular belief was framed by the dominance of cultural and religious life by the high caste elites at the top. '[C]ertain common denominators of Indian religion – the belief in reincarnation, the idea of retribution (*karma*), and the identification of virtue with ritual observance – influenced the masses through the social pressures of the caste system' (Bendix 1960, p. 195f.).

Once the concept of caste became the basis of the official British view of India, the category acquired a life of its own. As we have already seen, the census became a means of upward mobility. For their own part, having codified the differentiation of Indian society in terms of the caste system, the British could depict Indian society as a noble classical civilization in a state of 'arrested decay' where their role was to help the minorities and untouchables by setting aside official canons for positive discrimination. The whole idea of giving additional privileges officially to a segment of the population – known by the new terms of 'scheduled castes and scheduled tribes' that merit it – came to dominate colonial India from 1858 onwards. From Independence onwards, the revival of the pre-modern norms in Indian politics has led, on the one hand, to a questioning of the British categories of caste, while on the other hand, the race to compete for scarce resources has reinforced the caste system as a category of social differentiation.

Local castes, or *jatis*, are the basic social units that still govern marriages, social networks, food taboos and rituals in most parts of rural India. Even in towns, where caste sometimes forms the basis of the choice of residence or professional networks, whole neighbourhoods might belong to particular castes. In the past, caste regulated the choice of occupation as well, which were typically caste-specific and hereditary at the same time. This has changed rapidly because of modernization and urbanization. In addition, competitive examinations for entry into the civil service, where former untouchables and tribals have a quota, have opened up top jobs that once were the prerogative of the upper castes.

There are more than 2,000 *jatis* in India, traditionally divided into four hierarchically ranked broad categories called *varnas*: (1) the Brahmins, who originally performed the traditional function of priests; (2) the Kshatriyas, who were the rulers and the warriors; (3) the Vaisyas, who were the mercantile classes; and (4) the Sudras, who were the service groups, agriculturists and artisans. Untouchable castes were outside the Hindu *varna* system. Mahatma Gandhi, in an effort to integrate them with the Hindu society, called them *Harijans* – children of God. This has now been replaced with the more radical term *dalit* – meaning the suppressed ones. Originally, the caste system presupposed the interdependent relationship of occupational groups, referred to as the *Jajmani* system.[5] *Jatis* were linked to one another through ties of reciprocal economic, social and political obligation. In the centre of this scheme of reciprocity stood social groups with controlling interests in land, whom other castes provided with services, and from whom they received a share of the harvest. The relationship of the lower castes to the high-caste landowners was hereditary, but their dependent status also carried some traditional rights such as distress relief at the time of natural calamities. All behaviour within the system, however, emphasized social hierarchy and inequalities of power, wealth and status. Control over land was the critical lever of social status and power. These oppressive aspects of the caste system have been increasingly contested by those at the bottom of the pyramid, particularly the former untouchables and the lower castes, mentioned in the constitution, respectively, as Scheduled Castes (SC), Scheduled Tribes (ST) and Other Backward Classes (OBC).

High-profile national politicians like Mayawati or Laloo Prasad Yadav might give the impression that the problem of untouchability is past. However, for millions like Muli – the untouchable protagonist of Freeman's (1979) narrative of everyday life of an Indian untouchable – social discrimination is a constant presence. The former untouchables are often excluded from social interaction with the four *varnas*, traditionally because of the 'polluting' nature of their occupation as scavengers. They number more than 135 million people and make up about a sixth of India's population. Attempts to elevate them into full membership in society through legislation, affirmative action, and competitive politics have accelerated since Independence. The Bahujan Samaj Party, currently the most important advocate of *dalit* self-assertion, is an important factor in the politics of northern India. It has placed many of its members in major ministerial positions, thanks to the strategy of forging broad-based political coalitions. The strategy of the BSP is to build a coalition of the top and bottom-most layers of society against the middle castes. Figure 3.3 shows Mayawati at an election rally with the BSP secretary who is Brahmin by caste.

Many Indians see the caste system as the cause of India's social fragmentation and economic backwardness. But castes are also the only basis of identity and social interaction for vast numbers of people. Democracy and economic change have thus sometimes worked at cross-purposes, creating conflict, fragmenting large castes into new social groups, and fusing several existing groups into caste associations. As new opportunities for enterprise and political linkage open up, castes are increasingly the basis of community formation. The new 'political caste' is an instrument for the promotion of collective interest by social groups who come together for that purpose. The instrumental role that caste plays in raising consciousness and electoral mobilization actually undermines the ideological basis of social hierarchy and helps question the more odious aspects of caste domination.[6] The politics of North India has recently been dominated by coalitions of former untouchables and the 'Backward Classes', who usually belong to the Sudras, the lowest *varna*.

The situation of India's aborigines known as tribals (who represent 8.2 per cent of the population) parallels that of the former untouchables. The colonial policy of declaring tribal areas as reserved or 'scheduled areas', where tribal lands could not be easily acquired by non-tribals. This policy has increasingly come under pressure because of the expansion of the market, population growth and political mobilization, causing resentment among tribals. Although tribals exist all over India and some tribal groups living in non-tribal areas have caste-like status, the majority are

Figure 3.3 Mayawati and S.C. Mishra, BSP General Secretary, at a rally in Lucknow
Source: *Frontline*, 2007.

concentrated in three main regions – the North-East (in Nagaland, Meghalaya and Arunachal Pradesh), the hill areas of Central India, and Western India. Overall, these regions are socially and economically backward, but the spirit of political competition pervades them as well. Movements for the creation of autonomous regions and the spread of Maoist violence are indicative of this tribal self-assertion.

Religion: unity in diversity

The constitution of India recognizes a diversity of cultures, creeds and religions, none of which is accorded a status of superiority over the others. That makes India, in terms of the formal structure of the country, a multi-cultural and multi-religious state. The word 'secular' was inserted into the preamble to the constitution in 1976. In Indian usage, it implies both a wall of separation between the church and the state, and an equal status to all religions. Consequently, though in terms of the data generated by India's decennial census India is a Hindu 'majority' country (80.5 per cent of the population are Hindus according to the latest census), this fact alone does not give a special status or hegemony to Hinduism. Hindus themselves are divided into many sects and denominations as well, to the point where some scholars question the status of Hinduism as a distinctive religion altogether.[7] Additionally, all other major religions of the world are present in India as well. In three smaller Indian States – Nagaland, Meghalaya and Mizoram – there is a Christian majority, in Punjab a Sikh majority, and in Jammu and Kashmir, a Muslim majority. However, the rapid rise of the Hindu-nationalist Bharatiya Janata Party is a reminder of the political appeal of pan-Indian Hinduism as an ideology (Chapter 6). The idea of a politically mobilized Hindu majority threatening the plural and democratic character of the political process is a source of some consternation among the minorities (see Table 3.1).[8]

Table 3.1 Religion in India

Religious group	1961*		2001	
	Number (million)	Percentage	Number (million)	Percentage
Hindus	366.5	83.5	827.6	80.5
Muslims	46.9	10.7	138.2	13.4
Christians	10.7	2.4	24.1	2.3
Sikhs	7.8	1.8	19.2	1.9
Buddhists	3.2	0.7	8.0	0.8
Jains	2.0	0.5	4.2	0.4
Other**	1.6	0.4	6.6	0.6
Total	439.2		1028.6	

* Excludes Mizo district, now part of Mizoram.
** Including persons not identified by religion.

Source: 1991: *India 1998: A Reference Annual*. New Delhi: Publication Division, Ministry of Information and Broadcasting, Government of India, p. 17, and Tata Services Limited, Department of Economic Statistics, *Statistical Outline of India, 2004–2005*. Mumbai: Tata Services Limited, Department of Economic Statistics, January 2005, p. 34.
2001: Census of India 2001: Data on Religion, Government of India (Office of the Registrar General), retrieved 23 January, 2009.

India's political process is robust enough to inject a degree of moderation to extreme sectional demands. The logic of electoral politics, as we shall see later in this chapter, accounts for both the origin of such movements and, once in power, for the moderation of their more extreme demands.[9] In addition, cultural plurality is an integral part of Hinduism. Its many sects and their separate traditions influence one another, leading to the growth of new forms.[10] Many Hindus believe in the concept of 'unity in diversity'. While from the outside Hinduism appears as a vast phalanx that is internally undifferentiated and externally bounded, in reality it is far from being so. It has a rich diversity in spite of attempts to simplify and standardize ritual and social practice.[11] Each cultural-linguistic area has its own 'little' tradition and local gods, and it is within the local sects that most Hindus live their religious life. The classical ideals of Hinduism and local traditions have freely interacted with each other, and with Muslims, leading to the syncretistic Sufi tradition, and to the growth of regional traditions and cross-regional movements.[12]

An earlier generation of Indian analysts thought that religious beliefs impeded the functioning of the modern state and economy. Religion, some held, was a major obstacle to social transformation. By an extension of the same argument, they believed that with modernization, religion would decline in importance.[13] In contrast, recent political developments have shown that religion, as one can notice from the political mobilization of religious minorities, can also become a political vehicle for social mobility. It can impart a sense of identity to social groups feeling discriminated against or threatened by other groups. This confluence between the search for identity and political competition is seen in a number of ways.[14] When adherents of a religion are regionally concentrated, such as Sikhs in Punjab and Muslims in Kashmir, there is a convergence between religion and regional identity. This generates a corresponding demand that the regional government incorporate the sacred beliefs of the religion, which, in turn, severely stretches the limit of the secular state in India.[15]

Hindu nationalist movements extend this logic by demanding the embodiment of Hindu cultural ideals within the structure of the modern state at the national level. In general, political parties and movements that draw their strength from religious beliefs and aspirations are quite strong in political and cultural self-assertion. Following their impressive gains in the parliamentary elections of 1996 and 1998 at the expense of the centrist forces (the communist vote has remained low but stable), Hindu nationalist parties have formed the government at the centre and in several States. The result of the 2004 parliamentary elections which voted the Hindu-nationalist NDA coalition out of power at the centre appears to have arrested the growth curve of Hindu nationalism. The results of the parliamentary election of 2009 show a reinforcement of the position of the Indian National Congress at the core of the UPA coalition which has won the support of a majority in the Lok Sabha and was invited by the President to form the new government. The BJP, however, continues to be the main opposition party in the parliament. Still, religion, particularly the exclusive right to places of worship and the right to stage religious processions in a religiously mixed neighbourhood, is one of the main causes of conflict in India today.

North India is dotted with mosques that stand next to Hindu temples or are built on spots where Hindu temples once stood. This shows the residual legacy of the Islamic conquest of India from the eighth century onward. Many of these structures are now at the centre of the religious storm that, judging from the Gujarat riots of 2002, continues to incite religious fervour and political passion.

Muslims constitute 13.4 per cent of the Indian population. It is difficult to talk in terms of a national Muslim community because India's Muslims speak many different languages, and are divided by class, sect and social stratification, much like their Hindu brethren. However, despite this social heterogeneity, the Muslims of India are a vocal and increasingly assertive and politically organized minority.[16] The demand for a separate homeland for Muslims by the Muslim League during the British colonial rule led to the Partition of British India and the creation of Pakistan in 1947, a new state with the explicit purpose of becoming the homeland of South Asia's Muslims. About two-thirds of the Indian Muslims and the bulk of the leaders of the Muslim League left India for Pakistan following the Partition. Over the past decades, the political void that Partition left behind has been largely filled in by the emergence of a new generation of leaders. Muslim representation in legislative bodies and in public life has grown since Independence and political competition has enhanced the sense of group assertion and a substantial increase in the scale, intensity and geographic spread of Hindu–Muslim conflict.

Sikhism – born about 400 years ago as a resistance movement against Islamic invaders – took on many of the theological and organizational features of both Hinduism and Islam. Some Sikhs feel that their identity is threatened by modernization and assimilation with Hinduism. They envision the creation of a sovereign Khalistan state as an exclusive homeland for Sikhs. Although they form a tenuous majority in the North Indian State of Punjab, this is constantly being depleted through emigration of enterprising Sikhs to other parts of India and abroad. Punjab is also home to the Akali Dal, a Sikh political party that was a partner in the NDA coalition.[17] The party which once had separatist aspirations has become very much a party of the establishment. Some Sikhs also fear the further loss of the Sikh majority in 'their homeland' because of the influx of non-Sikhs from poorer parts of India, attracted to Punjab by better wages. Others perceive further threats to Sikh identity and traditions from new habits being inculcated by the youth through modernization and from the growth of revisionist sects within Sikhism. These anxieties fuelled a political movement that took an increasingly violent turn, leading to the army's siege of the Golden Temple in the holy city of Amritsar which had become the fortified headquarters of the Sikh separatist movements. The military operation against the Golden Temple led to the assassination of Prime Minister Indira Gandhi by two of her Sikh bodyguards on 31 October, 1984.[18] However, a firm combination of repression of dissidents and accommodation of some of their leaders has seen relative peace return to Punjab. The case of Punjab thus reveals the challenges that a multi-religious society poses to political stability and its solutions.

The political diversity of India is also enriched by its modern associations, trade unions and all manner of movements in which people come together for the purpose of obtaining material advantages. Group formation has frequently led to inter-community strife initiated or exacerbated by groups promoting their shared interest. Social solidarity has become an important means of political mobilization. Political groups, which are created out of fission and fusion of traditional social groups, define their newly found identity as a mechanism for gaining benefits.

The absence of nationwide, cohesive, homogeneous ethnic groups has impeded the growth of an equivalent kind of tribal politics which has stymied the growth of democracy and modern institutions in many post-colonial democracies. With the exception of Kashmir, the Indian state has contained separatist movements through a combination of firmness and flexibility. The direction and pace of the process depend largely upon the leadership that emerges, the nature of its demands, and how effective the central and regional governments are in dealing with them. India, with all its diversity, has been relatively successful in managing and containing these conflicts through a process of political bargaining, accommodation and institutional change.[19]

Language

Along with caste and religion, language is one of the key components of identity. Language is also one of the main social cleavages in South Asia, as one can see in the role that linguistic nationalism played in the break-up of Pakistan, leading to the birth of Bangladesh in 1971, and the role of Sinhala nationalism in fomenting civil war in Sri Lanka. India's 18 major languages, each of which has evolved over the course of many centuries, are concentrated in different regions. Consequently, the mother tongue has become the focus of regional identity. Although Hindi is common in northern India, the different regions (and sub-regions) have their distinct dialects. Many are very highly developed, and have their own distinguished literary traditions. In the 1920s, sub-national loyalties based on language developed simultaneously with the nationalist movement. One of the persistent demands of the Indian National Congress was thus to redraw the map of British India along linguistic lines. Indeed, the Congress itself was organized on the basis of regional languages as early as 1920. Later, in 1956, the administrative map of India was redrawn and since then the Indian States have been reorganized on the basis of mother tongue (see Tables 5.1 and 5.2 in Chapter 5). The elevation of the main vernacular to the status of official language of the region has reinforced the multinational character of the Indian political system.

Indian languages can be divided into two main groups: the Indo-Aryan languages of the North (e.g. Punjabi, Hindi, Kashmiri, Bengali, etc.) and the Dravidian languages of the south (e.g. Telugu, Tamil, Kannada, Malayalam). The largest single language in India is Hindi, which, along with English, is also recognized as an official link language of India. The languages of North India all have a common Sanskritic base. A complex three-language formula gives Hindi the status of the national language while equalizing the chances of non-Hindi speakers of India for public services by conceding English the status of a link language. Regional languages are the main medium for official transactions within regions. Linguistic movements in India have thus contributed to the greater differentiation of the political system as well as to the overall legitimacy of the state, without, at the same time, damaging the basis of national integration.

Languages are linked to one another through dialects and bridge languages. Hindi and Urdu have spread widely over North India, and increasingly, in the South and the North-East, thanks to the film industry. English has stayed on, very much a link language and an international window, thanks to the internet.

Social class

Unlike China and Vietnam, despite the presence of both mass poverty and radical politics, India did not develop a national revolutionary peasant movement prior to Independence. When radical movements inspired by Marxism appeared in southern India shortly after India's Independence and in West Bengal in the 1960s, they did not spread to other parts of the country. The nature of colonial rule and Indian resistance to it, particularly the role of Gandhi, the Indian class structure, and the country's social fragmentation, are responsible for the muted nature of class conflict in India. The slow pace of industrialization and urbanization has led to a highly uneven pattern of class formation, and castes, tribes and ethnic groups that cut across class lines. Cross-cutting cleavages, the catch-all character of India's political parties and the formation of broad-based political coalitions have further mitigated the sharpness of social polarization on an enduring basis. This pattern has severely inhibited the development of class identities and political mobilization based on class appeals.

India's slow industrialization is indicated by the fact that the industrial working class is quite small. Only a small segment of it is unionized. The wages and services of these unionized workers are protected by strong labour legislation. Surrounded by workers in insecure jobs, unionized labour constitutes a veritable labour 'aristocracy'. India's rural class system is also quite complex. The land reforms of the 1950s eliminated some but not all intermediaries between the state and the farmer. In their place, there emerged a powerful new rural force composed of a mixed-status group of middle-peasant cultivators. These middle peasants, described by Lloyd and Susanne Rudolph as 'bullock capitalists', control 51 per cent of the agricultural land, constitute 35 per cent of the rural households and 25 per cent of the total population of India.[20] They are a powerful political force in rural India. Championed by peasant parties like the Bharatiya Kranti Dal or the Lok Dal in the 1970s, they have challenged urban interests, upper-caste-dominated parties, and the formally dominant position of the older social notables and ex-*zamindars*. However, with the independent mobilization of the former untouchables, who constitute the social layer just below, their position is also gradually being challenged, and giving rise to new cross-class, multi-caste coalitions.

The landless and small landowners (those holding fewer than 2.5 acres of land), divided by caste as well as class lines, in States like Uttar Pradesh and Bihar, do not share a common interest. The small landowners also do not identify with the needs and aspirations of the rural landless population. Under the pressure of mechanization, which requires a larger unit of production, the pressure on land has increased, leading to more landlessness. The dominant social groups are being challenged in some parts of India through the independent political organization of the former untouchables who in most cases are landless agricultural workers. Such movements as, for example, the *dalit* movements in western India and the Bahujan Samaj Party in northern India, constitute an important challenge to the dominance of the upper social strata.

In summary, from a comparative perspective, India comes across as a highly pluralistic *and* segmented society where the twin processes of modernization and democratization have transformed a hierarchical society into groups that see themselves as legitimate political actors. The groups themselves are short-term coalitions. As such, fission – the differentiation of groups – and fusion – the temporary coming together of different groups – are the rule. Cross-class and multi-caste organizations do not necessarily have a national structure because social networks are often confined to region and locality. Regions have increasingly acquired their own distinct identity in terms of economic and political status, and cross-regional coalitions deeply influence the course of national politics.

Political socialization and political culture

Despite mass poverty (India's per capita GNP in terms of purchasing power parity is about 6 per cent of that of the United States) and low literacy (about 65 per cent according to the 2001 census) India has sustained the democratic form of government adopted at Independence over the past six decades. The hiatus between these two important 'preconditions' of democracy and Indian reality is puzzling. To explain this phenomenon, it is necessary to analyse the political attitudes that underpin political behaviour in Indian society and how people came to acquire them.

Box 3.2 The right to vote: power of the powerless

The following press statement provides an insight into the empowerment of the powerless through the electoral process. A 55-year-old Dalit woman, 'pointing to the stain of the indelible ink on her fingers', says, 'I voted for Laloo.' The reporters point to the gaping cracks on her roof, her grandchild who [has] nothing to wear, the medicine she does not have, the two meals she cannot afford, and ask, 'Why?' She replies, 'All that has been there for thousands of years.' Saying this, she remembers the day the chief minister's helicopter landed on the nearby paddy field. 'Laloo came to visit us,' she announces. 'Since I was born, not even a crow has flown over our village.' The second report is equally revealing. A 45-year-old landless labourer, when asked about Laloo, breaks into what looks like a strange dance. He falls on his knees and with hands stretched in front, presses his flat forehead against the ground and begins to crawl backwards. 'Now I don't do this when my landlord walks by,' he shouts, 'Because Laloo said so.'

Source: Raj Kamal Jha and Farzand Ahmed, 'Laloo's
Magic', *India Today*, 30 April 1995.

The interaction of tradition and modernity

The mingling of modern institutions and pre-modern practices and symbols is an important part of the Indian system. In his introduction to India's political culture, Morris-Jones explains this phenomenon in terms of three idioms – namely, the modern, the traditional and the saintly.[21] The modern idiom understands politics as a competitive process of articulation and aggregation of interests. This modern idiom of Indian politics consists of the constitution and the courts, parliamentary debate, the higher administration, the upper levels of all the main political parties, and the entire English press and much of the Indian language press. The main debates of Indian politics – on issues of federalism, economic development, planning or defence expenditure, for example – take place in the modern language of politics, and as such are accessible to Western students of Indian politics.[22]

However, there is rarely an occasion when Indian politicians do not have recourse to some traditional concepts like *jati* or *dalits* or *parampara* (custom) that are deeply embedded in Indian religions and values like *shaheed* (martyrs) or *ahimsa* (non-violence). The saintly idiom mobilized with insuperable skill by Gandhi's *satyagraha* reflects on the core values of society that cut across both modern and traditional cleavages but does not necessarily refer to the spiritual or the otherworldly. Messages from leaders like Gandhi expressed in this mode can reach the whole society and 'stir the imagination of the advanced radical and the conservative traditionalist alike'.[23]

Though the three idioms of politics are conceptually distinct, they are not necessarily apart in reality. In fact, the same individual may combine all three: a University of California-trained computer engineer based in Bangalore might have daily transactions with his business partner in California's Silicon Valley. He might have an arranged marriage within his *jati* and linguistic region, and follow the food taboos and social rituals of his caste punctiliously. He might also belong to an internet network, avidly exchanging messages with the worldwide network of the VHP, the World Council of Hindus. Depending on the region, locality, length and depth of colonial rule, and the individual's class, gender and age, one idiom may be more clearly pronounced than another. Strategic political actors manipulate all those idioms in terms of their perception of particular cases and contexts. Consequently, the three appear as functionally related to one another in the competitive political marketplace of India. The tribe or *jati* network – operating as a caste association – can very well carry the modern message of individual rights, entitlement and electoral preferences to people who are first-generation voters. Simultaneously modern satellite television, broadcasting the *Ramayana* and *Mahabharata,* Hindu religious classics, can spread the message of an indigenous Indian identity that claims to be unique, authentic and exclusive. Since Independence, such interactions have led to the creation of new political forms and processes as well as to the emergence of two new themes of Indian political culture: the instrumentalization of politics and the politics of identity.

Indians use a wide variety of forms of political participation such as voting, lobbying and contacting, and failing these (or sometimes in addition to these), the coercive methods of direct action. These forms are found all over the country, in areas where European powers first settled 400 years ago as well as in those that have never had any direct experience of European rule – among affluent elites well versed in the form of modern politics as well as among the poorest, illiterate peasants who were mobilized into electoral politics after Independence. Reports in the Indian media bear witness to such widespread attitudes of empowerment by village women or marginal peasants.

The simultaneous use of participation and protest drawing upon modern institutions and traditional symbols and networks has caused the three idioms of politics to conflate. Consequently, the political process in India acts as a channel for the expression of a collective identity. The power and position of the English-speaking elite that had hitherto seen itself as urban, urbane and secular are contested, but more Indians send their children to English-medium primary and junior schools than ever before. This search for identity expresses itself not only in terms of national movements like those associated with Hindu nationalism, but also in the assertion of Sikh identity in Punjab and the tribal Jharkhand identity in southern Bihar, now given constitutional recognition in the form of the new federal State of Jharkhand. Similar aspirations for welfare and identity also underpin politics in Kashmir and India's North-East, violently clashing against the Indian state in their determination to assert their own vision of the State and nation.

Open articulation of such discord and violent clashes over interest and identity might give the impression that there is no central or unifying theme behind political attitudes in India, no 'Indian way' of doing things. In the heyday of India's freedom movement, Gandhi and the Congress defined this central thrust of India's political culture. After Independence, Nehru and the Congress government articulated the core values of India's political culture in terms of secularism, socialism and democracy. Six decades later, the Congress party and its programme no longer occupy that central place it once held.[24] Instead, the political system is uneasily groping towards a redefinition of India's core values in terms of communal accommodation, capitalism and democracy. Once in power, cultural-nationalist parties have downplayed separatist themes like a Tamil homeland or an exclusive homeland for the 'sons of the soil', and they have gradually accommodated themselves within the Indian Union. The Communist Party of India, in power in West Bengal, is also trying to accommodate itself within the new political culture of enterprise.[25]

Political socialization

The range of attitudes mentioned above indicates the complex interaction taking place between tradition and modernity – a process that can be further investigated through specific questions: How do Indians acquire their political attitudes? How do the contenders for power communicate their positions on issues facing Indian society? How do the perception of authority and evaluation of political leaders vary across regions and sections of the population? Why have the electronic media achieved such prominence in India's electoral politics over the past years? The analysis that follows will illustrate the process of political socialization in the context of a traditional society undergoing rapid change.

Conventionally, in stable democracies the individual is politically socialized through family, school, secondary association and workplace. Totalitarian political systems usually inculcate the 'right' political attitudes by guiding the individual through school, youth groups, front organizations and, for the privileged few, party membership. Neither model is completely available to India. Modernization has greatly diluted the effective role that family, caste and kin once played in moulding attitudes. The totalitarian path is forbidden in theory by the constitution that guarantees the fundamental freedoms of thought, belief, faith, association and movement, and in practice, by a functioning and occasionally fractious political process.

Indian analysts started using public opinion surveys quite early, and this has made it possible to track changing opinions and attitudes that show a steady rise in political consciousness, a sense of empowerment and political information. Television, which is no longer a state monopoly, along with the internet, have accelerated the pace of the spread of political information in recent years.

Social change has influenced political socialization through means other than family, caste or tribe. But as far as the conventional instruments of political socialization are concerned, the state in India has two main institutional constraints. Schools, in the absence of a national curriculum (primary education, under the federal division of powers, is a state subject) and in the absence of a tradition of civics education, are not an effective means of imparting or inculcating a common set of national values. Thus, it is not possible for the state to suggest a national policy. Even regional governments have prudently avoided the temptation of interfering with the contents and administration of schooling, though recent attempts by some regional governments to introduce a new ideological bias into school books created a nationwide protest from educationists. A similar attempt by the communist government of Kerala in 1959 led the President of India to dismiss the Kerala government on the grounds that lawful government of the State was not possible. This act has restrained the enthusiasm of newly elected governments in India to seek to spread their ideas among the people by incorporating them into textbooks and school administration. As we learn from Lloyd and Susanne Rudolph, such attempts are ultimately self-defeating.[26]

The foregoing suggests that educational institutions, for constitutional and political reasons, are not an effective institutional medium for the Indian state to promote a cohesive national political culture. But that is not the same as saying that schooling has no impact on promoting legitimacy and personal efficacy. Formal education is associated with the legitimacy of the electoral process; the individual's sense of efficacy increases with education, as does confidence in politicians. However, there is a large body of illiterates whose evaluation of the personal accountability of individual politicians is at a lower level than the average, and a section of that group does not believe that elections are the only way to conduct politics. These are the parts of the population where leaders of mass movements are likely to find potential support.

In the past, mass illiteracy was the other main obstacle to state-sponsored political socialization through the print media. This has been overcome by the electronic media, which are restrained neither by the inability to read and write nor by the remoteness of villages from the capital, thanks to televisions, mobile phones and cheap internet access. Additionally, the introduction of competition into broadcasting has brought in diversity and sensitivity to consumer demands, and thereby vastly enhanced the appeal of the electronic media. An innovation in this respect is internet sites that expose corruption in high quarters.[27]

Until the onset of liberalization and penetration by the electronic media, the processes of political participation and electoral campaigns were the most effective tools of political socialization. New political attitudes and skills have evolved through participation. The pre-Independence legacies have also been enriched and sometimes replaced by developments since Independence. As a result, Indian society today is as affected by recent changes in its political and economic form as by its historical inheritance.

In the early years after 1947, the modernizing leaders around Nehru and the Congress leadership paid routine homage to a vaguely defined Indian nationalism, social democracy, economic self-reliance through import substitution, and secularism, understood as both the separation of state and religion and equal respect for all religions. But, in sharp contrast to other new states, these broad and abstract ideas were not made into a dogma. The Congress party itself harboured many factions that differed widely from one another in personal loyalties as well as ideological leanings.

As a result, in each of these major initiatives undertaken by the state, a significant variation of normative theory was used. The socialist aspirations of Nehru and the myth of the independent peasant producer were intertwined in the policies of land reforms. The neo-Gandhian approach, embodied in *panchayati raj* and community development, was juxtaposed with an equally powerful belief in the rational individual as the basis of voting decisions. Much reliance was placed on the ability of such individuals to identify parties as well as candidates as a result of their knowledge about the relationship of issues to voting choices. The market as the driving force behind production, consumption, credit and communication was promoted with as much vigour as central planning and bureaucratic implementation, and both aimed at achieving the same objective. These ideas, whether indigenous to India or gleaned from elsewhere, were formulated at the apex of the system and were expected to trickle down to the regional and local arenas.

Efficacy and legitimacy in India

Thanks to the availability of good and reliable public opinion data, we are in a position to observe the sense of efficacy within different subsections of the Indian population.[28] In response to the question 'Do you think your vote has effect?' one can notice the steady rise of the sense of efficacy in the population as a whole, going up from 48.5 per cent of the entire population in 1971 to 67.5 per cent in 2004 (see Table 3.2). Interestingly, the gain in efficacy has come from the steady decline in those who either do not have an opinion, or are not able to take a position on the question. The percentage of those who do not feel efficacious appears to have stayed low (less than a fifth of the population as a whole) but stable over the three decades between 1971 and 2004. Table 3.2 also reports on the sense of efficacy of the sub-populations. Thus, in 1996 as well as in 2004, those with a higher level of efficacy tended to be male, upper class, upper caste and highly educated. However, scheduled castes, Muslims and Christians also appear on the higher levels of efficacy. This, as we shall see later in the book, is the consequence of political mobilization, driven by ambitious leaders working out of special interest constituencies within the electorate.

A pattern similar to efficacy can be noticed in the case of legitimacy. Here, the question has been posed in the negative, in order to make sure that those who consider the existing political system, based on parties, elections and assemblies, preferable to one without these attributes of parliamentary democracy will answer the question in the negative – not an easy thing to do for interviewees facing college-educated young men and women, carrying clip boards, and ceremoniously writing

Table 3.2 Efficacy of vote (in per cent)

Question: *'Do you think your vote has effect on how things are run in this country, or, do you think your vote makes no difference?'*

	1971	1996	1999	2004
Has effect	48.5	58.6	63.0	67.5
Makes no difference	16.2	21.3	17.4	17.5
Don't know	35.3	19.1	19.6	15.0

Vote has effect	1996	2004
Illiterate	47.0	54.9
Scheduled tribe	47.8	58.4
Very poor	50.4	59.2
Female	50.8	61.3
Aged 56 years or above	51.9	62.6
Rural	56.9	66.2
OBC	58.0	67.8
Hindu	58.0	67.7
All India	**58.6**	**67.5**
Scheduled caste	60.0	65.1
Muslim	60.3	66.6
Aged 25 years or less	60.8	68.1
Upper caste	61.5	70.9
Upper socio-economic class	62.1	78.7
Urban	64.1	72.3
Male	66.2	73.0
Christian	66.4	69.6
College and above	79.6	82.4

Source: National Election Survey, CSDS (Delhi) 1971, 1996, 1999, 2004.

the answers down. Impressively, the percentage of those who see the political system as legitimate has gone up from 43.4 per cent in 1971 to 72.2 per cent in 2004. As in the case of efficacy, here also the gain has been made by a decline in those without an opinion or the undecided. A small percentage of the population, hovering around a tenth of the total, remains convinced that alternatives to parliamentary democracy might be better. Further analysis shows that those highly educated, upper castes and Christians, urban, male and younger sections of the population are on the higher levels of legitimacy.

Finally, the fact of an increase in personal efficacy and institutional legitimacy might still underpin rising group consciousness, and in the case of contentious issues such as the idea of having a single personal law for the entire Indian population, the sense of personal efficacy might actually enhance fragmentation of the national community. The question asked here is about having a separate personal law for each religious community rather than having one universal civil code for everyone living within Indian territory, regardless of religion. The results reported in Table 3.4 show a steady rise in those who do not see a problem with each community having its own civil code, their numbers having grown from 44.4 per cent in 1996 to 53.8 per cent. Here, too, the percentage of those who 'don't know' has diminished, thus empha-sizing the growing political consciousness of the people as a whole. Those opposed to this form of multi-culturalism – though the numbers are still small – argue in

Table 3.3 Legitimacy (in per cent)

Question: Suppose there were no parties or assemblies and elections were not held – do you think that the government in this country can be run better?

	1971	*1996*	*2004*
Yes	14.2	11.4	9.0
No	43.4	68.8	72.2
Can't say or don't know	42.4	19.8	18.8

Not better government without parties		*1996*	*2004*
Very poor		61.5	65.9
Illiterate		61.6	61.1
Sikh		62.7	66.2
56 years or above		63.2	68.4
Female		64.0	67.1
OBC		65.4	72.1
Scheduled tribe		66.3	68.0
Scheduled caste		67.3	69.0
Urban		68.1	79.6
Hindu		68.2	72.6
All India		**68.8**	**72.2**
Rural		69.0	70.3
25 years or less		71.3	73.2
Upper class		71.6	81.8
Muslim		72.1	72.9
Male		73.4	76.8
Christian		73.4	72.8
Upper caste		73.9	75.5
College and above		74.1	85.0

Source: National Election Survey, CSDS (Delhi) 1971, 1996, 1999, 2004.

Table 3.4 Need for separate civil code for every community by party support (in per cent)

	1996						*2004*					
	INC	*BJP+*	*NF*	*LF*	*BSP*	*Total*	*UPA*	*NDA*	*LF*	*BSP*	*SP*	*Total*
Disagree	29.9	36.5	29.4	22.1	30.4	**30.4**	27.4	29.7	22.4	20.2	22.3	**27.1**
Don't know	23.8	22.9	28.5	18.2	24.8	**25.1**	19.0	17.4	15.0	26.3	23.5	**19.2**
Agree	46.3	40.6	42.2	59.6	44.7	**44.4**	53.6	52.9	62.6	53.5	54.2	**53.8**

Support for separate civil code		*1996*	*2004*
Hindu		41.5	52.1
All India		**44.4**	**53.8**
Christian		50.2	61.2
Sikh		51.6	48.5
Muslim		67.1	66.0

Source: National Election Survey, CSDS (Delhi) 1971, 1996, 1999, 2004; Mitra and Singh (2009), p. 117.

favour of cultural nationalism, which demands a close liaison between the cultural basis of the community and the structure of law and order. The sections in the lower part of Table 3.4 provide a glimpse into the hiatus between the advocates of different religions. Muslim opinion is most in favour of separate laws for different communities, going up to 67 per cent in 1996 and 77 per cent in 2004, while Hindu opinion remains at 41.5 per cent. An even more interesting statistic is the support for separate civil codes among supporters of the Hindu nationalist BJP – impressive at 40.6 per cent in 1996 and 52.9 per cent in 2004 in the NDA, dominated by the BJP.

Conclusion

The chapter has discussed how social hierarchy as the basis of social exclusion and political dominance has gradually lost legitimacy. How successful has India been in achieving the kind of society which recognizes the legitimacy of difference and provides the moral and material means to different communities to assert their difference, and find a rightful and dignified position within the larger national community? Survey data and reports in the media provide some insights to this crucial aspect of India's political system and process. The traditional social structure, under the cumulative effect of positive discrimination, the electoral process where numbers rather than status play the key role and the logic of the competitive market in talents, skills and social networks have turned hierarchy into plurality and deeply affected India's political culture, particularly with regard to attitudes towards efficacy, legitimacy, trust and entitlement.

One of the consequences of the larger process of politial and social transformation brought about by Independence, transition to democracy, electoral mobilization and redressive social action is a social structure marked by extreme fragmentation and short-term political alliances for electoral gain. Some analysts see this fact as the indispensable basis for Indian democracy, responsible for the non-emergence of class or community as a polarizing political cleavage. Unlike China or Vietnam where peasant mobilization on the issue of class facilitated the rise of a political revolution led by the communist party, or Sri Lanka where the emergence of ethnic identity polarized society into warring camps of Tamils and Sinhalese, Indian society has segmented and coalesced in a manner which provides a constituency for every possible opinion while making it possible, nevertheless, for liberal democracy to function, thanks to the logic of coalition politics. The chapter that follows builds on the spectrum of cross-cutting cleavages that characterize Indian society today, and examines how and with what success Indian institutions have sought to weave the parts into a coherent state, a political community and an emerging nation.

Notes

1 See Dumont (1970) and Freeman (1979).
2 See Naipaul (1990), p. 517.
3 In his case study of the 'breast-cloth controversy', Hardgrave (1968) gives a brilliant demonstration of how the norm of legal equality, backed up by the might of British rule, cut into the rigid hierarchy that had relegated the untouchable caste of Shanans to the status of degraded pariahs, whose women were not allowed to cover their breasts in public. With growing prosperity from toddy-tapping, and with the support of missionaries, the Shanans could successfully resist the attempt of the local upper castes to enforce this taboo, and eventually got themselves registered in the census as Nadars.

4 'Caste was the "transmission belt" between the speculative ideas of the intellectual elite, and the mundane orientation of religious observance among the people at large' (Bendix 1962, p. 196). By its traditionalism, the caste system retards economic development, and conversely, inter-caste barriers become attenuated wherever economic activities attain an increased momentum. Thus, '*the spirit of the caste system militated against an indigenous development of capitalism*' (emphasis added, ibid.).

5 Beals (1963), p. 41.

6 Caste consciousness transforms caste from an ascriptive status to a politically convenient self-classification. For a discussion of the efforts to improve the material conditions of the former untouchables through the policy of reservation and the upper caste backlash against it, see Mitra (1987), pp. 292–312.

7 See Sontheimer and Kulke (1989).

8 Recent survey findings reinforce the impression that opinions on the issue of Ayodhya are polarized. Asked if 'only the Ram temple should be built on the spot where the mosque stood', 68 per cent of Muslims disagree compared to only 20 per cent of Hindus. However, support among Hindus for the proposition that 'India should make greater efforts for friendly relations with Pakistan' remains around 40 per cent, although support among Muslims has slightly decreased from the earlier 72 per cent to 65 per cent. Judging from the findings of opinion polls, while India's political process continues to reinforce group consciousness, thus creating a political distance between different communities, it also generates a sense of personal efficacy which leads to the emergence of new, short-term alliances among opposing groups. We shall come back to this theme later in this chapter. National Election Study (NES), 1999, CSDS Delhi.

9 See Malik and Singh (1992), pp. 318–36.

10 For an excellent study of the origin of political institutions and attitudes in India, see *Sources of Indian Tradition* by Embree (1991), vol. 1 and Hay (1991), vol. 2.

11 See also *Sources of Indian Tradition* for references to the attempts and movements to develop a standard form of worship, to simplify ritual, and to spread egalitarian norms within the Hindu community.

12 The Jagannath cult of Orissa is an example of this form of syncretism. See Mitra (1994), pp. 46–68.

13 'There is a good chance that 20 years from now, many of India's constitutional anomalies regarding the secular state will have disappeared. It is reasonable to expect that by that time there will be a uniform civil code and that Hindu and Muslim law, as such, will have ceased to exist. Legislation having already dealt with the most serious abuses in Hindu religion there will be little need for further interference by the state' (Smith 1963, p. 134).

14 Mitra (2005a), pp. 77–96.

15 Mitra (1991a), pp. 755–77.

16 Mitra (2005a).

17 See Jeffrey (1986).

18 See Singh (1993), pp. 84–105.

19 See Mitra (1995), pp. 57–78.

20 See Rudolph and Rudolph (1987), p. 49.

21 Morris-Jones (1987), p. 58.

22 This theme has been developed further in Jyotirindra Dasgupta, 'India: democratic becoming and combined development', in Diamond *et al.* (1989), p. 62.

23 Morris-Jones (1987), p. 61. The statement, first made in 1962, turned out to be prophetic, because J.P. Narayan became a rallying point for opposition to the Emergency in 1975.

24 The resurgence of the Congress as a national party in the parliamentary election in 2009 holds an important pointer towards a re-alignment of forces. See Chapter 6.

25 The press reported that the Left Front government at the height of its power in West Bengal was busy sending 'high-profile delegations to woo foreign investment and attract European investment in agriculture', while the draft resolution for the next party conference 'deprecates the trend towards liberalization which has resulted in a bonanza for foreign capital and Indian big business' (Manas Ghosh, 'Lack of identity: options before the CPI(M)', *The Statesman Weekly*, 22 April, 1995, p. 11). However, the recent conflict over the attempt of the communist government of West Bengal to set up a Special Economic Zone (SEZ) shows how arduous the task of repositioning a party can be.

26 Rudolph and Rudolph (1982), pp. 131–54.
27 In March 2001 the Internet News Agency 'Tehelka' uncovered a bribery scandal among leading government officials which caused the resignation of Defence Minister George Fernandes, BJP Party President Bangaru Laxman and the President of the Samata Party, Jaya Jaitly.
28 The data, collected from face-to-face interviews with a representative sample of the Indian adult population by trained interviewers, have been graciously made available by the Centre for the Study of Developing Societies, Delhi. For details about the method of sampling and fieldwork, see Mitra and Singh (2009).

4   Strength with democracy

Separation of powers and the imperative of leadership

It is by this mixture of monarchical, aristocratical, and democratical powers, blended together in one system, and by these three estates balancing one another, that our free constitution of government hath been preserved so long inviolate.

Bolingbroke, *A Dissertation upon Parties* (1733–34),
cited in Sabine (1975), p. 515.

. . . they [India's Prime Ministers] have often . . . achieved a kind of transcendence . . . and to provide moral leadership to the country, which is rather surprising for leaders who are partisan figures.

Manor (1994), p. 13.

Introduction

Following Independence, under the leadership of Prime Minister Jawaharlal Nehru, the government of India undertook an ambitious programme of social and economic reform. Similar projects in post-revolutionary countries like the USSR and China had relied on a cadre-based party to implement the agenda of modernization. In contrast, India at Independence did not have a revolutionary past or a cadre-based party comparable to the Communist Party of China. Instead, the constitution and the political institutions were expected to undertake the burden of nation-building. The chapter analyses how the institutional arrangement of India helped adapt the agenda of modernization to Indian conditions, and how its consequences – the legitimization of the norms of modernity, secularism, individual rights and independence of the judiciary, and the political recruitment of new social groups who were mobilized through this agenda – became, eventually, the bulwark of Indian democracy, and survived the passing away of the generation that was identified with the founding of the Republic. The chapter shows how the new state and its institutions succeeded in establishing themselves as the legitimate political centre of India's diverse society, and in bringing social organizations such as castes, tribes, religious orders and regional kin networks into a coherent national political community.

Modern political institutions and traditional society

India's success in making the transition from colonial rule to democratic governance has considerably benefited from the unintended consequences of colonial rule in the form of the growth of an elite well versed in the rules of parliamentary democracy – and the historical contingency which made it possible for them to play a key role in formulating the constitution. The unfolding of the institutional arrangement led to the development of countervailing forces which, in turn, secured the democratic ethos of the constitution. In particular, the intricate scheme of the separation and division of powers, the watchdog function of the judiciary and the parliament, and the bridging function of the Prime Minister (Figure 4.1) and the bureaucracy played crucial roles in the process of transition.

India emerged from colonial rule with a group of statesmen led by Jawaharlal Nehru. They united on a modern, secular, socialist agenda of nation-building, and were distinguished politicians and capable administrators in their own right. Nevertheless, they were loyal to the Congress party. Quite unusually for the emerging post-colonial states of their time, they shared a plural vision of the state and society that they were engaged in building. The Indian agenda and the line-up of these leading personalities responsible for its implementation were different from the totalitarian vision and authoritarian leadership of China and, in many ways, from Pakistan's. India's leaders sought to accommodate elements of traditional society within the framework of modern institutions. However, when specific individuals strayed too far off what the democratic and secular ethos required, the central leadership of the Congress party – deferentially referred to as the *High Command* – pulled them back to the mainstream. This method of reconciling regional and local autonomy within the framework of a modern state trying to assert its authority has been referred to as 'the rule by consensus' and 'accommodation'.

As one can only expect, from the outset, the political system faced a hiatus between authority vested in the modern institutions of the state and political power, which was dispersed among social groups.[1] The problem, staple of the scholarship on transitional societies,[2] was by no means peculiar to India. The relatively sudden withdrawal of the British colonial state which had kept a segmented society and several hundred princely states firmly together led to the chaos and large-scale violence that marked the Partition of the country.

In his classic study of the making of the Indian constitution – *The Indian Constitution: Cornerstone of a Nation* – Granville Austin (1966) sums up the problem of balancing the authority and legitimacy of the modern state with the power of traditional society to which it was held accountable by the constitution. Austin refers to it in terms of reconciling strength with democracy. Typically, the former requires the concentration of authority and the latter, its dispersion. The English polity has developed this delicate balance over the course of centuries since the signing of the Magna Carta in the year 1215 when a few aristocrats made King John concede to the principle of limitations on executive authority. India, where the traditional society was held under the tutelage of the colonial state with its attendant asymmetric power relations for close to two centuries prior to Independence, does not have the culture and tradition of the separation of powers on the English model. There are no indigenous equivalents to the likes of John Locke, Bolingbroke and Montesquieu. However, fortuitously, but also by design, India has found her own solution to the problem of authority and legitimacy, and put it to concrete practice in the office of the Prime Minister. By combining authority and accountability (see Figure 4.1 below) this office gives a central focus to the constitutional arrangement. The nature, components and limits of the Indian solution to the problem of authority in changing societies have considerable comparative significance.

The adoption of British parliamentary democracy as the model of India's governance at Independence in 1947 was in a way a natural consequence of the application of a series of legislative instruments with the British stamp on them, starting with the Council Act of 1830 (Chapter 2). The successive generation of Indian leaders who have had to act as intermediaries between the British and the Indian population were already familiar with the British statutes and the bargaining that characterized the political process. The real change, for many of them, came in terms of the vast number of jobs and governmental resources available.

In the event, the form of government that was introduced in 1947 included the main features of the British system, namely the accountability of the executive to the legislature, a professional and politically neutral military and career civil service, and the rule of law, all operating within the framework of a parliamentary system. Some salient features of the political system of the United States such as federalism, the separation of powers, and fundamental rights of individuals protected by a Supreme Court were also introduced. These constitutional and legislative measures reflected the visions of Prime Minister Nehru and Home Minister Vallabhbhai Patel as well as the leaders of the underprivileged – most notably Bhim Rao Ambedkar, the chief architect of the constitution, who wanted to give concrete shape to a broad vision

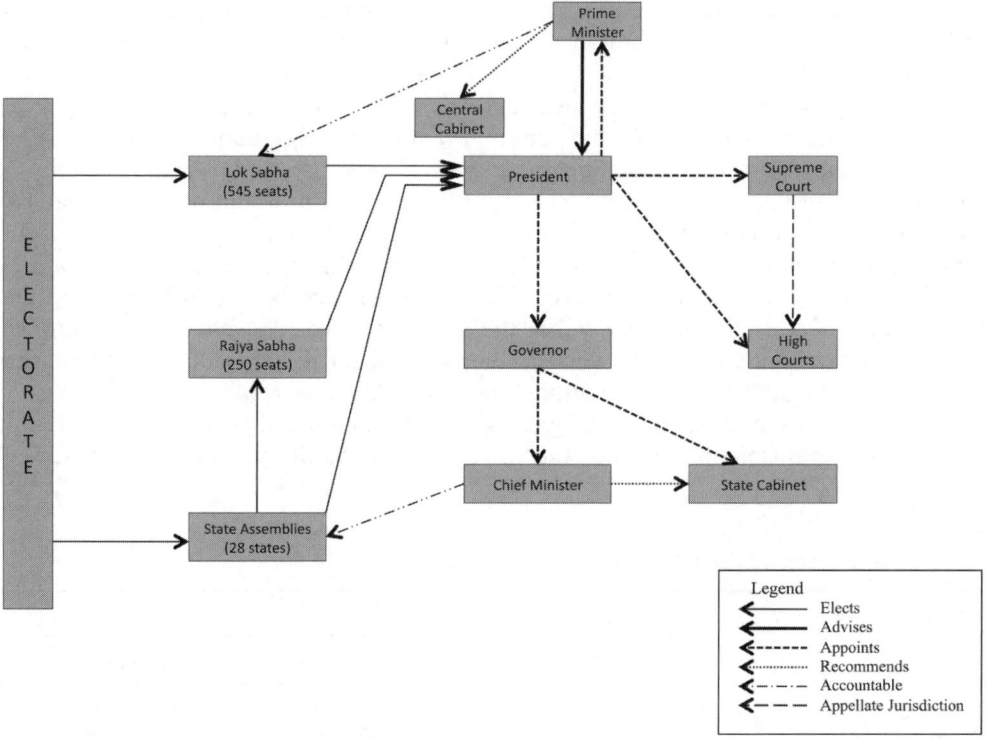

Figure 4.1 India's institutional arrangement
Source: Drawn by author.

of a modern, secular, democratic India, mobilizing its resources towards the twin objectives of growth and redistribution.

India in 1947, as we have already seen in Chapter 2, started with several advantages that eventually facilitated the growth of a parliamentary democracy. The transition from colonial rule provided a continuity of both the leadership and the institutional structure. The bureaucracy and security apparatus, both with a large contingent of well-trained Indians, were available for a smooth transition. Above all, the development of the Congress party organization into a nationwide electoral organization made for a unified exercise of power. The Partition of India, by removing the Muslim League which had been the main challenger to the Congress party in the political arena, produced a smaller state but a more cohesive political system. The leaders of the successor state quickly adapted themselves to the new, competitive political environment, based not so much on nationalist ideals as on the pragmatic politics of patronage and public policy. This led to the creation of a political system that institutionalized representation, competition, and accountability.

Finally, Nehru's adoption of non-alignment as the cornerstone of India's foreign policy created a conceptual symmetry between India's domestic and international politics. The result was the rise to prominence of a generation of inward-looking political leadership that saw elections and the growth of a self-reliant economy as the main basis of legitimacy. This basic institutional structure has survived the challenges of the past six decades, a period that includes the demise of the generation of leaders who were in charge at the time of Independence. The political system has thus been able to withstand the challenge by the newly-mobilized social groups, left- and right-wing radicalism, famine, mass poverty and large-scale changes in the economy, a major border war against China in 1962, and three wars against Pakistan.

One legacy of the Indian resistance to British rule was a deep distrust of power and a determination to secure the maximum possible freedom for citizens. The members of the Constituent Assembly gave shape to these aspirations in the institutions they devised. In some cases, they drew upon India's cultural and political legacies, but in others they borrowed widely from the major constitutions of the Western world. The result was the separation of power among the executive, the legislature, and the judiciary, at the national level. This is represented by the President and the Council of Ministers, the parliament, and the Supreme Court, respectively, to complete the system of countervailing powers; an equally robust division of power between the federal government and the regions was established as well (see Table 4.1).

The functional separation of executive, legislative and judicial powers – respectively, to tax and administer, to legislate, and to ensure that public life follows the rule of

Table 4.1 The separation and division of powers in India

Levels of Government	Powers		
	Executive	*Legislative*	*Judicial*
National	President-in-Council	Parliament	Supreme Court
Regional	Governor-in-Council	Assembly	High Court
Local	District Magistrate	*Zilla parishad*	District Court

Source: Drawn by author.

law – and their union in the person of the Crown is a quintessentially English idea with which India had made the first acquaintance as far back as the Council Act of 1830. The Constituent Assembly adapted this concept to the Indian context, but with an important modification. Significant amounts of executive and legislative power were set aside for the region, under a federal division of areas of competence. In its enthusiasm for the decentralization of power, the Constituent Assembly did not stop there. There were strong hopes for the devolution of power below the level of the regional governments, to be exercised directly by the representatives of the people. This hope took concrete shape in 1957 when the Balwantrai Mehta Committee recommended the creation of a *panchayati raj*, to set up representative bodies at the district, sub-district and village levels. Endowed with a measure of administrative autonomy, they were charged with developmental functions and were allocated adequate financial means to put these ideas into practice. The implementation of *panchayati raj* has been far from uniform, but thanks to the 73rd amendment of the constitution in 1993, all of India's half a million villages are covered by some form of direct exercise of power by the residents.

The resultant structure had tremendous potential for political fragmentation and social conflict. However, India's 'state-dominated pluralism'[3] – a political system where a powerful state functions as an honest broker among a multiplicity of social groups – provided the right balance between central direction and respect for regional and local autonomy. There are two further constitutional mechanisms to generate a dynamic balance between integration and differentiation. To cope with extraordinary situations where rapid action was imperative, the constitution gave a series of 'Emergency powers' to the national executive to meet the challenge of grave political crises. These make it possible for the central authority to step in to protect the territorial integrity of the state, maintain lawful governance, particularly in the regions, and a third, not yet tested provision – to maintain the financial viability of the state as a whole. These powers are meant to be exercised formally by the President but in practice guided by the recommendation of the Prime Minister. Similarly, although the constitution formally vested authority in the President, everyday exercise of executive power and legislative initiative was intended to be in the hands of the Prime Minister, whose accountability to the parliament ensures a bridge function between the law-making and administrative organs of the state. Similarly, the office of the governor – formal head of the regional government – appointed by the President at the recommendation of the Prime Minister, constitutes a crucial link between the central government and the States, so that both the autonomy of the State and its accountability to lawful governance can be maintained at the same time. This intricate institutional arrangement with large elements taken from the British practice to which a good measure of inspired borrowing from other traditions and a significant amount of indigenous innovation have been added is explained in detail in Figure 4.1.

The executive

The role of the President as the head of state was designed with the British monarch in mind, but in practice the office combines the ceremonial roles of head of state with some substantive powers. Under the Indian constitution, executive power is formally vested in the President, and he is expected to exercise these powers on the advice of the Council of Ministers, with the Prime Minister at its head. The real lines of control, as shown in Figure 4.1, nevertheless indicate otherwise.

The President appoints the Prime Minister and has the authority to dismiss him. But, unlike in neighbouring Pakistan, no Prime Minister has ever been dismissed by a President. By convention, the powers of the President are severely limited. The President invites the leader of the majority party or coalition in the Lok Sabha – the lower house of the parliament – to form the government. The President exercises his authority as advised by the Prime Minister. But that does not mean that the President is merely a 'rubber stamp'. The President might identify a potential leader when there is no clear parliamentary majority. This was the case in 1989 with V.P. Singh who was invited to form the government when Rajiv Gandhi, the leader of the Congress party, which had the largest number of seats in the Lok Sabha, stated that he did not intend to form the cabinet. More recently, after the parliamentary elections of 2009, the President invited Manmohan Singh to form the government again. Since 1989, the President has been extraordinarily watchful in upholding constitutional norms, and preventing the use of governmental powers for partisan purposes. This has greatly contributed to the growth in the stature of the presidency.

Though the Indian constitution successfully replicated the British method of the separation of the executive from the legislature and their union in the office of the Prime Minister, there was an important detail that was missing. In Britain, the Queen reigns and the Prime Minister rules, but India does not have a hereditary ruler who would combine the dignity of high office with its entirely ceremonial character. Unlike the British head of state, the Indian President needs to be elected but in a manner where the fact of election will not undercut the power and legitimacy of the Prime Minister. The election procedure involves the political representation and active participation of all regions of the country as well as the national and regional political parties.[4] The President is elected through proportional representation by single transferable votes, a complicated electoral procedure that has been explicitly designed to ensure uniformity among the States as well as parity between the regions as a whole, and the nation. The President's five-year term can be renewed and though no President of India to date has had to undergo it, the President can be removed through impeachment by the parliament.

The synchronization of the personalities of the President and the Prime Minister and the coordination of their roles are crucial to the successful functioning of the Indian political system. Quite fortuitously for India, Rajendra Prasad, the first President of the Republic, closely cooperated with Nehru as Prime Minister, which set the precedent for subsequent occupants of the office. Both – Nehru as the head of the interim government and Prasad as the chairman of the Constituent Assembly – had had considerable administrative experience prior to assuming office. Their long association with the Congress party had acquainted them with the culture of consensus and accommodation that were the characteristics of the party most of the time. Temperamentally, Nehru, the modernist, charismatic leader, hugely popular with the masses, could be in the driving seat of the new government, whereas Prasad, who ultimately deferred to Nehru, was a low-key, respected leader who was more attuned to the party organization than to the electorate. In office, he became a natural rallying point for conservative opinion within the ruling party. In this way, both modern and conservative opinion within the ruling party as well as in the parliament as a whole felt that they were represented at the highest level of government but neither felt exclusively in charge of the affairs of the nation. In sum, compromise and the ability to learn from experience became the method of functioning of India's first cabinet.

Looking back, one can sense that during those vital, formative years, most of the bickering was kept well under wraps so that the public could see the leadership as united and coherent. This increased the legitimacy of the first post-Independence government considerably. Finally, the early presidents like Rajendra Prasad and S. Radhakrishnan were eminent statesmen who, though elected, were not seen as politicians. That could help attain the ultimate goal of parliamentary democracy where the state is both intensely political and slightly above everyday politics. These early conventions were set under the long joint stewardship of Nehru and Prasad, and continued under Prasad's successor, Radhakrishnan. The convention has held fast as India has seen a succession of eminent men – from different walks of life, professions, religions and social origins – occupy the high office of the President, and now, with Pratibha Patil, India has her first female President. The combination of prime ministerial leadership and presidential vigilance has become India's own way of making parliamentary democracy work (see Figure 4.2).

The fact that the Congress party had already acquired governmental experience under colonial rule and lent a sense of cohesion to the small number of key elites who oversaw the transition from colonial rule are important aspects of the early years of the Indian Republic. As we have already seen, the fact that both offices were held by leaders linked to the Congress party facilitated cooperation during the early years of the Republic. This informal practice has become increasingly difficult to sustain as the hegemony of the Congress party has given way to coalition governments. But politicians have used other ways of achieving coordination, such as extensive multi-party negotiation before presidential elections. Thus, even as presidential elections have become contentious, once in office the President has slipped back into the aura of a dignified and detached authority with little real power in the everyday political life of the nation.

This sense of consensual outcome, in the face of potentially divisive elections to the office of the President, is important for the smooth functioning of India's political institutions, because the constitution confers an impressive range of powers on this office. The constitution provides the President with the authority to suspend fundamental rights and declare a state of National Emergency under Article 352, to impose the 'President's rule' in a region, under which the State is ruled directly by the Union executive (Article 356), and there is a provision for Financial Emergency under Article 360. But, in true republican fashion, even while leaving the decision to the President and the Prime Minister, the constitution requires the presidential proclamations to be laid before parliament for approval within two months, failing which it will lapse.

The appointment of the highest elected executive of India appears democratic in contrast to many developing countries where replacement of the chief executive often occurs by non-democratic means. However, some analysts point out that for 38 out of 60 years since Independence, India was ruled by members of the Nehru family.[5] A more serious criticism is the failure of democratic government leading to authoritarian rule and compromising India's democratic government through the imposition of a national Emergency in 1975 (see Box 4.1).[6] Dismissing elected governments at the regional level and applying direct rule from Delhi had become more frequent during the prime ministership of Indira Gandhi.

Prime Minister (Religion)	Year	President (Religion)
Jawaharlal Nehru (H) *Congress*	1947	
	1950	Rajendra Prasad (H)
	1962	Sarvepalli Radhakrishan (H)
Gulzarilal Nanda (H) *Congress* Lal Bahadur Shastri (H) *Congress*	1964	
Gulzarilal Nanda (H) *Congress* Indira Gandhi (H) *Congress*	1966	
	1967	Zakir Hussain (M)
	1969	Varahagiri Venkata Giri (H)
	1974	Fakhruddin Ali Ahmed (M)
Morarji Desai (H) *Janata*	1977	Basappa Danappa Jatti (H) Neelam Sanjiva Reddy (H)
Choudhary Charan Singh (H) *Janata*	1977	
Indira Gandhi (H) *Congress*	1980	
	1982	Giani Zail Singh (S)
Rajiv Gandhi (H) *Congress*	1984	
	1987	Ramaswamy Venkataraman (H)
Vishwanath Pratap Singh (H) *Janata Dal*	1989	
Chandra Shekhar (H) *Samajwadi Janata Dal*	1990	
P.V. Narasimha Rao (H) *Congress*	1991	
	1992	Shankar Dayal Sharma (H)
Atal Behari Vajpayee (H) *Bharatiya Janata Party* H.D. Deve Gowda *Janata Dal*	1996	
Inder Kumar Gujral (H) *Janata Dal*	1997	Kocheril Raman Narayanan (H)
Atal Behari Vajpayee (H) *Bharatiya Janata Party*	1998	
	2002	Abdul Kalam (M)
Manmohan Singh (S) *Congress*	2004	
	2007	Pratibha Devisingh Patil (H)
Manmohan Singh (S) *Congress*	2009	

Key: H=Hindu, M=Muslim, S=Sikh

Figure 4.2 Presidents and Prime Ministers
Source: Drawn by author.

Box 4.1 The national Emergency of 1975–77

The national Emergency from 1975 to 1977 led to the suspension of fundamental rights, postponement of the General Election by one year, and incarceration of numerous opposition politicians, journalists and political activists opposed to the personal rule of Indira Gandhi. This was the first major trial of strength and resilience of India's democracy. Both the motivation behind its declaration and the relative ease with which it could be imposed exposed the vulnerability of the Indian political system to authoritarian rule. However, the fact that Indira Gandhi was defeated at the polls in 1977 is a precedence against authoritarian rule and a valid piece of evidence for the resilience of the Indian political system.

However, K.R. Narayanan set an important precedent in 1998 by turning down a recommendation of the central cabinet to impose President's rule on the State of Bihar.[7] One can still point to the robustness of Indian democracy by showing that authoritarian rule, rather than becoming terminal as in many developing countries, is often used as a temporary measure. It is seen more as a self-corrective procedure written into India's Constitution.[8]

The connecting link between the cabinet and the President as well as between the cabinet and parliament is the Prime Minister. The Prime Minister's role continues to be, as Nehru used to describe it, 'the linchpin of Government' (see Figure 4.1). Nevertheless, the coalitional nature of contemporary Indian politics requires much more consultation with other parties, sometimes leading to the open articulation of defiance against the authority of the Prime Minister, a situation that would have been unthinkable during the days of Nehru. Together with the ministers, the Prime Minister controls and coordinates the departments of government and determines policy through the submission of a programme for parliamentary action. When the Prime Minister commands the majority in the Lok Sabha, his government is secure. If he is defeated on any major issue, or if a no-confidence motion is passed, he must, by the conventions of cabinet government, resign.[9]

Other practices of cabinet government have become institutionalized in India as well. Cabinet meetings, presided over by the Prime Minister with only ministers of cabinet rank in attendance, are the highest policy-making body in India. The cabinet provides a balance to the authority of the Prime Minister with its collective weight. The principle of collective responsibility was sorely tested during the tenure of Indira Gandhi, whose authoritarian tendencies and distrust of colleagues reduced the cabinet's role as a source of policy and administrative leadership, in sharp contrast to previous practice. The phenomenon was described as 'deinstitutionalization'.[10] Subsequent governments have restored the conventions of parliamentary government and the principle of collective responsibility.

The towering stature of Nehru as Prime Minister had overshadowed the principle of collective responsibility of the cabinet but subsequent occupants of the office have shown how the cabinet can project a leader into national prominence if the potential is there. Such was the case with the diminutive Lal Bahadur Shastri who, during the Indo-Pak war of 1965–66, swiftly rose in prominence as a national leader.[11]

More recently, the steady rise in the stature of Prime Minister Narasimha Rao was a testimony to the institutionalization of the office. Starting as a temporary replacement for Rajiv Gandhi and then as a compromise candidate for leadership, Rao brought about radical changes in the management of the economy, without a solid majority in the Lok Sabha. His leadership skills were immensely valuable in ensuring a smooth transition after the assassination of Rajiv Gandhi and during the post-Ayodhya period. He maintained a delicate balance between the opposing factions of the Congress party.

So deeply entrenched are the principles of consensus and accommodation as core values of the political system that even after the end of Congress dominance and the coming of non-Congress governments, there has been no radical discontinuity in civil servants, policy mechanisms or even policy orientations. As Prime Ministers, Rao's successors, first Deve Gowda and then Inder Kumar Gujral, followed very much in the mould of consensus and accommodation. The real test only came in 1998 with the Vajpayee government inducting into the central government some individuals who lacked previous ministerial experience. However, the BJP government maintained continuity in the areas of reform and security policy. The dexterity with which Prime Minister Manmohan Singh, supported by the UPA coalition consisting of 20 political parties, has continued the tradition of prime ministerial leadership, despite the long shadow of Sonia Gandhi as President of the Congress party on his government, are further testimony to the institutionalization of the practice of consultation and cohesion at the highest echelon of government in India.

The parliament

Even while they campaigned against British rule in India, the leaders of India's Freedom Movement aspired to a parliamentary democracy modelled on British institutions. For many of them, schooled in the British tradition, Independence brought the opportunity to design India's constitution. The main inspiration came from Britain, but with important differences. The principle of hereditary membership of landed aristocrats in the House of Lords has no equivalence in India. Besides, unlike Britain, India is a federation.

The parliament of India consists of two houses; the *Lok Sabha*, the lower house, and the *Rajya Sabha*, the upper house or Council of States (see Figure 4.1). As such, the Rajya Sabha has some features of the US Senate. In the same vein, reflecting the philosophy of social justice that underpinned the Freedom Movement, the system provides for some special features, such as the guaranteed representation of *dalits* – originating from castes that formerly carried the stigma of untouchability – and tribals in the Lok Sabha, through a quota system of 'reserved seats'. This practice, supervised by the independent Election Commission of India, ensures that the number of tribals and *dalits* in the Lok Sabha is close to their proportional weight in the electorate. The principle of guaranteed representation of former untouchables and tribals applies to lower legislations like State assemblies and village *panchayats* as well. In addition, women's representation – to the tune of one-third of the seats – is guaranteed by law in the lowest level of legislatures – the *gram panchayats* – in India. Efforts to extend guaranteed representation of women through a quota system to State assemblies and the national parliament have not yet been successful.

The Lok Sabha consists of 545 members: 543 are directly elected and two are nominated by the President of India as representatives of the Anglo-Indian community constituted of the progeny of the mixed race population – yet another legacy of colonial rule. Elections of the members of the Lok Sabha take place on the basis of general single-member constituencies with simple majority voting rule. The term of the Lok Sabha is five years, unless it is extended because of emergency conditions. The Lok Sabha can be dissolved before the end of its five-year mandate or extended beyond five years by the President on the advice of the Prime Minister (the latter has happened only once, during the Emergency of 1975–77).

The parliament is designed to be primarily an instrument of democratic account-ability. The constitution specifies that the Lok Sabha must meet at least twice a year, with no more than six months between sessions. The business of parliament, avidly reported in the press, is transacted primarily in English or Hindi, but provision is made for the use of other Indian languages as well. Keeping to the British practice, a number of parliamentary committees impart a sense of continuity and specialization to the functioning of the parliament. Some are primarily concerned with organization and parliamentary procedure. Others, notably finance committees – the Public Accounts Committee and the Estimates Committee – act as watchdogs over the executive. Specific committees scrutinize the budget and governmental expenditure, appropria-tions and allocations for specific purposes, the exercise of delegated power, and the implementation of ministerial assurances and promises. India has followed the British practice of inducting members of the opposition to senior positions in parliamentary committees. Since members of parliament usually stay with committees to which they are allocated in the event of their re-election, individual members, regardless of party affiliation, can acquire very senior positions within the committee structure. This practice has contributed greatly to the identity and autonomy of specific parliamentary committees and to the overall capacity and stature of the parliament as a whole.

The first hour of the parliamentary day (known as the 'zero hour') is devoted to questions that bring the ministers to public scrutiny. Written questions are submitted in advance – a process that extends the principle of parliamentary and public accountability to the bureaucracy – as well as supplementary questions, which test the minister's ability to master the technical details of governance.

The Lok Sabha's ultimate control over the executive lies in the motion of no confidence that can bring down a government. The parliament's right to dismiss a government which has lost its majority had remained in abeyance during the long years of one-party dominance. However, during the last two decades as the politics of coalitions has taken root and single-majority parties forming a government have become a distant memory, the power of the parliament to hold governments to account has come out in full force. Still, this has not created the kind of paralysis that occurred in the Fourth Republic of post-war France. The current number of leaders with ministerial experience both in the government and in the opposition ensures that the parliament is both the scene of continuous challenge to the government as well as an opportunity to collaborate in the interest of governance.[12]

The Rajya Sabha was seen merely as a 'talking shop' during the earlier periods of Congress hegemony when the party dominated both houses of parliament. Because most of the real power of accountability and finance are vested in the lower house, the centre of political gravity naturally lies beyond the reach of the smaller, and constitutionally less powerful, upper house. Still, the increasingly competitive char-acter of the Indian political process has enhanced the importance of the Rajya Sabha too.

The Rajya Sabha consists of a maximum of 250 members, of whom 12 are nominated by the President for their 'special knowledge or practical experience' in literature, science, art or social service. Reflecting the federal principle, the allocation of the remaining seats corresponds to the size of the population of the various regions, except that small States are given a somewhat larger share than their actual population proportion would imply. Thus, tiny Tripura with a population of 3,191,168 has one member in the Rajya Sabha, whereas Uttar Pradesh, with 190,891,000 people, has 31 members. This significant departure from the American practice where the states, regardless of size, have the same number of seats means that the members of the Rajya Sabha identify more with their parties than with the States they represent. The members of the State legislative assembly elect members of the Rajya Sabha for a term of six years. The terms are staggered, so that elections are held for one-third of the seats every two years. Thus, whereas the Lok Sabha becomes a static representation of the political profile of the country every five years, the Rajya Sabha remains a more continuous representation of the changing profile of the country as every second year it introduces new members. This, in the past, has been a boon to parties that have lost their majority in the Lok Sabha but have managed to keep some of their parliamentary influence intact because of their continued dominance of the Rajya Sabha whose support becomes necessary to get legislation through the parliament. The electoral procedure of the parliament thus ensures the empowerment of oppositions and curbs the potential of authoritarian use of power on the part of the ruling majority.

The role of the parliament is normally confined to the scrutiny of legislation for its technical aspects, because, reflecting the conventions of parliamentary democracy, most of the initiative for legislation lies with the cabinet. The legislators do not have the finance or the personnel that the political system of the United States bestows on its members of Congress. Indian committee hearings are not public occasions and therefore do not have the power of US congressional or Senate committee hearings. As such, they only provide a forum for wide political consultation.[13]

The legislative process follows the British practice on the whole. Laws are initiated in the form of government bills or private members' bills. The latter are more an opportunity to air grievances and to draw attention because few if any ever become law. The initiation of most legislation clearly lies with the government. All bills except money bills – with implications for spending, revenue, borrowing or India's financial reserves – can be introduced in either house. The Ministry of Law and the Attorney General of India are consulted on legal and constitutional aspects. Ordinary bills go through three readings in each house. The second reading is the most vital because it is at this stage that the bill receives the most detailed and minute examination and may be referred to a Select Committee or a Joint Committee of both houses of parliament. Again, these committees do not have the same standing or resources as the committees in the US House or Senate. They are neither called upon to investigate the affairs of the government in public hearing nor asked to approve executive appointments. Their strength within the Indian system derives from the tradition of bipartisanship which, as in the United Kingdom, creates great confidence and respect for them within the government as well as the opposition parties.

Once both houses pass a bill, it requires the assent of the President to become a law. This assent is not a mere formality. The President sometimes asks for technical details and expert advice in order to examine the constitutional implications of a bill before giving his assent. Potentially, this is a formidable threat in view of the fragility of coalition politics where a united stand by the cabinet against an adversary is relatively difficult to sustain. A President determined to delay or obstruct legislation can do so through the simple expedient of not returning a bill, with or without assent, before the end of the current session of the parliament. This, in effect, can kill a bill, requiring the government to go through the entire legislative process of introducing it in the next session. If the President withholds his assent and the parliament passes the bill again, he or she is obliged to give it the presidential assent. But these are exceptional situations. Unlike in the United States, the President is not expected to take legislative initiative, and there is no concept of the presidential veto as a source of influence on the policy process or an exercise of checks and balances.[14]

As a bill must be passed by both houses, joint sessions are provided in order to resolve conflicts. Because of its larger size, the Lok Sabha plays a dominant role in such meetings. In matters relating to money bills, the Lok Sabha even has exclusive authority. The Rajya Sabha may only recommend changes; it cannot initiate, delay or reject. When the majority of the ruling party or coalition in the Lok Sabha is narrow and the opposition has a majority in the Rajya Sabha, the potential peril of defeat in a joint session encourages the government to think in terms of cooperation rather than confrontation. This happened after 1977 when the Congress party lost to the Janata Party in the parliamentary election and thus lost its majority in the Lok Sabha. Because only one-third of the seats of the Rajya Sabha are up for election every two years, the Congress continued to hold a majority in that house. When the Janata Party set about amending the constitution to purge it of the authoritarian measures that the Congress had introduced during the preceding Emergency (such as the 42nd amendment of the constitution), it realized that it lacked the requisite majority in both houses. A compromise was struck and the Janata could achieve only part of its legislative objectives in the form of the 44th amendment. The parliamentary elections of 1996, 1998 and 2004 have produced situations where the two houses of the parliament do not have the same kind of majority coalitions. Consequently, the Rajya Sabha has gained in power and begun to play an independent role in the matters of scrutiny and accountability.[15]

On the whole, however, unlike the American senate, the Rajya Sabha is far from the co-equal of the Lok Sabha. Nor is it a hereditary 'talking shop' like the British House of Lords. But, over the years, it has acquired its own profile as a second chamber. With its less politically charged atmosphere and a more senior membership including people who are not professional politicians but represent special interests, the Rajya Sabha brings an additional element of representation to the parliament. Together, the two houses complement one another and add to the depth and complexity of the principle of popular representation.

The lack of party discipline is the nemesis of parliamentary democracy, especially in countries like India where modern institutions lack deep historical roots. Cross-party voting and defections can drive a government to paralysis and reduce parliamentary proceedings to personal rule or anarchy. The sudden governmental instability in the 1960s in Indian States that resulted from the end of Congress hegemony gave India a warning of this potential danger.[16] Since then, government control over legislation has been considerably strengthened by the passage of the Anti Defection Law. Under this act, voting against the party line is considered to be a defection, which leads to the loss of the seat by the member. That and the disapproval of political opportunism by the electorate have succeeded in inducing a degree of stability at the level of the central and State governments.

The parliament has constituted a number of committees to help discharge its functions, some of which are quite technical and require special expertise and experience. The committee system which draws on the British parliamentary committees as precedents goes back to 1854 when the Legislative Council, established by the colonial government, appointed its own committees to help with its functions. There are a number of ad hoc committees which include select committees and joint committees. The second type of committees are called standing committees and include those on petitions and privileges, those on 'government assurance', those dealing directly with the functioning of the house and, most important of all, the three financial committees, namely, the Estimates Committee, the Public Accounts Committee and the Committee on Public Undertakings. The main function of the Estimates Committee, set up in 1950, is to scrutinize the estimates of expenditure of the government and to suggest measures to introduce economy and efficiency. Its composition reflects the strength of political parties in the parliament. The Public Accounts Committee which first came into being in India in 1923 is a watchdog non-partisan body whose main function is to scrutinize the accounts of the government to see if the sums granted by the house for expenditure by the government of India have been spent in the manner and for the purpose for which they were granted. The Public Accounts Committee can draw on the expertise of the Comptroller and Auditor General of India to facilitate the technical aspects of its work. The Committee on Public Undertakings, constituted in 1964, consists of members drawn from both houses of the parliament. Its main function is to examine the reports and accounts of specific bodies involving public funds to see if they are being managed on sound business principles and according to procedure established by law.

The judiciary

The constitution of India committed itself to individual rights of equality and liberty. However, it did not incorporate the American concept of natural justice where the Supreme Court is the ultimate defender of the 'natural' rights of the individual, as interpreted by the Court. The schooling of India's leaders in parliamentary politics goes back to the period of colonial rule when parliamentary norms – necessarily restricted for the Indian colonies – became the basis of their complex relationship that alternated between competition and collaboration with the British rulers of India. The conciliation of the principles of parliamentary sovereignty and individual rights is facilitated by a judicial system that is both independent from external control and free to interpret the law. Originally, it was intended to be supreme only within the 'procedure established by law', law being the domain of the legislature subsidiary to it in authority. On numerous occasions, however, the court has vehemently defended its exclusive right to exercise control over legislation.

The Supreme Court has original and exclusive jurisdiction in disputes between the Union government and one or more States, and in disputes between two or more States. It has appellate jurisdiction in any case, civil or criminal, that involves, by its own certification, a substantial question of law in the meaning and intent of the constitution. The Supreme Court is the interpreter and guardian of the constitution, the supreme law of the land. Unlike the British system, where no court may hold an act of parliament invalid, all legislation passed in India's national or State governments must conform to the constitution. The constitutionality of any enactment is determined under the power of judicial review by the Supreme Court. Shortly after the promulgation of the constitution, litigation over the right to property had opened up a contest between the Supreme Court and the parliament over supremacy with regard to the final word on legislation. The court had conservatively defined private property in the sense of the value that it would fetch in the market whereas the parliament, seeking to promote egalitarian values, had enacted land reform legislation that set compensation for land acquired by the government at less than market price. The landmark judgment on *Golaknath and others vs. the State of Punjab* (1967) where the court had ruled a law *ultra vires* was eventually overturned by an amendment of the constitution.

The Supreme Court finally developed the doctrine of 'basic structure' in the case of *Kesavananda Bharati vs. the State of Kerala* (1973) in which it held that matters which are deemed to be basic to the constitution cannot be amended by the parliament. A remarkable feature of judicial review in India is the power of the Supreme Court to rule a constitutional amendment invalid if it violates the 'basic structure' of the constitution; but the scope of judicial review in India is not as wide as in the United States.[17]

Public Interest Litigation is another area where the Supreme Court has become active recently with regard to policy making. It is an innovative practice under which an aggrieved party (including judges of the court themselves) can file a case in the public interest and have it heard on a priority basis. The practice which has dispensed with some cumbersome practices associated with litigation gives citizens direct access to judicial intervention.[18] However, some allege that excessive judicial activism can undermine the goal of separation of powers which is vital to the constitution.

Although the modern legal system has largely displaced traditional customary law, traditional groups use the modern system for their own ends. The Supreme Court has dealt with such contentious issues as the Ayodhya case, which brought the dispute into the political system rather than let it slip out of the process of adjudication altogether (see Box 4.2). The Court's landmark decisions – for example, its ruling that *hindutva*, the core of the ideology of the BJP, was part of Indian culture and not necessarily of a religion – have deeply influenced the nature of political discourse in India. Recent survey findings rate the Indian Supreme Court along with the Election Commission as the most trustworthy of institutions[19] (see Table 4.2).

Since the core judicial doctrine of the constitution of India puts the 'procedure established by law' as superior to the American doctrine of 'natural justice', the Supreme Court was initially accorded a status below the parliament but above the national executive in terms of authoritative interpretation of the law. But gradually the Supreme Court has asserted its supremacy in such matters as well. This evolution was facilitated by the steady erosion of the massive legislative majorities since the early decades after Independence, the rise of media influence, and the mobilization of interest groups at the national level. The Emergency Rule of Indira Gandhi (1975–77) dented its authority and autonomy, but since then the Court has bounced back.[20] The Court has reached the highest level of esteem and trust in the eyes of the Indian public by drawing on the initiatives taken and innovations made in judicial practice and procedure. It exercises wide judicial review, including subjects ranging from the highly abstract and technical, such as personal law and industrial

Box 4.2 Inter-community violence, Ayodhya (1992) and its aftermath, Godhra (2002)

In the northern State of Uttar Pradesh, Ayodhya, famous as a city of Hindu pilgrimage, became the scene of an unprecedented conflict between Hindus and Muslims on December 6, 1992. A long-standing controversy between the two religious groups was the Babri Masjid, a mosque built in 1528 by the first Mughal emperor Babur, that Hindus claim stood where a temple once marked the birthplace of Rama. The Hindu nationalist Bharatiya Janata Party (BJP) – then head of the State government – launched a *rathyatra* (a holy chariot in ritual procession towards a holy site) to Ayodhya in order to destroy the mosque and to rebuild in its place a Hindu temple, but it could not discipline the frenzied crowd. The mosque was demolished by the *karsevaks* (activists) of two front organizations of the Hindu-nationalist movement, followed by communal riots in various parts of India. The BJP's dilemma became apparent again during the communal clashes in Godhra in February 2002, on the eve of the tenth anniversary of the Babri mosque's destruction, when an alleged attack by a Muslim mob on a train with Hindu activists returning from a demonstration in Ayodhya resulted in more than fifty dead, mostly women and children. This incident triggered a pogrom on the Muslim minority in the State of Gujarat, causing several hundred victims. The opposition accused the BJP-led State government of complicity with anti-Muslim mobs; the government on the other hand defended itself with statistics showing that about a third of the casualties were caused by the police shooting under orders, mostly against Hindu mobs.

Table 4.2 Trust in institutions

	Great deal	*Somewhat*	*Not at all*
Election Commission	45.9	31.1	23.0
Judiciary	41.6	34.2	24.2
Local government	39.0	37.8	23.2
State government	37.2	43.6	19.2
Central government	35.2	42.5	22.3
Elected representatives	19.9	40.4	39.7
Political parties	17.4	43.6	39.0
Government officials	17.2	40.4	42.3
Police	13.0	29.9	57.1

Source: Mitra and Singh (1999), p. 260.

jurisprudence, to topical and controversial issues like public interest litigation. The Supreme Court has also appointed itself as the guardian of vulnerable social groups and neglected areas of public life, such as the environment. This is one of the most celebrated and contested of the innovations of India's Supreme Court.

Today, the Supreme Court and the High Courts of India are seen as the most important symbols of liberty, secularism and social justice. It could all, of course, have turned out in a completely different way as in many changing societies where the pace of political mobilization overtakes the rule of law. That India did not follow this tragic course only goes to show the long evolution of the judicial procedure under colonial rule which continues to be an effective and important legacy, and it stresses the important role played by lawyers in India's freedom struggle.

The bureaucracy

One of the main achievements of the Indian political system is a bureaucratic apparatus that is both professionally organized and politically accountable. The Indian bureaucracy is an enormously complex system that combines national or all-India services with regional and local services, as well as technical and managerial staff running public sector undertakings. Public recruitment on merit with stiff competitive examinations is the general rule, with political appointments such as those in the United States being the rare exception.

The main services like the Indian Administrative Service (IAS) and the Indian Police Service (IPS) retain some of the features of their pre-Independence structures, but like the rest of the top services of India, they have been re-organized to create a federal balance in recruitment. Special attention is given to the representation of the former untouchables, tribals and women. Recruitment is supervised by the Union Public Service Commission – an independent advisory body appointed by the President – and extensive new facilities have been created for training new recruits. Although candidates are recruited centrally, the IAS is composed of separate cadres for each region. This helps strengthen federal links, because regional loyalties are balanced by the provision that at least half of the members of the IAS cadre come from outside the region. This practice creates language problems for officers who originate from outside, but it also encourages India's top administrators to learn the prevailing local language, contributing to the process of nation-building and cross-regional linkages. Members of a district administration seek to combine rule of law, efficient management and coordination, and, increasingly, local democracy. These values are often hard to reconcile in practice: the extent to which a regional government succeeds in achieving this ideal acts as a crucial parameter of how successful it is in achieving the goal of democratic governance.

Statutory commissions

There are a number of public commissions provided for by the constitution or set up by an act of parliament that are non-partisan and non-official in character and which assist the process of governance through authoritative expert advice and decisions. The main function of the Chairman and members of the Union Public Service Commission (UPSC) appointed by the President of India (Art. 315) is to conduct entrance examinations for the top civil service. Its main task is to ensure the professionalism and political neutrality of the civil service. The remit of the Election Commission, appointed by the President of India (Art. 324), is to ensure free and fair elections. The Auditor and Comptroller General of India who is appointed by the President for a period of six years (or up to the age of 65), is responsible for carrying out independent audits of the accounts of the government (Art. 148). The Finance Commission is an independent commission whose members are also appointed by the President. Its structure and function are laid down in Article 280 of the constitution; it has the vital function of arbitrating between the centre and federal

States with regard to the division of tax incomes between them. The National Commission for Backward Classes was set up in 1993 to oversee the implementation of the provision for the reservation of 27 per cent of jobs in central services for members of the Other Backward Classes as defined in the constitution. The Commission is appointed by the President under Article 340, which also provides for the conditions of work that ensure the autonomy and independence of the Commission. Other statutory bodies of this genre are the National Commission for Women, the National Commission for Minorities and the National Commission for Scheduled Castes and Scheduled Tribes. These commissions and statutory bodies have become an important part of the political landscape of India, and figures of avid interest for the media. They have added breadth and depth to the process of governance, rule of law and accountability.

The military

The case of the military and paramilitary forces of India deserves special attention. Although the number of armed military has increased significantly, the civilian government of India remains firmly in control. In contrast to many developing countries, especially in Africa, the Indian middle classes have opted for civil service and professional jobs under colonial rule, and political careers since Independence. In India, this has contributed to the professional and apolitical character of the army. Consequently, the officer corps of India, traditionally accustomed to civilian control and indoctrinated with the values of secular democracy and the rule of law in the course of their training, has remained nonpartisan even during political turmoil.

The absence of a leadership vacuum at the upper and middle levels of the system and the divided character of the command structure of the military in India are other contributory factors to the relative immunity of the Indian political system from a military takeover. A large police force of about a million men and women is the second line of defence of the political system against the danger of the breakdown of law and order.

Law and order is a State subject. As such, the basic components of the Indian police are recruited, trained and deployed by the regional governments. The central government also exercises considerable power over law and order management through different methods. In the first place, there are a number of special police forces who are recruited and trained by the central government. In principle, central forces can be sent to trouble spots in the regions at the request of the State governments, and once deployed they are placed under the orders of State officials. The district magistrate and the superintendent of police normally belong to the Indian Administrative Service and the Indian Police Service, both of which are central services. As such, these officials typically have some accountability to the central government in their professional judgements. However, as the situation in Ayodhya in 1992 and Gujarat in 2002 revealed, even the presence of a large paramilitary force is no guarantee of the effective management of law and order when the central and State governments do not agree on the policy to be followed. In extreme cases, therefore, the constitution provides for direct rule by the centre under Article 356 (President's Rule – as already mentioned earlier in the 'Executive' section). Central intervention in Punjab and Kashmir occurred under similar conditions where the regional government proved either unwilling or unable to take effective measures. Effective law and order management certainly contributed to the restoration of the political process in Punjab. The regions of India and the State itself continuously share knowledge of law and order management with one another, which results in the creation of new forces or major changes in equipment, training and service conditions.

Political recruitment

If political participation is a minimum criterion of democratic rule, then a persuasive case can be made that India has caught up with the West. However, to make the case for a high level of political socialization, participation on its own is necessary but not sufficient. For a population to be able to claim a high level of political socialization, participation needs to be ensconced within an appropriate normative structure and institutional arrangement. Here one can consider two further sources of evidence: political recruitment to the highest legislature of the country and the social composition of the local elite. Political recruitment is important because once people have knowledge of the normative structure of the system and the skill with which to engage in political transactions, they tend to elect representatives who reflect the main cleavages of society. Of course, the representative character of the elected elite is unlikely to reach a perfect statistical ratio with social cleavages because very small groups, thanks partly to the 'first-past-the-post' system of voting, tend to get penalized. However, by looking at the data over time and across different regions (see Table 6.3), one can draw some general conclusions.

The percentage of politicians of rural origin has grown over the years, and correspondingly, the weight of 'agriculturists' has grown as well. The percentage of women has doubled but is still far below their share of the population.[21] The percentage of Brahmins has dropped significantly. The former untouchables and tribals, who continue to occupy a little over a fifth of the membership, reflect their weight in the population of the country, thanks to the system of 'reservation' which sets a quota for these underprivileged groups. Quite interestingly, though there is no quota system for the election of Muslims to the parliament (and the electoral rules do not provide for proportional representation), their total number is not far below their proportion in the Indian population.

The picture of the social base of the national elite that we get from the Lok Sabha is reinforced by the data on local elites. The structure of *panchayati raj*, following the 73rd amendment of the constitution, which requires one-third of the seats in *panchayats* to be filled by women, has become an important recruiting ground for new leaders and a school for training these potential leaders in the art of governance.

Political participation and the recruitment of new elites act as powerful agents of political socialization. The data on efficacy and legitimacy present two interesting facets of political socialization in India (see Tables 3.2 and 3.3). Efficacy, which measures individuals' self-perception with regard to the State, shows a steady rise over the recent past. Legitimacy of the political system, as seen by a representative sample of all Indians, has also climbed, from 67.6 per cent in 1996 to 72.2 per cent in 2004. This creates an ironical situation where ordinary people feel empowered enough to 'kick the rascals out'. When the vital foundations of democracy are threatened by political adventurers, resistance growth and eventually democratic institutions re-emerge. Once again, as one can see from the example of the national

Emergency of 1975–77 (see Box 4.1) the Indian political system has experienced situations where this potential is transformed into the breakdown of democracy and the rise of popular authoritarianism, with democracy eventually bouncing back.

Conclusion

The doctrines of separation and division of powers which are crucial to democracy have evolved incrementally over centuries in European democracies. In India, democratic institutions are not the outcome of a similar evolution. Instead, democracy was to be built 'from above', under the guidance of the modern state. This was no mean feat. The chapter has shown the role of the constitution,[22] leadership, the institutional arrangement that combines strength with accountability and most of all, India's countervailing forces that juxtapose different wings of government against one another.

In spite of the trials and tribulations of the sixty eventful years that have followed, the modern, secular and democratic vision of the constitution, and its core components, have remained largely intact. With over a hundred amendments, the Constitution, both rigid and flexible, has succeeded in coping with a rapidly changing political and social environment. In consequence, despite local conflicts, insurgency in parts of the vast country and bouts of inter-community violence, the democratic state and the political process are firmly in control of the land. The main institutions such as the executive, the legislature, the judiciary, the organs of law and order and a plethora of independent commissions set up under the constitution have gone from strength to strength. The institutions have gained in autonomy but remained firmly integrated in the larger structure of the state. This singular achievement sets India apart from her neighbours with whom she shares the colonial origin of her modern institutions.

The founders of the constitution of India have instilled several core principles of Anglo-Saxon constitutionalism and rule of law into the letter and spirit of the constitution and the institutional arrangement of the country. These values such as the primacy of the individual, limitations on the power of the state, the legitimacy of social plurality, egalitarianism, the rule of law and accountability of the holders of power to the citizen sometimes militate against Indian tradition, steeped as it is in the values of social hierarchy.

Nehru's India was not alone among newly emerging democracies in undertaking such ambitious programmes but it was one of the few to succeed in making a successful transition to democracy and defending the institutions originally designed by the founding fathers. The chapter has argued that while the colonial legacy played a role in making this possible, the innovative and strategic use of institutions by the leaders of post-Independence India certainly helped the political system considerably in reaching its goals. India has known how to conquer social power and bring social actors into the legitimate political arena, transform rebels into stakeholders and find a political niche for most opinions and interests in the country within the space of the complex and dynamic institutional arrangement. The juxtaposition of separation and division of powers has created new political spaces, whose shifting boundaries are influenced by the countervailing forces at all levels of the system.

The leaders of modern India have been inheritors as much as creators. The institutions of India epitomize the re-use of institutional innovation of previous generations. Even when foreign designs have been used, they have been painstakingly and meticulously adapted to local conditions, context and culture. They are bound together in a functional whole, generating among them a field of countervailing forces that produce the capacity of the political system to maintain equilibrium. As we have seen in the case of Public Interest Litigation or the development of the Basic Structure Doctrine, the institutional arrangement has generated the resilience to make up for deficit in any particular corner. We move next to India's federal structure – yet another foreign design which India has been conspicuously successful in adapting to local needs.

Notes

1 Little realized at the time, in retrospect the frenzy of violence that marked Independence and the Partition of India can be attributed to this hiatus between authority of the state and social power.

2 Huntington's *Political Order in Changing Societies* (1968) is the best known of this scholarly genre.

3 Rudolph and Rudolph (1987), p. 247; pp. 255–58.

4 See Enskat *et al.* (2001).

5 The dynastic 'theory' of succession in India, popularized in the West by Ali (1985), has been questioned in Mitra (1988a).

6 The legal basis of the Emergency rule of 1975–76 has been the subject of an intense controversy. Most observers consider this period as a breakdown in the democratic political system in India. See Morris-Jones (1977).

7 President's Rule, under which a region is ruled directly by the centre for a specific period, is indicative of a failure of representative government. It happened relatively infrequently during the first two decades of Independence, the most celebrated case being the dismissal of the elected communist government of Kerala in 1959. It became more common during the governmental instability of the mid-1960s, bringing the total incidences of the imposition of President's Rule to eight during the prime ministerial tenure of Nehru and Shastri, from 1950 to 1966. However, during the two periods of tenure of Mrs Gandhi, President's Rule was imposed 42 times.

8 If the President of India is satisfied that a grave emergency exists whereby the security of the nation or of any part of the territory thereof is threatened, whether by war or external aggression, or internal disturbance, he may, by proclamation, make a declaration to that effect (Article 352). While a Proclamation of Emergency is in operation, nothing in Article 19 'shall restrict the power of the state to make any law or to take any executive action' (Article 358). Article 356 makes similar provisions for the suspension of democratic government in a region. It should be pointed out that emergencies are conceived of as temporary measures and the scope for executive and legislative accountability is not altogether absent.

9 This has already happened on several occasions. In 1998, the NDA government led by Prime Minister Vajpayee fell when a no-confidence motion came up for discussion in the parliament. More recently, the UPA government of Prime Minister Manmohan Singh escaped a similar fate. The government survived the 'trust vote' when a section of the opposition voted for it, making up for the votes of the communist members who withdrew their support on account of their opposition to the Indo-US nuclear deal, championed by the UPA government.

10 James Manor, who had earlier talked about the 'deinstitutionalization' of India, has more recently talked about the 'regeneration' of institutions. See Manor (1994).

11 Shastri's slogan – *Jai jawan, jai kisan* ('victory to the soldier, victory to the peasant') – galvanized the nation. His brilliant career came to an abrupt end by death from heart attack – in Taskent, USSR – just after the signing of the peace treaty with Pakistan.

12 The indepdence and institutional cohesion of the Lok Sabha was sorely tested in 2008 when Prime Minister Manmohan Singh, tired of the attempts of the Left Front members of the parliament who were then supporting the UPA government from outside, to control his room to manoeuvre with regard to the Indo-US framework agreement, demanded a trust vote from the paliament. In the actual vote, a politically surcharged event, there were accusations of misconduct on the part of some members. However, for the bulk of legislators, party discipline and probity prevailed, and the government of Manmohan Singh survived the trust vote.

13 For details, refer to 'The legislative process: how laws are made' in Kashyap (1989), pp. 121–56.
14 For a brief period during the last years of the presidency of Zail Singh, the presidential assent became an effective instrument to delay legislation. But commentators on Indian politics have attributed this more to the personal pique of Singh against Prime Minister Rajiv Gandhi than to any explicit policy difference between them.
15 Such situations are not unknown in parliamentary democracies. But the French solution of 'cohabitation' of a President and a legislative majority belonging to different parties or the German 'grand coalition' is not yet available, though they cannot be excluded in the future.
16 See Mitra (1978) for an analysis of the rapid rise and fall of governments in Indian States during the 1960s.
17 Thanks to this landmark judgement and the logic of coalition politics, the requisite majority to amend the constitution has become much more difficult to attain. Correspondingly, the relative power of the Supreme Court as the guardian of the constitution has grown.
18 Mehta (2006, p. 167) finds judicial activism as an invigorating act of poitical balancing.
19 The survey was conducted through face-to-face interviews during May to June 1996, in the aftermath of the eleventh parliamentary elections. A representative sample of about 10,000 adults was interviewed under the guidance of the Centre for the Study of Developing Societies (CSDS), Delhi.
20 Verma and Kusum (2000) narrate this success story.
21 The percentage of women representatives in India's highest legislature is low in terms of absolute numbers but does not compare too unfavourably to those in developed European democracies. Only 6 per cent of the current House of Commons of Britain are women. 'United Nations Economic Commission for Europe', *The Economist*, 18–24 March, 1995, p. 33.
22 India's constitution – the world's longest, with 397 articles and 12 schedules – was formulated by 299 men and women, indirectly elected under limited franchise but still representing a wide range of political opinions in India, after about three years of deliberation, and formally adopted on 26 November, 1949. Basu (1985), pp. 18–19.

5 The federal structure

Balancing unity and diversity

India, that is Bharat, shall be a Union of States.

Article 1, The Constitution of India.

Personally, I do not attach any importance to the label which may be attached to it – whether you call it a Federal Constitution or a Unitary Constitution or by any other name. It makes no difference so long as the Constitution serves our purpose.

Rajendra Prasad, President of the Constituent Assembly, in Constituent Assembly Debate V, cited in Austin (1966), p. 186.

No other large and important national government, I believe, is so dependent as India on theoretically subordinate, but actually rather distinct units responsible to a different political control, for so much of the administration of what are recognized as national programmes of great importance to the nation.

Appleby (1957), p. 22.

Introduction

This chapter concentrates on the structure and process of the Indian Union, which is, in many respects, a federal design of an unusual kind. It combines the classic features of federal government, with some unique characteristics born out of the Indian context. Its solicitude to balance local and regional interests on the one hand and national interests on the other has drawn the attention of specialists of federal theory.[1] In designing this institution and adapting it to Indian conditions, India's leaders have shown great flexibility and pragmatism.[2] The result has been a federal system that has evolved greatly beyond the original design, and, despite some conspicuous cases of dissidence as in Kashmir, has acquired a reasonably high level of acceptance from the population.

The federal structure

Political unrest in Kashmir, separatist movements in Punjab and in the North East in the 1980s and the occasional outbreak of inter-community violence have been the cause of anxiety about India's national unity. The fear of 'Balkanization' greatly concerned India's leaders who lived through the bloody Partition of the country during the early decades following Independence. They saw in demands for States' rights, reminiscent of the demand of the Muslim League prior to Independence, the thin end of the wedge that could eventually dismember India. The consequence has been a federal design and practice that combine serious attempts to pay attention to States' interests, firm opposition to secessionist movements and attempts to reconcile regional and national interests within the framework of the Indian state. Thanks to the successful accommodation of separatist demands which has seen the number of federal States rise to 28 (see Table 5.1), those movements are now seen as a democratic articulation of legitimate interests.

As one can see in Diagram 5.1, many demands for secession from the Indian state begin as very high-intensity movements, led by a handful of activists. The central government reacts with a double strategy of accommodation and repression, just as the secessionist movements promote their cause with a combination of protest and participation. Typically, such movements go through a transformation as they gain in strength. As the transformation of Assam into seven different States or creation of the three new States of Uttarakhand, Jharkhand and Chhattisgarh shows, such

Table 5.1 India's evolving federalism

Name of the State	Created in	Area	Principal languages	Population
Andhra Pradesh	1956	276,754 km^2	Telegu, Urdu, Hindi	76,210,007
Arunachal Pradesh	1987	83,743 km^2	Nissi/Daffla, Nepali, Bengali	1,097,968
Assam	1947	78,438 km^2	Assamese, Bengali, Bodo/Boro	26,655,528
Bihar	1912	94,163 km^2	Hindi, Urdu, Santhali	82,998,509
Chhattisgarh	2000	135,191 km^2	Hindi	20,833,803
Goa	1987	3,702 km^2	Konkani, Marathi, Kannada	1,347,668
Gujarat	1960	196,024 km^2	Gujarati, Hindi, Sindhi	50,671,017
Haryana	1966	44,212 km^2	Hindi, Punjabi, Urdu	21,144,564
Himachal Pradesh	1971	55,673 km^2	Hindi, Punjabi, Kinnauri	6,077,900
Jammu and Kashmir	1947	222,236 km^2	Urdu, Kashmiri, Dogri	10,069,917
Jharkhand	2000	79,714 km^2	Santhali, Hindi, Urdu	26,945,829
Karnataka	1956	191,791km^2	Kannada, Urdu, Telugu	52,850,562
Kerala	1956	38,863 km^2	Malayalam, Tamil, Kannada	31,841,374
Madhya Pradesh	1956	308,000 km^2	Hindi, Bhili/Bhilodi, Gondi	60,348,023
Maharashtra	1960	307,713 km^2	Marathi, Hindi, Urdu	96,878,627
Manipur	1972	22,327 km^2	Manipuri, Thado, Tangkhul	2,166,788
Meghalaya	1972	22,429 km^2	Khasi, Garo, Bengali, Assamese	2,318,822
Mizoram	1987	21,087 km^2	Lushai/Mizo, Bengali, Lakher	888,573
Nagaland	1963	16,579 km^2	Ao, Sema, Konyak	1,990,036
Orissa	1949	155,707 km^2	Oriya, Hindi, Telugu	36,804,660
Punjab	1956	50,362 km^2	Punjabi, Hindi, Urdu	24,358,999
Rajasthan	1956	342,239 km^2	Hindi, Bhili/Bhilodi, Urdu	56,507,188
Sikkim	1975	7,096 km^2	Nepali, Bhutia, Lepcha	540,851
Tamil Nadu	1956	130,058 km^2	Tamil, Telugu, Kannada	62,405,679
Tripura	1972	10,491.69 km^2	Bengali, Tripuri, Hindi	3,199,203
Uttarakhand	2000	53,483 km^2	Hindi, Garhwali, Kumaoni	8,489,349
Uttar Pradesh	1947	236,286 km^2	Hindi, Urdu, Punjabi	166,197,921
West Bengal	1956	88,752 km^2	Bengali, Hindi, Urdu	80,176,197

Source: *The Penguin Guide to the States and Union Territories of India* (2007) New Delhi: Penguin.

movements eventually lead to the creation of new federal States where the leaders of the separatist movement become the new rulers. The call for a federal division of powers, advocated by the Indian National Congress in the 1920s when it organized its provincial committees on the basis of linguistically contiguous areas, originated from the need to safeguard regional and sectional identity. But economic policy, especially in a country with formidable problems of development, required central coordination. Out of these contradictory needs has emerged what is known as the 'cooperative' federalism of India.

Table 5.2 Union territories: India's unconventional federal units

Union territory	Created in	Area	Principal languages	Population
Andaman & Nicobar Islands	1956	8,249 km²	Bengali, Tamil, Hindi	356,152
Chandigarh	1953	114 km²	Hindi, Punjab, Tamil	900,635
Dadra and Nagar Haveli	1961	491 km²	Gujarati, Hindi, Konkani	220,490
Daman and Diu	1987	112 km²	Gujarati, Hindi, Marathi	158,204
Delhi*	1956	1,483 km²	Hindi, Punjabi, Urdu	13,850,507
Lakshadweep	1956	32 km²	Malayalam, Tamil, Hindi	60,650
Puducherry	1963	492 km²	Tamil, Malayalam, Telugu	974,345

* National Capital Territory
Source: *The Penguin Guide to the States and Union Territories of India* (2007) New Delhi: Penguin.

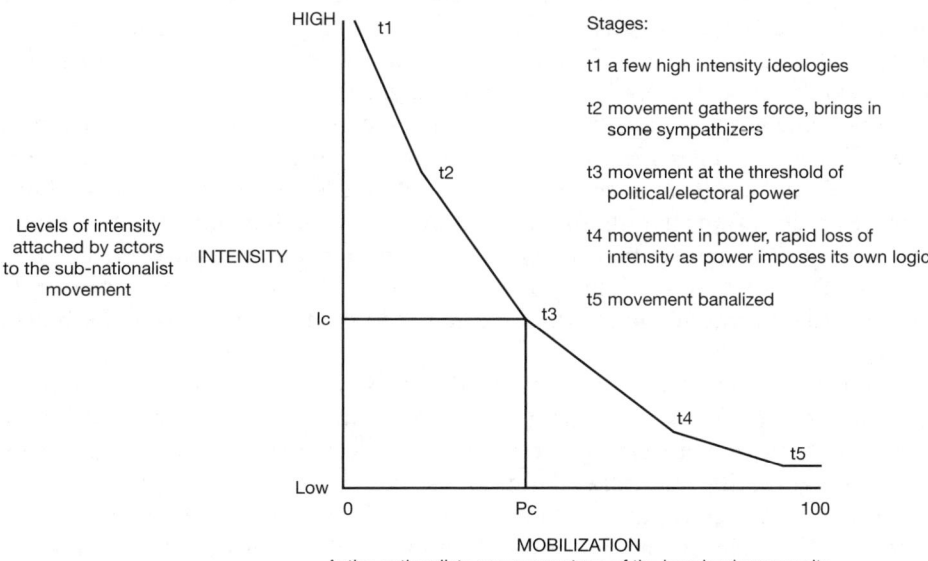

Stages:

t1 a few high intensity ideologies

t2 movement gathers force, brings in some sympathizers

t3 movement at the threshold of political/electoral power

t4 movement in power, rapid loss of intensity as power imposes its own logic

t5 movement banalized

Levels of intensity attached by actors to the sub-nationalist movement

MOBILIZATION
Active nationalists as a percentage of the imagined community

Ic Critical threshold of intensity, beyond which nationalism becomes 'visible' over and above 'mundane' politics
Pc Critical threshold of numbers beyond which those adhering to nationalism constitute a political force

Diagram 5.1 Sub-national movements
Source: Mitra and Lewis (eds) (1996), p. 27.

In addition, there are sub-states, district councils, and special districts with different levels of autonomy protecting them from outside interference (Table 5.2). The consequent structural complexity must create nightmarish scenarios of the whole system collapsing rather like the Soviet Union. Why has this not happened?

Sub-national movements and federalization: a coping mechanism

Numerous special features of the Indian constitution give it its highly centralized form. Of these, the two most important are the nature of the division of powers between the central government and the States with a bias in favour of the centre, and the financial provisions affecting the distribution of revenues. In India, unlike in the United States, the federal States do not have their own separate constitutions. The State of Jammu and Kashmir is an exception, because the Instrument of Accession on the basis of which Kashmir joined the Indian Union ordained that the central government would not interfere with the internal affairs of the State. Article 370, therefore, provides for a separate constitution for Jammu and Kashmir.

Kashmir has emerged as a test case of the integrative ability of the Indian political system. During British colonial rule, Kashmir was one of about 600 princely states, ruled by Indian princes under British suzerainty. As a part of the general arrangements for the Transfer of Power, Britain agreed to partition the territories under direct rule into the sovereign states of India and Pakistan, and to transfer the right to decide for themselves – 'paramountcy' – to the Indian princes who were then free to join either of the two successor states or to remain independent. Unlike most princely rulers who chose to join India or Pakistan, the King of Kashmir hesitated, because the King was Hindu, while the majority of his subjects were Muslims. Within about a year of Independence, however, when Pathan tribesmen, aided by Pakistan, invaded Kashmir, the King signed the Instrument of Accession to join India. India promptly airlifted troops to halt the invasion at the Line of Control (LoC) which became, thereafter, the unofficial frontier between Pakistan Occupied Kashmir (PoK) and the area under Indian control. As the State of Jammu and Kashmir has been accorded a special status under Article 370 of the Indian constitution, it possesses more autonomy than other units of the federation. However, in practice, many of these special rights have been whittled down, bringing the State almost to the same level of control from the centre as the federal States of the Indian Union.

Except for Jammu and Kashmir and parts of India's North-East, on the whole India has been more successful in coping with sub-national movements than her neighbours. Typically, these movements emerge on the basis of demands for regional autonomy raised by geographically concentrated minorities who share a collective identity, often backed by a sense of relative deprivation in terms of their share of material resources. Characteristically, such movements are voiced by small groups of activists who are prepared to make great sacrifices for their cause. However, as one can see from the cases of Tamil, Telegu, Gujarati, Marathi or Oriya nationalism, among others, a combination of factors has usually led to the swelling of the ranks of sub-nationalists and to a decline in the intensity of the movement as a whole. Electoral mobilization has often played a key role. Once successful in gaining a majority, the movements, which sometimes transform themselves into political parties, have taken over the responsibility of ruling their regions, make the oath of loyalty to the representatives of the state and are given free rein over their affairs under the watchful eyes of the central government. Thus, elections, creation of new States, central financial aid and the use of the army to rein in the more extreme wings of separatists have contained such movements within the Indian Union. However, as one can see from continued insurgency in Kashmir, the uneasy peace in Punjab and the appearance of new splinter groups of secessionists in the North-East, sub-nationalism, spilling over to outright revolt against the state, is not entirely off the agenda.[3]

The constitution of India, in the tradition of written agreements between the central government and the States, defines the division of powers between both sides in its seventh schedule. The fact remains, however, that in contrast to the case of the United States, the Indian federation is not the outcome of pre-existing units that came together in a federal union out of common interest. Instead, the Union is the result of the provinces of British India at Independence and their subsequent reorganization in 1957. The process of federalization continues, with the addition of new federal units in response to specific demands.

The Union List gives the centre exclusive authority to act in matters of national importance; this list includes 97 items of defence, foreign affairs, currency, banking, and income tax. Table 5.3 lists the most important of the powers. The State List, which allocates exclusive rights of legislation to the States, includes 66 items that cover issues of local and regional importance such as public order and police, welfare, health, education, local government, industry, agriculture and land revenue. The Concurrent List, a special feature of Indian federalism, contains 47 items over which the centre and the States share legislative competence. In case of a conflict, the central law prevails. Civil and criminal law and social and economic planning are the important items in this list as these subjects are crucial to issues of identity and economic development. The residual power lies with the Union.

Unlike the classic model of federalism, in India the central government, acting through the parliament, can create new States, alter the boundaries or names of existing ones, and even abolish a State by ordinary legislative procedure. Not only does the central government have a wide range of powers under the Union List, but these powers are also enhanced because the central government is vested with a variety of powers that enable it, under certain circumstances, to extend its authority to the domain of the States. These special powers take three forms: (1) the Emergency powers under Articles 352, 356 and 360; (2) the use of Union Executive powers under Articles 256, 257 and 360; and (3) special legislative powers granted under Article 249.

The Emergency powers in the Indian constitution can enable the Union Executive to transform the federation into a unitary state when the President makes a declaration to that effect. Under these Emergency provisions the central executive and legislature can simply substitute the corresponding organs of the regional governments. Even under non-Emergency conditions, the central government may assume executive powers over regional governments in the 'national' interest. These powers, used by the President on the advice of the Prime Minister, are closely monitored by the parliament, the media and the judiciary. In this context, the Rajya Sabha acts as the custodian of the States' interests.

Table 5.3 The federal distribution of powers

Lists (selected items)	Competence	Limits
List I – Union List (97 items) Defense of India – naval, military and air forces * Atomic energy * Central Bureau of Intelligence * Foreign affairs – treaties – war and peace * Citizenship * Pilgrimages to places outside India * Railways – national highways – Ports – Airways * Posts and telegraphs * Public debt of the Union – Currency, Foreign loans, Reserve Bank of India, Post Office *Trade and commerce with foreign countries * Inter-State trade and commerce * weight and measure * Industries – petroleum inter-State rivers – fisheries beyond territorial waters * Industrial disputes concerning Union employees * the National Library, the Indian Museum, Benares Hindu University, the Aligarh Muslim University and the Delhi University – the training of police officers * Ancient and historical monuments and records – archaeological sites and remains * Census * All-India Services – Union Public Service Commission * the Election Commission * Audit of the accounts of the Union and of the States * Supreme Court – High Courts * Taxes on income other than agricultural income – Corporation tax * Any other matter not enumerated in List II or List III including any tax not mentioned in either of those Lists.	Centre	None
List II – State List (66 items) Public order – Police – Prisons * Local government * Public health and sanitation * Pilgrimages * intoxicating liquors * Agriculture * Water *Land * Money-lending * Theatres – cinemas * State public services *Taxes on agricultural income, professions, luxuries, entertainments.	State government	1. Presidential assent 2. Parliament can transfer jurisdiction temporarily
List III – Concurrent List (47 items) Preventive detention * Marriage and divorce * Contracts * Bankruptcy * Trust and Trustees * Vagrancy – nomadic tribes * Forests * Economic and social planning * Population and family planning *Trade unions * Social security and social insurance * Education * Relief and rehabilitation *Price control * Electricity * Evacuee property.	Both	Central laws prevail in case of conflict

Source: *The Constitution of India.*

The centre's right to influence the federal division of powers is reinforced by the constitution's financial provisions. The central government has vast powers over the collection and distribution of revenue, which make the States heavily dependent on the central government for financial support. Financial assistance flows from the central government to the States in several ways. Most of the lucrative taxes like income tax, corporate tax, and import and export duties are collected by the central government. These funds are shared by the centre with the States under a formula devised by the Finance Commission, which is appointed by the President but guaranteed independence from interference by the centre as well as the States in its everyday functions. The centre alone has the power over currency, banking and international borrowings. The States also have their own sources of income, but these taxes, like land revenue or irrigation taxes, for example, have not been particularly lucrative. Agricultural income is notoriously difficult to ascertain and, for political reasons, taxation is difficult to enforce.

As a result of the financial provisions envisaged in the constitution and their evolution over the years since Independence, the States have been routinely short of funds. These shortfalls have been met through central assistance in the form of loans, grants-in-aid, and overdraft facilities – provisions that have compromised the autonomy of the States. This was further reinforced by the centralizing tendencies of the national Five Year Plans and the powers exercised by the Congress party on State governments, ruling both at the centre and in the States for virtually two decades without interruption following Independence. With the end of the hegemony of the Congress party, however, a new mutation took place in the federal arrangement, moving it towards a cooperative federation, away from the centre-dominated quasi-federation that it was to begin with.

India's cooperative federalism

Despite the centralizing tendencies, the Indian political system has developed a distinct pattern of cooperation between the centre and the States over the past decades. This was helped by the rise of language movements in the 1950s and the assertion of ethnic identity in the last two decades. Freed from the tutelage of central dominance because of the decline of the 'one-dominant-party system' of the Congress party, and liberalization of the economy since 1991, Indian federalism has become more robust in recent years. The adoption of regional languages as administrative languages has brought government closer to people. The regional languages have experienced a renaissance, spurred on by the textbook market, public funds for regional culture, cinema and TV, the National Sahitya Academy (the National Academy of Literature, which promotes the national language Hindi as well as the regional languages), and the national film festivals, which offer special prizes for the best regional films. The regional elite, confident in their language and identity, have also rediscovered the virtues of learning English and Hindi, which give access to competitive jobs under the central government, to prestigious national universities, and to business and industry in other regions of India and abroad. The process of national integration through the spread of link languages like English and Hindi has gone hand in hand with the assertion of regional identity. Thus the issue of language conflict, which split East Pakistan from West Pakistan and continues to threaten the integrity of Sri Lanka, has been largely contained in India.

The institutions that we have examined above show how the Indian political system has attempted to combine elements of a modern state with the historical legacies of the pre-modern past. The constitution includes countervailing forces – a wide spectrum of institutions with a sense of corporate identity, political power, agenda and political base – that would make it difficult, though not impossible, for a potential dictator to transform the political system into an authoritarian regime. In the process, the state has become the initiator of change, the author of a nation-in-the-making.

We will see below how the political process has helped produce a continuous interaction between the values of individualism, liberty, egalitarianism and secularism on which the system is based, and the hierarchical and organic norms of the society within which it is ensconced. The system has sometimes been stretched to the limit but without breaking down altogether. It has managed to bounce back in a transformed shape and with renewed vigour.

India's federal structure has matured considerably during the 60 years since Independence. The uneasy assortment of provinces directly ruled by the colonial government and native princely states whose rulers chose to join India has become a robust federal Union with 28 States and seven Union territories. The provinces, particularly since their reorganization on the basis of mother tongue, have become cohesive cultural and political units, effectively cooperating through a broad spectrum of federal bodies. These institutional changes are underpinned by growing popular trust in federal institutions. These achievements suggest two major puzzles.

First, while there is no denying the growing depth and complexity of India's federal institutions, what remains unclear is why India's federalism – given that it is a *modern* institution of exogenous provenance ensconced within a traditional society – *should* work at all. If the problems of governance in transitional societies arise from the hiatus between modern institutions and traditional society, then federalism – itself a modern institution based on a written constitution, States' rights, and judicial mediation in case of conflict of interests – should have been undermined by political practice, rather like it has been in neighbouring Pakistan. Despite having come to the brink of collapse time and again, India's federal structure has pulled back to continue as before.[4] Where does this resilience come from?

The second puzzle derives from the record of unseemly political behaviour particularly evident at the regional level. After all, if Indian federalism is the shining success that many claim it to be, then why do State governments – an integral part of the federal institutional design – produce chief ministers[5] whose communal, corrupt and venal regimes have sometimes excessively misused the power and autonomy granted to federal units? Considering that the States are an integral part of the federal structure and process, then why does the sum of parts, many of them damaged political goods by any reckoning, add up to the functioning whole? What federal 'brakes' operate to localize the damage and stop it from spiralling upwards and spreading horizontally, without at the same time compromising the principle of the autonomy of States?

The fortuitous combination of structure and agency best explains the coping mechanism that leads to the relative success of federalism in India. India's political geography, simultaneously marked by regional diversity and cross-regional cultural links and social networks, provides the countervailing pressures of regional autonomy and interregional bonds that are essential for a robust federal system. Both tendencies have been reinforced in the Indian case by the political process that characterized British colonial rule and Indian resistance to it. Masters of indirect rule through intermediaries, the British utilized a system of governance that required the transfer of the requisite degree of autonomy to regional and local units to provide some substance to their legal identities while simultaneously binding them together within the 'steel frame' of colonial rule.

The colonial tactic of 'divide and rule' found its match in the resolve of the leaders of the freedom movement to 'unite and oppose' – a strategy that combined institutional participation with rational protest. In retrospect, thanks to the insuperable political and administrative skills of leaders like Mohandas K. Gandhi, Jawaharlal Nehru, Sardar Vallabhbhai Patel and many others, the anti-colonial movement also evolved into a government-in-waiting. The second historical moment came after Independence. When the Muslim League, the main balancing factor against the hegemonic ambitions of the Indian National Congress, left India for Pakistan, the void was quickly filled by a succession of strong regional leaders who kept the expanding power of the central leaders in check.

This can be studied in terms of some empirical arguments, involving the political culture, institutional design, context, and policy process of federalism in India.[6] The success of a federal system is contingent on the perceived interest of federating units to stay within a federation rather than to strike out on their own. These arguments, discussed in detail below, suggest that the preponderant role of the Union in India's federal design responded to the need for unity in the wake of Independence and the scope for transfer of resources from the rich to the poor, thereby enhancing the legitimacy of the new postcolonial state. This was reinforced by the countervailing tendencies of Indian politics that gave federal institutions the necessary room to manoeuvre as well as a successful track record to draw upon once the binding mechanism of the 'one-dominant-party' phase of Indian politics – the period from 1947 to 1967 when the Congress party ruled supreme in all centres of power in India – was over. Following the liberalization of India's economy in 1991, interstate competition transformed the States from 'clients' into competing stakeholders which have since discovered a new *raison d'être* for federalism in the vast, rapidly expanding Indian market with its global reach.

What should propel rational actors towards federal institutions rather than away from them? Institutions, we learn from North (1991), are 'humanly devised constraints that shape human interaction'. They achieve legitimacy and strength by 'reducing uncertainty' and 'providing a structure to everyday life'. In a quickly changing political situation of the kind that one can expect in transitional societies, institutional durability depends on whether the institutions can provide a bridge between the indigenous political tradition and exogenous political designs through which the state attempts to shape them. The provision of incentives – material, symbolic and punitive – to abide by the federal rules of the game is of crucial significance. Crafty political leaders and their equally disingenuous followers can be constrained by rules only when they perceive compliance to be in their best interests. North puts it succinctly:

> The resultant path of institutional change is shaped by (1) the lock-in that comes from the symbiotic relationship between institutions and the organizations that have evolved as a consequence of the incentive structure provided by those institutions and (2) the feedback process by which human beings perceive and react to changes in the opportunity set.[7]

This might help us understand the strength, resilience, and effectiveness of India's federalism in terms of the culture, design, context and policy process that underpin it.

Measuring federalism's success

A detailed analysis of the functioning of India's federal institutions is beyond the scope of this book.[8] These include designated institutions such as the upper house

(Rajya Sabha), which represents States' interests at the Union level, as well as more specialized ones like the Finance Commission, an independent body appointed by the President to maintain a fair and efficient division of revenues between the centre and the States, and the Planning Commission and Election Commission, whose responsibilities indirectly affect the vitality of federal processes. One indication of the extent to which the economies of the States are affected by federal institutions is the provisions for sharing the national income. From 1998 to 2002, all the States together raised only 49.2 per cent of their current spending from their own taxes. The rest was raised through a variety of mechanisms such as tax devolution, grants (both plan and non-plan), and special loans from the Reserve Bank of India. These transfers were made on the basis of complex criteria that took into account distributive justice (the extent of poverty or special circumstances such as natural disasters, terrorism and population size) while rewarding evidence of efforts at self-help. In the event, high-income States covered 66.8 per cent of their current spending with their own resources, middle-income States covered 55 per cent, and low-income States covered 38.8 per cent.[9]

The findings from survey research show that enough profits from macro financial transactions have trickled down to the level of the mass public to bring the federal process a measure of legitimacy. A series of National Election Studies measured the interest of the Indian electorate in the political system at the central, regional and local levels, as well as loyalty to the respective political arenas. (See Tables 5.4 and 5.5.)

Analysis of these findings reveals a growing interest in regional matters from 1971 to 1999 (see Table 5.4). A notable and steady increase can be seen in the group of respondents who are equally interested in both levels of government. This table shows more and more people taking an interest in what their own region does while the focus on the centre has somewhat declined. The most remarkable increase has been in the public's interest in *both* central and regional government, accompanied by a stark decline in the percentage of those without an opinion. This can be interpreted as evidence of the internalization of the federal norm in that section of the electorate which appears to see the power-sharing arrangement as a part of normal centre–State relations.

One could infer from the results presented in Table 5.5 that loyalty first and foremost to the regions is in steady decline. Tables 5.4 and 5.5 show that both arenas are increasingly perceived as legitimate venues of political action, which need not be mutually exclusive. Regional political forces, having established themselves in the States as well as at the central level, have turned the issue of the relationship between national and regional identities from one of exclusive choice into one of inclusiveness. This has been accelerated through India's vigorous media and thriving telecommunications market.

Finally, the horizontal and vertical expansion of federal processes through the creation of new federal units that strategically co-opt regional and local dissidents and produce new stakeholders through the women's quota in the local *panchayats* (village councils) has brought greater legitimacy to the Indian state and cohesion to the Indian nation. Some evidence of trust in all three levels of government is presented in Table 5.6.

The breezy confidence with which some Indians explain the seeming contradictions of their country with reference to the political culture of 'unity in diversity' has been

Table 5.4 Interest in central and state government (in per cent)

Are you more concerned/interested about/in what the government in Delhi does or about what the (name the state government) does?	1971	1996	1999
Neither	24.9	39.7	26.0
Central government	21.0	11.0	14.8
Both	14.5	20.9	26.7
State government	18.9	23.0	25.6
D.K., N.A., Other	20.7	5.4	6.9

Source: National Election Studies, CSDS (Delhi) 1971, 1996, 1999.

Table 5.5 Loyalty to region first and then to India (in per cent)

('We should be loyal to our own region first and then to India.' Do you . . .?).	1967	1996	1999	2004
Agree	67.1	53.4	50.7	65.4
Disagree	22.3	21.0	21.4	19.8
D.K./No Opinion	8.4	25.6	27.8	14.8

Source: National Election Studies, CSDS (Delhi) 1967, 1996 and 1999.

Table 5.6 Trust in local/state/central government (in per cent)

How much trust/confidence do you have in the central government: a great deal, somewhat or no trust at all?	A great deal	Somewhat	No trust at alll
Local government	39.0	37.8	23.2
State government	37.2	43.6	19.2
Central government	35.2	42.5	22.3

Source: National Election Studies 1996, CSDS (Delhi).

sorely tested during the times of violence at Partition of the country in 1947, sporadic intercommunity riots, and the separatist movements and mass insurgencies that afflict Kashmir and the North East. Still, without a culture of compromise, consensus, and accommodation, the main hypothesis of structure-agency-new federal design will not succeed.

The expanding and successful Indian federation has helped transform the common adage 'unity in diversity' to something more akin to unity *and* diversity. All Indian religions have their specific concepts of a macro, binding structure. Each also has unique ways of accommodating latent conflicts of belief and practice, resulting in regional and local diversity. The same practice has been adopted by modern institutions like political parties and trade unions which, under the umbrella of a modern macro ideology and manifesto, embrace considerable divergence in doctrine and practice.

The legacy of British rule with regard to federalism can be best understood in terms of the British solicitude to reconcile administrative efficiency and cultural difference. The pre-Independence attempts by the British to institute a federal state, seen as biased in favour of the Muslim League, was perceived by the Indian National Congress as an attempt to weaken the centre. This path dependency of the pre-Independence context led to a 'union of States' (the word federation is not to be found in the Indian constitution) with the dual purpose of limiting the tyranny of the majority and generating strength through union.[10]

Combining strength with accountability: Indian federalism in cross-national comparison

Looking back to the Partition riots which cast their long shadow on the deliberations of the Constituent Assembly, one can see the reason for the top heavy institutional design of federalism that emerged. But what explains its continuation once the immediate peril had passed? Comparative federal theory tells us that a durable federal design derives its resilience from its success at reconciling the contradictory goals of cohesion and diversity.[11] Usually, one can assume such a design to be the product of a context with a tradition of political bargaining among autonomous units, and of a political culture leavened with the history of a 'social contract'. This is usually the case with the experience of Western federal states.

None of these *a priori* conditions prepares the student of comparative federalism for the Indian case. With a constitution that is more the result of a transfer of power than of a concerted, organized quest for independent statehood based on a contract, India stands apart from the world's major federations. After the 73rd amendment to the constitution in 1993,[12] India developed a three-tier system of government where authority is divided between the central level, the federal units, and about 500,000 village councils.

With a clear, constitutionally guaranteed division of power[13] effectively policed by an independent Supreme Court, direct elections to the *panchayats* and central and regional governments monitored by an independent Election Commission, and the capacity of the political process to sustain a dynamic balance between the levels of government, India exhibits many of the features of federalism. But India's membership in this exclusive club remains a matter of some dispute.[14] The political evidence with regard to the characteristics of a federal process[15] is present and can be seen in K.C. Wheare's brief review of the conditions of effective federalism that suggests four necessary conditions for a federal design.[16] The first requires at least two levels of government, each with independent spheres of administrative and legislative competence. This condition is more than fulfilled by the 73rd amendment to the constitution by which India actually has three levels of government. The federal division of powers allocates responsibility for matters of national importance to the union government, and regional matters to the State governments. Issues of national importance that nevertheless are of regional and local character are allocated to the concurrent list on the understanding that in case of conflict, the national law should prevail. Residuary powers are allocated to the Union government (Table 5.3). Second, the constitution recognizes the principle of independent tax bases, though with the combination of democratic pressure for tax reduction on land, education and healthcare, which fall under the scope of state legislation, States have lost out on the financial front, and expansion of the economy has benefited the central government more.

Third, a written constitution from which each side derives its legislative power makes sure that boundaries are clearly demarcated. Fourth, there must be a system of independent judicial courts to arbitrate between the centre and the constituent units.

Thus, in terms of the classic features of federal states, the Indian constitution fulfils the necessary conditions. However, the Achilles' heel of the institutional arrangement lies in the financing. The federal division of powers gives the Union jurisdiction over taxes that have an interstate base while taxes with a local base have been allotted to the States. The more flexible and lucrative sources of revenue – income tax, corporation tax, customs duty and excise duties – are allocated to the Union list. The constitution, however, has recognized the States' position of financial weakness and has provided a number of mechanisms to help them meet their deficit. The constitution provides three methods for the transfer of resources from the centre to the States, including:

(1) the transfer of net proceeds from certain taxes and duties such as stamp duties, duties on toilet and medicinal preparations, estate duty on non-agricultural property, duties of succession to property other than non-agricultural land, and taxes on railway fares and freight;
(2) the compulsory sharing of certain taxes like income tax; and
(3) permissive sharing of excise taxes as well as conditional and unconditional grants-in-aid.

The mechanisms for balancing the financial might of the union government and the needs of the States are the Finance Commission, a quasi-judicial body appointed by the President for a duration of five years, and the Planning Commission, whose recommendations are discussed by the National Development Council.

The institutional arrangements of federalism, carrying the double legacy of the euphoria of Independence and the fear of disintegration in the face of the Partition riots, show abundant evidence of a bias in favour of the Union. The central parliament enjoys the extraordinary power of legislation on state subjects that affect the national interest when authorized by the Rajya Sabha.[17] The consent of States is not required for alteration of their names or boundaries. The overwhelming financial power of the Union, already mentioned above, gives the Union government the edge when it comes to coercing state governments. Similarly, the comprehensive authority of the Union Planning Commission, very much Nehru's brainchild and an instrument of central initiatives with regard to development projects, plays an additional role in regard to central directives and guidance. The governor, formal head of the state government, was designed to be a central appointee rather than an elected, local official. The All India Services, a legacy of the British colonial framework, continued under central command. Finally the Emergency provisions in Articles 352, 356 and 360 became very much a part of everyday politics and not just the exception during the Congress hegemony and particularly under Indira Gandhi. In consequence, Wheare, voicing the scepticism of many experts, described the Indian case as 'a quasi-federation – a unitary state with subsidiary federal features rather than a federal state with subsidiary unitary features'.[18]

The ambivalent legal position that the Indian constitution accords to the constituent States of the Union must appear startling to the federalist. As mentioned earlier, the construction of the Union did not result from a decision by a group of independent political units to shed bits of their sovereignty out of shared interest to create a federal state. The Indian Union and the provincial governments were simultaneous creations of the Constituent Assembly in which the latter did not have any special representation. Furthermore, the central government gradually shifted the boundaries of the units that existed at the time of Independence and started to create new States. The first major redesign of State boundaries occurred in 1956 and 1957 through the States Reorganization Act, after prolonged agitation in South India for a reorganization of States along linguistic and cultural boundaries.[19]

Despite the misgivings of experts and the asymmetry in the structural relations between the union and the States, regional governments were not the mere minions of the union government. The Indian Supreme Court, vindicating the claims of Watts regarding the importance of an institutional arrangement to guarantee the autonomy of the constituent units,[20] declared that 'the fact that under the scheme of our Constitution greater power is conferred upon the Centre vis-à-vis the States does not mean that States are mere appendages of the Centre. Within the sphere allotted to them, States are supreme. The Centre cannot tamper with their powers.'[21]

Political dominance by a single ethnic group has been the bane of many postcolonial states. The dominance of Pakistani politics by the Punjabi people, or the great sense of insecurity that the Tamil minority of Sri Lanka feels because of the dominance of the Sinhala majority, both in terms of numbers and area, is enough evidence of the potential consequences of the structural asymmetry of the union. In the Indian case, the Supreme Court has confirmed the status of India's federalism as part of the basic structure of the Indian constitution.[22] Thus, the Supreme Court has codified this institutional design which was not expressly laid out in the constitution of India.[23]

Institutional changes since Independence

The framers of the Indian constitution were keen on federalism as a functional instrument for the creation of an Indian nation and a strong, cohesive state. The leading politicians of the immediate post-Independence state were faced with internal and external threats to India's security and confronted the challenge of development through centralized economic planning. Thus, for both constitutional and political reasons, the institutionalization of federalism in the Indian system appears to have been seriously compromised from the outset. In fact, the apprehension of 'fissiparous tendencies' and 'Balkanization' among the informed observers was so great that the professional predictions for the future of India as a democracy and a federation were pretty grim. Nonetheless, the political process has been able to adapt to this design and in many, though not all, cases to modify it when necessary, to safeguard regional interests.

The first phase of federation lasted from the time of Indian Independence to the mid-1960s. Nehru took democracy seriously enough to face the enormously expanded Indian electorate in the first General Election in 1951. The electorate significantly included the Hindu nationalists, one of whose members had assassinated Mahatma Gandhi, and the communists, who had just staged an armed revolution in Telengana in South India. Nehru took the chief ministers seriously enough to write to each of them every month, in an effort to keep them informed and to solicit their opinion in an effort to build a national consensus.[24] The Indian National Congress, which had already embraced federalism by organizing itself into Provincial Congress Committees based on the linguistic regions, institutionalized the principles of consultation, accommodation, and consensus through a delicate balancing of the factions within the 'Congress system'.[25] It also co-opted local and regional leaders in the national power structure[26] and sent out Congress 'observers' from the centre to mediate between warring factions in the provinces, thus simultaneously ensuring the legitimacy of the provincial power structure in running its own affairs and the role of central mediation.

The second phase of Indian federalism began with the fourth General Elections in 1967, which drastically reduced the Congress party's overwhelming parliamentary strength to a simple majority and saw half of the States moving from Congress control into the hands of opposition parties or coalitions, causing a radical change in the nature of centre–State relations. No longer could an imperious Congress Prime Minister benevolently 'dictate' to a loyal Congress chief minister. Even as the tone became more contentious, however, the essential principles of accommodation and consultation held during the crucial period of transition from 1967 to 1969. The Congress-dominated centre started cohabiting with opposition parties at the regional level. The tenuous balance was lost once the Congress party split in 1969 and Indira Gandhi, her party reduced to a minority in parliament, adopted a strategy of radical rhetoric and authoritarian leadership. In consequence, the regional accommodation, which had been possible through the internal federalization of the Congress party, eroded. After the authoritarian interlude of 1975 to 1977 (which in both law and fact reduced India's federal system to a unitary state), the system reverted to the earlier stage of tenuous cooperation between the centre and the States.

The third phase in the federalization of Indian politics began at the end of the 1980s. Regional parties, like the Dravida Munnetra Kazhagam (DMK) of Tamil Nadu and the Rashtriya Janata Dal (RJD) of Bihar, have asserted their interests more openly over the past one-and-a-half decades of coalition and minority governments. Even the Hindu nationalist Bharatiya Janata Party, which led the ruling coalition in the thirteenth Lok Sabha until 2004, has had to be solicitous in its at least symbolic adherence to the norms of centre–State relations established by its predecessors. As a matter of fact, the three newest States were created during the tenure of the NDA coalition, with the BJP as its leading member. The acceptance of the federal principle by Hindu nationalists was already evident in their acceptance of the three language formula in spite of the advocacy of Hindi as India's national language during the long years in opposition.

The fourth and the most recent phase of federalism started with the 'big bang liberalization' of the Indian economy. It has seen a radical transformation from the earlier 'ganging up of the States against the centre' to a free-for-all competition between all stakeholders – Union, States and mega-cities – to create conditions that attract investments from home and abroad. This has led to the decline of the centre-dominated developmental model that was implemented after Independence. By scaling back the State's involvement in the developmental process and as such reducing the functions of the central government, liberalization removed the safety net on which regional governments had depended. Consequently, the process of liberalization risked opposition from State governments. This opposition failed to materialize. Rob Jenkins even argues that part of the momentum for further liberalization comes from India's regions.[27]

The policies of liberalization launched in 1991 that started to dismantle the draconian rules of the command economy required a new regime to provide coordination in a rapidly changing financial environment.[28] The removal of subsidies and handouts held the potential to generate an anti-reform coalition of leftist parties. Why did this anti-reform wave, in spite of the rhetoric from its leaders, fail to block reform? Jenkins's analysis of the liberalization of coffee pricing makes the point.[29] Thus, centre–State conflicts have been at least partially displaced by *interstate* competition for investment from home and foreign capital markets. Lawrence Saez draws attention to changes in institutional arrangements and the process of political coordination of the economy: 'the most significant transformation of India's federal system is exemplified by the gradual shift from intergovernmental cooperation between the central government and the States towards inter-jurisdictional competition among the States.'[30]

Power-sharing and the federalization of national politics

The recognition of political coalitions as the most practised institutional form of politics in India has reinforced the concept of federalism as the most practical and effective method of centre–State and inter-State relations. The literature suggests four general conditions to explain the federalization of India's national politics with regard to the policy process. The first and foremost is 'elite accommodation'. Next is 'public involvement' though it may 'complicate the patterns of negotiation for the establishment of a federal system'.[31] An atmosphere of 'competition and collusion' between intergovernmental agencies is a third condition.[32] In the fourth place, drawing on Riker, Watts mentions 'the role and impact of political parties, including their number, their character, and the relations among federal, State, and local branches' as helpful in explaining the dynamism of federal processes.[33]

The pattern of elite recruitment employed by the Congress party during the period of its hegemony (1952–1967) shows that local and regional talent rose to prominence within the party organization and moved horizontally to government. Subsequently, new, upwardly mobile social groups entered the electoral arena as political parties, organized on the basis of caste and ethnic networks, which aspired to getting office in their own right. This shows a steady expansion of the social base of leadership in India. That satisfies the first two of the conditions mentioned by Watts. The competition for scarce natural resources among bureaucrats and political leaders from Indian States is a good example of the third condition at work. With the decline of the Congress party, however, intra-party federalization has been supplanted by an entirely different intra-party and inter-party system. Nevertheless, even though regional parties are viewed as champions of special interests in the States, leaders who aim to become national figures try to place the region in the larger context of the nation. Eventually, as members of national coalitions of regional parties, they start to pose as national leaders, ready to compromise and conciliate among conflicting regional interests. This places a measure of restraint on political impropriety and policing by coalition partners who do not wish to have their own political futures ruined through a partner's misconduct.

The shifting of Laloo Prasad Yadav from Bihar to the Railway Ministry in the central government is a case in point.[34] Thus even as the dominance of the Congress party has declined, the multi-party system that replaced it has produced the same institutionalized method of regional conflict resolution within a national framework.

The social origins of these 'new regionalist' champions who become born-again nationalists following the logic of the Indian political process help to identify the dynamic process that sustains the federal system in India. These new regionalists (who should be distinguished from the old regionalists who were given to taking non-negotiable positions during the period of Congress dominance) are likely to be upwardly mobile educated males, the erstwhile 'bullock capitalists'[35] who have now graduated beyond exclusive reliance on agriculture to other avenues of upward mobility. The new type of regional leaders has reinforced the link of India's centre with the periphery.

Having established themselves locally, regionalists have now set their sights on constructing the kind of nation that they want. They are using their alliances with similar forces from outside their region to define the nature of the national community in their own way. Recent events in different parts of the country have demonstrated that the pursuit of these goals cannot only coexist with similar aspirations elsewhere but that regional movements can, in fact, reinforce one another by pooling their political resources. Hence one finds the unprecedented scenes of political leaders from one part of India campaigning for regional parties in other parts of the country. The Congress system (1947–67) incorporated local and regional interests at lower levels of the internally federalized system. The new element in Indian politics has made the processes of regional and national consultation that are carried out within large coalitions of national and regional parties more systematic, transparent and institutionalized. The central government no longer holds a monopoly over defining what the nation is and deciding who has the right to speak in its name. This has opened up new ways of drawing in people from India's outlying areas and weaving them into a more composite, multinational culture of India.

As one can see from both the 1999 and 2004 Lok Sabha elections and the subsequent government coalitions,[36] regional parties have become part and parcel of government formation processes even at the central level. As in the case of the 2004 government formation process, some regional politicians have been able to secure more than their fair share of influence at the central level. While the 21-member RJD secured only two cabinet-rank ministries, the DMK, despite its limited strength of only 16 MPs, was allocated three cabinet ministries. At the same time, the RJD was able to secure a first tentative success with the inclusion of a Backward States Grant Fund – of which Bihar expected to be a major beneficiary – in the Common Minimum Programme of government after the 2004 elections.[37] This exposes the ambiguous nature of the federal bargaining process, where office means influence above and beyond the limits of the portfolio which a politician is allocated. Thus while some regions can hope that their interests are represented through regional power brokers at the central government level, other States fear being left behind whenever their regional parties are not included in the national government coalition.

The political processes of the 1990s show the integration of federal norms in the game plans of local and regional political leaders. Rather than taking a mechanical, anti-Delhi stance as their only *raison d'être*, the new breed of ambitious, upwardly mobile leaders of India have learned to play by the rules even while they challenge them, and thus have developed for themselves a new, federal space in which the nation and the region can coexist.[38]

Conclusion

The violent and chaotic situation caused by the Partition of British India and the Pakistan-backed invasion of Kashmir formed the background to the writing of the constitution. These danger signals for the new Republic called for a centralized, effective executive in Delhi, with the requisite flexibility to rein in unruly governments in the regions and localities. And yet, the need for evolving a democratic, collective agenda of social reform and economic development in a country of continental proportions required cooperation more than rule by fiat from above. The result has been a federal design that has endured the test of time, and has become, in its own right, a political tool of democracy, development and governance. The chapter has analysed this argument through the institutional arrangement of federalism, its anomalies and an evaluation of the practical results achieved by it.

In view of the high mortality rate of federalism in changing societies, the resilience of India's federalism leads one to ask: has India just been lucky? It can be argued that while chance, in the form of helpful structural conditions (and the fortuitous Partition of the country that made the political system of India more cohesive), has certainly played a positive role in the success of India's federalism, the agency of the post-Independence leaders and their successors built further on this foundation. Looking back, one can admire the prescience with which the framers of the Indian constitution equipped the Indian state to respond to the demands for autonomy through the dual mechanisms of individual and group rights, as well as the federal division of powers in normal times and the effective union of powers in the times of emergency.

During the first phase of India's constitutional development, some of these instruments were useful in empowering political majorities below the level of the national state through the effective enactment of provincial administrations. The second phase of constitutional development through the States' reorganization of 1956–57 created linguistically homogeneous States and counterbalanced the likely chauvinism. In its third phase, the process of constitutional development of federalism initiated by the 73rd amendment of 1993, India has witnessed the deepening of the power-sharing principle by the statutory power now accorded to village councils. Finally, in the fourth and current phase, the liberalization of the Indian economy has produced an atmosphere where State governments have emerged as stakeholders in the new economic order rather than clients of an almighty union, dependent on a handout to balance their budgets.

These institutional changes of India's federation explain the fusion of modern and traditional political cultures, historical contingency, and the fortuitous historical legacy of great political events like the Partition of India. During the critical years of transition from British rule and the consolidation of popular democracy in India, the Congress party provided the link between the modern state and the traditional society. Congress rule, both at the centre and in the States, provided informal channels of communication and the balancing of national, regional and sectional interests. The politics of coalitions that has replaced Congress hegemony has given a public voice to the new debate on the nature of the nation. In consequence, the search for regional allies has now become an imperative for all national parties.

The new group of highly visible and effective regional leaders, drawing on their power bases in the States which often include people from India's periphery (in terms of religion, elite caste status, or geographic distance from the centre), are able to generate a different concept of the nation-state that is better suited to the spirit of our times. When speaking in the national mode, regional leaders do not rule out the need to be well informed and decisive in the defence of the security and integrity of the nation. But in terms of actual policies, they are much more willing and (in view of their social bases) able to listen to the minorities, to regions with historical grievances, and to sections of society that entered the post-Independence politics with unsolved, pre-Independence (in some cases, pre-modern) grievances. It is thanks to these political 'fixers' – culture brokers who mediate between the union and the regions – and the emerging multi-party democracy of India that politics is not merely an anomic battle for power and short-term gain but the release of pent-up creativity and visions that provide a fertile and cohesive backdrop to the realignment of social forces as well. Far from being its antithesis, the region has actually emerged as the nursery of the nation.

The constitutional, legislative and policy instruments that India has drawn upon to reach the positive outcomes in the development of federalism have an important implication for the comparative analysis of the federal process. Whereas old institutionalists, such as Wheare, prescribed a given set of institutions as the necessary and sufficient basis of a federal State,[39] neo-institutionalists show the importance of being pragmatic in devising the institutions appropriate to specific cultural, religious and historical contexts.[40] The creation of sub-regional States like Gorkhaland (a result of protracted negotiations between the Congress government of New Delhi, the communist government of Bengal, and the Gorkha leadership) and, more recently, the creation of three new States during the regime of the NDA (considered opposed to further divisions of India) is in every sense a genuine and unprecedented innovation, guided by the heuristic notion of power-sharing and solid, political common sense. The rules of the federal system, rather than being exogenous to the federal process, have become endogenous to it.

In contrast to India, in Pakistan, also a successor state with the British legacy of an English educated elite schooled in the grammar of parliamentary politics for almost as long as the Congress party, federalism has followed a different trajectory. The undoing of federalism and consequent split of the Pakistani state in 1971 came through the combination of short-sighted leaders and trigger-happy generals, without the balancing factor of the regional and local leaders – the unshaven and ill-clad power brokers who throng the corridors of power in Delhi and the state secretariats. It is true that India, whose government-in-waiting was already forged in the 1930s and whose links with the constituencies remained intact even as the Partition wrenched the leaders of the Muslim League from their political base in India, held the better cards. But faced with the example of leaders like Nehru who, rather than taking short-term advantage of the preponderant role of the union and using this power to promote partisan advantage, used it with judicious discretion, taming the obdurate satraps of larger regions and reassuring the weak and insecure States of the rightness of their just demands, one has to admit that the Indians played their federal cards rather well. Of course, as the fragile state of the North-East and continued dissension in Kashmir show, the parallel processes of federalization and national integration are far from complete. A consideration of the Indian achievements from the dark days of the Partition riots of 1946–47, or the rising secessionist movements of the critical 1980s, however, shows that India's unfolding federalism is both robust and resilient. The next chapter takes up the formal and informal modes of articulation and aggregation of interest that criss-cross the country, individual States in a national grid which sustains the federal principle of 'self rule' leavened by 'shared rule'.

Notes

1 See, for example, the comment of Paul Appleby (1957).
2 See the comment of Rajendra Prasad, President of the Constituent Assembly, quoted on p. 87 above.
3 See Mitra and Lewis (1996) for detailed analysis of cases from India and her neighbours.
4 The anti-Hindi agitations in Madras in the 1950s were based on the fear of domination by North India and formed the basis of a movement for a separate state to be called Dravidstan. Similar anti-Delhi feelings were roused in West Bengal for much of the 1960s and 1970s, in Punjab in the 1980s, and, currently, in Kashmir and in the North East.
5 Some of the notable examples of regional autonomy being used for purposes that stand contrary to the norms of the Indian state can be seen in the cases of chief ministers Narendra Modi, Laloo Prasad Yadav, Kumari Mayawati and Jayalalitha Jayaram. The issue is why this regional habit of violating the constitution does not trickle upwards to the centre, reducing its legitimacy and integrative role, as is the case in other countries such as Nigeria.
6 These arguments draw on North's core insight regarding what makes institutions work (1991).
7 North (1991), p. 7.
8 Bhattacharyya (2001), Saez (2002), Arora (1995).
9 Rao and Singh (2004).
10 Article 1 of the Indian constitution puts it this way: 'India, that is Bharat, shall be a Union of States.'
11 Watts (1999, p. 7) famously put it as 'combining self rule and shared rule'.
12 In addition, the vertical expansion of the federal structure – to which a third tier was recently added through the inclusion of India's half million villages, with constitutionally mandated authority and financial autonomy and an obligatory minimum of 30 per cent of seats for women – deserves careful attention. This has turned the federal process into a major source of legitimization and democratization of power in India.
13 Following Indian usage, the constituent units of the Indian federation will be called 'States' and 'state' will refer to the central state.
14 Watts (1998, p. 118), in his comprehensive study of federal systems, counts 23 states as full federal states but one senses a certain reluctance to admit India as a full member of this club. 'India and Malaysia, marked by deep-rooted multilingual, multicultural and multiracial diversity, have nevertheless managed to cohere for half and a third of a century respectively, but are at a critical phase in their development.'
15 Following the usage of Watts, federal process is used in this chapter as a descriptive category which refers to the presence of a 'broad genus of federal arrangements' in a political system. These characteristics, which could in principle be composed into a scale, are drawn from the definition of a federation as 'a compound polity combining constituent units and a general government, each possessing powers delegated to it by the people through a constitution, each empowered to deal directly with the citizens in the exercise of a significant portion of its legislative, administrative and taxing powers, and each directly elected by its citizens' (Watts 1998, pp. 117, 121).
16 Wheare (1964).
17 Article 249 of the Indian constitution.
18 Wheare as cited in Basu (1985), p. 58.

19 For an assessment of linguistic and cultural diversity and its impact on federalism in India, see Mitra (2001).

20 Watts (1998), p. 126.

21 *S.R. Bommai vs. Union of India*, 1994 (3) SCC 1, 216.

22 A similar arrangement can be found in the German constitution (the *Grundgesetz* or Basic Law) which does not specify the number of states which constitute Germany and allows for the alteration of boundaries – albeit only with the consent of the people living in the territory concerned (Article 29) – but declares the abolition of federalism, i.e., the division of the country into constituent units as such, as beyond the power of parliament to amend (Article 79, Sec. 3, *Grundgesetz*).

23 Nonetheless, the alteration of boundaries, not least in the recent case of the creation of the State of Jharkhand out of Bihar, has invited protest on several occasions and this instrument, while creating opportunities for greater autonomy for certain ethnic or linguistic groups, has also placed constraints on the political process.

24 These letters, which are a veritable treasure trove on the politics of the early post-Independence decades, are now available in a five-volume set edited by the Jawaharlal Nehru Memorial Fund (1989).

25 Kothari (1970).

26 Lijphart (1996).

27 Jenkins (1999).

28 These issues have been discussed at length in Chapter 7.

29 In 1992, following the first generation of liberalization policies, coffee growers were for the first time permitted to sell 30 per cent of their crop in the open market, effectively ending the monopoly control of government coffee boards. The free sale quota was increased to 50 per cent in 1993. In April 1995, in a long-anticipated move, all obligations to the coffee board were removed for 'small growers' (those with land holdings of less than 10 hectares). As Jenkins puts it,

> 'In need of new sources of revenue, states with substantial coffee growing operations began to cast an avaricious eye on coffee growers who had received "windfall" profits. The Karnataka government, for instance, was able to raise resources in this way, justifying the new tax by saying that the coffee growers who had benefited would be prepared to contribute resources for the welfare of the poor.' These adaptations further delink States' economic fates from one another – contributing to the pattern of provincial Darwinism that 'has reduced the effectiveness of resistance among State-level political elites.
>
> (Jenkins, 1999, p. 132–33)

30 Saez (2002), p. 215.

31 Watts (1998), p. 128.

32 Ibid, p. 130.

33 Ibid.

34   Laloo Prasad Yadav, India's railway minister, was known during the 15 years that he and his wife, Rabri Devi, were successive chief ministers of the State of Bihar, for his earthy realism and rustic lifestyle, which included keeping cows in the garden of his official residence. He was also famous for failing to improve the lot of one of India's poorest and most lawless States, and for a raft of corruption charges that put him in jail five times. In May 2004, he was made railways minister in Delhi. . . . Mr Yadav is a wily and disarming politician and has confounded his critics by becoming one of the country's most successful railway ministers.

('India's Railway Minister with big ambitions', *The Economist*, 29 July–4 August, 2006, p. 54)

35 Rudolph and Rudolph (1987), pp. 49–55.

36 The BJP-led NDA coalition under Atal Bihari Vajpayee initially consisted of 16 parties in the Lok Sabha, out of which only the BJP was a national party, and the cabinet included many veteran regional politicians. In the fourteenth Lok Sabha, the 10-party coalition led by the Congress party under the name United Progressive Alliance and supported by the left parties included only two national parties, INC and NCP. Of the cabinet ministers, two key portfolios, IT (Dayanidhi Maran) and Railways (Laloo Prasad Yadav), were allocated to regional figureheads.

37 'UPA Government to adhere to six basic principles of governance', *The Hindu*, 28 May, 2004.
38 The integrative power of this model is at its best in Tamil Nadu where a federal 'deal' can be struck with a specific group of actors, such as the DMK. But when the actors themselves are fragmented or not a part of the negotiation (as in Kashmir), the model is no longer very effective in producing a legitimate, federal solution. Mitra and Lewis (1996).
39 Wheare (1964).
40 Watts (1998).

6   The articulation and aggregation of interests

India's two-track strategy

Like a shop-keeper in an Indian bazaar, it [the Congress Party] squats with its large, flabby shape in the middle of its wares, the heart of a political market place in which bargaining and dissent are the language of the discourse.

Morris-Jones (1966), p. 455.

In the 130 years or so since the Mutiny . . . the idea of freedom has gone everywhere in India. Independence was worked for by people more or less at the top; the freedom it brought has worked its way down. People everywhere have ideas now of who they are and what they owe themselves. The process quickened with the economic development that came after independence; what was hidden in 1962, or not easy to see, what perhaps was only in a state of becoming, has become clearer. The liberation of spirit that has come to India could not come as release alone. In India with its layer below layer of distress and cruelty, it had to come as disturbance. It had to come as rage and revolt. India was now a country of a million little mutinies.

Naipaul (1990), p. 517.

Introduction

In the search for legitimacy, political systems seek to link the policy output of the government to the demands emerging from society. The role of parties, pressure groups and other organizations like lobbies that help in the articulation and aggregation of demands is crucial for this purpose. However, the process does not always function smoothly in changing societies where these intermediary organizations are not well organized and where often the capacity of the state falls short of the scale of demands articulated by mobilized social groups,[1] leading to a chaotic dissolution of the political order. In these societies, institutions lack the requisite coherence and depth which would enable them to iron out differences between groups and contradictions in the multiplicity of problems that crop up. In this respect, India stands pretty much alone in the post-colonial world. India's elections, political parties, movements and the tradition of direct political action that dates back to the Freedom Movement combine to create a dynamic link between the government and the people. This chapter examines how interest and pressure groups, and an assortment of protest movements, help carry out political transaction at the national, regional and local levels in India.[2]

Institutional complexity, policy coherence and continuity

Despite the pressure on modern political institutions, caused by rapid social mobilization, India's political system has acquired a high level of resilience. India has multiple arenas where decisions that deeply affect the lives and identity of people can be taken. The system combines the vertical separation of powers between the executive, legislature and the judiciary with horizontal division of powers between the centre, regions and localities (see Table 4.1 above). During the early decades following Independence, the fragmentation of authority that this scheme gave rise to was overcome by the all-pervasive presence of the Congress party.[3] Conflict of interests and principles could be negotiated informally within the organization of the party. The period of the two decades of informal intra-party negotiation after 1947 set the basis for institutionalized conflict resolution which has made the coherence and continuity of public policy at the national level possible.

The formal and informal bases of policy making in India are enriched by three factors: first, the vast range of modes of representation, stretching from efficiently organized, modern organizations of employers, businessmen, industrialists and labour at the one extreme to traditional forms, involving caste, tribe and ethnic groups at the other. In addition, there are unconventional political forms like *satyagraha*, *dharna*, *boycott* or *rasta roko*, inspired by Mahatma Gandhi. Second, there is no practice of 'closed shop', where specific organizations have monopoly control over the representation of interests in a particular trade or activity. Instead, considerable competition among organizations seeking to represent the same interest leads to the fragmentation of labour unions and interest groups. This has stymied their growth. Third, India's political actors combine diverse forms of action and organizations such as parties, interest and pressure groups, and movements to pursue their goals in an effective manner. Consequently, India's levels of interest articulation and aggregation are comparable to what one might find in long-established and more prosperous Western democratic states.

The historical continuity between the political process, elite–mass linkage, and top leadership before and after Independence is part of the answer to the puzzling growth of representation in the context of a traditional society. This also partly explains why India has been more successful than neighbouring Pakistan in developing and sustaining a democratic political system. Several factors have contributed to this. Following Partition, the parts of India that had a long experience of British rule and Indian resistance to it remained within India. The Congress party found itself in a smaller country where it had deep political roots. Its top leaders, known as the High Command, took over the task of 'getting the vote out' in the first General Election of 1952 by transforming the party organization, spread out throughout the country, into an efficient electoral machine. The Congress organization became the fountainhead of patronage, earning for itself the sobriquet of the 'quota-permit-raj'.

Elections

After Independence, political transaction and election campaigns rather than ideology and organization became the main feature of India's political process. In a calculated move, India's leaders put everything on the auction block of electoral politics right at the outset, in the first General Election of 1951–52. Even the very definition of the nation, its physical boundaries, and the basic principles of its economic organization were not considered over and above politics. Since then, every election[4] has been an occasion for individuals to recognize the value of their votes (see Box 3.2 above). The result, as we shall see below, was that the great school of democracy quickly multiplied the numbers of its enthusiastic pupils and continued to produce both knowledge and skill even when the first generation, identified with the coming of Independence, left the scene.

Universal adult franchise was introduced in 1952. All political parties including communists and the Hindu nationalist Jan Sangh were authorized to participate in the election. Thanks to the extension of suffrage, the electorate rapidly expanded, bringing into the political arena a large number of voters with no previous experience of electoral participation. Such a sudden induction of new voters could have been a recipe for disaster for parliamentary democracy and political order, particularly in conjunction with the violence that accompanied the Partition of India. But the subsequent career of parliamentary democracy, thanks to the continuity of the institutions of state and the structures of leader–constituent relations, saw parties and elections becoming an essential part of the political culture of post-Independence India. Voter turnout, spread over all social classes, has gone up steadily.

The first General Election to the Lok Sabha was a veritable adventure in democracy. This was the first time that a mammoth electorate of 173.2 million electors was going to the polls. The voter registration, identification and, finally, the conduct of the polls were all to be arranged by the recently established independent Election Commission, with an electoral organization staffed by men and women drawn from many different branches of the public services because no specialized bureaucracy had been foreseen by the constitution for this purpose. The ballots had to be carted to far-flung polling stations, many located in areas not easy to access. Only a part of the electorate had previous polling experience but for the vast majority – such as those who could not meet the educational and property qualifications of restricted franchise under British rule as well as people from the princely states voting for the first time – the election was a novel experience. Finally, Nehru's India took the risk to lift the ban on communists and members of the Hindu right wing – imposed, respectively, after the violent uprising of peasants in Telengana led by communists and the assassination of Mahatma Gandhi by Nathuram Godse, a member of the Rasthriya Swayamsevak Sangh, a Hindu nationalist organization. The risk of permitting unfettered participation in the election to political forces of all ideological hues paid off handsomely in the form of an orderly and peaceful election, though with a rather modest turnout of 45.7 per cent of the electorate (see Table 6.1).

Subsequent elections have maintained the largely peaceful character of the polling process though the deployment of the army has become routine in recent elections. Under the constitution, elections to the popular houses – the Lok Sabha and the State assemblies – have to be held every five years or less and that has been generally the case except in 1977 when the term of the Lok Sabha was extended by one year on account of the Emergency conditions. Elections to the Lok Sabha and State assemblies were held together in the early elections but from the 1960s, the rhythm has been broken, which, in a way, has enhanced the pressure on the accountability of the party in power. As one can see from the statistics of the 2004 parliamentary election, with an electorate of 671 million with about 390 million votes cast, India's elections have assumed gigantic proportions, and have earned an international reputation for being largely free and fair.

Since regular and frequent political consultation was designed to be the most effective instrument of political socialization, we need to examine indicators of political participation. Revealing statistics can be found from participation in the General Elections to the Lok Sabha, the lower house of the federal legislature and the highest repository of legislative authority and governmental accountability in the country. These are illustrative of India's success at organizing an electoral process on a continental scale. Large-scale poverty and illiteracy notwithstanding, India, under the supervision of an independent Election Commission, has organized elections involving very large electorates who, by law, have to be provided with polling booths within easy walking distance. The campaigns themselves are strictly monitored.[5] It is not unusual for polling to be stopped and re-polling ordered in the event of electoral fraud or violence.[6]

General elections to the federal parliament and its regional equivalent, the State assemblies, and elections to popular bodies at the local level are crucial elements of policy making, political recruitment and inter-generational transition in India. The General Election of 1951–52 was the first time that a national electorate, the bulk of which had never voted before, took part in an election under universal adult franchise. The right to vote for all and a secure environment within which citizens can participate in polling freely have now been generally established. Men tend to turn out in greater numbers than women; but the participation of women has grown over the years. An equally interesting phenomenon is the participation of the former untouchable castes, which, both for men and women, keeps pace with the population as a whole. It is a significant achievement considering their oppressive exclusion by the upper social strata in the past.

The level of participation in India's parliamentary elections (see Table 6.1), which has stabilized around 60 per cent, is lower than in the longer-established and more affluent democracies of Europe. There is, however, considerable regional variation

Table 6.1 Parliamentary elections, 1952–2009

Year	Seats	Candidates	Polling stations	Electorate *(in millions)*	Votes polled *(in millions)*	Turnout (%)
1952	489	1,874	132,560	173.2	79.1	45.7
1957	494	1,519	220,478	193.7	92.4	47.7
1962	494	1,985	238,355	217.7	120.6	55.4
1967	520	2,369	267,555	250.6	153.6	61.3
1971	518	2,784	342,944	274.1	151.6	55.3
1977	542	2,439	373,908	321.2	194.3	60.5
1980	529	4,629	434,742	363.9	202.7	56.9
1984	542	5,493	479,214	400.1	256.5	64.1
1989	529	6,160	579,810	498.9	309.1	62.0
1991	534	8,780	588,714	511.5	285.9	55.9
1996	543	13,952	767,462	592.6	343.3	57.9
1998	539	4,708	765,473	602.3	373.7	62.0
1999	543	4,648	774,651	619.5	371.7	60.0
2004	543	5,435	687,473	671.5	389.9	58.1
2009	543	–	828,804	716.0	–	56.9

Source: Data Unit, CSDS (Delhi) and Election Commission India (2009).

in levels of participation. This is particularly visible in elections to the lower houses in the States. The level of participation in these elections has also gone up from the modest 45 per cent turnout of the first election to over 60 per cent in more recent assembly elections. Electoral participation in the North-East is among the highest. In the elections held during 2002–6, some of the States – such as Manipur (90.2 per cent), Nagaland (87.9 per cent), Mizoram (78.7 per cent), Tripura (78.7 per cent) and Assam (75.7 per cent) – produced spectacular results. Some other States have developed traditions of high participation because of factors specific to them. Thus, the skills of the Left Front coalition in West Bengal at mobilizing their electors contribute to the high participation rate of around 80 per cent in recent assembly elections. Puducherry – a former French colony called Pondicherry until its renaming in 2006 – and Goa, a former Portuguese colony, each has a rate of participation higher than the national average. Even in strife-torn Kashmir – a politically conscious electorate turns out in large numbers when conditions return to a semblance of normality. However, participation has remained low in some parts of India such as Bihar, Jharkhand, Madhya Pradesh and Orissa, and average in richer States of India such as Delhi, Punjab, Haryana, Maharashtra and Gujarat. Still, even in low partici- pation States, the right to vote is seen as a part of general empowerment by the poor and underprivileged.

The party system

Elections and political parties generate a tandem effect between them: one tends to reinforce the other. The introduction of limited franchise by the colonial government towards the end of the nineteenth century had spurred political competition for seats, leading to the mobilization of the electorate on communal lines. This has an important legacy for contemporary Indian politics. The party system of contemporary India is the result of the six decades of growth under British rule prior to Independence. It is a complex system with the continuous presence of the Congress party in the national political arena, the emergence of a powerful Hindu nationalist movement, the world's longest elected communist government at the regional level and the occasional lapse into authoritarian rule which, nonetheless, did not become permanent as in the case of the majority of post-colonial societies. The picture becomes much clearer if we divide the post-Independence period into the 'one-dominant-party system' period (1952–77) and its subsequent transformation into a multi-party system.[7] The relative ease with which India developed electoral democracy and a competitive party system might appear puzzling to those unfamiliar with the pre-Independence record of the Indian National Congress with regard to taking part in elections and its legacy of sharing ministerial office under the Government of India Act, 1935. The party, as one can see from Tables 6.2a and 6.2b, was handsomely rewarded in the elections to the national parliament, thanks to the inheritance of the aura of pre- Independence prominence and the efficiency of its party organization in candidate selection and getting the vote out.

Whether the individual should be the basis of political representation, or whether organic groups – religion, caste and ethnicity – should form the basis of representation and, as such, the exercise of power, is a question that had created heated debate among sections of Indians when the notion of restricted franchise was first mooted towards the end of the nineteenth century. The leaders of the Congress party, deeply

Table 6.2a Lok Sabha elections, 1952–71 seats (and per cent of vote)

Party	1952	1957	1962	1967	1971
INC (1)	364 (45.0)	371 (47.8)	361 (44.7)	283 (40.8)	352 (43.7)
BJS/BJP	3 (3.1)	4 (5.9)	14 (6.4)	35 (9.4)	22 (7.4)
JP/JD	–	–	–	–	–
CPM	–	–	–	19 (4.4)	25 (5.1)
CPI	26 (3.3)	29 (8.9)	29 (9.9)	23 (5.0)	23 (4.7)
BKD/LD/SJP	–	–	–	–	1 (1.8)
INC (2)	–	–	–	–	16 (10.4)
Socialist	21 (16.4)	19 (10.4)	18 (9.5)	36 (8.0)	5 (3.4)
Swatantra	–	–	18 (7.9)	44 (8.7)	8 (3.1)
Regional parties	14 (14.1)	20 (6.2)	20 (8.9)	32 (9.1)	41 (8.4)
Independents	38 (15.9)	42 (19.4)	20 (11.1)	35 (13.7)	14 (8.4)
Others	23 (2.2)	9 (1.4)	14 (1.6)	13 (1.1)	11 (3.6)
Total	489	494	494	520	518

Source: Data Unit, CSDS (Delhi) and Election Commission India (2009).

Table 6.2b Lok Sabha elections, 1977–2009 seats (and per cent of vote)

Party	1977	1980	1984	1989	1991	1996	1998	1999	2004	2009
INC (I)	154 (34.5)	353 (42.7)	415 (48.0)	197 (39.5)	244 (36.6)	140 (28.8)	141 (25.8)	114 (28.3)	145 (26.5)	206 (28.6)
BJS/BJP	–	–	2 (7.4)	86 (11.5)	120 (20.0)	161 (20.3)	182 (25.6)	182 (23.8)	138 (22.2)	116 (18.8)
JP/JD/JD(U)	295 (41.3)	31 (19.0)	10 (6.7)	142 (17.7)	59 (10.8)	46 (8.1)	6 (3.2)	21 (3.1)	8 (2.4)	20 –
CPM	22 (4.3)	36 (6.1)	22 (5.7)	33 (6.5)	35 (6.1)	32 (6.1)	32 (5.2)	33 (5.4)	43 (5.7)	16 (5.3)
CPI	7 (2.8)	11 (2.6)	6 (2.7)	12 (2.6)	14 (2.5)	12 (2.0)	9 (1.8)	4 (1.5)	10 (1.4)	4 (1.4)
BKD/LD/SJP/JNP	–	41 (9.4)	3 (5.7)	–	5 (3.3)	17 (2.9)	1 (0.1)	– (0.1)	– (0.1)	–
INC (2)	3 (1.7)	13 (5.3)	5 (1.6)	1 (0.3)	1 (0.4)	4 (1.5)	–	–	–	–
Regional parties	49 (8.8)	34 (7.7)	73 (13.3)	27 (10.5)	51 (13.3)	118 (20.6)	117 (24.2)	174 (32.0)	179 (33.4)	–
Independents	9 (5.5)	9 (6.4)	5 (8.1)	12 (5.3)	1 (3.9)	9 (6.3)	6 (3.2)	5 (2.6)	5 (4.3)	9 (5.2)
Others	3 (1.0)	1 (0.8)	1 (0.8)	19 (6.1)	4 (2.1)	4 (3.3)	49 (10.9)	10 (3.2)	15 (4.0)	–
Total	**542**	**529**	**542**	**529**	**534**	**543**	**543**	**543**	**543**	**543**

Abbr.: BJS–Bharatiya Jana Sangh; BJP–Bharatiya Janata Party; BKD–Bharatiya Kranti Dal; CPI–Communist Party of India; CPM–Communist Party of India (Marxist); INC (1)–Indian National Congress (–1967); Congress (Requisionist) (1971); Congress (Indira) (1980); INC (2)–Congress (Organization); Congress (Urs) (1980); Congress (Socialist) (1984–); JD–Janata Dal; JP–Janata Party; LD–Lok Dal; SJP–Samajwadi Janata Party.

Note: The 'Socialist' category includes the Kisan Mazdoor Party, the Praja Socialist Party, and the Samyukta Socialist Party.

Source: Data Unit, CSDS (Delhi) and Election Commission India (2009).

schooled in Locke and Mill, had early on opted for the same norms of electoral representation as in the British parliament with which they were familiar and which they much coveted. However, politicians from outside the group of Hindu, upper-caste groups that dominated the Congress party thought otherwise. They feared the tyranny of the majority, which they suspected would be the likely outcome of the introduction of electoral democracy based on majority rule in a society where caste and religion were the main basis of identity. Not surprisingly, political parties which drew their main support from among Muslims and the untouchable groups were keen on proportional representation, which they thought would be a safer basis for the protection of their interests and identities.

In the event, British policy makers were caught in a double bind – between majority voting rules that they were familiar with – and respect for minority rights, which enjoined the adoption of proportional representation. However, even as they resented the adoption of proportional representation as the basis of restricted franchise, they nevertheless participated in the elections under colonial rule, gaining in the process valuable experience of electioneering. The issue was finally settled through two fortuitous events. The Partition of India removed the Muslim League, which had been a main player in the Indian political arena and a trenchant advocate of proportional representation. The second event was the famous Poona Pact of 1936 between Gandhi and Ambedkar – the celebrated leader of India's untouchable communities – who was one of the main advocates of proportional representation. The agreement finally led to the setting aside of a quota of seats for the untouchables, and subsequently for tribal communities, under a rule known as 'reservation of seats'. There were thus no obstacles to the principle of majority voting after Independence and the Representation of People Act of 1947 gave due recognition to this rule as the basis of all elections in India except those to the Presidency and the upper house in the central parliament and State legislatures.

India's electoral campaigns are an excellent demonstration of how political parties develop their strategies to reconcile elections based on single-member constituencies and franchise based on individual preferences with the existence of castes, tribes and other groups based on collective identities. Factions, short-term alliances of individuals and, increasingly, broad-based coalitions are some of the consequences of this complex process of electoral mobilization. Elections and party competition have played a double role by empowering both individuals and groups, leading to the continuous creation of new groups and coalitions. The paradoxical co-existence of modern elections and caste alliances and caste consciousness is yet another outcome of the process of electioneering.

Rather than inhibiting the growth of party competition, social conflict, interwoven with political conflict, deepens political partisanship. However, elections based on first-past-the-post electoral rules, operating in large, single-member constituencies which are usually multi-caste and often multi-religious in character, ultimately lead to political moderation on the part of competing parties. Elections with limited franchise under British rule had facilitated political transition by acting as the institutional context in which power was transferred to elected Indian leaders. This experience had become an integral part of the culture and tradition of the Congress party which, as one can see from Tables 6.2a and 6.2b, was able to transform a minority of votes to a majority of seats in the early elections – thanks to a divided opposition. However, that was no longer possible towards the end of the 1960s in

State legislative elections and from 1977 in parliamentary elections because in the meantime the idea of political coalitions – an efficient method of transforming votes into seats – had become common currency among parties opposed to the Congress party. Its inability to come to terms with this new development cost its electoral prospects dearly, as one can see from the electoral outcomes in the 1990s. However, the Congress party eventually learnt to play the coalitional game and was handsomely rewarded for its efforts in the parliamentary elections of 2004 when Manmohan Singh became Prime Minister, leading the UPA coalition consisting of thirteen parties. After the 2009 election Manmohan Singh as the leader of the UPA was invited by the President to form the government. The UPA coalition which held together through the previous five years has once again shown its political acumen in terms of sharing out cabinet posts among its allies.

After Independence, electoral competition accelerated the pace of social change, leading to a second phase of political change when the generation of the Freedom Movement was replaced by younger leaders, many of whom came from upwardly mobile, newly enfranchised, lower social classes. The entry of the Bharatiya Janata Party, widely seen as the party of business and industry, into government brought these groups closer to power. All sections of Indian society thus have links to the structure of power at one time or another, if not in the national arena, then at least in one or more regional governments. Drawing on survey data provides the basic information about the distribution of support to the main political parties across social formations. One can notice the differential support that political parties receive from social groups in Table 6.3.

The social base of the Congress party cuts across all social groups and cleavages of India, making it India's quintessential catch-all party. Nevertheless, Congress has relatively greater support in the lower social classes and among religious minorities. The social profile of the Hindu nationalist BJP presents a sharp contrast. Initially, it was very much a party of the 'Hindu-Hindi belt' which normally means the north Indian Gangetic plains. Of late, it has spread out of this regional base and formed governments in the West (Gujarat), and the South (Karnataka). Table 6.3 shows that the BJP continues to be a party of the upper social order and Hindu upper castes, but has nevertheless already succeeded in extending its reach to the former untouchables, backward classes, tribals and even to a small section of Muslim voters as well. By the standards of its national support base, the left, consisting of both the communist parties (CPM and CPI), attracts proportionally more support from the lower social classes as well as support from the more educated voters. The rise of India's regional parties is a comparatively recent phenomenon. Like the Congress, in the regional context these parties cut across all social groups and compete with the Congress for the same social base, except for the Other Backward Classes (OBCs), a social group sandwiched between the Hindu upper classes and the former untouchables. The leaders of many of India's regional parties are drawn from the OBCs, which correspond to the service castes (Sudra in terms of the *varna* category). These groups which are not covered by India's programme for positive discrimination tend to extend proportionally more support to the regional parties.

At Independence, the introduction of universal adult franchise empowered under-privileged social groups with a new political resource. The right to vote by secret ballot, exercised at a polling booth conveniently located at a public place where one could vote freely, created an environment which was helpful for political participation.

Table 6.3 Social bases of political parties (1996–2004) (in per cent)

Background characteristics	1996					2004				
	INC+	BJP+	NF	LF	BSP	UPA	NDA	LF	BSP	SP+
All-India average	27.5	24.9	10.1	7.5	3.4	39.5	37.9	6.4	5.0	5.4
Gender										
Female	27.6	23.0	9.4	7.6	3.1	40.4	37.1	7.0	5.0	5.1
Male	27.4	26.8	10.8	7.4	3.6	38.8	38.5	5.9	5.0	5.7
Locality										
Rural	28.1	22.6	10.6	8.8	3.8	39.2	37.3	6.2	5.5	5.8
Urban	25.6	32.2	8.7	3.4	2.0	40.7	40.2	7.1	3.1	3.9
Age										
Up to 25 years	25.7	27.0	10.2	6.9	3.8	38.3	38.3	5.9	5.5	6.0
26–35 years	27.1	25.5	9.9	7.7	3.5	40.5	37.7	6.4	4.3	5.6
36–45 years	28.8	25.1	9.7	8.1	2.9	39.5	38.6	6.0	5.1	5.0
46–55 years	27.0	23.6	10.2	8.4	3.5	37.8	38.2	7.2	4.6	6.3
56 years and above	30.0	21.3	10.9	6.4	2.9	40.6	36.3	6.9	5.8	4.2
Education										
Illiterate	28.6	21.1	12.3	6.6	5.0	40.6	34.3	5.1	7.8	6.5
Up to middle	28.4	23.8	9.2	8.9	2.8	42.9	35.6	8.6	3.5	4.3
College, without degree	25.8	31.3	8.0	7.7	1.6	37.8	38.6	6.9	4.1	5.9
Graduate and above	21.1	36.7	6.1	6.0	0.9	34.9	46.7	5.0	2.8	4.4
Occupation										
Unskilled worker	30.6	17.0	9.9	10.8	5.2	42.6	27.4	8.0	9.8	6.0
Agricultural and allied worker	28.4	17.8	11.5	8.9	5.2	43.4	36.6	6.8	4.8	3.8
Artisan and skilled worker	27.3	24.1	9.3	7.7	3.0	43.9	34.8	6.8	3.9	5.3

Cultivator (less than 5 acres)	26.1	26.2	14.0	6.4	4.9	35.4	37.3	4.0	7.6	8.9
Cultivator (5 acres and more)	29.7	34.6	8.2	1.6	2.5	35.8	44.5	3.0	3.0	8.0
Business	23.3	33.0	10.1	7.6	0.7	37.0	42.7	7.1	3.0	4.5
White collar and professional	26.2	30.8	5.6	8.0	0.3	37.4	42.3	9.0	2.5	2.2
Caste										
Scheduled caste	31.6	14.4	5.6	11.0	12.1	39.7	25.9	8.8	18.4	2.9
Scheduled tribe	39.2	19.0	6.2	6.5	1.0	46.2	34.3	7.0	0.6	0.6
Other backward caste	21.7	23.6	16.3	5.9	2.3	40.7	38.7	4.4	2.8	7.6
Upper caste	28.4	33.6	7.1	7.3	0.4	36.0	44.6	7.3	1.5	5.5
Religion	26.2	28.9	8.4	7.4	3.7	36.8	42.3	5.9	5.3	4.4
Hindu										
Muslim	35.3	3.1	25.3	10.1	1.2	54.8	11.8	6.9	2.9	16.4
Christian	39.9	3.0	2.0	5.6	–	60.5	21.1	8.6	0.9	0.4
Sikh	18.3	14.3	16.7	2.4	5.6	30.4	48.2	6.9	4.9	2.7
Other	26.5	6.0	12.0	2.4	4.8	41.7	21.3	15.9	10.4	2.4
Economic class	29.6	16.0	10.7	11.3	4.4	42.9	32.8	7.5	7.0	4.3
Very poor										
Poor	28.3	23.1	10.5	6.7	4.7	39.6	37.3	5.8	5.7	5.8
Middle	26.1	31.1	10.9	5.6	2.2	37.6	40.9	5.8	2.8	6.9
Upper	22.4	40.1	7.9	3.4	0.4	32.8	49.3	3.7	2.4	5.6

Note: Parties here represent pre-poll alliances.

1996: *INC*+: INC + AIADMK; BJP+: *BJP* + Samata + Shiv Sena + Haryana Vikas Party; *NF*: JD + Samajwadi Party; *LF*: CPI(M) + CPI + RSP + FBL

2004: *UPA*: INC + TRS + RJD (Laloo) + LJNS(Paswan) + NCP + JMM + PDP + MUL + Kerala Congress (M) + JD(S) + RPI + RPI (Athawale) + PRBP + DMK + MDMK + PMK + PDS + Arunachal Congress;

NDA: BJP + TDP + JD(U) + IFDP + Shiv Sena + Biju Janata Dal + Akali Dal + AIADMK + Trinamul Congress + MNF + SDF + NPF; *LF* CPI(M) + CPI + RSP + FBL + Kerala Congress; *SP*+: SP + Lok Dal

Source: Data Unit, CSDS (Delhi) and Election Commission India (2009).

The right to vote in secrecy and without coercion acted as a direct challenge to social dominance posed by newly mobilized lower castes and religious minorities who felt empowered thanks to the value of the vote.

Social mobilization and its political containment, largely though not exclusively within the framework of political institutions, appear to have taken place in India as two independent but ultimately convergent processes. The pace of social change has accelerated through social reform legislation, recruitment of new social elites into the political arena and political mobilization through electoral participation. Their overall impact on the stability of the political system has been moderated by inter-mediary functions and parties at the regional and local levels. Lloyd and Susanne Rudolph have described the process as *vertical*, *differential* and *horizontal* mobilization.[8] Typically, as the marginal social groups discovered the negotiable value of the vote during the early years after Independence, they became avid players in the political arena at the local and regional levels. Established *Jajmani* systems – reciprocal social bonds based on the exchange of services and occupational specialization – broke down to create new groupings. Finally, caste associations, based on shared social and economic interests, emerged as links between the parties and society.[9] This has created useful room to manoeuvre in the hands of national, regional and local elites.[10]

The Congress System

The first two decades following Independence in 1947, roughly corresponding to Nehru's stewardship of Indian politics, were crucial to the transition from a colonial state to a democratic government. The years between 1950 and 1967 were the period of solid dominance of the Congress party. Although the opposition parties did not alternate with the dominant party in controlling the government, their exclusion from the formation of public policy was more formal than real. In fact, they were vital for the functioning of the Congress system. Their importance is amply demonstrated by the extent to which government policy was influenced (even though this influence was exercised indirectly) by opposition parties. This was the basic characteristic of the one-dominant-party system. It was not a one-party system in the sense that opposition parties were not legally barred from competing for power. However, during the first two decades after Independence, they hardly ever constituted a government on their own. These parties, which often had well-developed ideologies of the left and the right, were ranged on either side of the Congress party on the main issues of Indian politics like land reform and foreign policy (e.g. A–E, B–F, etc. in Figure 6.1). Situated in the middle, the Congress was the party of consensus, pinned down to a centrist position because of the pressure exerted on it by the parties of the opposition.

During the first two decades after Independence, the Congress party ruled at the centre as well as in the States. It had achieved this remarkable feat by drawing on its legacy as the party of Gandhi, Nehru and the Freedom Movement. But it also succeeded through patronage, the accommodation of often conflicting interests, and by developing an internal pattern of factions that made the party open to new interests. This unique achievement caused specialists of Indian politics to call this period the 'Congress system': 'a system of patronage [within which] traditional institutions of kin and caste were accommodated and a structure of pressures and compromises was developed'.[11] Ironically and fortuitously, the authoritarian ways of the Congress

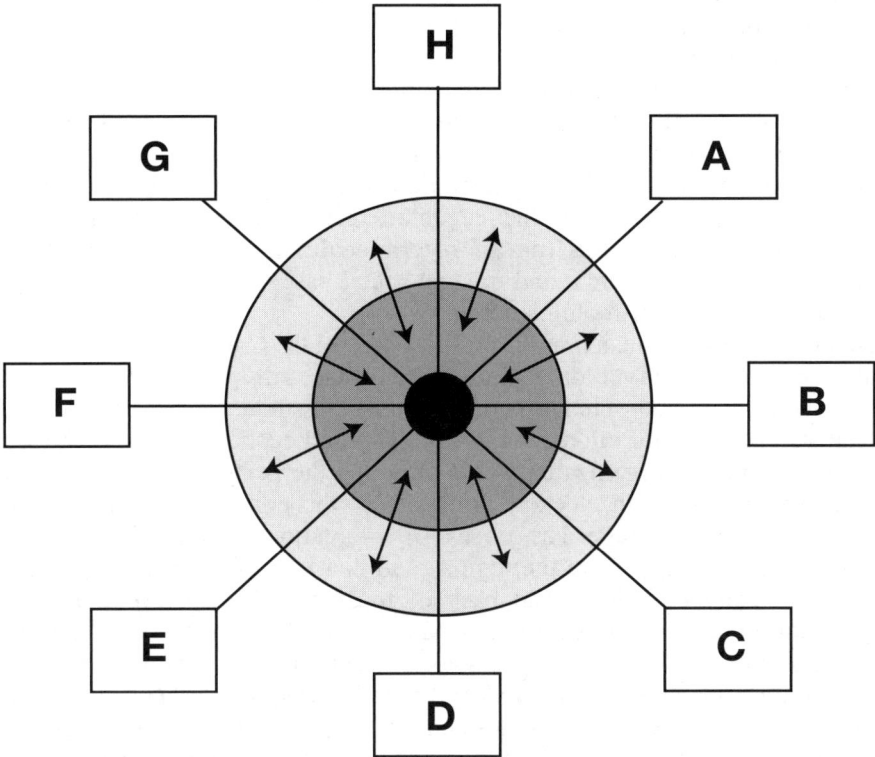

Figure 6.1 The Congress System
Source: Adapted from Morris-Jones (1966) 'Dominance and Dissent' in *Government and Opposition*, p. 219.

party facilitated the growth of a bargaining political culture and the recruitment of new elites – both of which are indispensable for the transition to democracy in developing societies. The system, thus, managed to achieve competition in spite of the fact that the Congress was the ruling party virtually everywhere in India. Individuals who had risen to power in the Congress organization sometimes constituted the chief opposition to the government and provided an alternative route to influence policy. In this process, elections at various levels of the party organization played an important role, as did the selection of party candidates for the General Elections.

The relative strength of political parties in the parliament meant that during those two decades following Independence, non-Congress parties had no possibility of exercising political power directly. Nevertheless, they had influence over policy as well as civil servants. The opposition parties in this system, therefore, were 'parties of pressure', operating outside the Congress but constantly criticizing, pressuring, censuring, and influencing opinion and interests both inside and outside the parliament. This restrained the Congress party from taking too intransigent a position on policy. The Congress contained factions ranging from the ideological left to the right, and encompassing various regional parochial interests as well as more secular and modern pressure groups. Furthermore, the opposition parties constantly exerted a latent threat to the Congress that, if the latter strayed too far away from the centrist position, it would be displaced from power by a coalition of the aggrieved factions. This element of internal competition facilitated the mobilization of new interests and the recruitment of new social groups into power.

The Congress succeeded in establishing its dominance essentially by a process of gradual expansion of its social base, so that new layers of recruitment and support were constantly brought into its fold, allowing it to garner a substantial number of votes in each region. Thanks to the fragmentation of the opposition, this could be transformed into a majority of seats in the legislature. This, in essence, was the basis of Congress dominance – emerging from short-term coalitions leading to a political majority rather than from a coherent and organic social base as a cadre-based party, wielding an ideology of social mobilization.[12]

The post-Independence expansion of the political base of the Congress party beyond its original emplacement in colonial India took place in phases. Soon after Independence, the Congress co-opted landed gentry, businessmen, peasant proprietors, new industrialists and the rural middle class – socially and economically entrenched groups in society – into its organization. This provided the party with a strong and ready structure of support, with electoral 'link men' who controlled various 'vote banks', serviced through patronage. The process of co-optation replaced higher castes that dominated the party machine in the regions and districts. Wherever the process was successful, it expanded the social base of the Congress and continued its ascendancy. In addition, the Congress developed an elaborate network of patronage, which made it possible to bargain political support in return for economic and social benefits with various social strata in rural and urban areas. The remainder of the Muslim community – bereft of its own elites and the Muslim League which migrated to Pakistan – turned largely to the Congress party. Finally, Congress espousal of positive discrimination endeared it to its beneficiaries – drawn particularly from the former untouchables and tribals.

All this enabled the Congress to be a catch-all party and further consolidated its electoral organization on the basis of the traditional social structure as well as the emerging structure of economic opportunities.[13] Both traditionally entrenched social groups and the new aspirants developed a stake in Congress, internalized the symbolism and procedures of the electoral and parliamentary systems, and got actively involved in the overall framework of authority and decision-making represented by the Congress. The resulting distribution of consensus proved highly functional to the development of democratic values and procedure among the large masses of the Indian electorate.

Such a process necessarily confronted the Congress with new issues and new pressures. These have been addressed by neutralizing the more glaring sources of conflict in Indian society by timely and often anticipatory legislation – abolition of *zamindari*, far-reaching protective labour legislation, removal of gross social inequalities through the granting of special rights and advantages to backward groups, and linguistic reorganization of the States. These progressive legislative measures were often supplemented with firm suppression of secessionist and violent activities in various parts of the country. Along with legislation, the Congress attempted both 'penetration' of labour unions and 'accommodation' of minority communities, and at the same time an informal but elaborate system of conciliation and resolution of conflicts and factional disputes through the mediation of prominent individuals at various levels. All these steps jointly led to a considerable strengthening of the party of consensus and a corresponding weakening of the potential sources of cleavage that might have gravely affected the stability of the political system.

The role of the Congress party in acting as a bridge between colonial India and post-colonial democracy is an important factor that explains India's relative success in transition to democracy compared to other successor states that emerged from the British Empire and which have not been similarly successful. Whereas in places such as Pakistan, post-Independence politics eventually led to the growth of anti-democratic social forces, in India it led to a fusion of cultural pluralism and political transaction, thus creating an authentically Indian political process. By making politics the great engine of mobilization and identity, the post-Independence political process brought wide sections of society into the fold of the new political order, dispersed the symbolism of parliamentary government and economic development, and socialized traditional and emerging elites into the norms of democratic politics.

The method of interest articulation and aggregation that took place within the framework of the 'one-dominant-party system' made the State the inevitable inter-mediary between competing interests in disputes involving labour and management (as conceptualized in the Industrial Disputes Act of 1947), landowner and peasant, student and university, and in every conceivable social conflict. This led to the multiplication of the number of unions, all competing for basically the same pool of workers. It did contribute to 'involuted pluralism' – growth in the number of unions and labour militancy accompanied by the diminution of average membership and financial viability.[14] This system of interest articulation, aggregation and conflict management was seriously challenged for the first time during the *Emergency* of 1975–77 (see Box 4.1 above).

Parties of Hindu nationalism and communism

In the early 1990s the Bharatiya Janata Party had confirmed its position as the main challenger to the Indian National Congress in northern India. Its presence outside the Hindi heartland of North India, where neither Hindi nor the religious dispute centred on a temple for Rama in Ayodhya, is a phenomenon of great significance. The steady evolution of the party in the national parliament is equally impressive. From the low point of two seats in the Lok Sabha in 1984, the party went up to 85 in 1989 and 182 seats in the parliamentary elections held in 1999. However, in 2004 the number of seats had come down to 138, and sank even further to 116 in 2009.[15] The downward trend has been caused by a variety of factors, such as the lack of a clear focus in its programme, organizational problems and desertion by some important coalition partners.

In the course of its rapid rise to power, the party had drawn on the desire of many Hindus to see a more prominent role for Hindu culture within the institutions of the secular state and to deny special treatment for minorities, such as a special status for the Muslim majority State of Jammu and Kashmir. The BJP came to power riding the crest of Hindu nationalism and promising to build a temple for Rama in the city of Ayodhya on the same spot where the Babri mosque stood. It failed to find a solution to the conflict between Hindus and Muslims for exclusive ownership of the site. When the mosque was demolished by a mob of Hindu zealots the State govern-ment of Uttar Pradesh, led by the BJP, accepted responsibility for its failure to uphold law and order and resigned. Subsequently, the imperatives of India's coalition politics have caused the party to moderate its stand on cultural and confessional issues. During the short-lived tenure of Vajpayee as Prime Minister (1998–99), the party spoke more of good governance and less of Hindu nationalism. Back in office in 1999 and with a clear majority for the National Democratic Alliance (NDA), of which the BJP was the largest partner in the Lok Sabha, Prime Minister Vajpayee announced the commitment of his government to follow the same moderate policies that he had launched during his previous tenure.

The General Election of 2004 to the Lok Sabha took place about six months before the end of the five-year term of the National Democratic Alliance government, led by the BJP. When the government called for early elections, nearly all opinion polls predicted a comfortable NDA victory on the strength of its record in office as well as the personal popularity of Prime Minister Vajpayee. In the event, the victory by the Congress-led United Progressive Alliance took everyone by surprise. In retrospect, the NDA's campaign slogan 'India Shining', which celebrated its achievements with regard to the unprecedented rate of growth of the economy, seemed to backfire. Those who had not gained from the liberalization of the economy, those who stood to lose from the removal of subsidies and the population in rural areas of India, as well as sections of religious minorities, appeared to vote against the coalition. The Congress party, which, for the first time, was able to make pre-election alliances on a 'secular' platform with regional parties opposed to the Hindu nationalist BJP, was able to use the votes cast in favour of the UPA efficiently. In the process, it could increase the number of its own seats in the Lok Sabha. The Congress party has reinforced this strategy – of appealing to the Indian voter from a national, secular and pro-poor platform while pressing ahead with the agenda of liberalization, nuclearization and diplomatic engagement with Pakistan. This yielded a rich harvest in the form of 206 seats in the Lok Sabha parliamentary election in 2009.[16]

Founded in 1927, the Communist Party of India is one of the oldest in the world. It was proscribed for most of the time under British rule except towards the end when the party came out openly in support of the war effort once the Soviet Union came under attack from Nazi Germany. The party went through factional struggle and several splits on ideological grounds following India's Independence. The Telengana uprising of 1946–47, modelled on the Chinese revolution, was rapidly put down by the Indian army. This discredited the leftist faction. Under the leadership of the right faction, the party came to terms with Indian democracy, took part in the first General Election, emerging as the second largest party after the Congress, though far behind it in terms of its actual number of seats. More success was to follow. The Communist Party won the regional election in the southern State of Kerala in 1957, a first victory for communism in a democratic election. Coinciding with the resolution of the Communist Party of the Soviet Union to support 'peaceful transition to democracy', the party looked poised for a bigger role in Indian politics. That was, however, not to be. The dismissal of the communist government of Kerala after two years in office by the Congress party in the centre under Article 356 of the constitution which provides for direct central rule when the deterioration of law and order threatens lawful governance showed the limits of 'bourgeois democracy', exactly as the left faction of the party had argued. More bad news was to follow. Differences with China on the boundary led to a border conflict in 1962 which caused the left faction to come out in favour of China, leading to their incarceration. The split was formalized in 1964 with the founding of the Communist Party of India (Marxist) (CPM) which followed a radical, pro-Chinese line compared to the Communist Party of India (CPI) which stuck with a more moderate, pro-Congress and pro-Soviet line. The CPM itself split five years later when its own left wing emerged as a new party – the Communist Party of India (Marxist-Leninist) – and initiated a peasant uprising in the Naxalbari district in the foothills of the Himalayas. The peasant uprising was put down by the security forces amid much bloodshed.

Two main trends have emerged since those turbulent times. The CPM, which came to power in West Bengal in the late 1970s, has stayed on, making it one of the longest serving, democratically elected communist governments anywhere in the world. At the centre, the 60 communist members of the parliament, whose support from 'outside' was crucial to the continuation of the UPA government until they withdrew their support on the issue of the nuclear framework agreement between India and the United States, in 2008 constituted an important source of influence on public policy. However, the urge for revolution, powerfully articulated by the 'Naxalites' – this is how the Indian Maoists named themselves – lives on, under different names in different parts of India. Their violent activities continue to be a source of anxiety for the Indian government, particularly in view of the success of Maoists in neighbouring Nepal.

Partisan conflict within the structure of overall systemic consensus

After Independence, when party competition with universal adult franchise began, the level of participation was relatively modest and parties approached voters, many voting for the first time in their lives, through village notables. Over the course of the past six decades, political competition has spread to every nook and cranny of the political system. Voters have become much more conscious of their rights and capable of pursuing their interests through a variety of means of participation which includes protest movements. However, politics has remained confined largely within the system. Anti-system parties and political violence have remained on the fringes of the political system. Political parties, as one can see in Table 6.3, have learnt to combine solid support in a specific social base with variable support from other social groups, depending on the nature of the coalitional arrangement they strike with other political parties. This has led to the formation of large, stable coalitions of parties within broad ideological labels at the national level while party competition at the local and regional levels has been more volatile.

The most important consequence of this configuration of party competition has been to induce a sense of moderation in Indian politics.[17] The fiery rhetoric and partisan outbursts among political parties that one often witnesses in televised debates in the Indian parliament or on the campaign trail might cause those unfamiliar with the inner dynamics of party competition in India to ask how the country manages to combine party competition and parliamentary democracy. In older democracies, particularly in the European continent, the coexistence of party competition and democratic governance has been made possible thanks to a large measure of consensus on the usefulness of parties in the first place, and an overall consensus on policy, within which parties chart out their specific positions.

In India, one can find plentiful evidence of the ability of political leaders to combine divisive rhetoric with united and purposeful functioning of governance. The UPA coalition led by Manmohan Singh was able to command a majority with the support of the Left Front for the first four years in office. During this period, there have been policy differences between the government and the Left Front on the pace of liberalization of the economy, and most of all on the nuclear issue. Finally, when the Left Front withdrew its support on the nuclear issue in 2008, the government was able to win support from the Samajwadi Party and survive the vote of confidence in an atmosphere marked by high drama, accusations of wrong-doing and breach of parliamentary norms by some legislators who voted against their party line. However, in a span of barely a few weeks, parliamentary government was back on the rails. The opposition NDA coalition held together during the tenure of the parliament that was elected in 2004 and managed to function as an effective and cohesive opposition, though there have been policy differences among the members of this body. Even in the regional arenas of India where the levels of rectitude are not always the same as at the national level, partisan politics and parliamentary governance have functioned together reasonably well. The absence of this deeper consensus has allowed party competition in countries like Bangladesh to get out of hand, paralyse governance altogether, and has facilitated the intervention of the army as a last resort.

Three factors – an awareness of the usefulness of political parties, overlapping social bases, and overall value consensus among party supporters – explain why this unusual combination of partisanship, governmental coherence, and policy continuity despite governmental change has been possible. The public opinion data on the usefulness of parties in Table 6.4 show that the overall support for parties, seen as 'a good deal' or 'somewhat useful', has gone up from 32.5 per cent in the 1971 survey to 42.5 per cent in the 1996 findings, though the level of disappointment ('not much useful') did also go up marginally as well. It is important, however, to note that the approval score for the usefulness of parties is higher than average among young voters, Muslims, upper castes, men and the highly educated (see Table 6.4). In other words, the 'opinion leaders' and voters from minority communities are supportive of parties as a legitimate institution for the articulation and aggregation of interests.

The second explanation for the coexistence of partisanship and overall consensus and political moderation comes from the fact that the social bases of Indian parties are largely overlapping (see Table 6.3). Though there is a tendency for the left parties to garner more support from lower social classes, and for the Bahujan Samaj Party to get higher than average support among the former untouchables and for the Akali Dal party to get substantial support among Sikhs, on the whole, one does not see the kind of binding contract between social cleavages and parties found in the case of European democracies. The Congress has remained India's quintessential catch-all party,[18] but the Congress example is imitated by others. Even the Bahujan Samaj Party has actively cultivated support among Brahmins in order to build a coalition between the upper and lower strata against the middle-status groups (see Figure 3.3 above).

This kind of loose relation between cleavages and parties has been made possible by two factors. In the first place, unlike in Europe, party politics did not emerge in response to the Industrial Revolution, where workers and owners rallied behind radical and conservative parties. In India, as we have already seen, parties emerged as elite initiatives to get electoral power, in response to the introduction of restricted franchise. When Islam emerged as a major political cleavage during the last decades of colonial rule, and the Muslim League used its identification with Islam and the

Table 6.4 Usefulness of political parties (in per cent)

Response	1971	1996
Good deal	10.9	9.5
Somewhat	21.6	33.0
Not much	25.7	27.2
Don't know	41.7	30.3

Usefulness of political parties – *Somewhat and Good deal (%)*	*1996*
Illiterate	27.7
Female	32.5
Scheduled tribe	33.0
Very poor	35.1
56 years or above	37.1
Rural	41.1
Scheduled caste	41.4
OBC	41.4
Hindu	41.9
All India Average	**42.5**
25 years or less	44.8
Muslim	45.4
Upper caste	46.9
Urban	47.0
Upper class	47.8
Male	52.2
College and above	65.6

Source: National Election Studies, CSDS (Delhi) 1996.

Muslims of the Sub-continent to position itself against the Congress party, the attempt at the communal polarization of Indian society was resisted by the Congress party under the leadership of Mahatma Gandhi. Eventually, the Partition of India, leading to the departure of the League to Pakistan, significantly lowered the salience of Islam as a national cleavage in post-Independence politics. The attempt by the movement of Hindu nationalism to revive it in recent times (see Table 6.5 below) has been only marginally successful. As such, Indian parties, despite their rhetoric that sometimes mimics western, programmatic parties, tend to be much more pragmatic and accommodating than one would expect from their rhetoric and their published manifestos. This is facilitated by the fact that the social cleavages in India tend to be cross-cutting rather than cumulative.

Finally, at the level of the supporters of the parties, when interrogated on their position on some of the salient issues of Indian politics, one finds considerable overlap in issue positions. This relative convergence of the followers at the level of issues (see Tables 6.5–6.7) provides the leaders of the parties with greater room to manoeuvre with regard to pragmatic compromises. Despite their formal ideological orientations, in practice all parties tend to converge towards the centrist position.

When cross-tabulated against partisan preferences ('Which party did you vote for?'), answers to the question 'Was the destruction of the Babri Mosque justified?'

reveal an interesting pattern. For the population as a whole, at 38 per cent, people saying that it was not justified form the largest category (see Table 6.5). The more educated and urban voters, and, not surprisingly, Muslims, tend to be opposed to the demolition. A large part of the Indian electorate (29 per cent) in 1996 had not even heard about the demolition which had taken place four years earlier. Only a little over one-fifth of the Indian electorate deemed the demolition to be justified. Quite interestingly, over a quarter of BJP partisans thought the demolition unjustified compared to 43 per cent among the partisans of the Congress party who thought so. Whereas the national leaders of Hindu nationalism had either supported the demolition or were equivocal about it, 25.7 per cent of the supporters of the BJP had opposed it and only two-fifths of its supporters found the demolition justified.

With regard to a negotiated resolution to the Kashmir conflict rather than a military 'solution', the number of people who prefer negotiation to force has gone up from 33.4 per cent in 1996 to 59 per cent in 2004 (see Table 6.6). Their numbers are even higher among BJP sympathizers in 2004 than in 1996. The symmetry of opinion in this case between the Congress and the BJP points towards the growth of a

Table 6.5 Partisan response to the demolition of Babri mosque (in per cent)

Response	INC	BJP+	NF	LF	BSP	Total
Unjustified	42.9	25.7	48.2	54.9	26.7	38.1
Don't know	8.0	11.4	7.6	9.2	19.9	10.2
Justified	16.5	40.7	24.1	9.1	27.3	22.7
Not heard about demolition	32.6	22.2	20.0	26.9	26.1	29.0

Source: National Election Studies, CSDS (Delhi) 1996.

Table 6.6 Partisan opinion on resolution of Kashmir problem (in per cent)

	1996						2004					
	INC	BJP+	NF	LF	BSP	Total	UPA	NDA	LF	BSP	SP	Total
Negotiation	33.8	34.7	32.6	32.9	25.5	33.4	58.8	61.7	63.0	46.4	57.8	59.0
Can't say	32.8	26.4	30.7	28.7	28.9	32.0	21.0	18.2	18.1	33.9	28.2	21.4
Should be suppressed	9.7	17.5	11.0	4.9	14.3	11.1	8.2	10.1	9.4	8.3	7.5	8.8
Not heard of Kashmir	21.2	19.8	23.3	32.2	30.7	21.6	12.1	10.0	9.5	11.3	6.5	10.8

Source: National Election Studies, CSDS (Delhi) 1996, 2004.

Table 6.7 India should develop friendly relations with Pakistan (in per cent)

Response	INC	BJP+	NF	LF	BSP	Total
Disagree	17.1	23.4	11.6	17.4	12.4	17.6
Don't know/No opinion	37.0	34.5	36.6	37.3	37.6	37.9
Agree	45.8	42.1	51.8	45.3	50.0	44.5

Source: National Election Studies, CSDS (Delhi) 1996.

Table 6.8 Need for separate civil code for every community by party support (in per cent)

	1996						2004					
	INC	BJP+	NF	LF	BSP	Total	UPA	NDA	LF	BSP	SP	Total
Disagree	29.9	36.5	29.4	22.1	30.4	30.4	27.4	29.7	22.4	20.2	22.3	27.1
Don't know	23.8	22.9	28.5	18.2	24.8	25.1	19.0	17.4	15.0	26.3	23.5	19.2
Agree	46.3	40.6	42.2	59.6	44.7	44.4	53.6	52.9	62.6	53.5	54.2	53.8

Source: National Election Studies, CSDS (Delhi) 1996, 2004.

bi-partisan consensus. Once again, the support for a negotiated solution is much higher among those with college education, the middle and upper classes and among Muslims.

India's relations with Pakistan – long considered a divisive issue nationally and particularly between the BJP and the Congress (see Table 6.7) – actually turns out not to be so. Whereas only about 18 per cent are against India's attempts to develop friendly relations, the bulk of the population is either for improved, peaceful relations or abstains from pronouncing an opinion. Quite contrary to what one might expect, the sympathizers of the BJP and the Congress are actually at the same level with regard to Indian attempts at being friendly to Pakistan.

Finally, on the issue of a separate personal law for each community (see Table 6.8), support for a multi-cultural solution – which permits the existence of different legal regimes for different communities within the structure of the same national state – has gone up nationally from 44 per cent in 1996 to 54 per cent in 2004. Whereas the difference between the support for this position among sympathizers of the BJP and the Congress had a difference of 6 per cent in 1996, by 2004 it had levelled off almost to the same proportion, which, interestingly, is the majority view among the respective groups.

Interest articulation: demand groups in India

Within the framework of an overall consensus about the basic values of the political system such as democracy, the rule of law, property rights and the right to representation, interest articulation is taken up by a number of institutions and forms of political action that combine modern and traditional features. In addition to a scrutiny of modes of interest articulation in India, the section also raises some questions about the impact of the liberalization and globalization of India's economy on the trade union movement. How has liberalization affected the structure and process of interest articulation in India? How do potential losers cope with the challenge of the 'new' political economy? These issues are salient for the smooth functioning of the democratic political system.

'Demand groups'[19] are one of the distinctive features of interest articulation in India. These have emerged as a response to the structural limitations of labour unions. Demand groups rely on ad hoc rather than bureaucratic organization and use mass mobilization more than expert knowledge and technical bargaining as methods. One finds shades of both movement politics and the politics of organized interests in their midst. Demand groups function through a two-track strategy which combines rational protest and institutional participation. Interest articulation and aggregation function best when wage demands follow the capacity of the enterprise to show a profit rather than preceding it.

Though the onerous task of the articulation and aggregation of interests is primarily the function of political parties, most societies provide for a number of other organizations – some large, with bureaucratic structures, and others ad hoc, with merely grass-roots organizations – to play a supplementary role. The contrast between the evolution of organized labour and labour legislation in the West and in India is important to the understanding of the Indian situation. How did the western world evolve from the grim life situation of industrial workers to peaceful and organized interest articulation by unions? In the West, the evolution of the modern state, democratic empowerment and the growth of institutionalized forms of interest articulation and aggregation have kept pace with the growth in surplus value. In India, recognition of workers' rights, first under British rule and subsequently by the post-colonial state after Independence, came before large-scale industrialization. Consequently, major trade unions such as the INTUC, CITU, AITUC and HMS became 'labour aristocracies', whereas the general capacity of interest articulation by labour remained weak.

Unlike in Europe,[20] in India right from the beginning capital became dependent on the state, through the Congress system and state domination of the economy. Consequently, the state took the initiative in the matter of labour welfare. These points can be illustrated with reference to the attempts to unionize students, workers and peasants. Student and labour organizations in India are both plentiful and active: but their evolution has taken a different direction compared to the form they have taken in liberal democracies. More than four million students are registered in some 7,000 colleges and universities in India. Most students are not politically involved, but the activists provide a reservoir from which political parties and protest movements can draw leadership and support. Campuses have long been centres of political opposition and student government elections are usually fought on party lines. The RSS student movement, the Akhil Bharatiya Vidyarthi Parishad, is now the largest student organization in India.

Labour unions in India, as in most developing countries, have been highly political. Reflecting the central role of the state in labour relations, union demands for better working conditions and higher wages are directed less often towards management than towards the government. Government tribunals for binding arbitration as well as wide ministerial discretion have made the government the critical focus of pressure. With both labour and management dependent on government intervention, collective bargaining is virtually non-existent, and the government has come to bear the brunt of all dissatisfaction. Government labour policy is guided, for the most part, by an effort to reduce the number of strikes and lockouts, and it handles labour disputes with a combination of the carrot and the stick.

No more than 10 million workers – roughly 3 per cent of India's labour force – are unionized at only a nominal level. However, because they are organized and are situated in strategic sectors of the economy, they command considerable power, if not influence – at least to disrupt. There are some 25,000 unions in India, most tied directly to political parties and affiliated with one of the major trade union federations. The Indian National Trade Union Congress (INTUC), the largest federation, is associated with the Congress (I) party and has often served as an arm of government labour policy. The fastest growing union has been the Bharatiya Mazdoor Sangh (BMS), with ties to the Bharatiya Janata Party. Much of its growth has come at the expense of the two Communist Party federations – the All-India Trade Union Congress (AITUC) associated with the Communist Party of India, and the Centre of Indian Trade Unions (CITU) associated with the Communist Party (Marxist). One of the more militant unions is the faction-ridden socialist Hind Mazdoor Sabha.

Trade unions and employers' associations

Under India's labour law, any seven workers can formally set up a trade union. State-appointed labour inspectors provide counsel and inquire into the conditions of work. Trade unionism in India today is built on the foundations of the continuous existence of some leading trade unions and employers' organizations. For example, the All-India Trade Union Congress (AITUC), established in 1920 and thus the oldest Indian trade union, is one of the largest central trade union organizations in the country. It was founded by the Indian National Congress as a mainstream labour organization during the Independence movement, in which it played a significant role. Since Independence, the AITUC has been affiliated with the Communist Party of India. A second example is the All India Railwaymen's Federation (AIRF), founded in 1925, which is today one of the largest labour organizations in India with a membership of more than a million railway workers.

Similar to that of workers, several well-organized interest representations of employers can be found in India. One famous example is the Confederation of Indian Industries (CII), founded in 1895 as the Engineering and Iron Trades Association. CII is now the most visible business association in India with over 4,700 member companies, 11 overseas offices and institutional partnerships with 216 organizations in 94 countries. Similarly, the Federation of Indian Chambers of Commerce and Industry (FICCI), founded in 1927 under the guidance of Mahatma Gandhi, together with the Associated Chambers of Commerce and Industry (ASSOCHAM), functions as the apex chamber for trade associations and industry in India. Both FICCI and ASSOCHAM are key actors in policy formulation and the socio-economic trans-formation of the country. They also have a significant role in the making of government economic policy.

Unlike in liberal democracies where interest groups concentrate basically on the conditions of work, which they seek to improve through collective bargaining, India's unions are closely affiliated to political parties and, thus, become specially active at the time of elections. The culture of effective collective bargaining is not deeply entrenched. Rather than thinking of organized strikes as the ultimate weapon, India's unions often resort to illegal stoppage of work (referred to as 'wild cat strikes'), and rely on state intervention on their behalf to win better conditions. Additionally they are highly fragmented, with an increasing number of unions competing for a stagnant pool of workers. Also, intra-union feuds reduce the effectiveness of the union movement as a whole.[21]

Trade unionism in India has gone through four broad phases since Independence, corresponding with structural changes in the economy. The first phase, 1950 to the mid-1960s, saw the government pursuing a planned economy and an import substitution strategy which corresponded to the rise of public-sector unionism. The second phase lasted until the late 1970s, and was a period of relative economic stagnation and political instability. It witnessed rising labour discontent, inter-union rivalries and industrial conflict. Organizations like the Hind Mazdoor Sabha emerged as leading voices in the labour movement. The third phase, 1980 to 1991, was characterized by uneven economic development during which decentralized bargaining and independent trade unionism both gained ground. Inter-State and inter-regional variations in the labour-management regimes grew wider with unions strengthened in the more prosperous economic sectors. The fourth phase started with the economic reforms of the early 1990s, and is characterized by demands for greater labour market flexibility, especially in employment and industrial dispute management. Reforms are considered vital to stimulate India's manufacturing sector but are resisted particularly by the left parties which, since 2004, have lent outside support to the ruling UPA coalition.

In addition to the modern forms of interest articulation, there are also indigenous variations of this as well. The tradition of unconventional direct action has spawned many variants.[22] Demand groups supplement their political repertoire with several modes of direct action. These include *satyagraha*, *hartal*, *bandh*, *dharna gherao*, *jail bharo*, and *rasta roko*. *Morcha*, a military term meaning battle formation, has been taken by the Akalis to describe their protest movements in Punjab and by V.P. Singh in his People's Movement, Jan Morcha. These are supplemented by social movements. For example, the *Chipko* movement in northern India fought for the protection of the Himalayan forests. Based on Gandhian principles, it used non-violent protest and attracted attention with its tactic of village women hugging trees to prevent them from being chopped down. Their first protest action took place in April 1973 and the movement had its major success in 1980 when it secured a 15-year ban on 'green felling' in the Himalayan forests of Uttar Pradesh.

There are also more specialized pressure groups, such as the Bharatiya Kisan Union (BKU), also known as the Indian Peasant Union, which has been active in organizing *kisans*. The *kisans* are divided between two broad sections, namely, the small self-sufficient landowners who cultivate land with family labour and do not employ outside labour, and those whose holdings are usually above the subsistence level.

Local politics: democracy at the grass-roots level

The Emergency of 1975–77 brought together a wide range of political forces for the defence of civil liberties. These groups, consisting of lawyers, journalists, academics, social workers and political activists, became an important pressure group starting in the 1980s. Their presence and intervention have publicized the struggles of vulnerable social groups and exposed acts of administrative injustice and, in more extreme cases, state repression. Thus, the greatly restricted scope for interest articulation and aggregation caused by the 1975–77 events to some extent produced non-party political movements, local protest movements and civil rights activists.

This has led to the emergence of a new social class of mediators in the political process, generally called the 'social activists', who are often upper and middle class in their social origin but who identify themselves with the lower orders of society, a whole variety of social strata ranging from the untouchable castes to the destitute among the tribes and ethnic minorities. There is a new genre of 'movements' in

India that, while having an economic content, are in practice multidimensional and cover a large terrain. This includes the high-profile environmental movements, the women's movement, the civil liberties movement, movements for regional self-determination and autonomy, and the peasants' movement. Other groups focus on peace, disarmament and denuclearization. Movement politics has appeared as the 'power of the powerless'. The coalition that brought the Janata Party to power in 1977 in many ways benefited from the widespread desire for democratic participation and access to the centre of decision making. The trend continues.

At a larger, systemic level, the rise of this new consciousness of civil rights provides a balancing factor to the potential for the growth of authoritarian tendencies and the advocacy of a muscular developmental state, committed to rational management and modern technology. These grass-roots movements also signify a new understanding of the democratic process, which has moved from an almost exclusive preoccupation with parties and elections to new issues that the political system has not addressed. The period of erosion of parliamentary, party and federal institutions and the decline of the authority of the state has been accompanied by the rise of new actors on the scene, new forms of political expression, and new definitions of the content of politics.[23] The growth of local protest movements as a method for articulating interests and demanding administrative redress was facilitated by the wide acceptance of lobbying and contacting decision-makers, and other techniques of direct action such as forcing public officials to negotiate by *dharna* or by physically surrounding them *(gherao)*.[24]

A survey of over 200 local elites in two Indian States revealed wide acceptance of collective protest as a means to get state officials to listen to local demands and meet local needs. The perception of this 'room for manoeuvre in the middle' gives a new focus and depth to democratic institutions because, simultaneously, it acts as a sanction against official complacency and inadequacy in implementation while undercutting the appeal of violent revolution as a more effective solution to social and economic problems.[25] The growth of political consciousness and the mobilization of interests have created a situation in India where the level of legitimacy and sense of individual efficacy exceed the trust that people have in politicians or in their ability to deliver the goods. This creates the potential for instability, because landslide victories can fizzle away at the first sign of failure on the part of the leader. This was the case for Rajiv Gandhi, who won the biggest victory the Congress party ever had at the polls in 1984 and then rapidly lost popular support when rumours about bribery by the Swedish company Bofors began to circulate. In a situation like this, politicians may attempt to escape popular wrath by recourse to abstract rhetoric and populist promises rather than concrete policy that might involve some sacrifice. The obverse side of chaotic populism is a dose of authoritarianism which offers to set things right and carries a disgruntled citizenry along with it. India has already had a taste of such methods during Indira Gandhi's Emergency rule.

The above discussion helps pin down the causes of the weakness of organized labour in India. In the first place, with regard to the interests of labour, just as in the case of students, peasants, women, tribals or any specific group, relative to their western counterparts, most of the time it is politics – more than the interests of the group in question – which is in command. The unions are penetrated by political parties because ambitious politicians often use positions in student unions, peasant movements or labour unions as stepping stones in their search for a political career.

The Pay Commission model sets the state up as the honest broker in wage conflicts between owners and workers. Rudolph and Rudolph explain how the Pay Commission model, set up in order to help labour, has in practice stymied the growth of labour unions.[26]

Indian liberal labour legislation is yet another factor that explains the weakness of India's labour unions. Under India's liberal labour laws, any seven workers can form a union. This creates competitive militancy, fragmentation and, finally, weakening of the labour union movement as a whole. There are no strike funds that could sustain the threat of the general strike, which has been the main weapon in the armoury of unionized labour in western democracies. Besides, the oversupply of labour makes it harder for those in employment to look for other alternatives because the owners can afford to replace striking workers without much difficulty. In addition, illiteracy and ignorance of complicated labour laws on the part of workers make it difficult for them to defend their interests through proper channels.

Rudolph and Rudolph have described this phenomenon as 'involuted pluralism'.

> This refers to the way in which the state dominates interest group pluralism in India. Involution refers to a continuing process and resultant structural condition, the excessive multiplication of less effectual units. . . . Such replication not only weakens each successive unit but also weakens all units collectively and thus the activity as a whole. In this sense, more becomes less. Involution is thus a regressive, debilitating process that results in decreasing effectiveness or entropy, the reverse of evolution.
>
> Rudolph and Rudolph (1987), p. 257.

The landscape of interest articulation and aggregation, according to them, comes across as a case of *'state-dominated pluralism'* – 'An Indian variant of pluralism which is dominated by the state. It leads to the excessive multiplication and fragmentation of interests.'[27]

The overall impression of the process of interest articulation and aggregation that one gets from India is thus that of a stalemated class conflict (Figure 6.2) where demand groups are able to express their interests without political hindrance. However, these interests do not cumulate to an unsustainable level. The limited capacity of modern institutions responsible for processing them and the limited financial ability of the state to satisfy them are thus not endangered by the freedom that demand groups and parties have to actively engage in the political process.

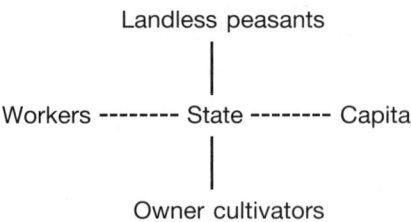

Figure 6.2 Stalemated class conflict
Source: Drawn by author.

This has two consequences. First, the trade union movement as a whole gets paralysed. Second, by drawing new talent into the political system, the demand groups bring greater depth and resilience to the political process. The process does break down from time to time, as unrepresented and unorganized labour has resorted to sporadic strikes and violence. However, to date, these threats have remained localized and the federal States have been able to cope with this challenge, often with the help of paramilitary forces sent by the central government.

Interest articulation and the 'new' political economy

The second-generation liberalization – so called because it involves the liberalization of specific sectors of the economy following the basic change in the economic regime – has entailed the liberalization of the labour market, introducing more flexible practices such as easier methods to 'hire and fire', bonuses linked to productivity, and flexible working conditions. Jenkins explains how India has managed to achieve some spectacular results in this area through the combination of 'big bang liberalization' and a 'special kind of gradualism'.[28] One specific measure he mentions is the Voluntary Retirement Scheme (VRS). Further, following the Chinese example, the setting up of Export Processing Zones (EPZs) and Special Economic Zones (SEZs), and classifying them as public utilities which require their employees to give 45 days' notice before going on strike, has become yet another practice to restrain militant tendencies on the part of workers. Some of these moves towards labour market reform have already got legislative recognition in the amendments of the Industrial Disputes Act (IDA). Finally, the federalization of labour market reforms through competition among State governments to attract investment, both from national sources as well as multinational corporations (MNCs), has pitted India's federal States against one another and in consequence has fragmented national labour unions.

The need to cut down on subsidies has now acquired a general if grudging acceptance. Jenkins gives a number of other indicators. Thus, employers have increasingly had recourse to 'de facto closures' and have obtained permission from the government under section 25 of the Industrial Disputes Act; labour disputes have also often been used as a pretext for effecting an 'indefinite lockout'. The ratio of strikes to lockouts (in terms of total man days lost as a result of industrial disputes) has fallen from 54:46 to 19:81 over the 20 years from 1978 to 1997. The statutory wages required by minimum wage laws have started falling behind real wages; the powers of labour inspectors are being effectively controlled; and finally, Voluntary Retirement Schemes are now being promoted in a big way by public as well as private sector employers.

Conclusion

The latest development in labour legislation and practice brings the focus back to the dilemma between growth and welfare that affects all post-colonial states that seek a democratic path towards modernity. There is enough evidence to show that Indian labour (and other interest and pressure groups) has learnt to adapt to changing conditions. Based upon the multiple roles of the post-colonial state, and a dynamic, neo-institutional model of governance (see Figure 1.1 above), one can argue that on the whole those in the organized sector have not done too badly. The success in the articulation of interest by workers in the unorganized sector is context dependent. The Rudolphs provide a macro-structure to these concepts by referring to the multiple role of the state in India. In their characterization of the state in India, Rudolph and Rudolph (1987: 400–1) show how it has successfully incorporated some apparently contradictory values in order to create a space where different social groups can periodically negotiate the priorities for the politics of the day.[29] The implications of these developments for economic growth will be taken up in the next chapter.

Notes

1 Naipaul (1990), p. 517.
2 Morris-Jones (1966), p. 455.
3 Ibid.
4 Practically every political office in India is open to election. Most of them are direct elections, but some, like the election of the President and members of the Rajya Sabha – the upper house of parliament – are indirect. The electoral principle has struck deep roots in India, to the extent that elections have become the most popular form of selection of members to district and local councils and even a myriad of school committees, youth groups and cooperatives. See Enskat *et al.* (2001).
5 The campaign pronouncements of Varun Gandhi, an estranged scion of the Gandhi family and the BJP parliamentary candidate from Uttar Pradesh for the 2009 Lok Sabha election, were considered anti-Muslim and landed him in jail.
6 Following allegations of irregularity in the North Indian constituency of Amethi where Prime Minister Rajiv Gandhi was a candidate, the Election Commission ordered new voting to take place. Thus, one can notice both the political will and institutional capacity at the systemic level to minimize cases of electoral tampering.
7 See Mitra *et al.* (2004).
8 Vertical mobilization refers to political linkages that draw on and reinforce social and economic dominance. Horizontal mobilization takes place when people situated at the same social and economic level get together to use their combined political strength to improve their situation. Differential mobilization refers to coalitions that cut across social strata. Rudolph and Rudolph (1967).
9 For the formulation of these ideas in terms of an analytical framework on elections and social change in India based on a model of electoral norms and organizational structures corresponding to them, see Mitra (1994a), pp. 49–72.
10 For an application of this concept as a framework for the discussion of political participation in India, see Mitra (1991).
11 Kothari (1988), pp. 164–65.
12 See Weiner (1968).
13 See Mitra (1994b), pp. 153–77.
14 Rudolph and Rudolph (1987), p. 255.
15 Khare, 'India gives Congress and UPA a clear mandate', in *The Hindu*, 17 May 2009.
16 Ibid.
17 Rudolph and Rudolph (1987, p. 58) describe this as the 'centrist multi-party system' of Indian politics.
18 Morris-Jones (1966), p. 455.
19 The Rudolphs use the generic term of 'demand groups' to connote interest groups, pressure groups, social movements and protest movements which undertake this function. Such groups are a regular presence on the political landscape of urban as well as rural India. Rudolph and Rudolph (1987), p. 247.
20 In Western Europe, as the contradiction between labour and capital got sharper, means of articulation on both sides grew through representative institutions, critical social knowledge, reform and legislation. Workers' wages kept pace with the growth of 'surplus value', unionization and the culture of collective bargaining.

21 Rudolph and Rudolph refer to the two phenomena respectively as 'state dominated pluralism' and 'involuted pluralism'. See Rudolph and Rudolph (1987), pp. 259–89.
22 See Mitra *et al.* (2006).
23 For a discussion on new social movements in India, see Omvedt (1993).
24 Mitra (1992).
25 See Mitra (1991).
26   State policy for the trade union sector has been fashioned not in response to the conditional of an industrial work force but by analogy to the regulation of the state bureaucracy. . . . In Western Europe state efforts to determine such policy are constrained by competition and bargaining among political parties, labour and industry federations and expert knowledge. Indian policy, by contrast, has remained largely a bureaucratic matter, relatively insulated from trade union and political pressures and relatively out of touch with the world of social research.

                          Rudolph and Rudolph (1987), p. 286.

27 Ibid, p. 247.
28 See Jenkins (2004), p. 339.
29 Mitra and Singh (1999) offers a model of state–society interaction where the new social elites, themselves the outcome of a process of fair and efficient political recruitment, play a two-track strategy and institute processes of law and order management, social and economic reform and accommodation of identity as an operationally testable model. The comparative study of Gujarat and Orissa by Mitra (*Power, Protest, and Participation*, 1992) shows how conventional participation and radical protest have effectively complemented one another.

7   Economic development and social justice

The tragic fact of the matter is that the poor bear the heaviest costs of modernization under both socialist and capitalist auspices. The only justification for imposing the costs is that they would become steadily worse off without it. As the situation stands, the dilemma is indeed a cruel one.

Moore (1966), p. 410.

Nehru's 'mixed economy' turned out to be a gravely flawed image of our future. . . . Nehru's blueprint of state-directed industrialization, based on publicly owned heavy industry and insulated from international competition was fundamentally wrong. . . . When ordinary human beings err, it is sad, but when leaders do, it haunts us for generations.

Das (2002), pp. 50–51.

Introduction

Poor countries rarely succeed in setting up a democratic form of government, and even more rarely, in sustaining one.[1] The combination of extreme poverty, inequality and ethnic diversity is fatal for the survival of democratic institutions. However, India has changed steadily from a colonial, agrarian economy into a capitalist, globalized economy but the country's democratic institutions have held their own. They have generated the political momentum that reinforces reform without upsetting the democratic and judicial due processes. Many had maintained that radical changes in India's economy and welfare would be unlikely as long as both are constrained by the liberal democratic constitution and the capitalist mode of production.[2] India has defied the norm. This chapter on India's economic development analyses how the country has been able to meet the challenge of the dilemma of economic growth versus social justice, and produced the economic basis for democratic consolidation.[3]

Incremental growth and redistribution

Rapid economic growth over the past two decades has transformed India's economy from a state of low growth to a level which has put the country in the company of emerging markets. India's economy has grown at an annual rate of about 7 per cent (see Diagram 7.1). Inflation, during the period of rapid growth, has remained relatively low. Measured in terms of the purchasing power parity (PPP), India has reached the level of $2,755 per capita (Table 7.1).[4] In terms of PPP, India surpassed Pakistan for the first time in the year 2000. In Asia, only the Chinese economy shows higher growth rates than the Indian.

India's economy had languished at a low level for several decades. However, economic growth has picked up momentum since the liberalization of the economy in 1991. The average growth that the Indian economy has achieved over the past two decades has stabilized at around 7 per cent. In spite of the financial crisis that

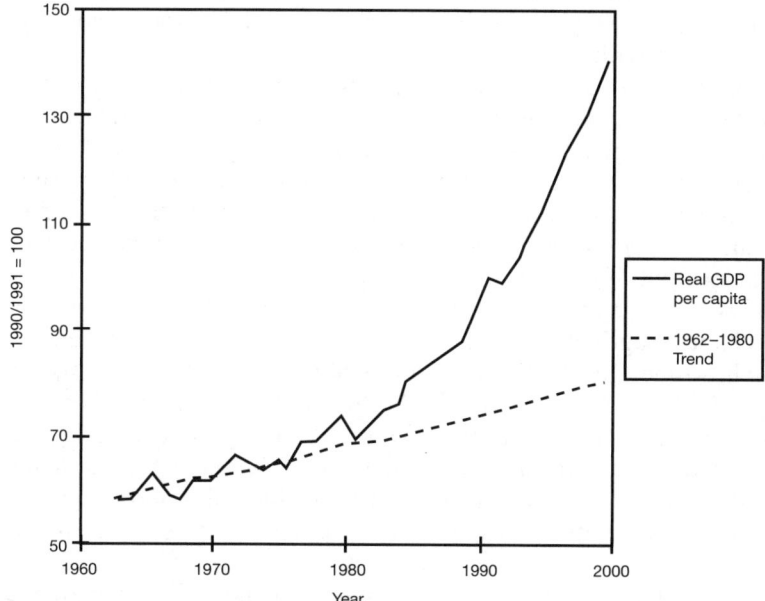

Diagram 7.1 Indian GDP per capita level compared to 1962–80 trend
Source: De Long (2003).

Table 7.1 The Human Development Index – India in comparative perspective

HDI ranking	Countries	Life expectancy at birth (years)	Adult literacy rate (% aged 15 and above)	Education: combined gross enrolment ratio	GDP per capita (PPP US$)
10	Japan	82.7	99.0%	86.6 %	33.632 $
13	United States	79.1	99.0%	92.4 %	45.592 $
21	United Kingdom	79.3	99.0%	89.2 %	35.130 $
22	Germany	79.8	99.0%	88.1 %	34.401 $
71	Russia	66.2	99.5 %	81.9 %	14.690 $
75	Brazil	72.2	90.0 %	87.2 %	9.567 $
92	China	72.9	93.3 %	68.7 %	5.383 $
132	Bhutan	65.7	52.8 %	54.1 %	4.837 $
134	**India**	**63.4**	**66.0 %**	**61.0 %**	**2.753 $**
141	Pakistan	66.2	54.2 %	39.3 %	2.496 $
144	Nepal	66.3	56.5 %	60.8 %	1.049 $
146	Bangladesh	65.7	53.5 %	52.1 %	1.241 $

Source: *United Nations Development Programme Report 2009*, p. 171–173.

affected most of the world in 2008, the Ministry of Finance and the Reserve Bank of India remain optimistic about India's capacity to sustain the pace of economic growth while keeping inflation low.[5]

Although average growth is an important indicator of the strength of an economy, it does not tell the whole story at the level of welfare. The Human Development Index (see Table 7.1), which takes into account such 'output' factors as life expectancy, adult literacy, gross enrolment ratio and per capita income, are important indicators of the standard of living of the population as a whole. In this context, India's performance is one of the best in South Asia, though Brazil, also a developing country, and China are better situated with regard to all these indicators.

Despite the rapid pace in the overall rate of growth, India still remains a predominantly agricultural country, with about two-thirds of its population dependent upon agriculture. Most are marginal peasants with small holdings or no land at all. The majority of these peasants draw their livelihood from rain-fed, subsistence agriculture. The economic legacy at the time of Independence included a small industrial base that, along with the business sector, contributed only 5 per cent of the GNP. However, the weight of industry as a component of the economy has vastly changed in recent times (see Diagram 7.2). Those fortunate enough to have made a breakthrough into mechanized agriculture, in the absence of a system of comprehensive crop insurance, remain vulnerable to the risks of bankruptcy, as one can see in the cases of farmers' suicide, avidly discussed in the Indian media. The needs of the economy in general, and agriculture in particular, are not adequately served by the transport and communication network. India inherited one of the largest rail systems in the world, which did not link, as already mentioned before, the ports with the economic hinterland, but rather with the capital cities, reflecting the security needs of a colonial power.

Though not quite as spectacularly as in China, poverty in India, in terms of the headcount ratio, has come down significantly compared to the levels two decades ago. According to a new measurement, the number of Indians living on less than

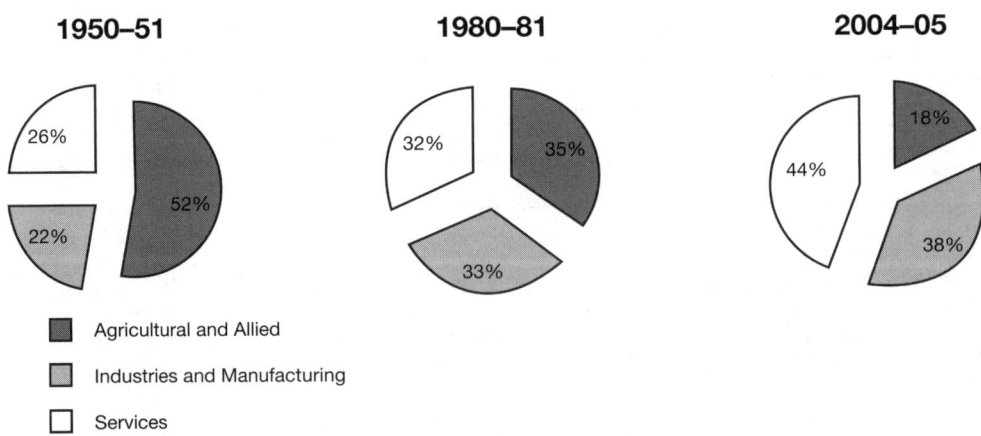

Diagram 7.2 The composition of GDP (in per cent) – agriculture, industries and services

Source: Reserve Bank of India, *Handbook of Statistics on Indian Economy 2006* (Table 3); components of Gross Domestic Product (at factor cost) available online at http://www.rbi.org.in/scripts/AnnualPublications.aspx?head=Handbook+of+Statistics+on+India+Economy.

US$1.25 per day is approximately 300 million (in 2010 this is approximately 28 per cent of the population). This is a dire indication of the resilience of mass poverty.[6] The picture is slightly better in terms of relative poverty, measured by the percentage share of the income of the lowest 20 per cent as compared with the United States, China or Brazil. However, the poor performance on the indicators of welfare such as access to sanitation, safe water or infant mortality, further reinforces the picture of enduring mass poverty in India. Though nationalism and communal harmony were the main organizing principles of India's Freedom Movement, the removal of mass poverty through democratic means was always high up on the nation's political agenda as well. While the symbolic articulation of this commitment to the welfare of the poor came from the austere lifestyle of Mahatma Gandhi, the anti-poverty programmes came from the Congress socialists, whose main leader was Jawaharlal Nehru, the first Prime Minister of India.

Upon taking power after Independence, the Congress government worked to create a mixed economy in which the state engaged in building the infrastructure and key industries. The private sector was to focus on manufacturing and distribution. National planning, conceived by technocrats but under the guidance of key members of the central cabinet and the state chief ministers who constituted the National Development Council, was charged with balancing the needs of growth with the imperative of social justice and redistribution. Besides introducing new notions of entitlement, the constitution promised a life of dignity and economic opportunity to the underprivileged, particularly to the former untouchables and tribal population. But while development remained high on the agenda, it was not placed outside the political arena as occurred in 'developmental' states[7] like Japan or South Korea, where development policy became the preserve of a technocratic and financial elite. In India, not only was economic policy an integral part of national and regional politics, but institutions like the Planning Commission, and the adoption of a mixed economy as the framework of development, guaranteed that economic policy was not shifted outside public control and accountability. This model of democratic planning (Figure 7.1) was further reinforced by a number of reforms that protected the rights of workers, extended electoral democracy up to the village councils (*panchayat* systems), removed intermediary rights of large landlords (*zamindars*) and princely rulers, and attempted to introduce land ceilings and cooperative farming.[8]

As a consequence of these policies, Indian development during the early decades after Independence was, broadly speaking, unspectacular in any specific area. Nevertheless, the policies and institutional innovations undertaken during this period strengthened India's modern political institutions, and eliminated famine and reliance on imported food in the span of one generation. The first gains came in the 1950s through an expansion of the area under cultivation and irrigation works. The 1960s accelerated agrarian production through a series of technical innovations like seeds of a high-yielding variety, new pesticides, chemical fertilizers and precise information on weather and market conditions. This 'Green Revolution' transformed India from a net importer of food to a country that was self-sufficient. Through the 1970s the government developed a complex system of storage and market interventions called 'Food Procurement' at guaranteed prices to maintain a steady flow of food production and supply to consumers. India's food policy, which evolved in reaction to chronic food shortage, necessitating food imports that meant huge financial and political costs, particularly during the Vietnam war when the

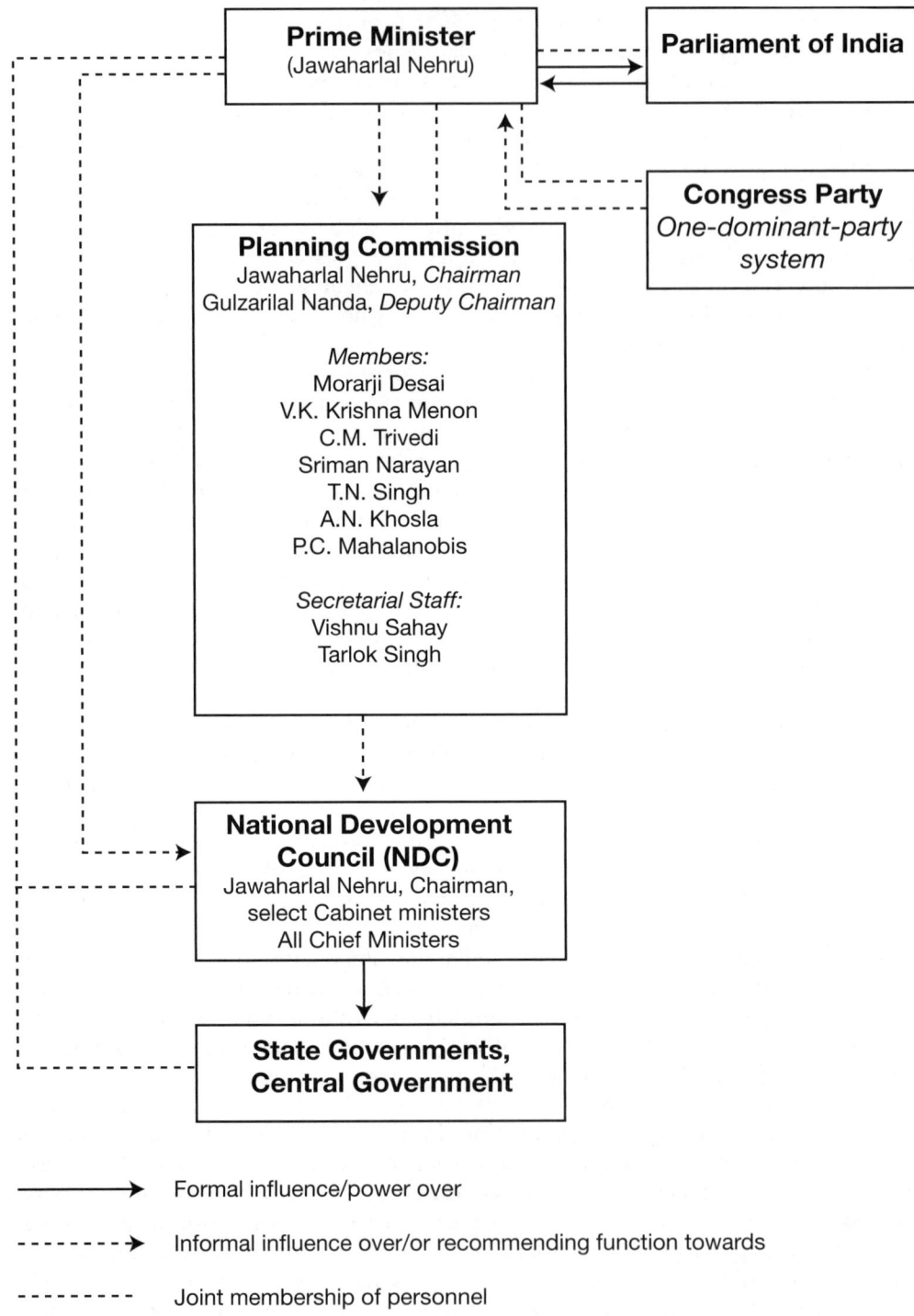

Figure 7.1 Structure, process and power in planning under Nehru
Source: Drawn by author.

Indian position was opposed to that of the United States, finally started yielding rich dividends in the 1980s. India's system of food security became so resilient that even the severe droughts of 1987 did not lead to significant fluctuations in the prices of agricultural commodities.[9]

The modernizing leadership around Nehru intended to raise the general standard of living and protect the country's newly won freedom through a mixed economy. This model, based on import substitution, planned economic growth, and a policy of self-reliance, did not leave much scope for integration with the international market. In part this reflected a certain Gandhian nostalgia for *swadeshi* – the consumption of goods made in India – but also a basic distrust of the capitalist West. Bitter memories of colonial rule underpinned this deep antipathy. During the first half of the twentieth century, from 1900 to 1946, Indian national income under colonial rule had risen by 0.7 per cent annually, while its population grew at the rate of 0.8 per cent. The lesson was not lost on the generation of leaders led by Nehru who saw economic development as the most important programme of the post-colonial state. Thanks to the developmental initiatives undertaken after Independence, during the period from 1950–51 to 1990–91 India managed to more than double the size of its economy. However, while its growth rate was well above pre-Independence levels, it fell far below expectations. India was considerably below the 8 to 10 per cent level of the fastest-growing parts of Asia – Japan, South Korea, Taiwan, Hong Kong and Singapore – and lagged substantially behind China.

In spite of its poor performance relative to worldwide economic growth, India did achieve some spectacular results. By the late 1980s, industry contributed 29 per cent of the Indian GNP. Despite the low level of industrialization, thanks to the sheer size of the economy, by the mid-1980s India was one of the 20 most industrialized nations in terms of total industrial production. India was by then self-sufficient in consumer goods and in basic commodities like steel and cement. It also produced a range of intermediate-level manufactured goods, ships, locomotives, trucks, machine tools and sophisticated electronic equipment. In a departure from its classic patterns of international trade based on primary exports, India had started a modest export of manufactured goods. However, the slowing down of India's economy and the visible inefficiency of the basic model of import substitution became compelling factors for radical change.

The model of planned development based on a mixed economy, where the 'commanding heights' of the economy were dominated by the public sector, did achieve a certain amount of welfare, but produced some less desirable side-effects as well. While state control over the market managed to simultaneously keep inflation and budget deficits low by the standards of developing countries, the system created what came to be known as a *Quota Permit Raj*[10] and generated unrestrained corruption and inefficiency, all but blowing out the spirit of enterprise. The result was a general slowing down of growth, which the government tried to stimulate in the early 1980s by borrowing from the international market, without, however, bringing about any radical changes in the structure of the management of the economy. The result was a serious financial crisis by the end of the 1980s. Most alarmingly for India's policy makers and the international financial establishment, the debt to GDP ratio of India went up by 100 per cent in the span of a decade. In 1991 Manmohan Singh, then Finance Minister, with the full support of Prime Minister Narasimha Rao, introduced the first structural reform of the economy that subsequently came to be known as 'liberalization'.

The first policies introduced by Manmohan Singh were aimed at a drastic reduction of state control over the market whether open or disguised. The government reduced subsidies on several items and relaxed strict import and export controls. The system of licensing new industries and closing those which were no longer profitable but could not be closed because of labour protection legislation was modified to bring a new flexibility with regard to the market. Areas of production which the government had brought under its control during the high period of nationalization in the 1970s under the concept of 'essential commodities' were gradually released back to the market, and important areas of production such as electricity generation, parts of the oil industry, domestic air transport, roads and some telecommunications were opened up for private initiative. The government welcomed foreign investment and participation in the process of production through 'joint ventures'. India attempted to make the domestic market attractive for foreign investors by lowering tariffs in a significant departure from the previous policy of import substitution and autarky. There was an easing of imports and Singh attempted to encourage exports through the devaluation of the rupee by 24 per cent in 1991. The rupee was also made partly convertible. The heavy taxes on entrepreneurs were gradually reduced, as was the direct tax on income. The top rate of income tax came down from 56 per cent to 40 per cent and corporate tax from 57.5 per cent to 46 per cent.[11]

These measures were reinforced by a communication revolution that saw a deregulation of broadcasting in India. This made it possible for Indian consumers to have easy access to foreign-made televisions and radios, and to hitherto unavailable programmes through satellite and cable channels. The state broadcasting itself took on the challenge and introduced a modest degree of variety through internal competition.

In some ways, the fiscal policies of 1991 to liberalize the economy and implement a policy of privatization of public sector undertakings went against the quintessence of Indian politics. As far as ancient Indian tradition goes, the *Arthasastra* – one of the earliest texts on statecraft in India[12] – had allocated a number of key sectors of the economy to the exclusive authority of the king. This tradition of state monopoly was continued by practically all the rulers of India, coming to a peak under British colonial rule. Indian commercial and industrial entrepreneurs had objected to the British monopoly and colonial obstacles to the expansion of their activities, and had enthusiastically supported the *swadeshi* programme of Mahatma Gandhi. They were content after Independence to find a secure niche for their products within the structure of the mixed economy. Each obstacle to free enterprise was also the visible tip of a powerful vested interest. As such, it comes as no surprise today that attempts to roll back the state have produced a powerful backlash from a formidable coalition. Groups that have informally come together include socialists who want to protect the poor and underprivileged from the devastation of capitalism, rich farmers who fear the loss of government subsidies, the *swadeshi* lobby, which is apprehensive about the loss of Indian political autonomy and cultural identity, and some regional leaders who fear the growing gap between rich and poor parts of India without the presence of a powerful redistributive centre.

Liberalization has thus sparked off a heated debate among India's political parties. India's communist parties, which have not gone through the process of de-Stalinization that marked their European counterparts following the decline of the Soviet Union, predictably came out with a firm opposition to the liberalization of trade regulations.

These reforms were seen as an attempt by the international financial establishments like the IMF and the World Bank to dictate terms to India. They demand that the entry of foreign capital be governed by the technological 'needs' of India, which are presumably to be determined by India's planners. For the left, the public sector as a whole and especially public sector employment needed to be defended against attempts at privatization that could lead to job losses. The Congress party, which had introduced the liberalization measures in the first place, was cautious in the defence of liberalization, having sensed its lack of electoral appeal. The Bharatiya Janata Party, which had traditionally drawn support from the trading communities and the better-educated urban populations, took a complex position on this whole issue. The party manifesto called for 'full liberalization and calibrated globalization'; it argued in favour of initiative and enterprise but wanted to retain the role of the state in protecting national industry and trade against 'unfair' international competition. The BJP also intended to exclude foreign intrusion from areas crucial to India's security interests, and foreign competition from consumer goods industries (using catchy slogans like 'computer chips yes, potato chips no').

In a context where coalitional politics is overly sensitive to popular mood swings, the uncertain feelings of the electorate are also reflected in the radical fluctuations of public policy. It was therefore remarkable that the BJP-led NDA government continued the policy of liberalization started by its predecessor in spite of the opposition among its ranks. In the wake of the nuclear tests of 1998, when sanctions against India threatened to restrain its economic growth, the BJP government sent its top troubleshooters to the finance capitals of the world and sought to salvage the situation by clearing the applications for joint ventures with accelerated speed. These efforts were partly neutralized by the nationalist euphoria created by the spectacle of India 'standing up' to the West, which some elements of the cultural-nationalist parties interpreted as the right moment to throw foreign products out of India. Still, the NDA government kept the momentum of liberalization intact, but the electoral dividends it had expected from its 'India Shining' campaign to illustrate its achievements did not materialize. In any case, following the electoral defeat of the NDA in 2004, the UPA coalition has kept the course of liberalization under the adroit leadership of Prime Minister Manmohan Singh, the original architect of India's liberalization in 1991, and Finance Minister Chidambaram, who was closely associated with Singh during the initial steps away from India's command economy. Going by the record of the past years, both have become quite skilful at balancing the pressure of a significant contingent of communists in the ruling coalition with the steady stream of successive reform.

There are still problems aplenty: poor infrastructure, political wrangling over educational quotas, deep pockets of poverty and illiteracy, and spectacular farmers' suicides as a form of protest against the side-effects of globalization. But over and above it all, there is also a sense of euphoria about close to double-digit growth and low inflation, and a widespread sense of opportunity knocking at the door. This sense of buoyancy is reflected in public opinion data.[13]

The long narrative of the evolution of India's economy from its post-Independence, regulated structure marked by low growth to one which has aspirations to be a global player, might give the impression of a smooth transition from the one to the other. In reality, that was far from the case. Transforming a colonial economy based on exploitation and geared to the needs of security into a productive, capitalist economy while keeping the structure of the democratic institutions intact is distinctive of the Indian case. This complex story of the transition is analysed below in terms of how a combination of planning, politics, coalitions of strategic policy-making elites and an element of chance helped transform the key components of India's economy.

Distinctiveness of the Indian model

A fine sense of politics, combined with attention to the requirements of economic growth and social justice, are distinctive of the Indian model of development. The political argument that evolved over the course of India's Freedom Movement privileged social justice over economic growth. It might have slowed the economy down in comparison to post-war growth worldwide, but it has spread the notion of being stakeholders widely within the population. This, in turn, has given a sense of legitimacy to modern institutions and strengthened state–society interaction.

The 'Indian model' of democratic development emerged from a series of strategic choices made during the early years after Independence. These choices, in turn, were based on a set of compromises that attempted to blend the experience of wartime planning and controls, domestic pressures for a policy of economic nationalism, and the liberal, Gandhian and socialist ideological cross-currents that existed within the nationalist movement. The model that grew out of these strategic choices evolved gradually into a set of policies that became the basis of India's development consensus. The objectives of India's development were to achieve rapid economic growth, self-reliance, full employment and social justice. It called for a system of centralized planning and a mixed economy in which a government-owned public sector would dominate basic industry and the state would control, regulate, and protect the private sector from foreign competition. Foreign capital would be permitted, but only under highly controlled and restricted circumstances.

The Constituent Assembly which wrote India's constitution was dominated by lawyers, politicians and members of the liberal professions inspired by the values of Fabian socialism. They recommended social change and economic development as the normative objectives of the modern state, and parliamentary democracy based on methodological individualism, as its preferred method of achieving it. Moore and others, who approached India from a leftist perspective, saw as the basic paradox of India's political economy that the modern state and economy were pitted against the traditional society. This the leftist canon has seen as the root cause of problems of disorder, slow growth, corruption, and caste and communal conflict in India.

In order to understand the distinctiveness of the Indian model which has made it possible for the traditional society to undergo radical change and economic development within a stable democratic political framework, one needs briefly to refer to the ideological environment of the 1950s that has deeply influenced the evolution of the Indian model. Two key concepts – social change and economic development – were crucial to India's planners, policy makers and vote-hungry politicians. These were understood as 'significant alteration of social structures (that is, of patterns of social action and interaction), including consequences and manifestations of such structures embodied in norms (rules of conduct), values, and cultural practices and symbols'.[14]

These key concepts were understood in the same sense as the European social history during the period of swift change which witnessed the rapid transformation of traditional agricultural society into the modern industrial society. The former was characterized by the predominance of ascription, multiplex social relations where one individual would play a variety of roles, a rigid hierarchical system, settled within primordial kin networks. A modern society, on the other hand, was seen as one based on the predominance of universalistic and specific norms, a high degree of social mobility, specialization, and an egalitarian society based on association rather than ascription.

The framework of analysis of India's planners and policy experts was based on these broad definitions of tradition, modernity and change. However, the political conditions of India and the attitudes and expectations that had grown around them did not fully conform to these premises. Traditional India was not identical to feudal Europe, nor were castes – endogamous status groups based on hereditary occupations, and degrees of purity and pollution – equivalent to feudal classes. Similarly, democracy and social change – in contrast to the state of affairs in Europe during the period of accelerated capitalist growth – were not considered subsidiary to economic growth but as integral parts of a unified concept of development. These values and consequent policies were strongly promoted by Jawaharlal Nehru – the undisputed leader and spokesman of modernity in post-Independence India.

In retrospect, the elements that emerged as constitutive of the Indian model took on Indian tradition as much as imported notions of modern attitudes, institutions, values and expectations. The caste system affected India's model of social change as much as the caste system was itself affected by the process of economic and political change. In his seminal analysis of the specificity of the Indian solution to the general problem of social change, Morris-Jones (1987) has described this as 'inter-penetration' of the modern state and traditional society in India. Why has India succeeded in achieving a generally peaceful and *orderly* transition? Rudolph and Rudolph formulate this in terms of the multiple role of the state, the relative autonomy of the state and state-dominated pluralism in India.[15]

The influence of British colonial rule on the model of India's political economy has been important, both in the material and in the cultural sense. British forms of production such as factories, mining, banks, audit and accounting, and securing autonomy of the market from political interference have left their mark on India's economy. Less marked has been the influence on agriculture, tea and coffee plantations being the exception. But India, unlike other parts of the British Empire like North America, Australia or parts of Africa, has been selective in appropriating British ideas. India's communitarian norms have set upper limits to profit as the motivating factor of the economy, just as interests of the needy and the socially marginal had continued to be a part of the agenda,[16] surfacing with renewed vitality after Independence.

The legacies of colonial rule have emerged as the outstanding features of the distinctiveness of India's political economy. These are: the rule of law, bureaucracy, economic planning, citizenship, industrialization, legislative and political moves against 'parasitic' landlords (*zamindars*), modern political institutions, a two-track tradition of protest and participation, and a neo-institutional, dynamic model of governance.

The origin and evolution of a mixed economy

The ideological reasons for the adoption of the mixed economy lie in the nature of Indian reaction to British rule. The 'moderate' strategy of engaging the British on the basis of a liberal political agenda, the 'extremist' rejection of this agenda in favour of a nationalist identity and economy and finally, the Gandhian synthesis of both characterized the course and content of Indian resistance to the British Raj.[17] The Congress party became the medium of this synthesis, and in the one-dominant-party system with the Congress at its centre as the framework of power, the successor state set about giving concrete shape to the visions of India's future that had emerged during the last decades of the Freedom Movement.

After Gandhi's assassination in January 1948, the debate focused primarily on the degree to which Nehru's vision of planning and socialism would prevail. The debate came to concentrate on several key issues, namely, the instruments government would use in guiding the economy, the size and scope of private sector economic activity, the role of Gandhian village and cottage industries, the role of state enterprises, nationalization, economic controls, and the future of foreign capital. The strategic choices made in settling these issues were based on a series of major compromises that ultimately came to shape the entire economic system of independent India.

What did Independence change? The year 1947 was a great divide: the new men wanted to leave their 'stamp on history', and started off an intense policy debate within the Congress party. The policy turmoil lasted from 1947 to 1951. During this period, Gandhi was assassinated, Vallabhbhai Patel died in 1950, communists rose in rebellion and failed, the Jan Sangh Party, the predecessor of the BJP, was banned, and the ban was subsequently lifted. Nehru felt strong enough to lift the ban on the extreme right and the communist left and the Congress party went to the polls on the platform of a mixed economy, secularism and non-alignment. The strategic choices made during this period became the basis of the Indian model of development.

The mixed economy gave an institutional shape to the liberal, socialist and communitarian values that constituted the three main strands of the Freedom Movement and dominated the proceedings of the Constituent Assembly. The liberal values were given a clear and incontrovertible shape in the fundamental rights to the freedom of trade, occupation and ownership – Article 19 of the constitution. The socialist values were less explicit, but nevertheless clearly discernible. Instead of the concept of 'due process' – an American practice that gave individual rights the highest value, defended by the Supreme Court through judicial interpretation – the constitution settled for the concept of 'procedure established by law' which made 'national' interest more compelling than the interest of the individual. This doctrine paved the way for land reforms and laws aimed at curbing the full play of capitalist enterprise. Articles 39, 41, 43 and 46 of the Directive Principles of State Policy recommended that the state pursue policies aimed at bringing about the right to an adequate means of livelihood, the distribution of the ownership and control of material resources of the community in a manner that best serves the common good and avoids the concentration of wealth, a living wage, decent standards of living and full enjoyment of leisure and social and cultural opportunities for the entire population. Finally, even though there was no staunch 'Gandhian lobby' in the Constituent Assembly, communitarian values such as welfare of *harijans*, backward classes, women and children, village and cottage industries, educational and economic interests of weaker sections, cattle welfare and the banning of the slaughter of milk cattle found their way into the body of this elaborate text.

The Industrial Policy Resolution of 6 April, 1948 gave a formal definition of the scope of the mixed economy. It suggested that public ownership would be confined to three industries – munitions, atomic energy and railroads. In six other industries – coal, iron and steel, aircraft manufacturing, shipbuilding, telephone and telegraph, and minerals – government reserved the exclusive right to start new ventures. Eighteen key industries of national importance would be developed under the control and regulation of the central government. Foreign capital and enterprises would be welcome but subject to government control and regulation. The resolution further announced that government would create a Planning Commission. Finally, in a symbolic recognition of India's communitarian culture close to the heart of Mahatma Gandhi, the resolution asked the government to encourage the development of village and cottage industries.

The second Industrial Policy Resolution, issued on 30 April, 1956, expanded the scope of public-sector development; guaranteed existing private-sector facilities from nationalization, and provided for their eventual expansion. Three categories or schedules of industries were created. Schedule A, consisting of 17 industries reserved for development by the public sector, included mostly basic and heavy industries. Schedule B contained a list of 12 industries in which public sector investment would supplement private-sector development. All other industries were open to private-sector development.

Politics, the Planning Commission and the policy process under Nehru, 1947–64

The philosophy dominating the thinking behind India's planning was a mix of Marxism, pluralism, functionalism and Gandhian moral economy. Economic development required the structural transformation of agriculture, transfer of the agrarian surplus to industrial investment and the rapid creation of infrastructure. However, a professional and neutral bureaucracy of generalists and career civil servants was expected to perform this task. The contradictions of democratic planning showed them at their most virulent in the problems of bureaucratic implementation of democratic planning within a post-colonial, non-aligned, federal and parliamentary context.

The Planning Commission was set up by the central cabinet on 15 March, 1950, as an *advisory* body. The Planning Commission was accountable to the National Development Council. The intention behind this was two-fold: to make up for the implementation gaps caused by the separation of powers, and to establish a division of powers. However, the system gave rise to corruption and inefficiency.[18] As a result, the idealistic assumptions and expectations behind India's democratic planning were not fulfilled.[19] The Industrial Policy Resolution was a carefully crafted compromise document that contained a series of strategic choices and established the basic outlines of Indian development. First, it envisioned the creation of a mixed economy and recognized that the private sector had an important role to play in the future economy of the country. Second, it declared that the state would be expected to play a progressively larger role in the industrial development of India. Third, it accepted the principle that private foreign capital would be allowed to participate in Indian industrialization. This participation, however, was to be regulated by the state, with major interest in ownership and control normally in Indian hands. Finally, it held out the hope that a place would be found for the development of Gandhian village and cottage industries. In short, it contained elements intended to satisfy each of the ideological pressures in India.[20]

The structure and functions of India's democratic planning, as depicted in Figure 7.1, reveal the main reasons behind the poor implementation of India's planning.

Despite the theoretical attraction of combining the dynamism of private initiative and the stability that long-term public funding of key industries and the infrastructure in a mixed economy model represented, in practice it turned out to be otherwise. The Third Five Year Plan – judging from the buoyant language of the document, a great achievement of planning – turned out to be disappointing in terms of the real rate of growth (see Diagram 7.3).

Contrary to the economic logic underpinning this model, the assumptions about the availability of resources for investment, consumption and the consequent reduction of poverty were not sustained. The prospects of growth deteriorated further as a result of the lack of political support for the fiscal discipline that a planned economy required. Rather than a method of transforming the economy, the mixed economy gradually came to be viewed as a means of generating support for the political machine of the ruling Congress party. The need for patronage as a means of garnering political support arose because of the vast change in the political environment in which the party found itself after Independence. The Congress discovered, once it acquired the mantle of the ruling party after the Transfer of Power, that it had lost a substantial part of its membership, including, in particular, a good number of idealistic workers. The void left by them was steadily made up by an influx of another type of member – people who valued the connection with the party because of the opportunity it gave to get close to those in power. This new vote bank quickly became symbiotic with the Congress-controlled governments which were the source of patronage, licences, quotas and permits and were responsible for new legislation. Those individuals and groups that had something to gain or lose by political and

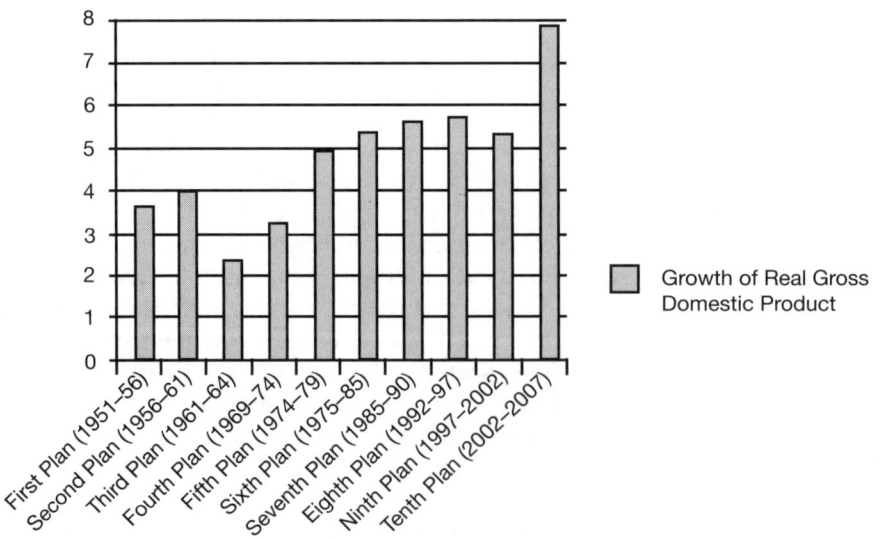

Diagram 7.3 Real GDP growth, 1951–2007

Source: *Statistical Outline of India 2005–06*, Tata Services Limited, Department of Economics and Statistics, Mumbai, 3rd edition, February 2006, p. 9 and p. 237.

administrative decisions and policies were interested in closer connection with the Congress, and many entered it. In other words, from a membership centring on 'have not' groups, the Congress began to attract the 'haves' – stakeholders of the new regime, those who would be affected by the decisions and policies of the government. The imperatives of democratic rule also required the ability to compromise and live with contradictions, which is opposite to the aptitude for agitation and opposition most valuable in a revolutionary movement. Many of those who had led the Congress movements, particularly socialists, found themselves with a greatly reduced role in the governing organization.

The introduction of a universal voting system raised the number of eligible voters from 35 million in 1937 to 170 million in 1952. The effect of property and education qualifications of the 1937 election had exaggerated the strength of the urban electorate relative to its proportion in the population. Universal suffrage shifted power to the rural elements in Indian society because the voters reflected the population distribution. With the relatively ineffective means of communication to the rural areas, the parties tended to rely on establishing contact with existing groupings – largely leaders of castes – to get votes. Thus elections increased the political role of rural elites who could deliver votes. Simultaneously, the existing village leaders who were members of locally dominant castes and cooperated with the government, both to deal with local problems and to get favours for their villages, now had to work with the Congress since that was the party in power. Inevitably there was a shift in power from more organized groups and leaders to those who were themselves rural or who represented rural groups. With universal suffrage, elections became far more expensive than earlier and the parties sought to attract support from these groups – largely urban – that could finance an election. Thus new coalitions were formed between rural groups that controlled votes and urban groups that controlled resources for elections. The alliance became the social basis of the Quota Permit Raj, which is how the Congress party itself came to be known.

In the final assessment, what were the main achievements and failures of the Indian model of the mixed economy? Was it, on the whole, positive or negative from the point of view of economic growth, development and democracy? On the achievement side one can point to slow but steady growth; political and democratic control over the economy and transformation of the rhetoric of development into an element of everyday political discourse. The legitimization of this discourse is found in the fact that even the less privileged sections of society have some progress to report.[21] The most important gain was possibly in legitimacy, if not in growth. The mixed economy became the socio-economic base of the post-colonial state. In the final analysis, it might have slowed India down economically but it kept the country democratic.

India's agrarian economy: from subsistence to subsidy

Over the past 60 years, India's agriculture has achieved a Green Revolution which, jointly with a national policy of food security, has effectively eliminated famine. The Green Revolution is seen by the advocates of agrarian modernization as a paradigm shift from subsistence farming to modern agriculture, involving the use of high technology and credit, in an integrated production system stretching from farming, distribution and financing to agri-business. It prompted a gradual shift from the classic problems of Indian agriculture – fragmentation of holdings, insecurity of tenure, uneconomic units of production, excessive dependence on the monsoon, low unit yield, and rack renting – to a modern agrarian economy. Scholarly opinion on the nature, extent and durability of the Green Revolution remains divided.[22]

A number of factors led to a re-appraisal of the agrarian policy in the 1960s. Massive food deficits in the early 1960s, famine in Bihar and the difficulty of obtaining food from abroad without compromising the sovereignty of the country brought the planners to question the marginal role accorded to agriculture in the overall economic model of India. Besides the half-hearted attempt to abolish *zamindari*, no comprehensive plan for agrarian development had been made. Agriculture was seen only as an adjunct to the industry–infrastructure-led, mixed-economy-based planning process. Public intervention, in the case of agriculture, extended only to control over production, distribution and financing. Planners believed in the Indian model which allocated the 'commanding heights' of the economy to industry, based on planning, and the trickle-down of resources and new ideas from the tip of the pyramid to the masses, based on the felt needs model.[23] Agriculture, following the classic model of growth drawn from European experience, was seen as the source of surplus capital, to be invested for greater industrialization, not the object of transfer of investment from industry. In India's federal system, agriculture is a state subject, and as such, beyond the scope of central planning. In consequence, not much direct investment was made, except in the form of initiatives like community development, *zamindari* abolition, land ceiling legislation and cooperatives.

During the early decades after Independence as India went through three successive Five Year Plans, the main approach to agricultural development was dominated by two irreconcilable goals: 'The economic aim of achieving maximum increases in agricultural output to support rapid industrialization; and the social objective of reducing disparities in rural life'.[24] One of the most difficult dilemmas arose from the obvious economic advantage of concentrating scarce inputs of improved seeds, fertilizers, pesticides and equipment in irrigated areas of the country where they could be expected to bring the greatest returns in output. Indeed the selection of the first community projects in 1952 was guided by this consideration. They were allocated only to districts with assured water from rainfall or irrigation facilities. Almost immediately, however, serious social objection was raised to the practices of 'picking out the best and most favourable spots' for intensive development while the largest part of the rural areas was left economically backward. Within a year, the principle of selective and intensive development was abandoned. The Planning Commission announced a programme for rapid all-India coverage under the National Extension Service and Community Development Programme with special attention to backward and less favoured regions.

The social goal of reducing disparities also influenced the selection of methods of agricultural development. The planners were inclined to give only secondary importance to the introduction of costly modern inputs as a means of increasing agricultural productivity. Instead, they devised agricultural development programmes based on 'intensive cultivation of land by hand – and improving conditions of living in rural areas through community projects, land reforms, consolidation of holdings, etc.'. Indeed, the planners' strategy for agricultural development rested on the capacity of the Community Development Programme to mobilize more than 60 million peasant cultivators for participation in labour-intensive agricultural production programmes and community works, including the construction of capital projects. The crux of the approach – the major inducement to greatest effort on the part of the small farmers – was the promise of social reform, held out by large-scale initiatives for institutional change. The highest priority was assigned to rapid implementation of land reforms, including security of tenure, lower rents, transfer of ownership rights to tenants, and redistribution of land. Meanwhile, state-partnered village cooperatives were created to fortify small farmers with cheap credit facilities and economies of bulk purchase and sale of agricultural commodities.

In retrospect, it was probably inevitable that a development strategy requiring extensive land reform and institutional change as preconditions for success should meet with powerful opposition from landed groups; and that in a political democracy, where land-owning interests are heavily represented in the legislatures, this resistance should manifest itself in a go-slow approach towards agrarian reforms. By the early 1960s, most legislation on tenancy reform and ceilings on land ownership had not been effectively implemented. Yet in the absence of agrarian reform it proved imposs-ible to provide attractive incentives to the majority of small farmers for participation in labour-intensive agricultural production programmes.

There was, in fact, no dearth of policies. Following the recommendations of the Balwantrai Mehta committee in 1957, *panchayati raj* was adopted as the overall administrative structure for rural development. The Congress party passed a resolution proclaiming a modified version of cooperative farming in 1959 as a goal for the future. But as Moore notes drily, the implementation was not at the same level as the rhetoric. The Community Development Programme took no note of the reality on the ground: '. . . official instructions to program officials in contact with the villagers made no mention of caste, property relationships, or surplus manpower in the village – in other words, any of the real problems.' Though local elections, in some parts of the country, had some effect on weakening the authority of hereditary social notables, as a whole, Moore found the experiment a dismal failure.[25]

As a matter of fact, as early as 1958, lagging growth rates in the agricultural sector became a serious limiting factor on the overall rate of economic advance. By the middle of the Third Plan, years of relatively static production levels (1960–61 to 1963–64) convinced the Planning Commission that continuation of shortfalls in agri-culture would jeopardize the entire programme of industrial development. Of necessity, some retreat from the social goals of planning had to be contemplated. In 1964, therefore, the planners announced 'a fresh consideration of the assumptions, methods, and techniques as well as the machinery of planning and plan implementation in the field of agriculture'. Two major departures from previous policy were initiated as a result of this re-evaluation:

1   development efforts would be subsequently concentrated in the 20 to 25 per cent of the cultivated area where supplies of assured water created 'fair prospects of achieving rapid increases in production' and
2   within these areas, there would be systematic effort to extend the application of science and technology, including the adoption of better implements and more scientific methods to raise yields.

In October 1965, the new policy was put into practice when 114 out of 325 districts were selected for an Intensive Agricultural Areas Programme (IAAP). A model for the new approach already existed in the 15 districts taken up under the pilot Intensive Agricultural Development Programme (IADP), beginning in 1961. Initially pioneered by the Ford Foundation, the IADP emphasized the necessity of providing the cultivator with a complete 'package of practices' in order to increase yields, including credit, modern inputs, price incentives, marketing facilities and technical advice.

The economic rationale of an intensive agricultural areas programme was considerably strengthened by the technical breakthrough reported from Taiwan and Mexico in 1965 of the development of new varieties of paddy and wheat seeds, with yield capacities of 5,000 to 6,000 pounds per acre – almost double the maximum potential output of indigenous Indian varieties, and also by the development at Indian research stations in the late 1950s of higher-yielding hybrid varieties of maize, *bajra* and *jowar*. In all cases, the availability of controlled irrigation water and the application of the package of modern inputs, especially very high doses of chemical fertilizer and pesticides, were essential preconditions for realizing maximum yield potential. By November 1965, the Food Ministry was ready with a full-blown version of the New Strategy: in essence it called for the implementation of a High-yielding Varieties Programme in districts that had already been selected for intensive development under the IADP and IAAP schemes, following the same extension concepts embodied in the Package Programme.

The missing link in the chain of agrarian production was soon identified in the person of the 'progressive farmer'.[26] These link men, with some measure of literacy, contacts with the world outside and enough status within the local society to arouse the trust of their fellow men, caught the imagination of the bureaucracy responsible for producing results. Soon, in various parts of the country, the liaison of the progressive farmer and the VLW (Village Level Workers, also known as *gram sahayaks*) produced a critical mass which cut through the local 'bottlenecks' – to use a favourite jargon of Indian planners – and the Green Revolution was born. The statistics of food production tell the story of the agrarian political economy in a nutshell. By 1966–71, food production had increased massively. In 1972–75, bad weather conditions led to the decline of food production to 101 million tons, causing imports of 7.41 million tons. By 1975–76, however, thanks to good weather, production went up to 116 million tons.

The Green Revolution was marked by the introduction of a new group of actors – the *bullock capitalists* – into the political arena. Agrarian entrepreneurs, these farmers from the middle and backward castes quickly learnt to combine their numbers, social network and political contacts to garner power in local institutions. They formed farmers' parties and movements to promote their interests – in subsidized energy, loans, agrarian inputs and slowing down the trends towards collective farming.[27]

Overall, the Green Revolution is considered to have been a mixed legacy. On the positive side, it certainly contributed to the improvement of the quality and quantity of food supply, self-sufficiency and the Public Distribution System.[28] On the negative side, increasing volumes of agrarian subsidies have become a drain on the public exchequer. Increasing prosperity on the part of the rural rich and their lifestyles based on conspicuous consumption has widened the gap between the rural haves and have-nots, exacerbating class conflict, both of the right and the left. However, *kisan* movements cutting across regions and social classes have mitigated the worst. Finally, with technological progress has come its pathology – in the form of growing pollution, terminal decline of local resources and degradation of local biodiversity.[29] Most of all, many on the left argue that the conviction that agrarian problems of productivity can be solved through technology and massive investment distracted attention from the imperative of land reform.

The dilemma of democratic land reform

The post-colonial state and popular democracy, with their commitment to fundamental rights to property on the one hand and social justice and empowerment of marginal groups on the other, have been both a stimulant for and a constraint on land reform in India. In view of its centrality to India's political discourse, land reform is one of the most discussed problems of India's political economy. Every major author or policy maker active in this field has felt obliged to respond to the reality of millions of insecure, indebted peasants under the constant threat of a bad monsoon, illness, and pestilence, by offering a diagnosis and a solution. Unlike capital, land is static, concrete and visible, giving the impression of being more accessible to political control from above. As such, land reforms, already on the agenda of the colonial government and the Congress movement that opposed it, have attracted the attention of all shades of reformers. This section is intended to define the concept, to summarize the measures taken, engage in an evaluation and develop broad questions about the political gains and economic costs of land reforms in India.

Though the rhetoric of land reform in India has consistently revolved around the slogan of 'land to the tiller', in practice land reform has meant more than the transfer of property rights to the poor. The broad range of meanings grouped together under this generic concept has included legislation aimed at (1) *tenancy reform*, (2) *abolition of intermediaries*, (3) *ceiling* on landholdings and (4) *consolidation* of landholdings. On the whole, however, India's land reforms have involved only limited efforts at land redistribution, implemented mostly through ceilings on land holding. Agrarian land belongs to the State List under the federal division of powers. As such, state legislation aimed at regulating tenancies, improving tenurial security and reducing the power of absentee landlords and intermediaries has been the most common method.

Independent India inherited a complex and diverse system of land tenure from the British Raj. Das (in Pushpendra and Sinha, 2000) reports that in 1947, Indian agricultural land was administered under three systems: *zamindari* (57 per cent) – *zamindars* were also known as *talukdars*, *jagirdars* and *malguzars* – *raiyatwari* (38 per cent) and *mahalwari* (5 per cent). Between the *zamindars* and the tillers, there was a layer of intermediaries numbering up to 50 in some places.[30] These *zamindars* used to collect several times the intended revenue, though they had a fixed tax to pay to the government which was permanently fixed as land tax back in 1793 (rack renting). This generated, in practice, a system which looked as shown in Box 7.1.

Life for most people engaged in agriculture under colonial rule was precarious at the best of times. In addition to the exploitation by landlords and intermediaries, the money-lender was always in the background. What was left to the actual cultivator after the claims of various superior rights holders were satisfied was subject to the collection of unpaid debt by money-lenders. The mechanism for enforcement of this withdrawal of the great bulk of the product from the primary producers was provided by the new body of written law, the courts, the police, the promulgation of ordinances and so forth.

Box 7.1 Lines of control and exploitation in the *zamindari* system

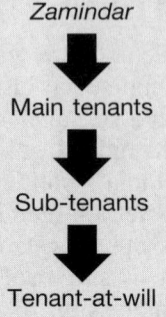

Zamindar

Main tenants

Sub-tenants

Tenant-at-will

Source: Drawn by author.

The main goal of land reform after Independence was to generate both growth and justice in agriculture, as indeed in all areas of the economy. This meant, in practice, to establish a direct relationship between the state and the cultivator and to provide the latter with optimal conditions of production. Following Independence, the autonomy to initiate legislation and enforce the new order, in view of the fundamentally political nature of the enterprise and the diversity of conditions prevailing in Indian States, ensured that there would be significant regional variations. The success of land reforms depended on a number of factors. In States like Kerala where the potential beneficiaries – the rural masses – were highly organized, politicized and capable of fighting for their rights, there was a measure of success. However, as subsequent developments showed, under the watchful eyes of the Supreme Court defending the right to property, and the central government making sure that political unrest would not reach a level which would obstruct lawful governance, the autonomy of the States to undertake land reforms was quite limited.[31]

Following Independence, all States of India undertook legislation for the abolition of *zamindari*. The main consequence of *zamindari* abolition was the creation of a new class of 'rich peasants', mostly from the cultivating castes, who took advantage of the provision for resumption of land under 'personal cultivation' (i.e. transfer of property – *bhumidari* – rights to superior tenants) to displace tenants-at-will (inferior tenants). In addition, the capital that they gained through compensation helped them further consolidate their hold on the agricultural operations and went into the making of the Green Revolution and bullock capitalists at a later stage.

The Rudolphs (1987, p. 314) describe the key policies that evolved in response to the double challenge of growth and justice, resulting from the interplay of local conditions and state and central legislation. The first policy regime, characterizing the agricultural strategy of the Nehru era (1947–64), consisted of land reform (mostly, the abolition of intermediaries between the state and the peasant) and the centrally sponsored and funded Community Development Programme that saw the whole village as its unit of operation and strived to improve general welfare. The second strategy, geared mostly towards improving agrarian productivity through new technology which began soon after Nehru's death, continued till 1971. The third strategy, focused on basic needs and income redistribution, began with Mrs Gandhi's *garibi hatao* (abolish poverty) appeal in the 1971 parliamentary and 1972 State assembly elections. The fourth was launched in 1977 by the Janata Party's agrarian-oriented government. It emphasized rural employment and asset creation, paving the way for agri-business. However, the rhetoric of income redistribution and nostalgia for agrarian socialism continued to be voiced by vote-hungry politicians and intellectuals of the left, and got a boost with the return of Indira Gandhi to power in 1980. The contemporary situation is a combination of all four of these strategies.

In the absence of a large-scale rural exodus and of manufacturing to absorb surplus labour, a consensus has grown that India will need to solve the problem of rural poverty on the land itself. Hence, 'land reform' continues to be on the political agenda still, after six decades of Independence. However, the consequences of various forms of land reform have left their stamp on the rural landscape. The attempt to abolish intermediaries has generated some surplus land that has been redistributed (Diagrams 7.4a and 7.4b). However, the overall consequence of reforms appears to have been a general reduction in the number of large holdings and an increase in the number of small holdings. As such, while reforms might have had some effect on poverty reduction, it is not clear if they have also contributed to the growth of agrarian productivity. As a unit of production, one learns from the limitations emerging from the Green Revolution, land has a particular limitation. Beyond a particular point, at a given level of technology, investment in agriculture reaches a point of decreasing marginal utility. While industry also has a point beyond which additional investment brings in lower levels of output, factories can take in more investment than agriculture before diminishing returns set in. Besides, the technological environment in factory production is more dynamic, justifying the case for investment to be made on a regular basis.

The debate between the advocates of land reforms and agri-business as the better solution for India continues. The First Five Year Plan expressed the commitment to redistributive land reforms in terms of a recommendation to the state to 'reduce disparities in wealth and income, eliminate exploitation, provide security for tenant and workers, and finally, promise equality of status and opportunity to different sections of the rural population'.[32] These sentiments have been echoed by all successive plan documents. The fact that *implementation* turned out to be the fatal weakness in the causal chain built into the structure and process of plans did not deter the Planning Commission, given an opportunity, from coming up with similar recommendations. The key point here remains that, thanks to democratic empowerment and India's half-hearted land reforms, the message of a right to ownership, if not the capacity to make a profit out of the little parcels of land, has certainly spread all over India. However, this has also created the phenomenon of 'poor' land-owners – people owning small parcels of land – who cannot put their land to profitable use, either because they do not have the means or because they do not see the need and hold on to their land merely as an investment, letting it lie fallow rather than rent it out, for fear of losing ownership altogether.

The debate on land reform has now become a part of the larger issue of the pace of liberalization of the economy. Some suggest that a more rational strategy for India's agrarian policy would be to create legal mechanisms that would facilitate renting out, so that one can retain tenancy in a rational and efficient form, while trying to avoid its exploitative dimensions. Seen from this angle, Indian agriculture can be positioned not necessarily as a drain on her economy but as a potential strength.[33]

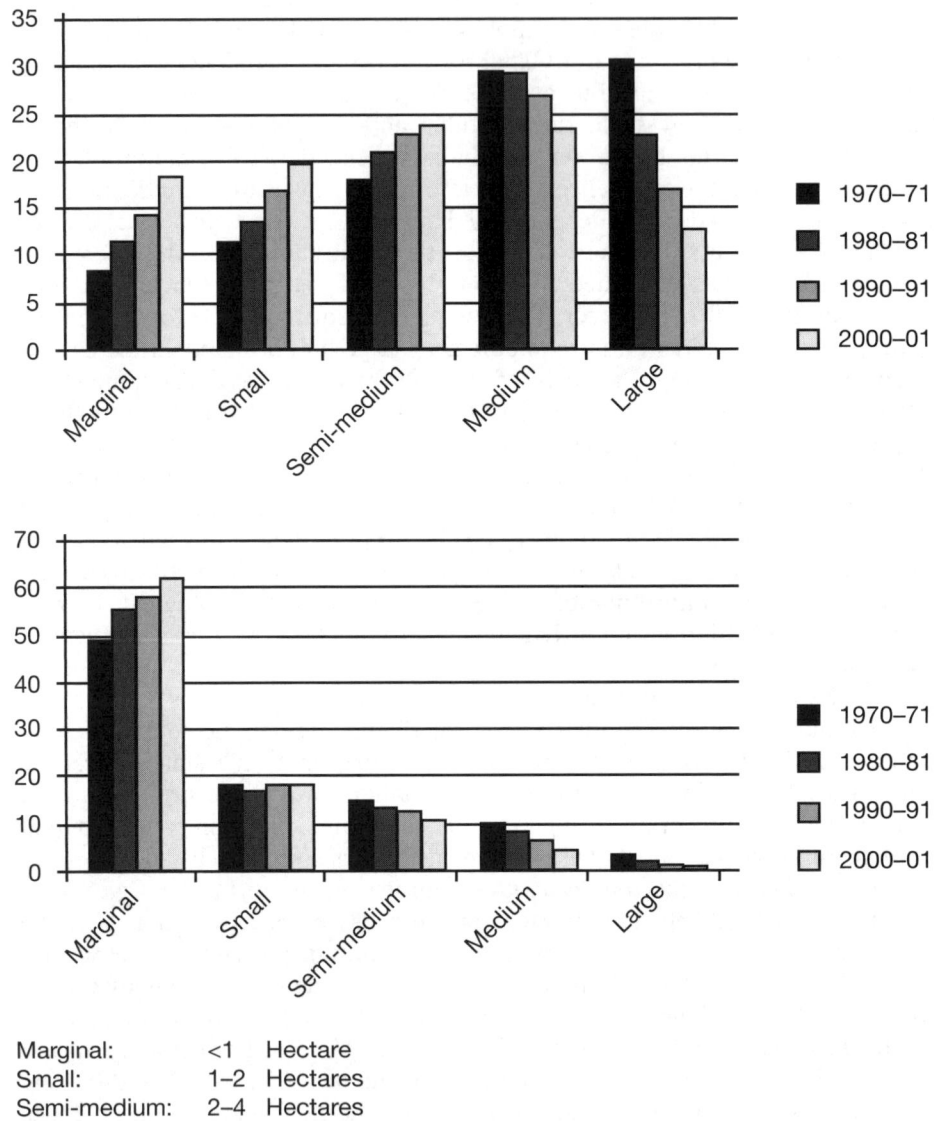

Marginal: <1   Hectare
Small: 1–2 Hectares
Semi-medium: 2–4 Hectares
Medium: 4–10 Hectares
Large: >10 Hectares

Diagram 7.4a (*Top*) India – area of holdings (per cent of population)
Source: Tata Services Ltd, *Statistical Outline of India, 1996–1997*, p. 59.

Diagram 7.4b (*Bottom*) India – number of holdings (per cent of population)
Source: Tata Services Ltd, Department of Economics and Statistics.

Democracy and liberalization of the economy

Though as a policy the liberalization of the non-agricultural sectors of the economy has been far more successful than land reform, both have some strong parallels. There is the same complexity of conceptualization, polarization of opinion around them, and comparable uncertainty about their pace, sustainability and prognosis. Ubiquitous signs of liberalization hide the fact of its inner complexity both as a concept and as a process. Essentially indicative of a culture of enterprise rather than of control, the policy of liberalization shows substantial reduction in direct state control in terms of administered prices and regulation of economic activity. It promotes the *market* rather than *state*, i.e. lowering bureaucratic control as the main basis of economic decision-making. Liberalization leads to the rationalization and reduction of taxes, not necessarily on income but on enterprises. In addition, it leads to the privatization of state assets, down-sizing public sector undertaking (PSUs); easing rules for foreign direct investment (FDI), allowing non-residents to hold domestic financial assets, providing easier access to multinational corporations (MNCs) and to foreign commercial borrowing by domestic firms, and allowing domestic residents to hold foreign assets. Further, politically controversial aspects of liberalization indicate the need to remove subsidies, restrictions on foreign exchange, travel, import and export and fiscal deficits, and to generally increase competition. Further, liberalization entails cutting back on public investment and certain types of social expenditure, trade liberalization, a shift from quantitative restriction on tariffs and, typically, reduction of export subsidies and moving to market-determined exchange rates.

The chronology of development policy since Independence shows that rather than being a sudden, radical innovation, the tendency to let the market play a salient role in India's economic development existed right from the outset. The period 1947–51 witnessed a policy debate within the Congress party with regard to the role of the market in India's economy. The advocates of the market did not lose outright to those keen to give the state the leading role in development. In the end, the mixed economy, strongly supported by Prime Minister Nehru, emerged victorious, but it did not exclude private enterprise from participating in national development. An implicit state–private sector partnership emerged during 1952–63 which saw the implementation of a model of development based on planning, political control over resources, import substitution, the public sector, and industry as the 'leading sector'.

There was a discernible shift to the right during 1963–69 when the policy debate was revived, and the rise of the Green Revolution marked a new, distinctive phase in India's political economy. The years 1969–73 witnessed a populist surge under the leadership of Indira Gandhi. However, once she consolidated her power, the tendency to let market forces assert themselves slowly set in. Even under the shadow of the National Emergency of 1975–77, there was, despite the radical rhetoric, a surreptitious and incremental liberalization. The Janata Party coalition government, which came to power following the electoral defeat of Indira Gandhi in 1977, once again saw the conflict of liberalism, socialism and Gandhism. The government fell back on the 1956 industrial policy resolution. Token emphasis was given to agriculture, cottage industries, employment generation and poverty alleviation. Indira Gandhi's return in 1980 brought back the commitment to economic development through industrialization. But cautious liberalization was swallowed up by bureaucratic inertia. However, surreptitious liberalization continued once Indira Gandhi was back in power (1980–84). Under Rajiv Gandhi, Indira's son and successor as Prime Minister, the policy of liberalization became explicit, though, at the level of implementation, it tended to be 'half hearted', and lasted from 1985 to 1991.[34] The initiative to liberalize India's economy took the final leap towards becoming a full-fledged policy of the government of India under the Congress Prime Minister Narasimha Rao. Following the massive changes in the law in 1991, India has developed a steady, bi-partisan consensus on the goals of liberalization, but with discernible differences on the pace of reform.

The government of Narasimha Rao, constituted in 1991 as a minority government after the Congress (I) won 226 seats in the Lok Sabha in the June election following the assassination of Rajiv Gandhi, is usually given credit for the initial push towards extensive liberalization of the economy. India was then running a current account deficit of around $10 billion. Foreign exchange reserves were down to two weeks of imports despite an IMF loan of $1.8 billion in January 1991. The credibility of India's financial strength had reached rock bottom, and commercial borrowing had become impossible. Inflation was running at an annual rate of 13 per cent and the inflow of foreign currency from non-resident Indians had been reversed. The crisis had been simmering since the mid-1980s with the government relying on unsustainable levels of foreign and domestic borrowing. It was brought to a crisis point by the Iraqi invasion of Kuwait in August 1990 resulting in a rise in the price of oil. The Janata government of V.P. Singh and the successor 'lame duck' government of Chandra Shekhar failed to take action commensurate with the rapidly growing crisis. Immediate drastic action, including a large devaluation and deflationary fiscal measures were essential to prevent default by securing the cooperation of officials, donors and lenders. Many countries have been forced to take similar measures when the borrowing that they relied on dried up. But the almost simultaneous announcement (by a minority government) of a long-run programme of deregulation and liberalization is not so common and calls for some comment.[35]

A key element in the reform package was the New Industrial Policy (NIP), announced in July 1991. The NIP abolished industrial licensing for all but a select list of 18 sensitive industries; removed asset limits for companies that used to fall under the domain of MRTP – Monopoly and Restrictive Trade Practices – and eliminated phased manufacturing programmes. Further, it eased location requirements for industries; promised 'automatic' permissions for foreign direct investment up to 51 per cent; increased foreign equity limits from a maximum of 40 per cent to 51 per cent; created a special board to negotiate with the top 40 to 50 international firms to invest in India; and developed incentives for small-scale industry and promised to begin disinvestments in the public sector.[36]

This had come to be the case in India by July 1991. The change of 'mind-set', to use a fashionable cliché, during the previous five years, had been remarkable, although it was also remarkably slow to come. For nearly 20 years any mention of South Korea or Taiwan resulted in signs of amazement that anyone might think that India could learn from such small economies. It was more than a decade since China's liberalizing reforms could be seen to be highly successful. But at last, the total collapse of the Russian communist system must have convinced many people that a highly regulated economy with centralized planning was not a model to copy.

Is liberalization irreversible? The failed attempt by the Tatas to set up a factory to produce the Nano – reputedly the world's cheapest small car – in Singur in West

Bengal because of trenchant opposition by displaced peasants, mobilized by parties opposed to the Left Front government of West Bengal, holds a cautionary lesson for the advocates of liberalization in India. The forces opposed to rapid liberalization today are the Swadeshi Jagran Manch, an umbrella organization with core support from the RSS, the main labour unions, rich peasants and the left parties. The question that arises is whether there is a national consensus behind liberalization and how to interpret the political objection to SEZs – Special Economic Zones – where specific facilities like loans at advantageous rates, infrastructure facilities and some relaxation of India's stringent labour laws are made available to entrepreneurs. Generally speaking, however, while the emphasis on the pace and the choice of location varies, there is broad bi-partisan support for the direction of liberalizations as one could see in case of the recent bill to liberalize insurance.

Globalization of India's economy

As in the case of liberalization, democracy has turned out to be both an incentive for and an obstacle to the integration of India's domestic economy with the global market. Just as in the case of liberalization, the issue raises the same questions about the definition of the concept, its perception by the Indian people and the pace of its implementation. Globalization is of course much more than merely an economic process because mere integration of the economy of a nation with the international market economy cannot necessarily be equated with globalization. That, as we have already seen in Chapter 2, is exactly what happened under colonial rule. A more appropriate definition of the process of globalization should necessarily draw on the values and interests of a much wider range of stakeholders than merely the integration of capital markets. Finally, one should ask if globalization is a mixed blessing, and what might be appropriate for India in an inadequately integrated and poorly governed world.

With the radical reforms in legislation that the government of Narasimha Rao introduced in 1991, India took the first definitive steps in the direction of liberalization of her economy and its integration with the international market economy. However, in spite of the robust performance of her economy, there are many in India who are unsure about the future.[37]

Definition and measurement of globalization

Many economists measure the concept as the ratio of trade to GDP. The World Bank, which defines it in terms of the *openness index* (trade to GDP ratio) (see Diagram 7.5), believes that the progress of India is 'slow but in the right direction'. The Bank recommends that India should stay the course and accelerate the pace of integration of her economy with the world market through *reforms* and *good governance*. However, the international financial crisis of 2008 has brought back some of the initial resistance to the integration of the Indian economy with the international market, voiced particularly by the political parties of the left. There is some resistance on the part of India's left and trade unions who fear job losses. Sections of the cultural right are against further integration of India's economy with the international economy out of a fear of losing autonomy.

Liberalization was an elite-initiated policy with little popular support or knowledge at the time of its original inception: it certainly was so after a full term in office by

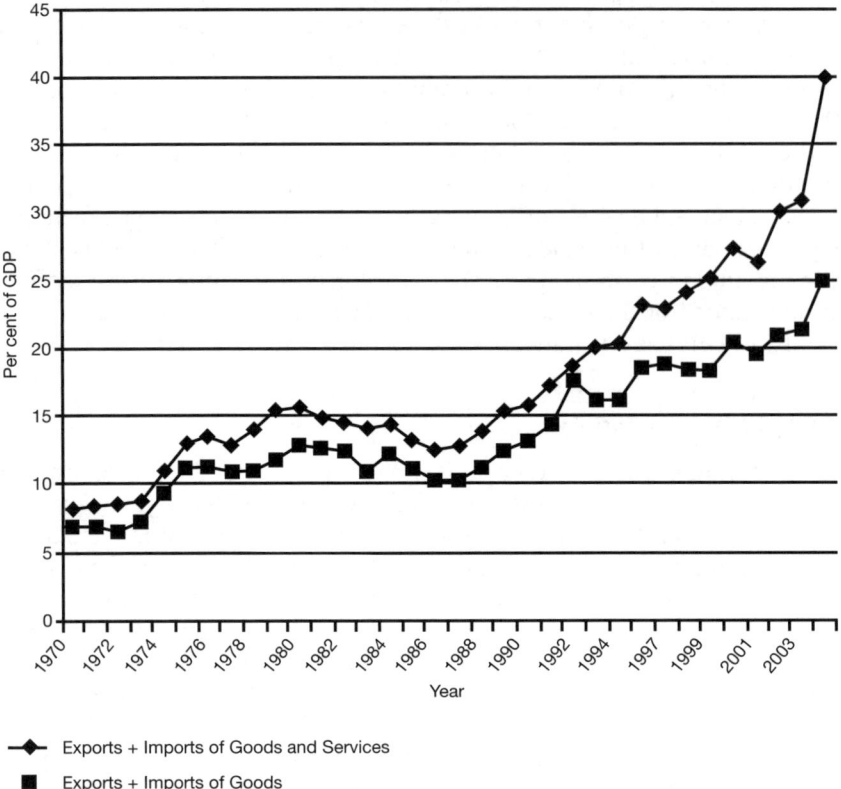

Exports + Imports of Goods and Services

■ Exports + Imports of Goods

Diagram 7.5 Openness index
Source: *World Development Indicators*, World Bank.

the Rao government which made it the cornerstone of its politics. Early responses to the initiative, measured by the 1996 survey of the Indian population, show the lack of majority support for both liberalization of the economy and its integration with the international economy, particularly through the agency of multinational corporations. In this survey (see Table 7.2 and Table 7.3), only about a fifth of the population approved of the policy of integration with the international market economy, particularly with regard to open access to multinationals, and 37.3 per cent were opposed to this policy. Roughly two-fifths of the population were not aware of it or considered it so far removed from everyday life that they had no opinion on the issue. However, strong support for this form of liberalization did exist within some vocal and articulate sections of the population, namely, the higher secondary- and college-educated, urban, upper-class people and the high achievers. The second question, 'Government companies should be given into private hands. Do you agree or disagree with this?', was asked to test popular opinion on the other important aspect of liberalization, namely, privatization. The results show a marginal increase in popular support *both* for liberalization and against it, while the percentage of those without an opinion on the issue has gone down, indicating a growing polarization of opinion in India.

The contrast between the reality of India's economic policy and popular opinion is striking. Compared to the past, India has emerged as an economic giant, and the

Table 7.2 No free trade for foreign companies (in per cent)

Do you ...	1996	2004
Disagree	21.8	30.1
Don't Know/No Opinion	41.1	31.1
Agree	37.1	38.8

Source: National Election Survey, CSDS (Delhi) 1996, 2004.

Table 7.3 Privatize government companies (in per cent)

Do you ...	1996	2004
Disagree	34.5	46.2
Don't Know/No Opinion	42.2	30.2
Agree	23.3	23.6

Source: National Election Survey, CSDS (Delhi) 1996, 2004.

high rate of growth has been sustained over the past two decades. Major change in legislation has made it easier for Indian entrepreneurs to collaborate with the international market. However, the overall perception of the twin processes of privatization and globalization that made it possible in the first place remains negative. This shows the complex interaction between state, society and market in the context of a post-colonial society. The contrast between the patterns of support and opposition to liberalization shows the deeper dimensions of the problem.

Support for globalization comes from international capital, on the look-out for best investments. Indian high-tech industry such as IT and other export-oriented sectors and India's skilled manpower looking for foreign employment also favour rapid integration with the international market economy. Many have already learnt how to apply a form of 'putting out' – as one can see in the case of tomato and green pea cultivation in Punjab – in order to take the maximum advantage of local conditions such as skilled manpower, lower wage rates, climate and subsidies offered by the regional governments, and connectivity and transport facilities that help link supply and demand. Citing the Chinese example, these advocates of globalization argue that the process can also become an instrument through which to challenge the exclusive Western domination of the international economy.

The Indian author Gurcharan Das argues in the same vein that the integration of parts of the Indian market with consumers abroad – be it in the service industry or handicrafts – has brought new resources, technology and hope for a rapid improvement of conditions.[38] The combination of new technology and entrepreneurship can help entire societies make strides in economic development. However, there is deep resistance as well, which comes from India's public sector, some private sector concerns which fear foreign competition, and the farm lobby which fears the loss of domestic subsidies and competition from abroad. These strident voices, avidly mobilized as part of the electoral campaigns by practically all political parties, act as a brake on rapid liberalization. In the process, the fact that globalization stands for the free movement of ideas and commodities across national frontiers and can, thus, become an instrument of challenge against western hegemony gets lost in the minutiae of current political coalitions and their links to external powers, national issues like farmers' suicides, farm subsidies, labour legislation and international financial crisis.

Poised between *swadeshi* and internet, India has the potential to become a 'bridging power' in the next millennium. It has certainly reinforced the eagerness of a part of Indian society, more among the privileged than among the poorer sections of the population, to enjoy the commodities and lifestyles that one has come to identify with the affluent West. But much more overwhelming is the evidence of resistance from those likely to be worse off – at least in the short run – on account of the policies of privatization and the integration of the internal market with the aggressive profit-oriented corporate culture of multinational companies. Several NGOs are at the forefront of this form of resistance and critical discussion of the agenda of globalization. In a society where the right to participate is taken seriously and popular support has become the sole basis of legitimacy, such resistance is bound to contribute to transparent, effective, legitimate and sustainable globalization. India, with her continued commitment to *Panchasheela*, her resilient democracy and multicultural society and with her new-found economic and military power, as Khilnani (2005) argues, can become a 'bridge power' in a multi-polar world, able to ease the transition into a properly globalized world based on capital market integration, shared values, and a global civil society of stakeholders.

Mass poverty and India's 'new' political economy

The issue of mass poverty brings back, once again, the core issue of India's political economy, namely, growth vs. redistribution. Scholarly opinion remains divided. Many critics of the Indian model of development consider the continued existence of mass poverty as evidence of the shortcomings of Indian democracy and the political economy of development. Others point in the direction of the relative improvements in India's infrastructure, GDP and rate of growth as a sign of progress. In theoretical and methodological terms, mass poverty raises issues of incredible complexity, pitting quantitative methods against the qualitative, and problems of politics and public policy against the moral issue of poverty in the midst of plenty. The issue raises a host of questions – specific to the Indian case – as well as problems of cross-cultural significance. First and foremost among these is how successful India has been in reducing poverty. This question, in turn, raises the broader question of how to measure poverty. Is it objective and universal, or is poverty a state of mind, dependent on local conditions, culture and context?

The analysis of poverty in India uses both objective and subjective measures. The most important of the objective measures is the headcount ratio (HCR = $q/n \times 100$, where q is the number of persons below a pre-defined poverty norm, called the Poverty Line, and n is the total population). Yet another example is the Gini-coefficient which compares the actual distribution of income in the population to an ideal, egalitarian standard. These *objective* measures include income, possessions (e.g. land, enduring goods), food consumption and human resources such as education, health and access to infrastructure.[39] The *subjective* or qualitative measures attach more importance to perception, and the social construction of the self. How the 'poor' themselves think about their financial situation becomes the leading criterion of measurement in this case.[40]

Visible symbols of unequal distribution of wealth – the run-down infrastructure of cities, shanty towns, beggars and reports of farmers' suicides in the media on the one hand and the lifestyles of India's nouveaux riches – inevitably lead to a China/India comparison where the former comes off as significantly more successful in combating mass poverty. The contrast, significant as it is, needs to be put in context. While the Chinese record of lifting about 400 million people out of poverty in the span of one generation is not contested, one needs nevertheless to remember that the Chinese path to poverty reduction has been marked by large-scale killings – in the great Maoist campaigns such as the Great Leap Forward and the Cultural Revolution – and famines. India's performance, though not as dramatic as China's, is nevertheless respectable. In terms of percentage, though there is some controversy between Indian and external measurements, the fact remains that the poverty ratio has radically come down from nearly half the population to little over a quarter in the span of about two decades. In terms of numbers, since liberalization began, India has been able to reduce the number of people under the poverty line by about 100 million (Diagrams 7.6a and 7.6b). In contrast to China, where the combination of authoritarian policies and the expansion of manufacturing have achieved the breakthrough, in India the progress has been achieved through the policies of redistribution and market forces.

The subjective measurement of poverty reinforces the picture that emerges from the objective measurement. Whereas about a fifth of the Indian population feel worse off financially compared to before, the rest either manage to hold their own in a rapidly changing economy, or even feel that they have improved their position. A roughly similar situation emerges when people are asked a question about their current financial situation or, for that matter, their prognosis about the state of their finance in a foreseeable future. About a third of the population turn out to be dissatisfied as compared to the rest who are either satisfied with the status quo or expect things to get better.

Further analysis of the survey data makes it possible to establish a socio-demographic profile of the sections of the Indian population who consider themselves winners or losers in the new political economy (Table 7.7). Comparing the findings from 1996 and 2004 one can see that men are more likely to feel satisfied with their financial situation than women. The same is the case with the urban population as compared to the rural. Younger people are more likely to be optimists than pessimists. Educated people see their financial situation in a more optimistic way than the less educated, though it is quite significant that even among the illiterate – usually a reliable indicator of poverty – in the 2004 survey, about 40 per cent expected their financial situation to get better. Two minority communities – Christians and Sikhs – tend to see themselves as better off than the average whereas the opposite is the case with Muslims, though in percentage terms they are not too far behind their Hindu brethren. The upper castes perform better generally though here also there are particular twists in the data. In 2004, only 13 per cent of the scheduled castes saw themselves as satisfied with their financial situation compared to 20 per cent among the upper castes, but when it came to the perception of future financial situation, though the relative gap of about 7 per cent persists, in absolute terms, close to a majority of them saw themselves in the camp of the optimists! Finally, the perception of the financial situation, using a composite measurement of

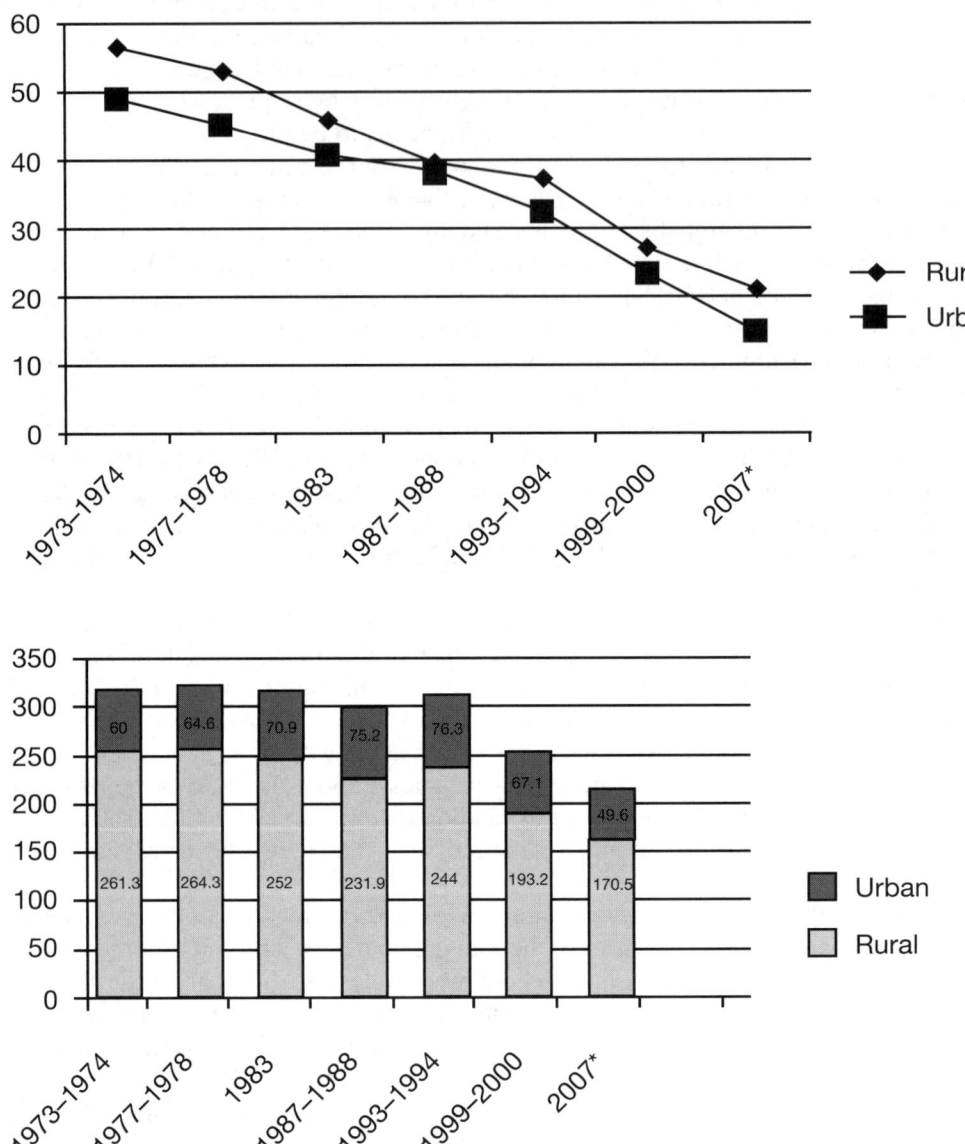

Diagram 7.6a (*Top*) Official poverty estimates (quinquennial surveys): poverty ratio (in per cent)
* Estimate.
Source: Tata Services Limited, Department of Economics and Statistics, Statistical Outline of India 2007–08 (Mumbai: 2008).

Diagram 7.6b (*Bottom*) Official poverty estimates (quinquennial surveys): number of poor
(in millions)
* Estimate.
Source: Tata Services Limited, Department of Economics and Statistics, Statistical Outline of India 2007–08 (Mumbai: 2008), p. 224.

Table 7.4 Financial situation of respondents during the last few years (in per cent)

Situation has . . .	1971	1996	2004
Improved	20.2	29.2	26.5
Same	40.1	53.8	51.1
Worsened	39.7	17.0	19.0
No opinion	–	–	3.4

Source: National Election Survey, CSDS (Delhi) 1971, 1996, 2004.

Table 7.5 Present financial situation of respondents (in per cent)

Respondent is . . .	1971	1996	2004
Satisfied	10.7	28.4	16.0
Somewhat satisfied	28.6	41.2	47.4
Not satisfied	60.7	30.4	33.4
No opinion	–	–	3.2

Source: National Election Survey, CSDS (Delhi) 1971, 1996, 2004.

Table 7.6 Future financial situation of respondents (in per cent)

Situation will . . .	1971	1996	2004
Get better	38.6	47.9	49.2
Remain the same	20.9	27.0	19.4
Get worse	18.8	8.9	6.2
Don't know	21.7	16.2	25.2

Source: National Election Survey, CSDS (Delhi) 1971, 1996, 2004.

the economic class of the respondents that takes into account the ownership of a number of assets, shows the 'very poor' as far less satisfied with their present financial situation both in the 1996 and the 2004 surveys. However, the relative gap between the classes narrows when it comes to the perception of the future: in both surveys, close to 40 per cent of the very poor report an optimistic view of their financial future.

Modest by the standards of the tiger economies of East Asia or China, India's achievements nevertheless question the pessimistic predictions of Moore that saw no possibility of a breakthrough for India within the political and technological constraints that prevailed at the time.[41] Similar sentiments led Dandekar and Rath (1971), at the peak of the period of the populist rhetoric of Indira Gandhi, to suggest that poverty alleviation needed higher taxation and employment generation through public works. True, the new agrarian technology that made the Green Revolution possible have certainly increased the room to manoeuvre of poor democracies struggling against mass poverty. Still, India has yet to lift a lot of people out of poverty, particularly in the countryside. The problem with these people is that they are mostly without saleable skills, and are dependent on subsidies of various kinds for their basic survival. Consequently, radical politics and populist policies of vote-hungry politicians have found a niche in these sections of the Indian population.

Table 7.7 Perception of financial satisfaction by socio-demographic groups (in per cent)

Groups	1996			2004		
	Financial situation has improved	*Satisfied with present financial situation*	*Financial situation will get better*	*Financial situation has improved*	*Satisfied with present financial situation*	*Financial situation will get better*
All Groups	**29.2**	**28.4**	**47.9**	**26.5**	**16.0**	**49.2**
Gender						
Men	31.6	31.0	50.5	28.7	17.0	51.8
Women	26.7	25.7	45.3	24.3	15.1	47.0
Locality						
Rural	26.6	25.8	45.1	25.8	15.7	48.2
Urban	37.3	36.6	56.9	29.8	17.7	54.7
Age						
<= 25 years	32.9	29.9	52.5	30.2	17.0	55.3
26–35 years	31.2	28.0	50.1	28.9	16.6	51.8
36–45 years	27.4	27.5	45.7	24.8	15.4	49.2
46–55 years	25.9	29.1	46.9	24.1	14.9	45.9
56 years +	24.3	27.4	40.1	22.5	16.1	41.2
Education						
Illiterate	22.3	22.0	39.5	19.6	11.8	39.7
Up to middle	27.8	27.1	47.5	26.0	16.1	51.5
College, no degree	39.9	38.7	60.0	34.0	20.8	58.5
College +	49.0	47.4	69.4	41.0	22.9	61.1
Religion						
Hindu	29.1	28.6	47.9	27.4	16.7	50.2
Muslim	26.6	25.9	45.2	21.1	12.6	45.8
Christian	34.6	31.2	59.1	24.0	9.6	51.0
Sikh	48.4	34.1	52.4	32.9	24.8	49.9
Caste						
Scheduled caste	24.5	28.6	47.9	22.3	12.8	45.6
Scheduled tribe	25.3	25.9	45.2	24.9	11.2	49.9
OBC	25.7	31.2	59.1	25.8	15.3	49.1
Upper caste	36.4	34.1	52.4	30.7	20.2	52.2
Class						
Very poor	18.1	17.7	37.5	17.5	10.6	41.9
Poor	27.5	25.8	46.7	24.6	14.0	49.0
Middle	34.6	43.0	54.3	34.9	21.0	56.3
Upper class	51.2	50.2	68.7	42.9	29.2	61.1

Source: National Election Survey, CSDS (Delhi) 1996, 2004.

As a matter of fact, the struggle between the market and the state – driven by the concern for social justice and populist politics – has been characteristic of Indian development right from the outset. India's Five Year Plans directed public funds towards private enterprise and infrastructure building, not employment generation. Nehru's model – import substitution, industrialization, modernization of agriculture, and planning – was a model based on the 'felt needs'[42] and the trickle-down theory of development. So *zamindari* abolition was followed by less enthusiastic but not very effective land reforms. Cooperative village management became the preferred jargon. By the late 1960s, the land situation was getting polarized. Bullock capitalists on the one side and radicalized peasantry on the other were producing an environment many thought to be ripe for a Maoist revolution.

The split in the CPM, rise of Naxalite violence and political instability in many Indian States indicated the deeper problems of the Indian model of development. But the much heralded revolution did not materialize. What followed instead was a spate of radical legislation, nationalization and some conspicuous programmes under the 20 point programme, e.g. land to the landless, homestead land, and target group programmes. These measures were introduced by Indira Gandhi during the eighteen-month Emergency. Many of these social-democratic policies were put on hold when the Janata Party came to power after the end of the Emergency and the fall of Mrs Gandhi. Rich peasant parties dominated. Then came the stagnation of the late 1970s, and finally, the 'half-hearted' liberalization of the 1980s. Current poverty policy straddles between target approach, subsidies, special election-oriented policies by State governments and the programmes launched by NGOs and activist groups.

The poor in India have neither disappeared nor formed themselves into a political party or movement, but continue to exist as a demand group whose presence is a brake on rapid and radical liberalization. These demand groups have expressed themselves through sporadic violence which has spurred the state – acting through the union, State and local governments, central agencies and NGOs – to generate anti-poverty policies and programmes. Following Independence, a centre-dominated developmental model and a centralized federal system operated in a complementary fashion. The constitution provided for several methods to transfer resources from the centre to the States, such as assigning in full the net proceeds of certain taxes and duties like stamp duties, duties on toilet and medicinal preparations, estate duty on non-agricultural property, duties of succession to property other than non-agricultural land, and taxes on railway fares and freight; compulsory sharing of certain taxes like income tax and permissive sharing of taxes like excise. The *Finance Commission*, appointed by the President for a duration of five years, and the Planning Commission (whose recommendations are discussed by the National Development Council) are responsible for the sharing of revenues.[43] There are two conflicting principles that govern these transfers: should the hardworking and productive be rewarded, or should the poor and backward be helped? Once again, we are faced with the dual challenge for political economy in the context of a poor, post-colonial, democratic state which must balance the conflicting principles of accumulation and legitimacy. The discretionary grants-in-aid are made by the central cabinet; there are no fixed criteria for these.

The policies of liberalization which were launched in 1991 to start dismantling the draconian rules of the command economy required a new regime – informal arrangements among sets of actors – to provide coordination in a rapidly changing financial environment. By scaling down the involvement of the state in the developmental process and thereby reducing the functions of the central government, the process of liberalization risked generating opposition from the poorer State governments which were dependent on central grants and subsidies. However, in practice it has not been so. Jenkins even argues that part of the momentum for further liberalization actually comes from India's regions. The removal of subsidies and hand-outs has not produced an anti-reform coalition of left parties which must have been aware of the lack of popular support for reform. However, the effective management of the transition from the command economy to the market economy has helped India avoid the chaos that has blighted liberalization in post-communist states of Eastern Europe and Russia.[44]

That poverty will continue to be a salient issue in the deliberations over economic policy in the foreseeable future is more than likely. The percentage of people who supported the need for a ceiling on property and social control over ownership was a staggering 70 per cent of the population in the 1996 survey, and this remains almost unchanged in 2004. Even more significantly, these sentiments seem to be almost equally spread out among different social strata, testifying to the basic communitarian character of the Indian political system.

Conclusion

The political context and the technological environment in which the initial design of India's political economy evolved have changed substantially over the course of the past decades. The dismantling of India's command economy and the revolution in the technology of communication, particularly the internet, have helped India jump into the ranks of main players in this field. Harnessing these new technological inventions has been possible because of the innovative capacity of the structure and process of India's political economy. With regard to agriculture in particular, India, like other developing countries, has had access to the fortuitous invention of the HYV – the high-yielding variety 'miracle seed' – which made the breakthrough in food production possible in the 1960s. However, poverty still persists and the dilemma between the need for rapid growth and the imperative of social justice still mark the process of development in India.

The annual budget for the financial year that the UPA government presented in February 2008 to India's parliament provides some insights into how the state seeks to reconcile the exigencies of growth and need for short-term welfare, linked to the chances of re-election.[45] The thresholds for income tax were raised from Rs110,000 (US$2,800) to Rs150,000 for men and Rs180,000 for women. The peak customs duty was left unchanged but the central value added tax rate was reduced from 16 per cent to 14 per cent. The measures to accelerate growth and respond to the financial crisis were supplemented with attempts to promote long-term investment and short-term welfare. The allocation for Bharat Nirman, a rural infrastructure development plan, was to be raised to Rs313 billion, and the National Rural Employment Guarantee Scheme was to be implemented in all districts of the country with a budget provision of Rs160 billion. The government committed itself to increasing funds for education and undertaking institutional measures to boost exchange-traded currency and bond markets. Most significant of all, in response to the crisis affecting India's farming sector which reportedly led to 17,000 farmers' suicides in 2007, the government allocated the sum of US$15 billion as a one-off loan waiver for farmers.

The careful balancing of the policies geared to growth, investment and electoral politics has been succinctly summarized by the Economist Intelligence Unit.

> Large spending increases on health, education and rural infrastructure are part of the government's strategy to spread the benefits of economic growth to India's poor. Another priority is to reduce inflationary pressures, including cuts in import and fuel excise duties. However, efforts to liberalize the economy will be limited by the practicalities of coalition politics and by the Congress's focus on subsidizing the rural sector.[46]

The minor fluctuations around a generally cautious policy aimed at sustaining growth and welfare can count on a solid base of financial expertise, economic reserves and managerial talent that characterizes the political economy of India in the twenty-first century. In the euphoria over liberalization one tends to forget that the gains of the first decade of planning, 1951–61, were not inconsiderable. There was a sizeable increase in public investment in major and medium irrigation projects, power, transport, basic industries and higher education. Agricultural production rose by 41 per cent and industrial production by 94 per cent; steel production increased from 1.4 to 3.5 million tons. Domestic savings as a proportion of the Gross Domestic Product (at 1960–61 prices) rose from 10 per cent in 1954–55 to 15 per cent in 1964–65. Life expectancy went up from 40 years in 1951 to 50 years in 1966. By Rosen's conservative estimate, India's total stock of wealth grew by 65 to 75 per cent in the ten-year period after Independence.[47] On the negative side, hard-core poverty and illiteracy were barely touched; growth was sluggish; agriculture stagnated; and a patronage-driven, corrupt party machine (the Quota Permit Raj) spread its tentacles across the length and breadth of the country. The crisis hit in the 1960s, bringing in its wake a populist counter-attack and the authoritarian rule of 1975–77.[48] India got cut off from the dynamism of the international market and wrong priorities caused the under-investment in infrastructure and education which hindered its transition from a subsistence-based economy to one based on skills.

The events and economic statistics of the past two decades provide a contrasting picture to that which preceded it. Whereas some sectors of the Indian economy have taken rapid strides in productivity and competitiveness, social and material vestiges of a backward economy persist in others. The situation is still replete with puzzles and anomalies for those unfamiliar with India.[49]

The combined processes of electoral mobilization, positive discrimination, judicialization and political movements have succeeded in providing the necessary economic space to those who have fallen out of the safety net of the welfare state in the face of the sustained assault of the policies of liberalization. The politics of India's political economy have thus generated enough countervailing forces to sustain citizenship and democratic consolidation. Finally, there is a re-assessment of the role of the state. Even the radical advocates of liberalization assert the importance of the state as the careful observer, and the site of political negotiation among competing groups, and most important of all, as the arbiter of the authoritative allocation of values, and as such, it is a key player in development. The discussion of the state as an international actor, particularly with regard to economic diplomacy, builds on these salient features of India's political economy, as we shall see in the next chapter.

Notes

1 Students of comparative politics from Aristotle to Seymour M. Lipset have argued that a degree of political moderation and equitable distribution of property are necessary conditions for the viability of representative democracy.

2 Moore (1966) was most closely identified with this line of reasoning. This pessimistic prognosis was sustained by Myrdal's concept of the 'soft state' (Myrdal 1968), incapable of taking urgent measures to reform the economy.

3 The chapter also responds to the critics of the Indian model from the left such as Barrington Moore, who could only predict a future of economic stagnation and 'democratic paralysis', as well as the neoliberal critique of socialist planning which may have slowed down growth in the early years after Independence but nevertheless provided the economic basis of democratic consolidation.

4 Purchasing Power Parity is a composite measure that takes into account the local cost of essential services and consumer products. Economists argue that the PPP, rather than the mere monetary equivalent of local incomes in international currencies, is a better indicator of income relative to standards of living.

5 India's economy appears to be withstanding the impact of the global economic crisis.

> India's real GDP is projected [to] grow by seven per cent in financial year 2009–10, which can be partly seen in the signs of recovery in the data available for January 2009, the Centre for the Monitoring Indian Economy (CMIE) said in its monthly review here. Economic think tank CMIE expects the growth rate to climb slowly from around six per cent in the first half [of 2009] to about eight per cent in the second half of the financial year. The global liquidity crisis in late September 2008 has suddenly brought the economy's story of nine per cent growth to a grinding halt. Financial year 2010 would gradually recover from this jolt. . . . While the global economy seems to be getting into a deep crisis, the domestic Indian economy is likely to see a smarter and quicker recovery in the financial year.
>
> 'GDP growth to stabilize at 7 per cent', *The Statesman Weekly*, 28 May 2009, p. 14.

6 India Country Overview April 2010, World Bank. See: www.worldbank.org.in

7 See Johnson (1983) for the concept of the 'developmental' state where the agenda of economic growth was above and beyond the pale of partisan politics.

8 The Indian model of development most identified with Nehru has had sharp critics like Moore (1966) who has described it as 'an out-an-out failure' (p. 395), 'rather long on talk and quite short of development' (p. 407). For a positive evaluation of Nehru's model of development see Dasgupta (1989).

9 See Wall (1978), pp. 88–9.

10 A pejorative epithet, usually implying the tendency of the Congress regime to practise patronage politics. Literally, a regime based on disbursing largesse such as quotas for commodities whose supply is controlled by the government, and giving permits to set up industries or run specific businesses for which government permission is needed. Liberalization has attempted to put an end to this by removing these areas of enterprise from the control of government.

11 *The Economist*, 21–26 January, 1995, p. 7.

12 The *Arthasastra* ('Science of Material Gain') is thought to have been written by Chanakya (also known as Kautilya) in the fourth century BC.

13 When asked in a national opinion survey in 2004 about the financial prospects they expected, 49.2 per cent of the national sample thought their financial conditions would improve, 6.2 per cent thought they would worsen, 19.4 per cent thought they would remain the same and about 25 per cent were not sure. In the same survey, 67.5 per cent thought their vote had an effect on how things are run in the country, compared to 17.5 per cent who thought the opposite. National Election Survey, CSDS, Delhi 2004.

14 Wilbert Moore (1968), p. 366.

15 In their characterization of the state in India, Rudolph and Rudolph (1987) show how it has successfully incorporated some apparently contradictory values in order to create a space where different social groups can periodically negotiate the priorities for the politics of the day.

16 Here, the British legacy is mixed. The original British-made famine acts provided for minimum welfare to the indigent, though it is state inaction that led to the avoidable deaths of three million people in the Bengal famine of 1943.

17 See Chapter 2 for the discussion of these ideological strands and their synthesis as the ideological basis of the Congress party from the 1930s onwards.

18 Commenting on this general problem, Rajiv Gandhi had remarked:

> . . . and what of the iron frame of the system, the administrative . . . services . . . and the myriad functionaries of the state? They have done so much and can do so much more, but as the proverb says there can be no protection if the fence starts eating the crop. This is what has happened. The fence has started eating the crop. We have government servants who do not serve but oppress the poor and the helpless . . . who do not uphold the law . . . but connive with those who cheat the state, and whole legions whose only concern is their private welfare at the cost of society. They have no work ethic, no feeling for the public cause, no involvement in the future of the nation, no comprehension of national goals, no commitment to the values of modern India. They have only a grasping, mercenary outlook, devoid of competence, integrity and commitment. . . .
>
> Prime Minister Rajiv Gandhi, Bombay 28 December, 1985, cited in Pant and Gupta (1990), p. 13.

19 After working in central government for more than 20 years, Ram (1978) framed the following laws of bureaucratic behaviour: (1) never do anything on your own for the first time (i.e. find a precedent), (2) avoid responsibility if you can, (3) pay is a function of the number of hours spent in the office and not that of productivity or achieving results.

20 David Potter, about this attempt to satisfy each of the dominant ideologies:

> That orientation was a weakness. It was widely recognised that successful implementation of development programmes initiated by government required a bureaucracy which was (a) innovative, (b) could bring to bear on local problems a wide range of specialist expertise, and (c) could respond quickly to local demands for such expertise. It was also widely recognised that these characteristics were not 'natural' within the Indian bureaucracy as a whole. Many IAS [Indian Administrative Service] individuals were staunch proponents of development and gave it a high priority. It was even argued that an IAS generalist in district or secretariat, when viewed as an individual, could be considered an effective development man or woman. But to make these points about IAS individuals was to miss the broader consequences of the general administrative tradition which these individuals sustained. What even the most enlightened IAS officers failed to see was that their own tradition resulted in a more general orientation throughout the bureaucracy as a whole that de-emphasised these characteristics which were important for sustained, successful development administration.
>
> Potter (1986), p. 243.

21 Refer to the opinion of the poor about their welfare from Mitra and Singh (2009).

22 Is the 'Green Revolution' yet another example of the Indian penchant for catchy slogans, heady rhetoric or, as Barrington Moore put it, an Indian habit of being tall in talk and short in action? As Frankel (1971) says:

> The phrase 'green revolution' has all the qualities of a good slogan. It is catchy; it simplifies a complex reality; and most important, it carries the conviction that fundamental problems are being solved. Agriculture, it suggests, is being peacefully transformed through the quiet workings of science and technology, reaping the economic gains of modernization while avoiding the social costs of mass upheaval and disorder usually associated with rapid change.
>
> p. V.

23 'The basic assumption of the Community Development Programme . . . has been that the Indian peasant would of his own free will, and because of his "felt needs" immediately adopt technical improvements, the moment he was shown them' (Moore 1966, p. 401). Moore explains why it did not happen that way. '"Felt needs" in any society are in large measure the product of the individual's specific social situation and upbringing. They are created; not simply the gift of nature' (ibid., p. 402).

24 Frankel (1971), p. 3.

25 Fundamentally, the notion of village democracy is a piece of romantic Gandhian nostalgia that has no relevance to modern conditions. The pre-modern Indian village was probably as

much of a petty tyranny as a petty republic; certainly the modern one is such. To democratize the villages without altering property relationships is simply absurd. . . . Finally, the real sources of change, the factors that determine the fate of the peasantry, lie outside the boundaries of the village. Through the ballot box and through their pressure on state and national politics, the peasants can do something about those questions, but not within the framework of village politics.

Moore (1966), p. 394.

26 Frankel (1978), pp. 197–98.

27   At least in the short run, the dominant landed castes were successful in manipulating the majority of subsistence cultivators and landless workers fragmented by vertical factional structures to capture the village institutions. They increased their access to scarce development resources and strengthened their position as strategic intermediaries, linking local markets and power structures to the state and national economic and political systems.

ibid, p. 200.

28 Leaf (1980/81), p. 620.
29 Shiva (1991), p. 200.
30 Moore (1966).
31 The Uttar Pradesh Zamindari Abolition Act (1950), which covered the most populated State of India, was the first act on this subject. However, the manner in which it was passed severely compromised its objectives. The bill was under preparation for a very long time. Since it was debated for years it gave enough opportunity to most of the *zamindars*, *talukdars* and other intermediaries to sell off or dispose of their landed property to near relatives, family-controlled trusts or through *benami* (false-name) transactions. Subsequently, the act was struck down by the High Court of Uttar Pradesh as ultra vires. Consequently, the constitution was amended, for the first time, in early 1951, and the act was incorporated in the Ninth Schedule of the constitution itself, and only thereafter became enforceable. By that time, the political context had changed significantly.
32 First Five Year Plan (1953), p. 178.
33 Once agricultural capitalism gains legitimacy, the next step would be to think of land as *convertible*, depending on the *market opportunity*, and to let the logic of the market spread into lucrative fruits, vegetables and other cash crops like cashew nuts. The Indian producer can then link up with the international market in a competitive way. India can ignore the 'niche-marketing' strategy at her own peril. However, as the successful resistance to the acquisition of agricultural land for the Special Economic Zone in West Bengal shows, the case for land rights of small peasants is far from lost.
34 See the chapter on 'Managing the economy: halfhearted liberalization' in Kohli (1990), pp. 305–38.
35 A crisis is an opportunity for introducing a new style of government pursuing a new model of development when the old style and the old model can convincingly be presented as having led to a disaster. But in a democracy there must also be a sufficient body of influential opinion already convinced or very ready to be convinced of the need for radical change. Jenkins explains the strategies as 'liberalization by stealth', through which Indian elites achieved a policy change. See 'Political skills: introducing reform by stealth', in Jenkins (1999), pp. 172–207.
36 Joshi and Little (1996), pp. 1–2.
37 This, as we can learn from the Nobel prize-winning economist Stiglitz, is also the position of many international experts on globalization.
38 See the chapter on 'A million reformers' in Das (2002), pp. 228–43.
39 Kohli, (Lorenz curve/Gini coefficients, based on land holdings), and NSS-based consumption data Kohli (1987), pp. 82–3.
40 For subjective measurements of poverty please refer to Table 7.3 'Perception of financial satisfaction by socio-demographic groups' in Mitra and Singh (2009), pp. 155–56.
41 Moore (1966), p. 410.
42 Ibid, p. 392.
43 Commenting on the Finance Commission, Austin (1966, p. 220) says that it is a guardian 'of the equitable and fiscally sound distribution of the revenue from the shared tax heads and of the

effective use of grant-in-aid . . . the Finance Commission – quasi-judicial bodies of five members appointed by the President'.

44 Jenkins (1999) citing the case of windfall profits arising out of the ending of the monopoly of the Karnataka coffee board over the entire coffee crop (pp. 132–33) shows how in the new environment where the state government and provincial elites can make money, rather than ganging up on the central government, State governments have started competing against one another in order to enhance their incomes. Their ability to adapt themselves to the new political economy has further delinked States from one another – contributing to the pattern of 'provincial Darwinism' that has reduced the effectiveness of resistance among State-level political elites. The potential for centre–State conflicts has thus been transformed into inter-State competition for investment by Indian and multinational capital.

45 The statistics are taken from the Economist Intelligence Unit country report on India, April 2008, p. 11.

46 The Economist Intelligence Unit, Monthly Report, January 2008, p. 5.

47 Rosen (1966), p. 135; Table 10.

48 Frankel (1978, pp. 188–9) gives a further catalogue of the shortcomings in implementation.

49 Thus, one often hears why caste survives, even thrives on the interaction of the modern state and the economy and traditional society. A closer inspection of the ground reality reveals that while caste as status continues, caste as occupation or as a determinant of life expectation has pretty much disappeared. The combined effects of legislation and political action have succeeded in detaching caste status from caste consciousness. Consequently, the closed world of the *jati* is slowly opening up to political and economic opportunities, bolstered by the myriad methods of advancement – through open competition in the market place or through the politics of positive discrimination.

8 Engaging the world

Foreign policy and nation-building in India

> One is ... tempted to ask whether India is destined always to be 'emerging' but never actually emerging.
>
> Cohen (2001), p. 2.

> At the global level we must devise instrumentalities to deal with imbalances built into the functioning of the international political and economic order. We should aim to expand the constituency that supports the process of globalization. ... To meet these challenges and constraints, we must respond in a manner worthy of the Bandung spirit. Just as that historic meeting redefined the agenda for its time, we must do so once again here today.
>
> Manmohan Singh Bandung Address, commemorating the 50th anniversary of the Non-aligned Conference, 2004.

Introduction

India's foreign policy can come across as enigmatic to those who are unfamiliar with the political context that underpins it. Apparent contradictions abound. The country of apostles of peace like Buddha and Gandhi, India is a member of the nuclear club. An impressive arsenal of conventional weapons complements India's bombs and missiles, many of them indigenous in origin (see Table 8.1 below). However, despite the possession of this deadly stockpile, India does not have an explicit doctrine stating whom these weapons are aimed against.[1] The Indian nuclear test of 1998 undertaken by a Hindu nationalist-led ruling coalition was not, as the subsequent events have shown, merely a flash in the pan. Despite the political bickering over details, a bi-partisan consensus has grown over the need for India to acquire nuclear weapons and delivery capacity.[2] Still, despite the stable and bi-partisan character of India's nuclear policy, there is no coherent doctrine that underpins it.[3] A similar incoherence marks India's use of 'coercive diplomacy', usually against Pakistan, involving the mobilization of large numbers of troops who are, after a while, recalled, without any demonstrable goals having been achieved. This lack of clarity over broader goals (Mitra 2009) affects the global perception of India's foreign policy as a whole.[4]

The uncertainty of India's diplomatic and strategic objectives has not gone unnoticed by experts. Cohen (2001: 2) describes India's foreign policy as Janus-faced, straddling both the single-minded pursuit of self-interest like any other nation state and a 'civilizational' outlook, committed to the ideal of a world community governed by democratic values and institutions. The spirit of Afro-Asian solidarity, voiced by

Table 8.1 Tools of persuasion: who has what?

Tools of Power	India	Pakistan	China	United States
Nuclear weapons	45–95	30–52	400	9,200
Tanks	3,978	2,451	7,580	7,821
War ships (frigates)	13	7	49	34
Fighter aircrafts	1,430	523	1,471	2,604
Submarines	16	8	55	74
Active troops	1,325,000	650,000	2,255,000	1,380,000
Available military manpower	584,141,225	82,747,782	729,323,673	144,354,117
Military spending	US$22.4 billion	US$4.2 billion	US$121.9 billion	US$711.0 billion
Gross Domestic Product	$1.099 trillion	$143.8 billion	$3.251 trillion	$13.84 trillion
Major ports/harbours	9	2	8	10
Airports	346	146	467	14,947
Territory	3,287,590 sq km	803,940 sq km	9,596,960 sq km	9,826,630 sq km
Population	1,147,995,904	172,800,048	1,330,044,544	303,824,640

Sources:
CIA World Factbook 2008
China: National Security
   URL: http://www.mongabay.com/reference/new_profiles/496.html (accessed January 2009)
The Asian Conventional Military Balance in 2006
   URL http://www.csis.org/media/csis/pubs/060626_asia_balance_powers.pdf (accessed January 2009)
World *Military* Strength Comparison
   URL http://www.globalfirepower.com/countries_comparison.asp (accessed January 2009)
The Federation of American Scientists (FAS): Intelligence Resource Program
   URL http://www.fas.org/irp/threat/wmd_state.htm (accessed January 2009)
The SIPRI Military Expenditure Database
   URL http://milexdata.sipri.org/ (accessed January 2009)
International Institute for Strategic Studies, *The Military Balance 2008*, US Department of Defense.

Prime Minister Manmohan Singh on the occasion of the fiftieth anniversary of the launching of the Non-aligned Movement in Bandung in 1954 (see the statement at the beginning of this chapter), echoes this apparent duality of India's foreign policy. Not surprisingly, the 'peaceful nuclear explosion' of 1974 and subsequently the nuclear tests of 1998 have both been a source of intense speculation about India's real intentions.[5]

The ambiguity of India's foreign policy leads to questions about specific issues as well as those of a general character. Is Indian foreign policy, steeped in the 1950s jargon of non-alignment, out of sync with India's growing economic presence in the global arena? Has her diplomacy kept in step with her growing arsenal of conventional and nuclear weapons? Is India still the Quixotic lone warrior, seeking a form of world politics without power, despite her recently acquired nuclear teeth? Finally, is India's moral grandstanding merely a pragmatic gambit to put a foot in the door of the nuclear club without quite appearing to want to do so? In other words, is India 'playing poker', albeit in the name of justice and international order?[6]

The chapter responds to these questions through an analysis of the evolution of India's foreign and security policy from the early days when Jawaharlal Nehru gave it the stamp of his personality, to the emerging power that India has become in the twenty-first century. India's foreign policy no longer reflects the preference of one individual or a party but is the result of complex manoeuvres within large political coalitions. The chapter considers India's evolving foreign policy in the light of the constellation of political forces in the domestic arena, the country's military capacity, arms procurement and deployment, threat perception, and India's relations with the South Asian region and the wider world. The comprehension of these problems is crucial for a proper appreciation of the dilemmas and tribulations of India's foreign policy, particularly with regard to the challenges and opportunities of the twenty-first century.

Strategy and context in the making of India's foreign policy

India's international relations revolve around some core issues, each of which impinges on the South Asian region. The most important of these are, in order of importance, borders and territory disputes (with Pakistan regarding Kashmir, and China with regard to the disputed status of Arunachal Pradesh, shown as Chinese territory on Chinese maps[7]), international rivers (India–Pakistan, India–Nepal and India–Bangladesh), energy (prospective oil pipe lines to run over Iran–Pakistan–India, and/or Myanmar–Bangladesh–India), and security – particularly cross-border terrorism – and the smuggling of drugs. These, in turn, raise two important questions. How does India's 'hegemonic presence' in the centre of South Asia's geography affect interstate relations and the regional politics of South Asia? And, following from this, why have the states of South Asia even six decades after decolonization not succeeded in instituting an effective regional framework for peace and cooperation despite the existence of SAARC – the South Asian Association for Regional Cooperation?

The dilemmas and contradictions that mark India's foreign policy should be seen in the larger context of her location at the geographic centre of South Asia, the disputed status of Kashmir (already indicated in Chapter 1) and the tradition of non-alignment as the basis for India's foreign policy. The conflict over Kashmir led to war between India and Pakistan in 1947–48, 1965 and 1999. In addition, there is an ongoing 'proxy war', fought between the Indian army and Kashmiri militants, and cross-border terrorism. In retrospect, the politics of conflict and insurgency in Kashmir appears as a mute testimony to the ideological battle between two different theories of state in South Asia. The controversy, as we saw in Chapter 2, was started by Muhammad Ali Jinnah, the founder of Pakistan, and Mohandas Gandhi before Independence through the advocacy by the former of the 'two nation' theory and opposition to it from the latter. After the Partition, Kashmir became the new symbol of this old struggle. The State of Jammu and Kashmir, which has a Muslim majority, is claimed by Pakistan as proof of the rightness of the 'two-nation' theory. Challenging the Pakistani claim to Kashmir on account of its Muslim majority, India justifies her claim to Kashmir as an evidence of the credibility and sustainability of her status as a secular state. In 1948, in the face of an invasion of Kashmir by armed tribals from the North-West with the backing of regular Pakistani troops, Nehru, instead of letting the much better-equipped Indian army push the Pakistani invaders all the way back to the north-western frontier of the princely state of Kashmir, referred the issue to the United Nations. However, instead of ordering the invaders to go back to where they had come from as Nehru had evidently hoped, the UN dispatched monitors to supervise the actual Line of Control (LoC) which separated the troops. From then on, the Kashmir issue got embroiled with the Cold War, becoming a pawn in the

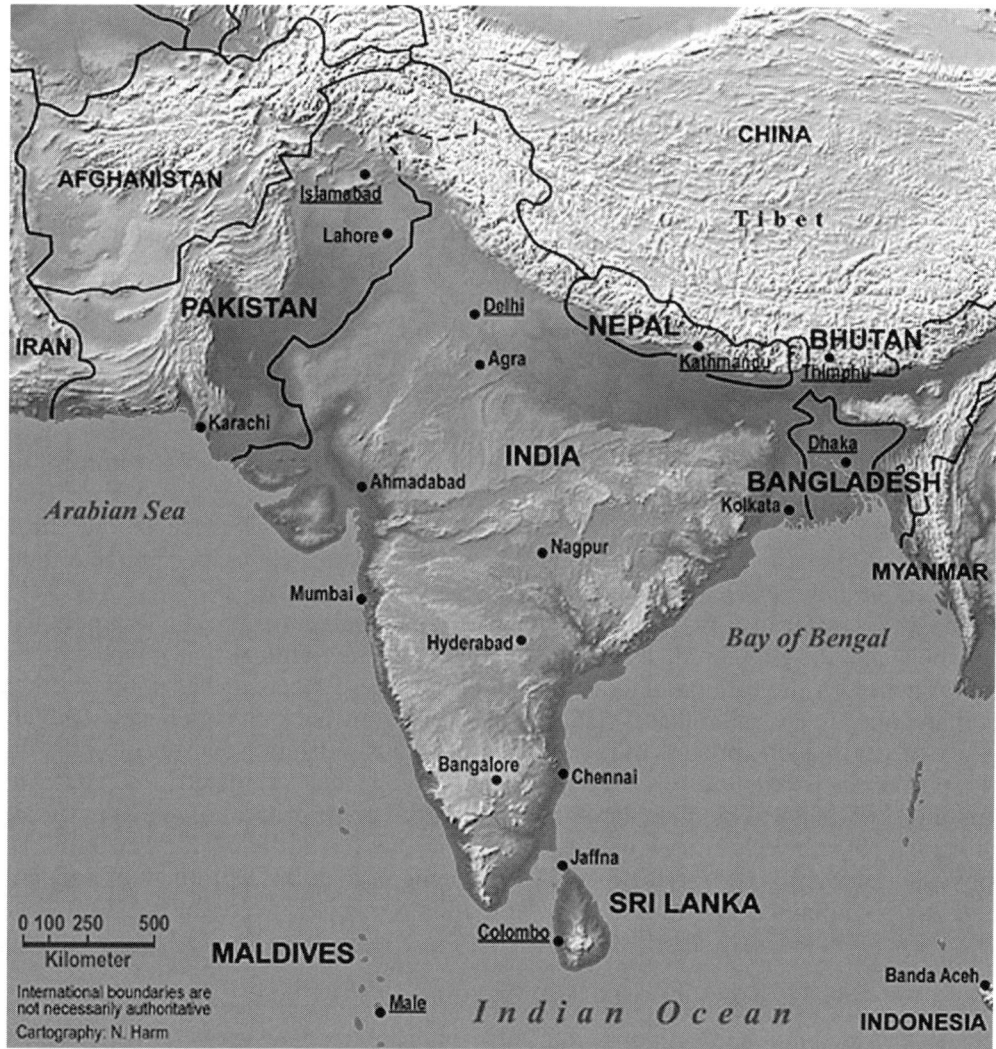

Map 8.1 Physical map of South Asia
Source: Department of Geography, South Asia Institute, Heidelberg University.

rivalry between India and Pakistan, supported, respectively, by the Soviet Union and the United States. The struggle to regain Kashmir, militarily at first, and through a plebiscite when the separatist movement in the Kashmir valley gained momentum in the 1980s, became the major focus of Pakistani policy. As an ally of the United States in the war against terrorism, Pakistan has become the beneficiary of American support on a broad range of issues including that of Kashmir.

Current developments point in the direction of cautious optimism with regard to a solution to the Kashmir problem that might be acceptable to India, Pakistan and the majority of the people of Kashmir. Public opinion in India continues to be in favour of a negotiated solution to the Kashmir problem. The initiative taken by the Hindu nationalist BJP at the head of the NDA coalition to negotiate with Pakistan has been followed by the successor, the Congress-led UPA. A negotiated outcome to the Kashmir problem has emerged as the second best option for the government of Pakistan, continuously in search of domestic legitimacy and international acceptability. The acquisition of nuclear weapons and missiles has helped Pakistan overcome the handicap of her relatively smaller arsenal of conventional weapons against India. Finally, Pakistan's nuclear threat has given further salience to the Kashmir problem by drawing the attention of a world keen to avoid regional nuclear conflict.

In the aftermath of the attack on the World Trade Center in New York on 11 September, 2001, Pakistan has re-emerged as the key strategic partner of the US government in the South Asian region. This has reversed the middle-term trend of US policy to improve Indo-US relations, and inducted the US as a key player in South Asia's regional politics. The attraction of India as an emerging market and a possible balancing factor against China, and the efforts of the Indian government to gain recognition of its nuclear status have induced a sense of moderation and pragmatism to Indo-US relations. On the Indian side, in the place of the shrill ideological rhetoric of the past, one now finds a more moderate, pragmatic and nuanced approach to the United States, as well as to Pakistan.

India's colonial history, the post-colonial attempts to revive pre-modern political symbols, and the democratic and federal structure of the political system are sources of influence on the foreign and security policies. These facets of her politics affect Indian policy in a manner that is radically different from Western nation states, which are products of a long process of nation building, industrialization and state formation. They seek the promotion of national interest through their diplomatic and strategic initiatives. As a post-colonial 'state-nation', engaged in the process of nation creation, India is comparatively more complex in its rhetoric. For India, as for others in her position, international politics, in addition to being used as an instrument of national interest, also plays a symbolic role in the building of collective identity.

Domestic and international constraints on foreign policy

Students of the international politics of India can get a heuristic grasp of this complex process in terms of a 'tool box' (see Figure 8.1) which takes into account the input, and the processing of this input, in the form of a two-level game where the national decision makers seek to identify an option that would be best for domestic opinion and acceptable to the international arena. The alternative courses of action typically consist of capitulation to the demands being made on the country, aggression and war against the adversary or the assertion of national interest in international organizations. The national leadership is the interface of domestic and international politics. Their choices are influenced by interests – of their own support base and what are considered national interests, the symbolic value of the issues at stake, deeply held values that are culturally embedded and the personal propensity of leaders to take risks or to be risk-averse. The choices also seek to balance the costs and benefits deriving out of treaty obligations and the likely gain is of the choices made. A feedback loop connects the outcome of a given foreign policy decision for future sequences of the game.[8] The chapter will draw on the tool box to analyse the unfolding of India's foreign policy under successive Prime Ministers from Nehru to the present day.

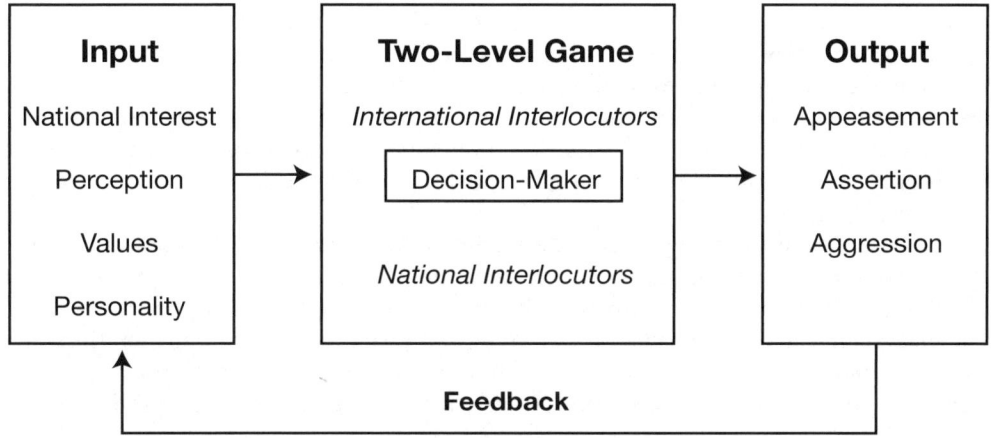

Figure 8.1 Tool box: domestic and international constraints on foreign policy
Source: Drawn by author.

A chronology of wars and treaties of 'non-aligned' India

During the early decades after Independence, foreign policy rarely featured as an issue in India's political life. Though Nehru saw foreign policy as an integral part of nation-building, and the logic of non-alignment underpinned his worldview in both arenas, foreign policy choices were seen as the preserve of the policy-making elites and not the mass electorate. The contrast between the tepid national debate following the Chinese debacle of 1962 and the national debate on the course of India's nuclear policy in 2008 that rocked the nation[9] show how foreign policy has become enmeshed with domestic policies in the course of six decades of post-Independence politics.

India is the biggest power in South Asia, and her significance, in terms of how she sees herself and how others see her, is a key consideration for regional politics, though there is considerable force to the argument that the dynamics of security and international politics of the region are crucially contingent on the India–China–Pakistan triangle.[10] India is a democratic state and an open society, both of which give a false sense of visibility to her security profile and malleability to her policies towards her neighbours. Foreign observers, depending on their own national origin and the context, place their bets on predictions of India's next move either as the 'regional bully' or the 'regional push-over', and the country, in her contradictory style, often proves both speculations to be right, appearing in the process to be either mystical-moral, or utterly devoid of principle or doctrine.[11]

India's foreign policy is affected by a number of forces unique to South Asia as a geographic region. First and foremost, the dominant presence of India at the centre of South Asia's geographic location and her power relative to the other states of the region creates an asymmetry within the region that has adversely affected the chances of closer regional integration.

The nuclear rivalry between India and Pakistan on the one hand, and India and China on the other, focuses international attention on India. Indian policy is scrutinized with more alacrity and censure than one finds in the case of her rivals – Pakistan or China. Politics of the region is marked by inter-state wars, intra-state conflicts requiring the use of armed forces to quell secessionist movements, and cross-border terrorism as well as low-intensity conflict (see Box 8.1).

While the switch from exclusive reliance on conventional weapons to a mixed arsenal with unspecified numbers of nuclear warheads has brought a sense of stability reminiscent of the cold war to the region, the warring neighbours have devised their own form of low-intensity war that has transformed the borders of South Asia into areas of high tension.

The lack of significant regional trade accounts for the absence of incentive towards the amelioration of relations. Further, there are constant allegations of the use of militancy and cross-border terrorism by the governments and rogue elements to enhance their interests, producing a no-war/no-peace situation, degenerating into overt conflict from time to time. The internationalization of domestic problems (e.g. treatment of religious or ethnic minorities), the entanglement of domestic politics

Box 8.1 War, military operations and terrorist attacks, with implication for foreign policy 1947–2008

A. Inter-state wars

1947–48	The First Indo-Pak Conflict
1962	Sino-Indian Border War
1965	The Second Indo-Pak War
1971	The Third Indo-Pak War: creation of Bangladesh
1998	Kargil conflict (a limited war between India and Pakistan)

B. Other internal/international military operations

1947	Punjab Boundary Force deployment
1947	Junagarh deployment
1948	Hyderabad police action
1961	'Liberation' of Goa
1984	Operation Bluestar
1987	The sending of the Indian Peace Keeping Force (IPKF) to Sri Lanka

C. Counter-insurgency operations

1954–74	Anti-insurgency operations in Nagaland
1965–67	Anti-insurgency operations in Mizoram
1971	Anti-insurgency operations in Tripura and Mizoram
1985–90	Anti-terrorist deployments in Punjab
1989	Anti-terrorist deployments in Jammu and Kashmir
1991	Anti-insurgency operation in Assam: Operation Rhino

D. Terrorist attacks, with an impact on foreign policy

2000	Attack on the Indian parliament
2007	Samjhauta Express bombings
2008	Suicide bombing of the Indian Embassy in Kabul
2008	Terrorist attack on Mumbai

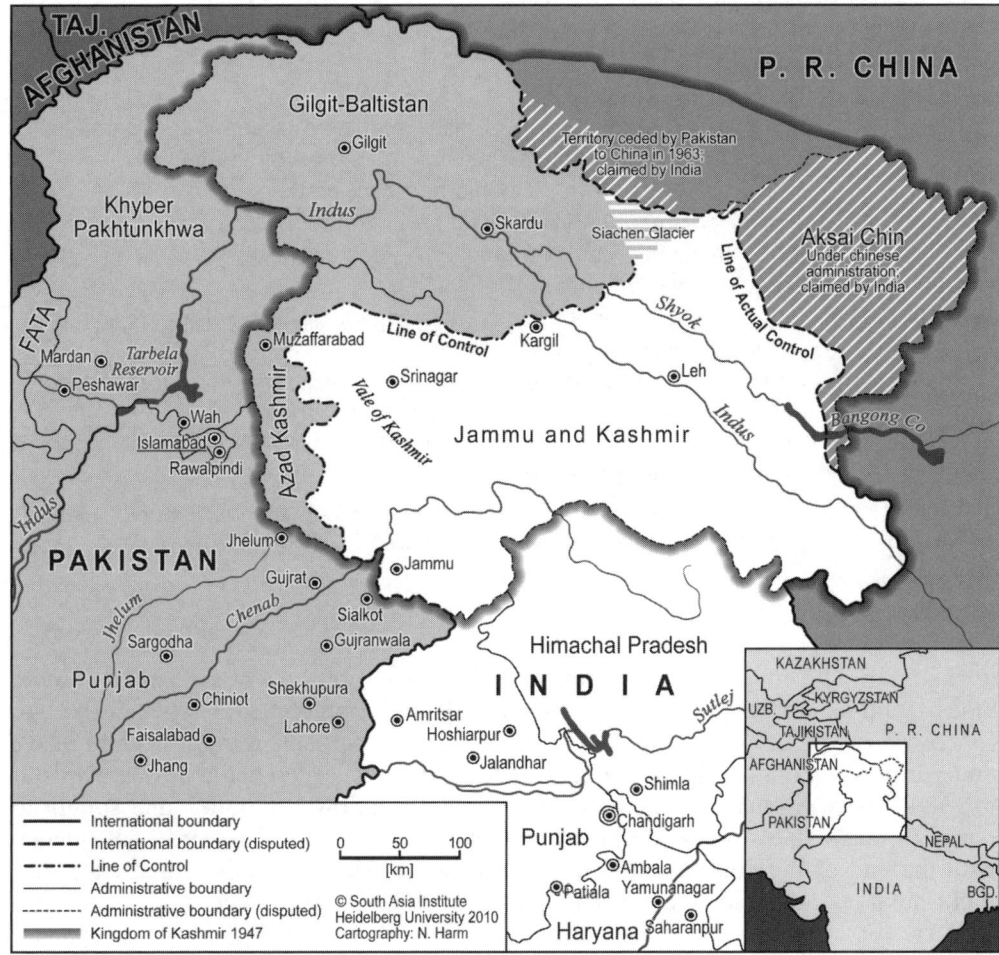

Map 8.2 Parts of Kashmir under Indian, Pakistani and Chinese control

with international relations (e.g. status of Kashmir) and the absence of a regional conflict-solving body further lower the chances of regional cooperation.

To cope with these manifold challenges, India, the key player of the region, has constantly sought to balance her declared policy of non-alignment with treaties that the country has signed with regional and extra-regional powers. Each of the major wars of South Asia, or war-like incidents, has sparked off both bouts of doctrine elaboration by the government and political controversies around them. Often they have played the role of a catalyst for new alliances.

The evolution of India's foreign policy

Since Independence, India's foreign policy has evolved through roughly three different phases. The first phase was the period of classical non-alignment when India sought

Box 8.2 India's major treaties (1947–2008)

1954	Bandung Declaration
1960	Indus Water Treaty (India–Pakistan, mediated by the World Bank)
1966	Taskent Declaration (India–Pakistan, mediated by the USSR)
1971	Indo-Soviet treaty of Friendship and cooperation
1972	Simla Agreement (India–Pakistan)
	India–Bangladesh Land Boundary Agreement (LBA)
1987	Indo-Sri Lanka Accord
1990	Agreement between India and Pakistan on Prohibition of Attack Against Nuclear Installations and Facilities
1993	(India–China) The Agreement on the Maintenance of Peace and Tranquillity along the Line of Actual Control (LAC)
1996	India–Bangladesh Ganga Waters Treaty
2005	India–China Border Agreement
2008	(Fully approved) USA–India Nuclear Cooperation Approval and Non-proliferation Enhancement Act (initiated in 2006)

to chart a middle course between the two rival camps – of the western and the Soviet blocs – and sought to generate influence by playing a pivotal role between the two superpowers, the USA and the USSR. The policy was jettisoned in the second phase under Indira Gandhi and her son Rajiv Gandhi who succeeded her as Prime Minister in 1984, following her assassination. Both of them followed a policy that sought to portray India's status as the dominant power of South Asia. The third phase began with the end of the cold war, the fall of the Soviet Union and the emergence of a multi-polar world. With the nuclear tests of 1998, the phase acquired its distinct character of a mixed strategy – of investment in nuclear weapons, carrying capacity, purchase of conventional weapons – combined with economic diplomacy, strategic alliances and negotiation with the United States, EU, China and Pakistan and international organizations like the WTO.

Over two decades before India's Independence, Jawahahrlal Nehru had emerged as the person in charge of the foreign policy of the Indian National Congress. His succession to the stewardship of the foreign policy of India after Independence was, in this sense, only natural. Nehru's approach to foreign policy, which went through many metamorphoses under his successors, namely Lal Bahadur Shastri (1964–66), Indira Gandhi (1966–77, 1980–84) and Rajiv Gandhi (1984–89), represents a mix of liberal internationalism and a 'norm driven' realism. It was originally characterized by a sceptical view of the United States, reliance on the Soviet Union and support for other anti-colonial movements. Nehru acknowledged the problems facing a weak state in the international system and consequently aimed at cooperation where possible and necessary. This approach got a rude jolt in India's defeat in the 1962 Indo-Chinese border war, and started generating resentment against an unbalanced international power system. For Nehru's successors, sub-continental hegemony became the overriding goal of foreign policy. Pakistan, China and the United States were seen as basically hostile towards India. This thinking, which reached its peak in the

Indo-Pak war of 1971, persisted until 1991–92, when the liberalization of India's economy created a radically new strategic environment for foreign policy.

According to Cohen, the Nehruvian origins of strategic thinking in post-Independence India have been enriched by two additional currents which he calls, 'realist' and 'revitalist', to distinguish them from the overall idealism of Jawaharlal Nehru. The realists started as offshoots from the generally liberal, market-oriented, pro-American Swatantra party in the mid-1960s. They held a pragmatic view of Sino-Indian and Indo-US relations and supported increased economic openness and integration with the international market forces. The revitalists take a more regional perspective, stemming from their preoccupation with spreading Indian influence over South Asia, which they see as essentially the main theatre of action for Indian foreign policy. They, like the realists, deem nuclearization necessary. The synthesis of realist and revitalist perspectives was represented by the NDA Prime Minister Atal Behari Vajpayee.[12]

The period during the Indo-China war of 1962 and the Indo-Pak war of 1971, when Pakistan gradually came closer to China, caused major re-thinking, because India had to confront the possibility of a war on two fronts. The increase in defence allocation during this period (Table 8.2), and increased military cooperation with the West, saw the beginning of a greater security consciousness. After Indira Gandhi came to power in 1966 she displayed a greater willingness to link politics, foreign policy and security.

Table 8.2 Military expenses (1996–2006)

Year	India		Pakistan		China [estimated]		USA	
	US$ million (2005)	% of GDP	US$ million (2005)	% of GDP	US$ million (2005)	% of GDP	US$ million (2005)	% of GDP
1996	12,178	2.6	3,430	5.1	[16,614]	[1.7]	337,946	3.5
1997	14,144	2.7	3,285	4.9	[16,808]	[1.6]	336,185	3.3
1998	14.757	2.8	3,281	4.8	[19.273]	[1.7]	328,611	3.1
1999	17,150	3.1	3,311	3.9	[21,636]	[1.8]	329,421	3.0
2000	17,697	3.1	3,320	3.7	[23,778]	[1.8]	342,172	3.1
2001	18,313	3.0	3.553	3.9	[28.010]	[2.0]	344,932	3.1
2002	18,256	2.9	3,819	3.9	[33,060]	[2.1]	387,303	3.4
2003	18,664	2.8	4,077	3.7	[36,552]	[2.1]	440,813	3.8
2004	19,204	2.6	4,243	3.5	[40.278]	[2.0]	430,451	4.0
2005	22,273	2.8	4,412	3.4	[44,322]	[1.9]	503,353	4.0
2006	23,615	2.7	4,465	3.2	[51.864]	[2.1]	511,187	4.0

Notes:
1. The figures for India include expenditure on the paramilitary forces of the Border Security Force, the Central Reserve Police Force, the Assam Rifles and the Indo-Tibetan Border Police but do not include spending on military nuclear activities.
2. Figures for these countries are for current spending only (i.e. exclude capital spending).
3. The figures for China are for estimated total military expenditure. On the estimates in local currency and as a share of GDP for the period 1989–98, see Wang, S., 'The military expenditure of China, 1989–98', *SIPRI Yearbook 1999: Armaments, Disarmament and International Security* (Oxford: Oxford University Press, 1999), pp. 334–49. The estimates for the years 1999–2002 are based on the percentage change in official military expenditure and on the assumption of a gradual decrease in the commercial earnings of the People's Liberation Army (PLA).
4. The figures for the USA are for financial year (1 Oct.–30 Sep.) rather than calendar year.

Source: *Stockholm International Peace Research Institute. The SIPRI Military Expenditure Database.* http://milexdata.sipri.org (accessed 19 May 2010).

Indira Gandhi also turned India firmly in the direction of the Soviet Union with the Indo-Soviet Treaty of Peace, Friendship and Cooperation, signed on 9 August, 1971. After 1971, the balance of power in South Asia was altered significantly, with the defeat of Pakistan in 1971, the emergence of Bangladesh and the 'peaceful nuclear explosion' of 1974 which gave yet another indication of an 'Indira Doctrine', which visualized India as the hegemonic power of South Asia.[13]

Though the onset of liberalization of the Indian economy prepared the ground for a rapprochement with the United States and China, the contradictory pulls within India's strategic thinking continued from 1990 to 1999. The collapse of the Soviet Union required a radical change in policy, while economic reforms in India necessitated budget cuts, affecting the military adversely. This might have opened a window of opportunity for Pakistan, which, taking advantage of the onset of militancy in Kashmir, started supporting cross-border insurgency and covert military operations there. On the political front the unilateralist Gujral doctrine and subsequently the BJP initiatives for a diplomatic opening to Pakistan through the Lahore bus trip (see below) and subsequently the Agra summit continued the Indian policy of putting India's relationship with Pakistan on a normal footing. However, Pakistani policy operated on more conservative lines and sought to take advantage of the perceived weakness of the Indian military establishment. One consequence was the war in Kargil in 1999, but the forceful reaction of India's army once again underscored the need for a coherent Indian strategic doctrine. The section below will discuss some of the pivotal figures and events under successive Prime Ministers in more detail.

The foundational years: Jawaharlal Nehru, 1947–64

Utopian visionary, realist Congressman, patrician populist and authoritarian democrat, Nehru's foreign policy presents a unique blend of strategy, vision and tactical errors, ensconced in the context of his understanding of Indian history. The evolution of India's foreign policy during Nehru's watch can be split into three phases. The first phase, from 1947 to 1953, saw Nehru as a key leader of Third World politics. The second phase lasted from the Bandung Declaration of 1954 to the debacle of India's China policy as India stood defeated in 1962. One of the key domestic factors was the disputed status of Kashmir. In retrospect, two elements dominated Nehru's Kashmir policy: (1) popular will rather than religious composition as the basis of the state, and (2) the Instrument of Accession signed by the King of Kashmir in favour of joining India. However, the representatives of western powers did not see the Kashmir problem in the same categorical terms and rejected India's claim. Nehru attributed the support by western states of the Pakistani position to their acceptance of the 'two-nation theory' which saw Pakistan as the designated home of the Muslims of British India which, in their eyes, reinforced the claim of Pakistan on Muslim-majority Kashmir. The whole idea of religion as the basis of state formation was anathema to Nehru's firm belief in the principle of secularism. His second disappointment was the radical shift in position of Sheikh Abdullah (the most important Kashmiri leader in the 1940s and an ally who fell foul of Nehru when he declared Kashmiri independence as his goal). These forces led to the third phase, 1963–64. The traumatic events of 1962 created an occasion for national stock-taking and the resignation of a substantial number of chief ministers and important members of Nehru's own cabinet.

Nehru saw himself first and foremost as a great modernizer and as such, social and economic development was the cornerstone of his political thinking. Defence as a political and strategic issue was mainly used to advance these objectives. Nehru was deeply distrustful of the military. Not surprisingly, no coherent security doctrine developed during the period of Nehru's stewardship, non-alignment being an overall guide to the ways and means of avoiding conflict rather than a strategy of the enhancement of national power and security. India established good neighbourly relations with her smaller neighbours on the basis of treaties with Bhutan 1949, Sikkim 1950, Nepal 1950, Burma 1951 and Ceylon 1954/1964. Force during this phase was used primarily for domestic purposes, the military action against the Portuguese colony Goa in 1961 and its subsequent union with India being the exception.

The first official declaration of a policy of non-alignment by Nehru took place in 1946. At the same time, similar moves were also made by Burma, Indonesia and Yugoslavia. 1950–54 was the formative period. The role of India gradually shifted to that of the pivot between competing sides in the intensification of the cold war and the break-up of hostilities in Korea (June 1950). The Korean War as such led in turn to further intensification of the cold war. The western strategy consisted of containing communism by military pacts. The outbreak of the Korean War put the non-alignment policy to a severe test, but also offered an opportunity to demonstrate its utility. The policy of the non-aligned countries, contributed in some measure to the lessening of tension and to creating the necessary atmosphere for peaceful negotiations between the two blocs. Both blocs recognized the value of the peace efforts initiated by non-aligned nations, leading to the emergence of an Afro-Asian group in the UN. Since 1954, the consolidation of this policy took place in terms of its ideology and recognition by the two blocs. The full conceptual implications of the non-aligned policy emerged by the end of the period as a doctrine opposed to military pacts, committed to expanding the zone of peace in the world, as summed up in *Panchasheela* – the Five Principles of Peaceful Coexistence. Later, these were incorporated into the ten principles in the final communiqué listed at the Bandung Conference, announced a joint statement. This indicated agreement on the five principles by these countries.

The Non-aligned Movement (NAM) was never meant to be a uniform policy for all its adherents on all occasions. It represented a broad similarity in approach to contemporary international situations, expressed in similar policies on certain questions among these nations. Basically, it implied not aligning oneself with either of the two superpowers *permanently* and being non-aligned from one another. It suggested a case-by-case approach: each time there was a crisis, a series of consultations was

---

Box 8.3 *Panchasheela* – the Five Principles

- Mutual respect for other nations' territorial integrity and sovereignty
- Non-aggression
- Non-interference in internal affairs
- Equality and mutual benefit
- Peaceful coexistence

undertaken to decide how to vote in the UN, how to act with regard to conflicting parties, what facilities to accord the aggrieved nation, whether to lend support to UN intervention and to send troops for peace-keeping. It worked on the basis of a conventional anti-colonialism which sometimes facilitated concerted action.

Nehru's foreign policy, a joint product of domestic policy and international context, was moderately successful in meeting his main goals: democracy, development, secularism, socialism and peaceful conflict resolution. The paradigm of non-alignment had seemed optimal in view of Nehru's commitments at home and abroad. China's friendship, however, came with a price tag spelt out by Mao which was, first and foremost, the priority of the national interests of China. These were: the national security and territorial integrity of China, abolition of all unequal treaties, liberation of all China's lost territories, such as Taiwan, Tibet and Hong Kong, readjustment and legitimization of the northern and southern territorial boundaries, making China economically and militarily strong, and reasserting China's historical and cultural greatness. In terms of its foreign policy, China wanted the leadership of the newly emerging Afro-Asian and socialist blocs, which Nehru's India wanted as well. In retrospect, a conflict between these two emerging Asian giants was inevitable.

Unlike China, which was a revolutionary state, led by a new leadership with a new set of revolutionary objectives, seeking a radically different profile in international politics, India was a 'successor state' to which the outgoing British had transferred power. India was a status-quo power whose main objective was to secure the territorial boundaries that the country inherited from the colonial rulers. To meet this goal, India was willing to go some way to accommodate China. The slogan *Hindi-Chini-bhai-bhai* ('India and China are brothers') was evolved by New Delhi, with the connivance of China, basically to accommodate the demands of China over Tibet. Shortly after Independence and the establishment of the People's Republic of China, India withdrew the military and trade presence in Lhasa set up by the British which had seen Tibet as a buffer between the colonial state and China. However, whereas India saw the McMahon Line, the colonial boundary between India and Tibet, as India's international boundary with China, the Chinese did not recognize it and demanded negotiation of the border. They also demanded political solidarity at an international level, privately viewing Nehru as a stooge of neo-imperialism. India, for them, had choices to make between continuing on the path of bourgeois-feudal democracy or making a revolutionary break with the past. The radicalization in India's domestic politics, particularly the growing splits within India's communist movement, opened a window of opportunity for China to export its brand of revolution.

Nehru's perception of India in the world arena was a contrast to that of the Chinese. Nehru wanted India to play a pivotal role between the USA and the USSR, a posture which had yielded an enhanced profile to India in the Korea conflict. India could bolster her economic and political situation through foreign aid from the West and support from the USSR in the Security Council. With regard to China, this required Nehru's India to turn a blind eye to the steady incursion of the Chinese into Aksai Chin. However, when these incursions became public and the Indian parliament demanded action, Nehru, following the so-called 'Forward Policy', ordered the sending of Indian troops to occupy isolated posts located in areas that the Chinese claimed as theirs. Nehru's statement in parliament that the Indian army was under instruction to 'throw the Chinese out' has been depicted as evidence of Indian intransigence and aggression by the Chinese and scholars sympathetic to the Chinese view.[14]

The results of the 1962 border war showed the asymmetry of India–China relations in terms of national strategic capabilities. The casualties on the Indian side were approximately 5,000 dead, and 4,000 taken prisoner. The casualties on the Chinese side are uncertain as figures were not available, but these were considered to have been far less. China declared a unilateral ceasefire and withdrew, thus demonstrating Chinese readiness for negotiation as opposed to Indian intransigence.

The contributions of the 1962 border war to developments in Indian and regional politics were enormous. India's ignominious defeat accelerated the polarization of opinion both on the ideological left and the right, and started the process of questioning the Nehruvian consensus, accelerating the search for a more robust foreign policy, based on national power. India's image suffered a serious lack of credibility in South Asia, setting off steady overtures by Pakistan towards China, which had come across as the clear winner in terms of its more successful policy of domestic development and nation-building. India's defeat lowered Nehru's stature and raised larger questions both at home and abroad about India's stability, the appropriateness of her institutional arrangements, and the suitability of non-alignment as the basis of her foreign policy.

Ironically, the debacle of 1962 set in motion forces that prepared the ground for the 1965 war against Pakistan, producing an unlikely hero in Lal Bahadur Shastri, successor to Nehru as India's Prime Minister. Short in stature, hailing from a modest background and relatively unknown in national politics except for a short stint as a cabinet minister, Shastri, with his slogan *jai jawan, jai kisan* ('victory to the soldier, victory to the peasant'), left behind a legacy of war as an integral part of national politics and foreign policy, necessary when just, and portent of glory and national honour. Indian troops crossed the international frontier to attack Pakistan – Shastri's biographer informs us[15] – for the first time in the history of the nation, under instructions from the diminutive Shastri. The groundwork for the decisive 1971 war against Pakistan was set.

The Pakistani game plan in 1965 was to fight a quick war in which, with tanks playing a key role, cutting Kashmir off from the Indian mainland seemed an attractive option. The military regime of Pakistan found in Kashmir a ready-made alibi, excellent to rally the people of Pakistan. The alliance with China was sealed with the 1963 Sino-Pak treaty which ceded part of Pakistani-occupied Kashmir to China, and helped build the Karakoram Highway, creating a direct road link between Pakistan and China. At the same time, US–Pak relations were in good functioning order, with a steady supply of American arms and training for Pakistani military, as a conspicuous counter-example to India's non-alignment.

The perception on the Pakistani side was to strike India at her most vulnerable, at a time when the new leadership had not yet settled down, to create conditions to 'defreeze' the Kashmir issue, and force India to come to negotiation. The parallel with the Chinese strategy in 1962 was uncanny. Much like the Chinese incursions of 1959 prior to the invasion of 1962, the Pakistani action started with 'probing' encounters. Pakistani strategists chose to engage Indians at vulnerable spots such as in the Rann of Kutch on the Gujarat coast, preliminary to an 'all-out' but disguised invasion of Kashmir by the Pakistan army. It was to start in the form of 'guerrilla warfare', camouflaged as 'revolt' by the local population, to be followed by a full-scale assault by the Pakistan army in the Chhamb area of Kashmir, leading to a massive lightning armoured attack to capture Amritsar in Punjab, and as much more Indian territory as possible. These were to be eventually exchanged for Kashmir.[16]

In retrospect, it was Shastri's tactical thinking and a stroke of good luck that foiled the Pakistani grand strategy. One of Shastri's first acts in office was to establish a personal rapport with defence chiefs, leaders of the opposition as well as main voices within the Congress party. This helped him build up a strong national consensus to meet the Pakistani challenge in Kashmir. Simultaneously, he took new initiatives in political as well as military matters, relying on populist symbols rather than high policy, and crucially, deciding in favour of the open and unabashed use of force to come to terms with the political problems of the day. It was under Shastri's orders that the Indian army crossed the international frontier, and marched in the direction of Lahore (to relieve pressure on the Chhamb sector in Kashmir). The Indian air force was launched into the battle right at the outset in spite of the risk of superior Pakistani aircraft. Finally, Shastri was willing to trade land against security when the need for it arose.

In the 1965 Indo-Pak war, the Indian strategy greatly benefited from the failure of the 'spontaneous' mass uprising in Kashmir. In the short run, there were no clear winners to the war, although India more than held her own against superior Pakistani armaments and fighter planes. That, from the Indian point of view, was the significant outcome. The Tashkent agreement was a successful attempt by the USSR to increase its influence in South Asia; and to develop a concept of a collective Asian security system by weaning Pakistan away from the United States, and paving the way for a '20 Year Treaty of Peace and Friendship' with India under Indira Gandhi. In terms of civil–military relations, 1965 initiated closer integration of the two. On the Pakistani side, in the long run, 1965 resulted in a loss of authority of the military leaders and eventually contributed to the rise of a political leadership under Zulfikar Ali Bhutto.

Indira Gandhi and the realist turn in Indian foreign policy

The sudden death of Shastri in 1966, just after he had signed the Tashkent agreement with Pakistan, left Indian politics in disarray because there was no clear successor and, though the country was riding high on a surge of patriotism, there was no clear policy or institutionalized policy-making body to coordinate security and foreign relations. Besides, the indicators of domestic growth were grim. The Third Five Year Plan (1961–66) had ended with a drought bringing catastrophic agricultural failure and the need for food imports from the United States. The World Bank, as part of an aid package, had enforced devaluation of the rupee in 1966, rudely shaking national confidence in the soundness of the economy. Shastri's successor Indira Gandhi was seen as a weak and provisional leader who, the scheming power-brokers of the Congress party expected, would eventually pave the way for a member of the 'Syndicate', an informal body consisting of important regional leaders and members of the Congress organization. For her part, as subsequent events proved, Indira Gandhi had other ideas.

Meanwhile, Pakistan, under the leadership of General Yahya Khan, seemed well poised to raise its international profile as an agent brokering a rapprochement between the United States and China, during this period of domestic instability in India. However, a major domestic crisis emerged in Pakistan following the General Elections of 1970 in which the Awami League swept the polls in East Pakistan, winning an overall majority in Pakistan's national assembly and staking its claim to form the government, generating a regime crisis and a confrontation between East and West

Pakistan. On 25 March, 1971, an army of 40,000 West Pakistani soldiers descended on East Pakistan, unleashing a systematic reign of terror. The leader of the Awami League, Sheikh Mujibur Rahman, was arrested and airlifted to a jail in West Pakistan. The bloodshed unleashed by the Pakistani army created a massive flight of refugees to India, eventually reaching the figure of 10 million.

There were important changes afoot in the diplomatic environment of South Asia. The dominant position that the USSR had achieved in 1966 as the peacemaker between India and Pakistan was challenged by an emergent Pakistan, and the new USA–China–Pakistan axis. China was challenging the USSR for leadership of the communist world, and building an anti-India alliance with Pakistan. The Indian response had been to seek to counter-balance it with the Indo-Soviet treaty of Peace, Friendship and Cooperation of 1971, which guaranteed mutual consultation in the case of attack on either of the two and appropriate measures to ensure peace with security for its partners. Indira Gandhi had, in the meantime, following the split of the Congress party in 1969, consolidated her hold over the party in alliance with the Indian left and won a resounding victory in the 1971 parliamentary election.

In the event, when India entered the war in East Pakistan to fight the Pakistani army jointly with the Bangladeshi freedom fighters, the USA–Pakistan–China axis swung into action, putting India under pressure to restrain the freedom fighters while manoeuvring to get the UN to send observers to East Pakistan. At this juncture, the USSR came to India's rescue, blocking the US and China in the Security Council by applying the veto three times and balancing the American seventh fleet, and, according to some accounts, threatening to attack Sinkiang in China. At home, Shastri's policies – the 'nationalization' of the security issue – were adopted by Indira Gandhi, who, following the military success of India, reaped great electoral dividends in terms of an important victory in the elections to regional assemblies in 1972.

In military terms, the war was a complete victory for India. The Pakistani army in Bangladesh capitulated and a total of 93,000 officers and men were taken prisoner. However, the political outcomes were not as clear. The 1971 war temporarily established Indian supremacy over South Asia. India signed a 25-year Treaty of Friendship, Cooperation and Peace with the People's Republic of Bangladesh in 1972, and appeared poised to enter a period of undisputed Indian hegemony over South Asia. But this was not to be. The main reason for the ambiguous political consequences was that the Simla Agreement, 1972, between India and Pakistan did not paper over the wide gulf that separated the perceptions and policies of the two neighbours. India failed to secure a lasting solution to the Kashmir dispute. The territory on the Western front that the Indian army had brought under its control was transferred back to Pakistan, without, as some Indian commentators have alleged, any commitment from Pakistan to giving a semblance of permanence to the Line of Control.

In fact, the rump state of Pakistan regrouped its forces swiftly, maintained its pivotal role between the USA and China, securing support from both. When the United States and the USSR got engaged in Afghanistan, Pakistan became the main beneficiary of massive American support. Indira Gandhi, who got embroiled in domestic politics, the state of Emergency and then her unceremonious ouster from power, ceased to be a player in regional politics for a while. The assassination of Mujibur Rahman in 1975 removed a source of support for India and swiftly brought Pakistan back in. The smaller neighbours took the initiative to launch the South Asian Association for

Regional Cooperation which India perceived mainly as an attempt to set firm limits to any hegemonic ambitions she might have developed as a result of 1971.

The only formal clause of the Simla Agreement (1972) that came across as in the interest of India was a provision for conflicts to be solved bilaterally, without any third-party intervention – a tactic that Pakistan had often resorted to in the past against India. Both sides also committed themselves to refraining from the organization, assistance or encouragement of any act detrimental to the maintenance of peaceful and harmonious relations. In Jammu and Kashmir, the Line of Control (of 17 December, 1971) was to be respected by both sides without prejudice to recognized positions of either side, neither side was to 'seek to alter it unilaterally, irrespective of mutual differences and legal interpretations, both sides were to refrain from the threat or use of force in violation of this line'.

In retrospect, the 'Indira Doctrine' appears to have been more rhetoric than reality. The gains of 1971 to India's international profile and her capacity were short-lived. Within two years of signing the Simla Agreement, Pakistan was busy mobilizing support within the UN and among Islamic countries to bolster its claims to Kashmir and was engaged in buying arms from the USA. The American tilt towards China counter-balanced the enhanced stature of India as South Asia's dominant force – and reduced the significance of the close ties between the regime of Indira Gandhi and the Soviet Union.

The assassination of Indira Gandhi in 1984 by her two Sikh bodyguards, seeking revenge for the attack on the Golden Temple in the holy city of Amritsar by the Indian army – put to the test the survival of the attempt by India to work out a sphere of influence that would bring the whole of South Asia under Indian hegemony. Rajiv Gandhi, Indira's son and successor to the position of Prime Minister, was a relatively new face in South Asian politics, whom many expected to bring a new era of peace, cooperation and progress to South Asia. The ascent of Benazir Bhutto to the prime ministership in Pakistan – she was also a relatively youthful leader with modern ways – reinforced these expectations. Anointed with a massive majority in the parliamentary elections of 1985, Rajiv Gandhi set about putting India's political landscape in order. But the grand initiative did not last beyond a couple of years. By the late 1980s, the regime was tainted by the Bofors scandal. The accusation of financial kickbacks by the Swedish firm to the Congress party was never proved but continued to sap the legitimacy and vitality of Rajiv's leadership. The old difference with Pakistan on the status of Kashmir resurfaced, leading eventually to the massive mobilization of the Indian army known as Brasstacks. But the final blow came with the debacle faced by the Indian Peace Keeping Force (IPKF) sent to disarm the Tamil Tigers and help Sri Lanka solve the ethnic conflict peacefully.

In 1984, upon taking up office as Prime Minister, Rajiv Gandhi had expressed concern at the deteriorating ethnic situation in Sri Lanka, and stated that India did not want to interfere in the internal affairs of that country. However, the steady flow of Tamil refugees into India had put pressure on the government for a credible reaction. The Sri Lankan government agreed to undertake secret talks with Tamil 'terrorists' (under Indian persuasion), but by early 1987 there had still been no progress in negotiations. Meanwhile, Sri Lanka imposed a military blockade on Jaffna peninsula, and in response, India's air drop of food to Jaffna (violating Sri Lanka's air space) showed Indian determination to play the role of regional peace-maker. The 'Indo-Sri Lanka Agreement, 1987, specified the conditions needed to establish peace and normalcy in Sri Lanka', which, under this agreement was to recognize Tamil as the official language, lift the state of emergency, and to search for military help from any other country. In return, India was to ensure that Indian territory would not be used for 'activities prejudicial to the unity, integrity and sovereignty of Sri Lanka', and to provide military assistance in implementing the accord.

Accordingly, Indian troops (organized as the IPKF, whose numbers would soon reach 70,000) were airlifted to Sri Lanka. The IPKF was dispatched to Sri Lanka under the Indo-Sri Lankan accord (1987) signed by Rajiv Gandhi and President Jaiwardhane of Sri Lanka. In retrospect, the move was deeply flawed because there was no consensus on the perception of the mission by the key players. Indian policy was dictated by the double commitment to the peaceful resolution of the ethnic conflict in Sri Lanka – a process to be brokered by India and not by any other extra-regional force; the commitment of the Sri Lankan government was limited to the use of the IPKF to counterbalance the Tamil Tigers, but not necessarily to a genuine federal power-sharing as in India. The Tamil Tigers themselves welcomed the IPKF as a short-term respite from the Sri Lankan army. The Tamil Tiger leader Velupillai Prabhakaran was not a party to the accord. The Tamil Tigers were only biding their time; once they thought the time was ripe, they turned against the IPKF. Fresh elections in Sri Lanka brought the Sinhala nationalist government of Premadasa which was strongly anti-Indian. Upon taking office, Premadasa asked the Indians to leave which they eventually did, having lost 1,100 men. 'The verdict on Rajiv Gandhi's Sri Lanka accord can only be that it was a dismal failure.'[17]

An analysis of the limits to India's power under Rajiv Gandhi reveals the structural constraints and shortcomings that have been characteristic of Indian foreign policy. There were four main factors at play. In the first place, Indian policy was identified too much with the personality of the Prime Minister and not seen as the cohesive outcome of institutional decision-making. Prime ministerial domination of foreign policy kept it from becoming professional. The failure of the Indian initiative in Sri Lanka can partly be blamed on the lack of coordination between government and intelligence agencies (at one time, India had three Sri Lankan policies simultaneously). Second, the doctrine of *Panchasheela* set an ideological limit to national power, offering a blend of liberal goals and enlightened self-interest in principle, but in practice India's policy managed to combine the worst of both worlds. Third, India's international profile and size produce an asymmetry in her relations with her neighbours. India is both too large compared to any given neighbour and yet not big enough to unambiguously dominate Pakistan or the combined diplomatic strength of the neighbours in regional and international organizations. Finally, the considerations of domestic politics, countervailing forces and democratic restrictions constrained India's foreign policy, denying it cohesion and strength.

India's failure to put her 1971 dominance of South Asian politics on an enduring basis has both domestic and international explanations. The replacement of Indira with her inexperienced son and Rajiv's failure to develop a cohesive foreign policy were the main causes of India's decline. Indian foreign policy aimed at maintaining India's status as a non-aligned country, making short-term adjustments under extreme necessity but bouncing back to the lonely posture of the moralist, surrounded by interest-seeking, power-maximizing nation-states. In their different ways, Nehru, Indira and Rajiv gave substance to this posture which became increasingly tenuous with time. Did the coming to power of the Hindu nationalist BJP in the parliamentary elections of 1999 as the leading element in the NDA coalition change this mould? This will be the main theme of the next section.

India's search for power in a post-cold war, multi-polar world

The early 1990s introduced three major developments that radically affected the main parameters of Indian foreign policy. The end of the cold war and the chaotic disintegration of the Soviet Union deprived India's stance of non-alignment of its main *raison d'être*. In a world no longer polarized along the lines of the capitalist western bloc and its socialist opponents, non-alignment made little sense. Nor could India rely on Soviet backing in the Security Council, Soviet armaments or softer terms of international trade. The second major change that sent India searching for allies in the western world was the liberalization of India's economy (see Chapter 7), and its integration with the international market economy, opening up a new, competitive world full of challenges and opportunities for global alliances. Finally, the emergence of Hindu nationalism as a political force in India's domestic politics, and into governance, brought in long-time critics of non-alignment as the main decision makers of Indian foreign policy.

A brief analysis of the key events during the Hindu nationalist-led NDA government shows that the paradigm shift many expected of India's foreign policy did not quite materialize during Vajpayee's watch. Though it took a Hindu nationalist government to give the decisive push for the actual tests, the nuclear tests of 1998 were the culmination of a programme that had started long before, under Congress governments. More than the nuclear tests, the opening up to Pakistan, symbolized by the 'bus diplomacy', which saw Prime Minister Vajpayee riding a bus into Lahore in February 1999 and being personally received by the Pakistani Prime Minister Nawaz Sharif, and the signing of the Lahore Declaration, gave a more surprising twist to the new direction of Indian foreign policy. However, the rebound to the older way of suspicion and hostility came swiftly with the Kargil war when Indian troops discovered, accidentally as it turned out, the presence of well-entrenched Pakistani troops on Indian territory in July 1999. The setback that Kargil introduced to India–Pakistan relations took a turn for the worse with the Hindu–Muslim riots in Gujarat in 2002. The Kargil war, with the potential to spread into a regional nuclear war, induced American intervention – behind the scenes to accommodate Indian sensitivity to third-party intervention in regional conflicts – and started the process of an Indo-US rapprochement which eventually led to the Indo-US Framework Agreement of 2006.

The fact that the Kargil war broke out so soon after the signing of the Lahore Declaration raises important questions about the stability of Indo-Pak relations. The tactic of occupying the high-altitude areas of Kargil vacated for winter by the Indian army – a standard practice hitherto – appears to have been mooted as part of a strategy by the Pakistani army, alarmed at the attempts of the civilian government to normalize relations with India before the resolution of long-standing conflicts over Kashmir and the Siachen glacier. It was a political-strategic move which consisted of disrupting vital supplies to Leh by cutting off the Srinagar–Leh road and outflanking India's defences from the south (see Map 8.2); it gave a fillip to militancy in Jammu and Kashmir, and a boost to the morale of militants in the Kashmir valley. These factors accelerated the proxy war in Kashmir – which started with the outbreak of insurgency in 1987 – and activated militancy in the Kargil and Turtok sectors by opening new routes of infiltration into the valley. These military tactics drew political support from the fundamentalist lobby in Pakistan. India's decisive and restrained reaction (unlike the previous wars in 1965 and 1971, the Indian army and air force did not cross the international frontier and invade Pakistani territory or airspace) and American pressure on Pakistan foiled the grand strategy of the authors of the Kargil war. Specialists' comments show the grim reality of unresolved issues that underpin the apparent diplomatic success of the bus diplomacy.[18]

Paradoxical as it may sound, on the whole, during the watch of the Hindu nationalist party, the prospects for peace between India and Pakistan were at their highest since Independence, though as Kargil shows, the future remained fraught with uncertainties. India's nuclear status invited sanctions and gave an opportunity to the trouble shooters of the NDA to show that India could walk her way around it. The bus diplomacy proved the point that once in power extremists can become moderate. Perceptions of Vajpayee and evaluations of his foreign policy vary. But three legacies stand out. In the first place, the bomb as symbolic of the search for power has now become accepted Indian policy. The second was the opening up to Pakistan by a Hindu nationalist government through the bus diplomacy. At the time, it had come across as paradoxical, raising further questions. The third was the resolve to continue with the global economic diplomacy of the previous government.

In retrospect, it is seen as the tendency of extremists to become moderate once in office, as seen in the diplomatic initiatives of the NDA, particularly with regard to Pakistan. The Lahore Declaration, unlike the Simla Accord, while still paying obeisance to bilateralism with regard to regional conflict, explicitly recognized Kashmir as an 'issue', recommended a composite integrated dialogue and Confidence Building Measures (CBMs) and the joint resolve to combat 'terrorism'. Most of these policies have been continued by the UPA government that succeeded the NDA in 2004. The UPA has managed to achieve policy continuity in spite of governmental change, secured a nuclear deal with the United States without having to sign the Nuclear Non-Proliferation Treaty (NPT), and continued the 'composite dialogue' with Pakistan which has made a real difference in the level of hostility between the two neighbours.

Why has India, long an advocate of nuclear disarmament, turned into a candidate for nuclear status? The question takes us back to Nehru. In retrospect, one can argue that India has had a double nuclear strategy from the outset. The nuclear programme of India, started in 1946 under the leadership of Homi J. Bhabha, got an institutional shape in 1948 with the establishment of the Atomic Energy Commission (AEC). The first two civilian nuclear reactors opened in 1956 and 1960. The Chinese testing of a nuclear bomb in 1964 caused anxiety in India's policy community but the internal leadership struggles did not prove conducive to national policy making in this vital field. The fact that the nuclear 'haves' had no intention of giving up their ownership and control of these ultimate weapons of mass destruction had started making many in India question the Indian policy of nuclear disarmament.

Once the issue of political leadership was resolved, the programme took off, leading finally to the 1974 test of a 'peaceful nuclear device'. However, it led to an embargo on India to the detriment of the development of nuclear research and industry and a set-back in technical terms. In the 1980s the nuclear doctrine of 'recessed deterrence' came into vogue. This managed to avoid sanctions while letting it be known that should there be a need for it, the last stage of putting the bomb together could follow easily.

The actual tests of 1998 once again led to renewed international embargos, but India was prepared for it this time around. Concerted and successful attempts to engage India in international structures for non-proliferation and India's active cooperation in the war on terror led to the partial lifting of trade embargos and the Framework Agreement of 2006 with the United States. However, several complications arose from International Atomic Energy Agency (IAEA) regulations that prohibit the export of nuclear technology into states that are not signatories of the NPT; a policy which India finds discriminatory, as she has had to get a special exemption from this body and the Nuclear Suppliers Group (NSG) to make it possible for her to fully engage in nuclear research, commerce and industry. The growing energy needs in India and nuclear power, perceived as essential to the growth of the economy, is an additional argument. For this, particularly in view of the dual-use character of the military and civilian forms of nuclear research, Indian diplomacy has to assuage the international apprehension that South Asia's regional conflict could escalate into large-scale nuclear war, or that weapons of mass destruction could get into the hands of non-state actors, and that civilian facilities could become military ones. The fears about the aggressive military use of nuclear power masked under a programme of research and development and about the Indian ability to protect non-safeguarded facilities from terrorists continue to underlie the reluctance of the nuclear powers with veto rights in the UN Security Council to extend full recognition to India's nuclear status.

Challenges for Indian foreign policy in the twenty-first century

Some observers of the Indian scene have interpreted India's recent policies as indicative of her ambitions for great power status. At least in terms of rhetoric, quite discernibly, an attitude to that effect often lurks behind the moral postures and grandstanding by India's leaders when they are asked to pronounce on global problems. How much of this is empty rhetoric and how much indicates the real interests and intentions of India will be discussed in this section with reference to a series of specific issues.

Global and regional security regimes

Under the impact of the new contextual and indigenous developments, India is re-examining its approach to international and regional organizations. Nehru was a great supporter of international peacekeeping and mediation initiatives,[19] and a staunch advocate of Asian regional cooperation. It was he who organized the Asian Relations Conference even before India achieved Independence. In the new scheme of things, with much of the world clamouring for mediation in Kashmir and India holding out obstinately, claiming that Kashmir is an internal problem of India, the Indian position seriously needs to be looked at afresh. This holds out both a challenge and an opportunity. A proper deal can expedite India's case for a seat on the Security Council. The problem is similar in nature though different in scale with regard to threats to India's security links with her South Asian neighbours. Although the sources of India's insecurity often lie within the territories of her neighbours, India has so far refused to have the issues discussed as a common problem of South Asia, preferring, instead, to take things up at the bilateral level. There is a structural problem here that India needs to solve.

It can be argued that a regional body like the South Asian Association for Regional Cooperation (SAARC) could perhaps facilitate India's room to manoeuvre. However, regional cooperation can work only when either one of two conditions exists. The first is the presence of a benevolent, dominant regional power that can regulate regional behaviour. The second is the existence of a set of regional players with roughly similar resource endowments, or similar threat perceptions from outside the area. The leading role of the United States in the western hemisphere and the successful regional organizations in Europe and South East Asia are pointed out as examples of these conditions. Neither condition obtains in South Asia.[20] A successful solution to the issue of joint management of security threats at the regional level will reduce India's security burden and increase her support from regional powers at the international arena, but, for reasons to be discussed below, India might not find it easy to move in that direction.

A thaw in India–China relations

The easing of tension in India–China relations can help India free up some of the resources tied up in the North-East. From all indications, such efforts are afoot. But the traumatic legacy of India's defeat in 1962 is hard to live down. In addition, the relative freedom of political expression and association in India, periodic movements in favour of human rights in Tibet, particularly on the occasion of high-level visits from China, set limits to India's room for manoeuvre. Beijing has supported separatist and autonomist groups within India in the past. Cohen is sceptical of any chances of early breakthroughs. 'As its own requirements for Middle Eastern oil draw it into the Indian Ocean, China could also emerge as a naval rival to India. The realists in Delhi see China continuing its strategy of encircling and counterbalancing India, preventing it from achieving its rightful dominance of the Subcontinent. This next decade is seen as a transition period, when India must cope with expanding Chinese power, achieve a working relationship with the Americans, and cautiously use each to balance the other's military, economic, and strategic influence. India's new balancing act combines appeasement of China on the issues of Tibet and Taiwan with the pursuit of improved ties with China's other potential balancers, especially Vietnam and Russia.'[21]

India's Arunachal Pradesh which the Chinese regard as disputed territory continues to be a bone of contention. The Economist Intelligence Unit reported an exchange between the two neighbours in 2008 that indicates the high tension that characterizes this dispute.[22] But the pragmatism that characterizes the policies of both countries suggests that the dispute is unlikely to boil over into open conflict.[23]

There are shared interests such as the threat of terrorism combined with increasingly restive Muslim minorities. Both sides clearly need to search for a political formula that will allow for minor adjustments in their respective claims so that political honour is satisfied on both sides.

India and her South Asian neighbours

One of the main factors that have blighted India's chances of gaining a seat in the Security Council is the lack of support for the idea in her own neighbourhood. India's neighbours have been constantly wary of her intentions, seeing India alternately as a 'regional bully' or a 'vulnerable giant'. Why do the relationships between India and her 'small' neighbouring states not run smoothly and, instead, continue to be mired in mutual suspicion? What might be short-term and long-term departures from the low-level equilibrium trap in which the relations seem to be permanently trapped?

The 'small' neighbours, namely Nepal, Bangladesh and Sri Lanka, are comparable in terms of population to larger European states. The epithet 'small' is indicative of an approach that is part of India's problem in the region. In addition, there are historic and demographic reasons that contribute to the complexity of the problem. Soft borders, illegal immigration, terrorism, smuggling, drugs, water resources and the treatment of minorities are among the factors that create pressures on India to intervene in what these countries perceive strictly as their domestic affairs. Cohen reports two positive developments in this regard. First of all, the revolution in economic policy that has swept over India makes it a far more attractive country for all of its neighbours and the more developed states of South-East Asia. Indian management expertise, technology and organizational skills are now widely exported to the rest of Asia, giving substance to the Indian claim that she is a major power. Second, India's democracy is having a great impact on many of its Asian neighbours. For the smaller states of the region, India is something of a model of how to peacefully manage a multi-ethnic, multi-religious state.

The evolution of India's relationship with her South Asian neighbours has gone through several phases. The first phase was that of the classic non-alignment during the tenure of Jawaharlal Nehru as Prime Minister, 1947–64. During this phase India hardly had a policy towards these countries. Despite the first Kashmir war of 1947–48, India saw no need to develop a South Asian policy, pitching herself, instead, as a world player, engaged in bringing about peace and a just world. The penalty for this was paid by Nehru's successors, as relationships with Pakistan worsened, leading to a war in 1965. After the acrimonious exchanges with Sri Lanka with regard to Indian Tamils rendered stateless in the early 1960s, the Shastri–Sirimavo pact saw the repatriation of two-thirds of them to India – a move that planted the seeds of bitterness among the Tamil minority of Sri Lanka and acted subsequently as a catalyst for Tamil discontent in India with regard to their compatriots across the Palk Strait. Indian victory in the 1971 war against Pakistan and the continuation of the 'Indira Doctrine' contributed to fear and suspicion among India's neighbours and added in no small measure to the founding of SAARC, the initiative for which was taken by Bangladesh, with the support of Nepal, as a measure to restrain the hegemonic ambitions of India. India's economic diplomacy in the region following liberalization of the economy in 1991, the 'Look East Policy'[24] and founding of the Bay of Bengal Initiative for Multi-Sectoral Technical and Economic Co-operation (BIMSTEC), associate membership of the Association of South-East Asian Nations (ASEAN) and efforts to accommodate the interests of neighbouring countries within the framework of the South Asian Free Trade Area (SAFTA) are indicators that there is a realization of the need for a coherent South and South East Asian strategy among Indian policy makers. This new realization stems from India's need for transport facilities across Pakistan and Bangladesh for oil pipelines, management of international rivers, a concerted strategy to combat terrorists – many of whom use the neighbouring countries as a base for attacks on India – and generate support in international organizations.

The Ganges Waters Treaty with Bangladesh (1996) shows that a successful model of conflict resolution and a balanced relationship with small neighbours are possible.

Institutional solutions through intergovernmental negotiations have been found to strike a balance between the Bangladeshi complaint about the unilateral diversion of the waters of the Ganga by India to the detriment of Bangladesh and the Indian perception that Bangladesh over-pitched its water need and exaggerated the effects of reduced flows. Of course, it is not a straightforward issue of conflict over interests because the tone one takes towards India is itself a contested issue in the domestic politics of Bangladesh – just as in Sri Lanka, Nepal and Pakistan – and that makes a negotiated settlement of bilateral conflicts so much more difficult.

In addition to the complex interplay of domestic politics and issues of bi-national relations, the South Asian security dilemma and the India–China–Pakistan strategic triangle is a second factor that deeply affects India's relations with her neighbours – particularly Pakistan. The problem arises from the fact that India needs to strike some form of balance with *both* Pakistan and China. Even if India were to arrive at a balance of force with Pakistan, in view of the fact that Indian strategists must anticipate the need to engage both countries in action at a given time, India will need to acquire an additional capacity over and above what the India–Pakistan balance of forces minimally requires. From the Pakistani point of view, since there is no guarantee that India would not mobilize the additional units putatively meant to meet the Chinese threat against Pakistan, Pakistan needs to provide for this contingency by acquiring a suitable counter-force. Thus, the probability of long-term stability under a balance of force breaks down, which leads to the competitive acquisition of additional military capacity. The problem is not insurmountable. If India's relations with Pakistan, United States and China could reach some semblance of trust and normality, the rapidly spreading Indian market of goods, services and entertainment would do the rest in terms of creating a South Asian common market.

The Kashmir imbroglio is a good example of the cost of the security dilemma to both India and Pakistan, the former because of the steady attrition of the costs of internal war, and the latter because it hinders the potential for the benefits of trade and bi-national cooperation. In consequence, India is still at war in Kashmir, though at a reduced scale compared to the recent past. It is a war of attrition, which India cannot manage to win and Pakistan cannot afford to lose.

India and the Indian Ocean

Unfortunately, it seems that up to now India has not actually developed an Indian Ocean policy. Despite some efforts of some institutions like the Institute for Defence and Strategic Analyses (IDSA) or the Society of Indian Ocean Studies (SIOS), both in Delhi, there is no maritime strategic doctrine as such in India.[25] India is part of the Indian Ocean region, but that has not played a very important role in its foreign policy, especially since all conflicts with neighbouring states are situated at India's land borders. In the perception of most Indian specialists on maritime affairs, an Indian Ocean awareness began to develop because of the importance of SLOCs (Sea Lines of Communication) and the EEZ (Exclusive Economic Zones) only very recently. The recent spate of piracy emanating from the coast of Somalia has led to a coordinated effort by India and several other countries whose maritime interests have been adversely affected, to police the sea lanes. Virtually all of India's foreign trade, some 97 per cent in volume, is transported by sea; in 1994–95 this accounted for an estimated 20 per cent of GNP. In addition, as much as 80 per cent of India's

Box 8.4 EU to request new WTO consultations on Indian wine and spirits taxes

Press Releases (P&I/2008/012) Geneva, 22 September 2008

The EU will today request WTO consultations with India on its domestic tax regime for spirits and wines. The request follows a similar WTO panel in 2007, also on India's wines and spirits duties, which was suspended when India changed some elements of its law. These new consultations will seek clarifications from India on the way tax legislation and other measures on market access for wine and spirits are applied in states such as Goa, Maharashtra and Tamil Nadu. These states are among India's largest markets for wines and spirits.

The custom tariff for imported bottled wines and spirits at the Indian border is already as high as 150%. Discriminatory internal taxation in some Indian states adds further to this burden for importers. For example, Maharashtra imposes a special fee on imported wines and exempts locally-produced wines and spirits from excise duty. Goa adds an import and 'label-recording' fee to the cost of imported wines and spirits. In both cases, internal taxes are applied only to imported wines and spirits, or at a much higher rate for imports than domestic goods. This is a breach of the WTO's national treatment principle, which requires that WTO members treat imports and domestic goods the same.

Despite recent amendments to legislation, there are no clear indications that the restrictive retail and wholesale practices in Tamil Nadu have ceased. A special fee also appears to be being imposed on imported wines and spirits only. As part of its 2007 Market Access Strategy the European Commission has focused new resources on removing unfair barriers to trade in key growing markets such as India.

In 2007, EU pressure and a WTO case led to the elimination of the discriminatory federal Additional Duty on wine and spirits in India. This removed the excessive duty burden that India had imposed on imports of spirits and wine, which rose as high as 550% for spirits and up to 264% for wines.

According to EU industry, the Indian market for spirits is one of the largest in the world, amounting in 2007 to about 130 million nine-litre cases. The corresponding figure for wine is 1.5 million nine-litre cases. In 2007, EU exports of spirits to India amounted to about Euro 57 million out of a total Euro 7 billion exported to more than 150 countries. EU exports of wine to India amounted to about Euro 11 million out of a total Euro 6 billion in the same year.

Source: European Commission Daily Press Release cited on: http://europa.eu/rapid/pressReleasesAction. do?reference=IP/08/1382&format=HTML&aged= 0&language=EN&guiLanguage=en.

demand for oil is met from the sea, either carried aboard ships (46 per cent) or extracted from offshore areas (34 per cent). Experts emphasize the need for Indian foreign policy to concentrate efforts on this area.[26]

India and the United States: from ambivalence to engagement

The Indo-American rapprochement is a recent development. The Indian public and policy makers alike have problems understanding why the United States, itself a secular state and a democracy, has not been able to support India against Pakistan, and to a limited extent, against China. The fact that the United States has a firm policy of war against terrorism but condones cross-border terrorism emanating from Pakistan makes many question its real intentions in Asia.

India has remained ambivalent with regard to the United States in the recent past. Thus, during Operation Desert Storm against Iraq, the world was first treated to pictures of a smiling Indian Foreign Minister in Baghdad, then the grant of refuelling facilities to American aircraft which were promptly withdrawn when the Indian anti-American lobby got wind of it. Americans, who had their fall-back arrangements anyway and had only needed an Indian show of support for propaganda purposes, were not amused. With regard to economic diplomacy, in WTO negotiations India often sides with China and Brazil against the United States on the issue of agricultural quotas. However, while the United States tacitly accepts the opposition, it finds India's moral grandstanding with regard to American dominance particularly irritating. On the other hand, Indian policy makers remember with particular resentment the long American support to the Pakistani position on Kashmir in the United Nations, and the supportive rhetoric of the United States in the 1962 India–China war which did not translate into actual support on the ground. The sending of the *USS Enterprise* to the Bay of Bengal at the height of the India–Pakistan war of 1971 remains a reminder of American incomprehension of South Asian realities and insensitivity towards Indian sentiments. The increasingly visible and politically active Indian–American lobby in the United States and accommodation of American interests in the Indian Ocean are two factors that the current government appears to have taken on board with regard to the conceptualization and implementation of Indian policy.

American perception of India during the cold war (1947–89) was influenced by what US policy makers saw as India's irritating show of neutrality and pro-Soviet leanings in real terms. Pakistan was portrayed as the linchpin of American alliances in South/Central/East Asia and the USSR was seen as an Indian ally. The Indo-China war in 1962 did not in any way turn Indo-US relations in India's favour. The Vietnam War cemented the ideological distance between India and the United States. The events of the 1970s, beginning with the Pakistan-brokered Nixon visit to China, the Indo-Soviet Treaty of Friendship (1970), the Indo-Pak war of 1971 where the United States intervened in favour of Pakistan at a late stage, and finally the Soviet invasion of Afghanistan (1979) reinforced the distance between India and the United States. The end of Soviet rule in Afghanistan led to the US loss of interest in South Asia, just as post-liberalization India, an emerging market for the United States, became an interesting trading partner. Following the re-emergence of the Taliban and the need to counter-balance, India has emerged as a potential ally – a fact that has led to unprecedented levels of American support for India's nuclearization.

In addition to their growing proximity, Indian diplomacy has increasingly sought to engage the allies of the United States such as Israel in strategic partnerships. In some cases, India has been able to engage powers which the United States sees as rivals, such as France, or hostile, such as Iran, in deals of mutual interest. Close on the heels of the approval of the Indo-US Nuclear Agreement, India signed a similar agreement with France. As for the nuclear ambitions of Iran, India has sought to maintain a middle position between herself and the United States which wants it curbed altogether and has pursued the idea of an oil pipeline that would run overland across Pakistan. Even with China, despite some difference on the boundary issue, bilateral trade is booming compared to the past.[27] India has started actively linking trade and diplomacy. The 2006 Joint Statement Towards Japan-India Strategic and Global Partnership could counterbalance China's influence in the area. On a larger plane, India is active at the international level as well; it is involved with the India–Brazil–South Africa Dialog Forum (IBSA). Finally, as one can see in Box 8.4, the transformation of India's agrarian economy is opening up new vistas of challenge and opportunity, making it possible for her diplomats to work closely with counterparts from other countries.

India – still an emerging power?

India's contested status as a nuclear power,[28] the scale of her armaments (see Table 8.2),[29] and the huge deployment of ground troops on the western front, particularly in Kashmir, are issues of immediate concern to her South Asian neighbours. Since tension feeds on tension, war in Afghanistan, terrorist attacks in cities all over India – Mumbai, Bangalore, Jaipur, Ahmedabad, Guwahati, Kolkata, Delhi, Jammu and Srinagar – mounting tension between India and Pakistan over the issue of cross-border terrorism in Kashmir, and the formal policy of Pakistan to consider the first strike option as part of her strategic response to Indian aggression have contributed to the seriousness of the state of affairs. The probability of the regional conflict escalating into large-scale nuclear war, or weapons of mass destruction finding their way into the hands of non-state actors, have drawn world attention to South Asia, which has had visits in quick succession by political leaders and military delegations from the United States, the UK, Germany, France, Russia and China. India's ambiguity – building up a stockpile of arms and political rhetoric to match, but not followed up by consequent action – has contributed to the uncertainty of placing India in the hierarchy of powers. This section, based on a brief analysis of India's military capacity and public opinion, seen as an indicator of national will, delves into this issue.

India's military capacity

India, with a huge economy and a poor population, thus presents a somewhat contradictory picture. The picture has changed since the beginning of liberalization in the early 1990s, and the quality of life is slowly going up. But, in terms of relative power, this does not help India, for both GNP per capita and the quality of life are going up even faster among her competitors. It is also an intensely politicized society, and a contentious democracy, which affects the ratio of potential power to effective force negatively, contributing to the overall ambiguity of India's international presence.

With regard to India's defence outlay, the state spends approximately 2.5 per cent of its Gross Domestic Product (GDP) on defence, amounting in 2008 to only US$21 per person.[30] By comparison, India's adversaries spend more. Pakistan spends around 3.1 per cent of its national income on the armed forces, – about US$24 per person, while China spends 2 per cent – US$48 per person.[31] In comparison to these Asian figures, the United States is, with US$1,786 per person, which equals 4 per cent of the GDP, far ahead of them all. In terms of aggregate figures, India spent about US$25 billion in 2008.[32] This is modest compared to China's US$64 billion or Japan's US$43 billion. Russia spends US$38 billion, but the United States, which spends around US$548 billion in military equipment and personnel, is ahead of everyone else.

How do these figures translate into actual power? Cohen (2001, p. 29) mentions a multiplier effect of 'low wages and generally high quality of Indian armed forces' which 'magnify the effect of India's mere US$14 billion in defence spending'. India has the largest volunteer military establishment in the world, with well over one million regular soldiers, sailors and airmen, and nearly the same number of paramilitary forces. But, in terms of effective logistics, as we learn from Jaswant Singh's influential *Defending India* (1999), a large part of this force is tied up with other tasks and, as such, should be discounted when it comes to the calculation of national power.

In real terms, the effective power of the Indian army to wage war is less than one might deduce from its strength because the army is deployed in policing activities (e.g. riot control, providing security for elections). This opinion is echoed by a high-level inquiry commission set up by the government of India which states that the withdrawal of paramilitary (army) forces from the borders has in the past exacerbated the problems of border management. This internal-external security link persists in recent discussions of India's security management and underscores the necessity for analysts to see the two themes as connected. India's contentious democracy and the worsening communal relations have greatly exacerbated the need for effective policing. The police are a State subject under the federal division of powers and, being under the control of India's regional governments, are not always considered politically neutral. At the slightest outbreak of communal violence, therefore, there is a clamour for the deployment of the army. Already overstretched in view of its engagement with anti-insurgency operations in Jammu and Kashmir, Punjab, the North-East and sundry other trouble spots where the state is engaged in fighting Naxalites (left-wing guerrillas), the additional demands on its personnel greatly reduce the effective fire power of the armed forces.

India had sought in the past to increase her room to manoeuvre against Pakistan through diversification in arms procurement which lowers dependence on any particular arms supplier, and through a programme of indigenization which required supply contracts to include a provision for their production in India under licence. The 1965 Indo-Pak war had demonstrated the advantage of this strategy, for India, unlike Pakistan, was not dependent on an outside supplier for spare parts or for continued supply. But these advantages have been neutralized through nuclearization, which has helped Pakistan bridge the gap of 'strategic depth' against India, assisted further by the ability of Pakistan to draw on both China and the USA against India. In addition, there have been allegations that Indian armed forces are suffering from waste and corruption and are under-equipped compared even with Pakistan.

In consequence, modest increases in defence spending have a limited impact on India's power projection capabilities.[33]

India and Pakistan are self-declared nuclear powers and their devices, with the multiplier of delivery vehicles, must also be factored into the regional military balance. China is supposed to have nearly 300 deployed nuclear weapons. While the question of deployed nuclear weapons in India is still subject to speculation, India is estimated to have the capacity for building between 25 and 100 warheads,[34] and Pakistan to have enough fissile material to produce between 10 and 15 'devices', although recent reports suggest that Pakistan holds the larger inventory.[35] It remains unclear how many weapons are deployed at a given time, but one can safely assume that both have at least a few devices and could produce many more on fairly short notice. China is believed by some Indian analysts to have several nuclear weapons deployed in bases in Tibet. As for delivery, aircraft still remains the main mode, but Pakistan is assumed to be moving towards a missile-based capability. Some experts assert that India lags behind Pakistan in this category, with only a few short-range missiles (the Prithvi) in its inventory, and a medium-range missile (the Agni) still under development. China has a few intercontinental ballistic missiles (ICBMs), nearly 70 medium-range missiles and a dozen sea-launched ones (India has neither an ICBM nor a sea-launch capability, although programmes of both are under way). Most of these Chinese systems could theoretically target major Indian cities or Indian nuclear weapons based in northern and eastern India.[36]

In terms of naval power, India's fleet is smaller than China's, but anecdotal evidence suggests that it is better trained and more experienced. Indian ships range throughout the Indian Ocean, paying regular calls on ports in East Africa and South-East Asia. Although in terms of quantity, the Indian navy is shrinking, since many obsolete vessels are being retired, and although a new carrier[37] may be out of (financial) reach for the Indian navy, the quality of the Indian warships is gradually improving through the acquisition of Russian *Kashin*-class destroyers or Russian *Granit* Submarine-Launched Cruise Missiles (SLCMs) for their Kilo-Class submarines. So the Indian navy may currently not be able to conduct sustained operations far from base (for example in the South China Sea), but it is definitely well positioned to defend India's interests in the Bay of Bengal and in the Arabian Sea. India's capacity to deploy a substantial air-sea operation within 48 hours of the tsunami catastrophe demonstrates this point.

In terms of gross indicators of size of the population and the economy, India is among the leading states in the world. As regards the number of inhabitants, India has the world's second largest population, having passed the billion mark, and on current trends could surpass China in the next few decades. India is far ahead of the United States (270 million), and other points of reference like Russia, Indonesia, Japan, Pakistan, Brazil and Nigeria, all of which are home to between 100 million and 250 million people. India's economy is gigantic in terms of overall Gross National Product (GNP) and, along with China, is well placed to become one of the major economic powers in the near future. When measured by *purchasing power parity* (PPP) taking into account local rates of exchange, India scores higher with US$1,661 billion, the fourth largest in the world. As international politics recognizes states as the main actors, these figures should rank India among the leading 'powers' of the world. But from the point of view of relative power, they are misleading, for the transformation of GNP to power must take into account the ability of an actor to mobilize the economy to a war economy, and for the population to be able to sustain a war over an indefinite period. Seen in this light, the impact of India's size is modest on her relative power position because of the poor performance on the per capita indicator. India ranks low in terms of GNP per capita, with a figure of only US$430, far below China's US$750. On social indicators, the picture is just as dismal, for India does rather badly on the Human Development Index of the United Nations Development Programme (UNDP).[38]

India's ambiguous profile results from the hiatus between self-perception and evaluation by others. Perception based on the nostalgia for the *Hindi-Chini-bhai-bhai* days where there was a semblance of equality between the two neighbours is widely out of sync with the reality on the ground. Parity with China will require the deployment of resources at a scale that India does not possess. Besides, India's engagement with South Asia keeps her troops tied down to the region. Consequently, in terms of translating force potential into actual power, India faces a considerable degree of slippage. This uncertainty about the real power at the disposal of India causes the country to shuttle uneasily between grandstanding on the one hand, and inexplicable acquiescence in situations that are contrary to her interests or declared principles on the other, lowering her credibility even further.

Soft power: foreign policy and popular perception in India

An analysis of data on popular perception of the nuclear programme gives some credence to Stephen Cohen's contention that the Indian nuclear programme is 'without clear purpose or direction'.[39] Three factors, namely, the cohesive nature of public opinion about national security commitments and priorities, the clarity of a national security doctrine and the actual possession of the resources to wage war, constitute the variables in the perception of national power. As the following information about public perception and attitudes shows, India's exact rank as a power remains uncertain. Indian public opinion supports the bomb, but not for warlike purposes (Tables 8.3 and 8.4 below). India is engaged in the production of weapons and missiles but, unlike other countries similarly engaged, there are no plans for or policies about sale or diffusion of such technology.[40]

India's active media and contentious democracy provide effective conditions for an influential role for Indian public opinion in the formulation and implementation of strategic decisions. The data reported in Table 8.3 show that Indian security and foreign policy are both firmly in the realm of national political consciousness, a fact that no government in politically contentious India can afford to ignore. But, while the Indian public appear to be conscious of the problem of security, what do they really want from their government?

The data reported in Table 8.3, possibly reflecting the effects of Kargil, show a public that is agitated but indecisive, whereas Table 8.4 shows the perception of Pakistan as India's 'public enemy number one', although with regard to the right course of action to follow, the Indian public is surprisingly conciliatory. Significantly, many more people agree that 'India should make efforts to develop friendly relations with Pakistan' than disagree (Mitra and Singh 2009, p. 115). On the general issue of 'war as the only solution to the Indo-Pakistan problem', the number of those who

Table 8.3 Public opinion on state-to-state relations

Now I will read the names of some countries. Have you heard the name of these countries?		*(If yes) How is their relationship with India – Friend, neither friend nor enemy or enemy?*		
	Yes	*No*	*Friend*	*Neither*	*Enemy*
Nepal	65.3	34.7	41.3	16.8	1.7
America	70.3	29.7	27.1	25.9	11.1
Pakistan	82.9	17.1	6.9	7.4	64.2
Bangladesh	65.5	34.5	32.5	21.4	5.7
China	64.3	35.7	21.7	23.4	13.0
Sri Lanka	66.5	33.5	36.1	21.0	3.3
Russia	61.9	38.1	42.1	12.7	1.4

Source: Post-poll Survey of the Indian Electorate, CSDS (Delhi) 1999.

Table 8.4 Public opinion on security issues

Q: Now I will talk about some specific issues on which different people have different opinions. I will read out some statements to which you may agree or disagree.

Statements	*Agree*	*No Opinion*	*Disagree*
India should make efforts to develop friendly relations with Pakistan. Do you . . .	42.4	33.9	23.7
Country should increase spending on army even if it increases the burden on ordinary people. Do you . . .	50.1	32.6	17.3
War is the only solution to Indo-Pakistan problem. Do you . . .	25.2	35.6	39.1

Source: Post-poll Survey of the Indian Electorate, CSDS (Delhi) 1999.

disagree far exceeds those who agree (while a substantial number express no opinion), but these conciliatory and peace-like opinions are contradicted by the strong support for 'increased spending on the army even if it increases the burden on ordinary people', with over half of the total sample agreeing to the proposition and less than a fifth expressing their disagreement.

Conclusion

In the course of the six eventful decades since Independence analysed in this chapter, Indian diplomacy has changed greatly in its tone and content. The shrill undertone of morality has now been replaced by a new pragmatism that keeps India's foreign policy nuclear, internationally engaged and non-aligned, all at the same time. Compared to the sharp moral reactions to world events, the general tone today is more nuanced. Rather than standing alone on issues that affect both long-held principles and material interests of the country, such as the failed attempts by the King of Nepal to scuttle democratic development in the country, India has chosen to act in concert with the UK and the United States. The country now refrains from direct interference while still making it clear that it stood by democratic transition. Further, the approach to international relations has become more complex, capable of conducting diplomatic business in spite of existing conflicts, as one notices in the case of flourishing Indo-Chinese trade despite differences over territory, and the Chinese reservations about the Indo-US Nuclear Framework Agreement and India's growing nuclear arsenal. In the third place, within the general norms of the five principles of co-existence, Indian diplomats have been busy negotiating the terms of trade in international organizations such as the WTO, often making alliances with like-minded countries. However, the apparently anti-western rhetoric that sometimes characterizes these dealings has not affected the support that India has received from the United States in difficult negotiations with the International Atomic Energy Agency or with the Nuclear Suppliers Group.

These significant changes in India's diplomacy have come about as a result of the contributions of successive generations of leaders, who have added their innate ideas and perceptions of national interest to the cumulating fund of Indian diplomacy. The main framework of non-alignment has remained, but the contents have been reshuffled, repacked, enriched and occasionally jettisoned by Nehru's successors. Their strategic moves have been influenced by the joint consideration of their perception of choices open to them in the international arena and the advantages that the given choice could deliver in domestic politics. Just as the decision of Indira Gandhi to intervene in Pakistan's internal conflict in 1971 at the risk of international opprobrium, particularly from the United States and its allies, generated great enthusiasm within India, so did the move of Atal Bihari Vajpayee to authorize the nuclear tests and the subsequent bus diplomacy with Pakistan. The alacrity with which the UPA government has pursued the nuclear deal, and has attempted to balance the sentiments of articulate Hindu opinion in Jammu with the interest of the Kashmir valley in direct trade with Pakistan across the Line of Control indicates the continuation of engagement and affirmation of national interest.

How does India's status as a nuclear power affect her self-image as a non-aligned country, committed to international peace?[41] *Panchasheela*, the five principles of peaceful coexistence to which Jawaharlal Nehru gave an institutional expression in terms of the Non-Aligned Movement, provided a complete if not coherent statement of India's strategic doctrine at the height of the cold war. Following the decline of Nehru's *Panchasheela*, despite attempts by Indira Gandhi and Gujaral to formulate a general framework for India's engagement with the world, no explicit single coherent doctrine has emerged. New generations of policy makers, voters, parties and major changes in the regional and international contexts have influenced the development of strategic thinking. These have yielded significant changes but overall, Indian foreign policy retains an aura of uncertainty about it.

Two significant aspects of recent developments in Indian foreign policy should be mentioned here. In the first place, one should remember that three key elements – liberalization of the economy and a consequent integration with the world economy, nuclearization, and engagement with Pakistan and China in negotiation – have become enduring features of Indian diplomacy. Second, there is a strong bi-partisan consensus around these initiatives. Once in power, Hindu nationalists took the initiative for the bus diplomacy with Pakistan, and invited General Musharraf – for many, the main architect of the failure of Lahore and the betrayal of Kargil – for a dialogue with India. The Congress, long identified with the 'firm India' policy of Indira Gandhi and Rajiv Gandhi, has come back to where the NDA government located itself.

Analysed critically, the recent statement by Prime Minister Dr Manmohan Singh at the Asian–African Conference,[42] evocative of the heady days of the Bandung spirit not seen since the 1950s euphoria of *Panchasheela* and Afro-Asian solidarity, reveals an important, new and potentially enduring step in the evolution of an Indian doctrine. Once one gets past the familiar litany one finds a fine balance of national self-interest and idealism. The idea of Afro-Asian solidarity is pragmatically adapted to the imperatives of our times. The commitment to justice and solidarity is tempered with the imperative of change. The difference in tone and content of the new *Panchasheela* from the old is remarkable. Whereas its invocation during the earlier phases started, continued and ended with idealistic evocations of Afro-Asian solidarity and abstract goals of peace, an instrumental approach to abstract goals triumphs in the current form. The declaration on a new Asian African Strategic Partnership outlines guiding principles for joint action to achieve our goals in a changed global environment. With his insuperable command over the technical aspects of the international political economy and the newly acquired aura of confident actor in international politics, under the leadership of Manmohan Singh, India has come up with a series of specific measures that should be at the top of the international agenda. These measures include the demands to phase out trade-distorting agricultural subsidies in developed countries and to remove barriers to agricultural exports from developing countries; lowering of tariff barriers to other exports; to balance the protection of the environment with the development aspirations of the developing nations; urgent measures to generate additional financial resources for development, especially for the least developed countries and the highly indebted poor countries. India has effectively couched the country's long-standing goal of a permanent seat in the Security Council of the United Nations with the right to veto under the rhetoric of the 'democratization' of the United Nations and its specialized agencies.

With Manmohan Singh continuing the Bandung spirit very much in the Nehruvian mode, and the stream of international visitors calling by, those with long memories of the early years after Independence might ask if Indian diplomacy is back in its well-worn, noble-minded but effete grooves. However, broad similarities can be deceptive. Beyond the constants of Indian politics such as familiar faces in high places, and familiar rhetoric, Indian diplomacy has acquired a new pragmatism and a tone of confidence that distinguish it from its earlier avatars. The 1998 tests which brought India opprobrium from all possible quarters, deftly handled in its conceptualization, implementation and subsequent damage-limiting diplomacy, have produced an environment conducive to a new sense of realism in Indo-US strategic relations, which, in turn, has become a leading element in similar arrangements with the EU, Russia, China and Pakistan.[43]

With the emergence of a complex multi-polar world, international politics has entered a context where the rules of international conduct on issues of technology, multilateralism, environment and terrorism are being rewritten. A new coalition of major powers is at the forefront of efforts to reorganize the Security Council. Once again, as at the height of the cold war, fortuitously, Indian policy has gravitated towards placing her interests in the international arena with the right combination of structural realism and constructivist principles. Rather than being self-consciously unique and aloof, this policy is increasingly drawing on national identity (culture and ideology), and liberal values of peace and plurality without at the same time ignoring the assertion of legitimate national self-interests.

Notes

1 If a doctrine is understood in terms of a cohesive construct that reduces uncertainty by pulling together clear objectives, an institutional mechanism for implementation and the capacity to match action to policy, then India's 'doctrine of minimum nuclear deterrence' is an epitome of ambiguity. Key statements such as 'India will not be the first to initiate a nuclear strike, but will respond with punitive retaliation should deterrence fail' are capable of diverse interpretation. See 'Draft record of National Security Advisory Board on Indian Nuclear Doctrine', http://www.indianembassy.org/policy/CTBT/Nuclear_doctrine_aug_17, accessed on 1 June, 2005.

2 In a remakable demonstration of its commitment to the Indo-US Nuclear Framework Agreement, the Congress-led United Progressive Alliance government of India risked its very survival in the trust vote of 2008 where the communist allies of the ruling coalition withdrew their support. The government survived the trust vote by recruiting other allies to replace the communists.

3   The UPA government is committed to maintaining a credible nuclear weapons programme while at the same time it will evolve demonstrable and verifiable confidence-building measures with its nuclear neighbours. It will take a leadership role in promoting universal, nuclear disarmament and working for a nuclear weapons-free world.

> UPA's Common Minimum Programme;
> see Internet sources.

4 Incredible as it might sound, a month after the attack on Mumbai by terrorists who are suspected of having been trained in Pakistan, it was India which was being called upon to be restrained in her reaction! Despite circumstantial evidence indicating a link between the terrorists and the Pakistani army, Pakistan, with the support of China, has manoeuvred to get India to assure a world weary of war between the nuclear-powered neighbours of its peaceful intentions.

> Buoyed by the entry of traditional ally China in the role of the peacemaker in the region and feeling 'vindicated' by the toned down Indian statements, Pakistan proposed on Tuesday that New Delhi should send it 'positive signals' by deactivating its forward air bases and relocating troops to 'peace time' positions.

The best that Indian embassy officials have managed by the way of response to this demarche on the part of Pakistan is to issue a statement: 'We have been asked to undo what we have not done' ('Relocate troops to "peace time" positions: Pakistan' in *The Hindu*, 31 December, 2008).

5 The statement by Prime Minister Vajpayee, that 'the tests . . . provided a valuable database for the design of nuclear weapons and of different yields for different applications and different delivery systems', went beyond the ad hoc extemporizing of Indira Gandhi in front of the world media about peaceful uses of nuclear power. This was a step in the direction of greater clarity but was still short of the standards set by the nuclear establishment as it failed to nail it to some visible target. The NDA appeared to be speaking in two voices – with the Defence Minister Fernandes holding forth about China being India's enemy number one whereas the rank and file greeted the tests as a fitting symbolic victory against Pakistan (Bertsch *et al.* 1999, p. XIV).

6 'It would seem that for India, and Singh, it was poker all along, and that Singh bluffed the man who held the stronger hand' (Finan 2005, p. 96).

7 The Economist Intelligence Unit's country report on India sums up the situation as follows:

> A long standing dispute between India and China over the Indian State of Arunachal Pradesh flared up once again in March [2008]. The dispute has been festering since the war between the two countries in 1962. Both sides agreed in 1993 to maintain peace along the McMahon Line (the existing Line of Control) regardless of their divergent views regarding the sovereignty

over the territory. The 1,030 km unfenced border is separated by the McMahon Line which China has not recognised since it was determined during the British Colonial rule in 1914. China claims 90,000 sq km of the territory – that is, nearly all of Arunachal Pradesh.

Monthly Report, April 2008, p. 10.

8 The tool box draws upon the two dominant modes of thinking in international politics, namely, (neo-) realism and (neo-) liberalism (many going back to the Kantian notion of perpetual peace) as well as constructivism, which seeks to bridge the chasm between the former two. Indian policy strikes a balance between national interest and deeply held values. For a guide to understanding its complexity, see Wendt (1999, p. 1): 'the structures of human associations are determined primarily by shared ideas rather than material forces, and ... the identities and interests of purposive actors are constructed by these shared ideas rather than given by nature'. See also Mitra and Schoettli (2007).

9 The Economist Intelligence Unit country report on India (Monthly Report January 2008, p. 3) highlighted this as part of its outlook for 2008–9, emphasizing the linkage between domestic politics and foreign policy. The political crisis was precipitated when the Left Front parties led by the communists whose parliamentary seats were crucial for the stability of the UPA government served an ultimatum on the government to withdraw from negotiations with the International Atomic Energy Agency (IAEA) or forfeit support on the floor of the parliament. The crisis spurred Prime Minster Manmohan Singh to ask for a 'trust vote' from the parliament to prove that the civil nuclear deal with the United States had the confidence of a majority of members. In the final voting where the Left Front withdrew its support from the UPA coalition, the government survived by gaining support from the Samajwadi Party.

10 See Mitra (2001).

11 Notice, for example, the tremendous costs in terms of lives and prestige paid for an Indian stand on Sri Lanka and the utter silence of the Indian regime on the most important settlement just concluded between the Liberation Tigers of Tamil Eelam (LTTE) and the Sri Lankan government.

12 Cohen (2001), p. 47.

13 See Mansingh (1984).

14 See Neville Maxwell (1970) on India's 'forward policy', pp. 173–74; 232.

15 Srivastava (1995), the secretary to Shastri who was with him in Tashkent and followed events closely, provides valuable insights into the thinking of Shastri.

16 See Srivastava's 1995 biography of Shastri for details of the Indian perception of the unfolding scenario.

17 Nugent (1990), p. 116.

18 'Kargil ... was emblematic of a malaise in India–Pakistan relations that threatens, in the absence of serious and concerned efforts to put these relations on a more productive footing, to darken their passage well into the twenty-first century' (Wirsing 2003, p. 39).

> [T]he most important lesson of the two-month crisis ensues from the disastrous consequences of unstructured governance. The Kargil affair has exposed systematic flaws in a decision-making process that is impulsive, chaotic, erratic and overly secretive ... playing holy warriors this week and men of peace the next betrays an infirmity and insincerity of purpose that leaves the country leaderless and directionless.

'Anatomy of a debacle', *Newsline*, July 1999.

19 In fact, the constitution of India mandates cooperation with international bodies, including the United Nations. See Constitution of India, Article 51.

20 Cohen (2001), p. 58.

21 Cohen (2001), p. 56.

22 In early March [2008] Mr Mukherjee [India's foreign minister] said that China's claim was illegal and made clear that Arunachal Pradesh was 'an integral part of India'. Mr Mukherjee's comments followed Mr Singh's first visit to the mountainous State, during which he called Arunachal Pradesh 'our land of the rising sun', much to the annoyance of the Chinese. China has consistently refused to issue visas to Indian passport holders hailing from Arunachal Pradesh, arguing that they do not need such documentation to visit "their own country". India has been alarmed by what the army chief of staff, General Deepak Kapoor, has called

a "tremendous" build up of infrastructure on the Chinese side in the past few years. The Indian government has vowed to speed up the development of the State.

Economist Intelligence Unit Monthly Report, April 2008, p. 10.

23 The EIU reports wryly,

Both countries know that the cost of war over the territory would be prohibitively high (the state's GDP is less than 2 per cent the value of India–Chinese bilateral trade) and would derail the process of closer bilateral economic integration and co-operation – unlike in decades past, when such a process was ore or less non-existent. But long-running negotiations on Arunachal Pradesh have yielded no real progress that would reflect these improved bilateral ties and new economic realities.

Economist Intelligence Unit Monthly Report, April 2008, p. 10.

24 The Look East Policy is a generic name for a cluster of initiatives undertaken by the Government of India to strengthen Indian interests in South-East and East Asia.

25 According to, for example, Commodore C. Uday Bhaskar there is neither an understanding of India's maritime history nor an Indian Ocean awareness. Interviewed by Peter Lehr and Maike Tuchner on 27 August, 2000 for the research project 'Panchayati Raj in the Indian Ocean – Towards a Maritime Security Regime?', funded by the Fritz Thyssen-Foundation, Cologne.

26 Roy-Chaudhury (1998), pp. 19–27.

27 The Nathula trading post, for example, which was closed following the war in 1962, was opened again in 2006.

28 Neither the five recognized nuclear weapon states, nor the signatory states of the NPT and CTBT and the members of the IAEA formally recognize India's and Pakistan's nuclear status. However, at the informal level, the major actors, above all the US administration, follow a rather pragmatic policy by engaging India in tacit negotiations and increasingly intense cooperation on nuclear safety and restrictions on technology transfer.

29 India, as Cohen (2001) reports,

has been in the midst of a major arms buying spree. A recent purchase from Russia for more than $4 billion worth of equipment will augment India's tank force and air fleet considerably and permit the acquisition of several important ships, including a second aircraft carrier. This included a $3 billion agreement to produce aircraft under license and acquire modern tanks and an aircraft carrier' (p. 31). See 'India, Russia sign $3 billion arms deal', *Times of India*, 29 December, 2000.

Also 'India, Russia ready military arms dealer', CNN.com, 4 October, 2000. India has just purchased more than 1,000 man-portable radar systems from Israel and is negotiating a deal on Hawk jets with the UK.

30 See Cohen (2001), p. 29.

31 Own calculation based on Stockholm International Peace Research Institute data. See the SIPRI Military Expenditure Database. http://milexdata.sipri.org (accessed 19 May, 2010) and *CIA World Factbook* (https://www.cia.gov/library/publications/the–world–factbook/) (accessed 19 May, 2010).

32 See Table 8.1 above.

33 See the scathing pre-Kargil critique by Mohan Guruswamy, 'Modernise or perish', *Indian Express*, 26 January, 1998. After Kargil, he and others pointed out the considerable qualitative disadvantages held by India's larger forces when confronted with the Pakistani forces.

34 Tellis, in Ganguly (2001) gives estimates by various specialists.

35 For an analysis, confirmed in part by recently retired US officials, see Windrem and Kupperman, 'Pakistan Nukes Outstrip India's, Officials Say,' MSNBC News (2001). See also Tellis (2001, p. 730) 'Pakistan, though nominally weak (compared to India) is actually stronger than it is commonly perceived'.

36 Cohen (2001), p. 30. See Perkovich (1999) for a detailed account of the development of India's nuclear programme. For a projection of future growth of India's nuclear weapons programme, see Tellis (2001), p.720.

37 In January 2004, India finalized a deal with Russia for the purchase of the 'Admiral Gorshkov' (IISS 2004–5, p. 144).

38 See Cohen (2001) for details.
39 Cohen (2001), Chapter 6.
40 Former President A.P.J. Kalam, one of India's leading military scientists and the 'father' of India's missile programme, had urged India to get into the business of missile sales in order to break up the 'monopolies' of the dominant powers and their unfair regulating mechanisms, such as the Missile Technology Control Regime.
41 Indians, apparently, see no contradiction between India's brand recognition as a country of peace and her status as a nuclear power. See Mitra and Singh (2009).
42 Manmohan Singh (2005) speech delivered on 23 April.
43 Ibid.

9   Conclusion

Some general lessons from the Indian case

India is the one place in the world where a man can do as he pleases and nobody asks why.

Kipling (1895), 'The Miracle of Purun Bhagat', *The Jungle Book II*, p. 23.

If we possess our *why* of life we can put up with almost any *how*.

Nietzsche (1889), *The Twilight of the Idols*.[1]

Introduction

A perusal of India's print media – in English as much as in the vernacular languages – and the lively political debates on the television help illustrate the arguments relating to the democratic structure and process of India's politics made in this book. The rich harvest of events, statistics and cultural vignettes that one encounters in India's politics are a testimony to the vigorous reach of the Indian state, the market and the civil society. This concluding chapter seeks to draw these mobile elements into a common narrative. In addition, it considers the Indian case in cross-national comparison, with a view to drawing some general lessons.

The political context of Indian democracy

Well into its seventh decade following Independence, democracy in India thrives even as it gets fuzzy at the edges.[2] The constitution holds the Union of India to be 'indestructible', but violent dissent persists in Kashmir, in the North East and in other parts of the vast land. The economy sustains unprecedented growth. This has now been dented by the financial crisis that struck the world economy in 2008, but India appears to be coping with this effectively. Efficient financial management has kept inflation within manageable limits. But the issue still remains of how to redistribute money to the increasingly assertive poor without eroding the incentive to work, take risks and expect to earn higher wages and profits. Thanks to television, the new culture of buying and selling has trickled down deep into Indian society. In consequence, share prices have risen steadily, despite the turbulent history of periodic scams. More alarmingly, however, the dark sides of democracy – corruption, violent crime and other challenges to governance – do not show any signs of abating. In some parts of India, civil society languishes, as assertive majorities threaten to appropriate the public sphere in the name of their collective identity, pitching democracy and secularism at odds. Yet – defying logic, dark forebodings and in apparent contradiction with itself – India, seemingly, goes on. Why?

The question has engaged many celebrated observers of India,[3] as much as scholars of general and comparative theory who have found a foil for their arguments in the case of India. India's *otherness*, particularly the idiosyncratic nature of the caste system, the peculiarities of Hindu ritual, and Hinduism itself – more a cultural system than a religion – have made India an interesting case in point for a wide variety of observers. In writing this book, I have drawn on this scholarly heritage in order to understand how far India's political system can cope with the challenges that the country faces at the start of the twenty-first century. The chapters on India's institutional arrangements, the interaction of the modern state and traditional society, the policy process, the economy and international relations have each engaged with the contradictions that have become trademark features of India. The book has responded to these issues with an 'Indian model' which pinned the Indian miracle – democracy and development in a post-colonial context – on strategic reform and a policy process based on elite agency, accountability, state–society linkage, individual rationality and institutional arrangements (Figure 1.1 above). I have argued that the diligent performance of India's modern institutions – the veritable work horses of democracy – backed up by the political process, a relatively new coalitional arrangement for power-sharing, constitutional recognition of basic rights and their assertion by potential beneficiaries, and empowerment of social groups who have long remained at the margins of the political system, have brought meaning and substance to formal procedures of democracy. Working together, India's institutions and political process have transformed the country from a British colony into a bustling democratic society in the span of six decades. Indeed, such is the nature of Indian democracy that even political groups which do not necessarily share the liberal premises of democracy nevertheless articulate their demands in terms of the extension of *their* democratic rights.

Therein lies a paradox. Democracy might offer the best solution to politics *within* the system, but how good is it at coping with politics *of* the system? Does the democratic process, particularly in a post-colonial context, have the strategic room to manoeuvre to reform the political system of which it is a part? What additional resources might India need to 'repair the ship, while keeping it afloat' as storm clouds gather on the horizon? In my study of the structure and process of India's politics, and the attempt at generalizing beyond the Indian case, I have pointed towards strategic reform, accountability, and social policies that balance efficiency with justice as the best solution for sustaining the progress achieved over the past two decades. The concluding chapter looks beyond the distributional issues and draws attention to the as yet unresolved problem of collective identity. India's incomplete project of nation-building requires her to look beyond her borders, for the Indian problem cannot be seen in isolation from that of the subcontinent.

Many of the distributional conflicts analysed in this book result from the success of India's democracy, and more recently, of her economy. That, by itself, is a portent of hope. The judicious and efficient solution of these conflicts over resources has enhanced the legitimacy of the system as a whole. The spate of mass movements of the 1950s based on language could be contained through negotiation. The eventual redrawing of the map of India, thanks to the States' Reorganisation Commission (1957–58), enhanced the legitimacy of the State and the federal structure.[4] However, while effective management of the conflict based on language produced attractive opportunities for emerging social groups, new cleavages based on ethnic identity have emerged in the course of time. Using existing constitutional methods and innovating new ones such as the creation of new administrative and political units within existing federal States, the Indian state has succeeded in bringing a satisfactory solution to these conflicts.[5] The growing economy and the hunger of the middle class for cars, electronic gadgets and other symbols of affluent living have vastly intensified India's energy needs and led to consumer frustration. The two-pronged strategy that the government has developed to address this category of conflicts has consisted in an elaborate system of controls and subsidy to customers on the one hand and efforts to enhance capacity through exploration, international alliances and the price mechanism on the other. Social mobility and the growth of population make the infrastructural needs – such as transport, communication, education, health, clean drinking water and prevention of communicable diseases like AIDS – sharper. Simultaneously, however, the liberalization of the economy and the steady integration of the Indian market with the international market economy threaten to disenfranchise parts of the population, and prevent others from joining the consuming classes.

India's conflicts and cleavages often manifest themselves in complex combinations – such as ethnic conflict, secessionist movements, inter-community violence and terrorist attacks. Students of comparative politics, equipped with the competition over scarce resources as an all-purpose key to social conflict, might look askance at India because so often these demands and potential conflicts are articulated in a form and an idiom that are deeply embedded in culture. From their location in villages, urban localities and peripheral regions, India's national, regional and local elites, leaders of ethnic groups and all manner of social activists have mastered the art of political manipulation through a deft combination of protest and participation, drawing on political strategies that encompass the symbolic and the material. In order to make these indigenous modes of politics in Indian society accessible to the tools of political analysis, one needs to consider the norms, modalities and language of India's everyday life, indispensable to the students of comparative politics as a point of entry to the minutiae of the country's complex political landscape.

The non-linear modernity of India: the distinctive style of Indian politics

Those unfamiliar with India would be amazed to see how far and how much India's pasts live on in the midst of modern institutions and practices, not necessarily as exotic rituals but as competing partners. Like all large and complex societies with a settled, continuous political process stretching over millennia, India has also developed some distinctive features and a style specific to her. The insiders use this idiom as a code, as much to fend off intrusive outsiders as to conduct their internal transactions in an effective way. The style of Indian politics – a mode of communication that politicians, legislators, senior administrators and police and army officers, and newsmen share in common – has been a constant backdrop to this text on the political system and a connecting link for the chapters.

To the baffled eyes of the Western observer, India might still come across as a self-contained geographic landmass and a distinctive chain of interacting cultures with codes of conduct that differ radically from the Western norm, and vary widely from one region to another. Students of comparative politics, approaching the complex kaleidoscope of Indian society and state for the first time, might find the sheer scale of the political space, the wide spectrum of parties, movements, religious and ethnic leaders actively engaged in politics quite baffling.[6] For early observers of India – Kipling and Forster are archetypal here – there was a deeper level of mystical inner world underlying this rich surface and not accessible through political norms. At Independence, the Indian Constitution recognized both the individual and the community as building blocks of the political system. Morris-Jones saw the normative basis of Indian politics in terms of the modern and the traditional, with a third *idiom* – the saintly – connecting both. Louis Dumont, also formulating the normative basis of India's society and politics, found in religion and the community the main source of *homo hierarchicus* – interpersonal relations organized along the power of the ritually superior over the inferior as in the caste system. More recent observers such as Lloyd and Susanne Rudolph have acknowledged the existence of this very Indian idiom of politics in a series of highly evocative concepts such as the 'modernity of tradition', 'caste associations' and the modern state as '*avatars of Vishnu*'.[7]

The continuity of the past in the midst of change is yet another element that is distinctive to India compared to China or Western democracies. These states have experienced large-scale dislocation and discontinuity, thanks to the Marxist or the Industrial Revolution, in the course of their transition from agrarian society to the modern world. India's incremental change (Chapters 2 and 3) has entailed frequent re-use of the past, which has become a general practice, and as such, is not confined only to ambitious politicians drawing on the legacy of illustrious predecessors, or on Indian tradition in general. The memory of mythical events – the Ram Temple of Ayodhya for example – permeate current politics. Visitors to India are often amazed at the apparent ease with which the past and the present live side by side in cities, rural towns and villages. Four generations might live under a roof, eat from the same kitchen and yet have different lives. The *Dak* bungalows, outposts of the British Raj out in the country, temporary homes for the British civilian officers and their post-Independence successors on tour, are tended with the same attention to detail by the PWD – the Public Works Department, also of British vintage – as are the post-Independence guest houses of the national and state governments. The departments of religious property – the Devaswam boards, set up during the British rule to regulate religious property in the South and their equivalents in other parts of India – are still in charge of administration of the old temples as of the new. Government ministers of democratic India hold court – much like their colonial and pre-colonial predecessors held *durbar* – and transact state business with a motley crowd of visitors, with the same display of power, privilege and outdated pomp.

Survival of the past, of course, is by no means unique to India. One need not go further than the British monarchy and its arcane rituals to sense the presence of the past in the midst of the present. But India is different. The past in this country is present, not just as exotic relics of distant memory but instead, as a contender, jostling for space, attention and power within the modern structure and public sphere. Why is the past more significant for the present in India than in other comparable countries, and how do the legacies of the past affect modern institutions? What gives India's pasts their peculiar resilience? And does the continued presence of the past lend legitimacy to contemporary institutions, or does the endurance of the past by modern institutions constitute the Achilles heel of modern politics in India?

The unresolved normative-ontological issue of identity which drags the past into the present and makes India's modern institutions vulnerable to challenges in the name of tradition will be taken up more fully later in this chapter. The discussion of the rise of Mahatma Gandhi to power and his central role in moulding the course of India's struggle for Independence perhaps best answers some of these questions regarding continuity, change and re-use in Indian politics. But, as we have already seen in the analysis of the institutional basis of British rule in India, Gandhi received the incentive to develop his unique synthesis from his main adversaries – British colonial rule and Hindu nationalists. They, in their own ways, also contributed concepts, institutions and processes that linked the modern present to the mythical past. The fortuitous departure of the Muslim League for Pakistan left the Indian National Congress the hegemony over Indian politics – for a while at any rate – but did not resolve the issue of what kind of nations and neighbours India and Pakistan were going to be. This political environment has made it possible for India's political system, fuelled by the vote-hungry politicians, to transform colonial subjects into participating citizens – quickened by the new notions of enfranchisement, entitlement and empowerment – that have become the three basic building blocks of Indian politics. This, as we shall see in the next section, has made it possible for India to achieve democracy before development.

Democracy and development reconsidered

Barely a decade after India's Independence, Selig Harrison, voicing the pessimism of many Western observers, had warned: 'odds are almost wholly against the survival of freedom ... the issue is, in fact, whether any Indian state can survive at all.'[8] Harrison was giving voice to the apprehension in conservative circles about self-rule leading to chaos.[9] After six decades of democratic rule and 14 national elections, the issue of India's survival as a democracy could probably be taken off the agenda. The key question that now confronts us is, instead, what kind of Indian democracy will emerge over the next decades? Will it be an affluent, secure and democratic India, a responsible member of the international community of nations, able to sustain the pace of reform and the current rate of growth? Or will it be a democracy divided along the fault lines of inter-community conflict, mired in obstinately resilient mass poverty, living in the shadow of a powerful state, armed with nuclear teeth, threatening its neighbours and scuttling the chances of nuclear non-proliferation, wishing, nevertheless, to enjoy the benefits of trade and scientific exchange with the rest of the world?

Drawing on the development of institutions and the policy process in India during the past six decades, I have argued in this book that the likelihood of the collapse of the Indian state and its democratic political system is slim.[10] The sense of optimism is reflected in public opinion. The national elite, evolved over years, has understood the benefits of cooperation with all sections of the population. In consequence, consensus has prevailed over conflict. India's leaders of all political shades increasingly articulate their concerns about national security and prosperity in one voice. India's experience contrasts with the political experience of other countries of the subcontinent such as Pakistan, Sri Lanka and Myanmar, which share some of India's cultural, political and historical legacies. The difficulties faced by the democratic process in these countries confirm the postulates of conventional social theory: that successful political democracy requires the preconditions of literacy and economic development,[11] institutionalization of political power prior to the introduction of popular participation,[12] or a victorious bourgeoisie acting as the social base for democratic institutions.[13] The Indian 'counter example' thus raises a main question. Why has India, despite a culture based on social hierarchy and authoritarianism, mass poverty and high illiteracy, succeeded in establishing a successful democratic political order?[14]

In responding to this question, the book has pointed away from Indian 'exceptionalism' as an explanation for the resilience of democracy. India's record at successful state formation and more recently, state contraction, without the ensuing chaos that has blighted the end of Soviet rule, speaks positively of the vitality of her institutional arrangement and political process. The book has provided insights into the functioning of modern institutions in a country of continental proportions and dramatic extremes, where spirituality is juxtaposed with religious hatred, mass poverty with affluence, philosophies espousing multi-culturalism and universality with those committed to sectarianism and bigotry. Unlike the majority of post-colonial countries, India has retained the territory, constitution and political system that marked its emergence as an independent country in 1947. In spite of external conflicts and internal insurgencies, elections based on universal adult franchise have been held regularly. The fact that in spite of terrorist attacks and insurgency, an election could be held in Kashmir in 2008 speaks of this particular strength of India's democratic institutions and process.

The achievements in other areas have been less spectacular but, in comparison to her own colonial past and that of a large number of post-colonial countries, they are still respectable. India has achieved a minimum of welfare and food security, inflation and explosive population growth have been tamed; and now, with the liberalization of India's economy, international business confidence in India remains generally high despite fluctuations in response to specific crises. However, some dark spots continue to blight the democratic credentials of India – mass poverty and illiteracy persist. Just as the electoral need to build broad-based coalitions had forced Hindu nationalists to moderate their stance, so has the political temptation to garner the votes of hard-core supporters of *hindutva* provided the incentive for more extreme stances for some Hindu nationalist leaders.[15] The puzzles of India's democracy are rooted in these contradictions.

This book has formulated answers to some of these questions by drawing on India's political resources – its social and cultural diversity, its experience of colonial rule and the resistance to it, the efforts of a modernizing and visionary leadership at nation and state building, its major institutions and policy process since Independence. These were the main components that facilitated democratic rule and, in the present context, orderly state contraction. With its political parties, movements, elections, multiple conflicts and conflict-solving mechanisms, India is a rich source of data for students of comparative politics, especially with regard to an illustration of the main theoretical concepts of the discipline – from interest articulation, aggregation and adjudication, to the interaction of politics, policy and economic development. For those interested in the resilience of democratic political systems, particularly by turning rebels into stakeholders through their enfranchisement, empowerment and eventual integration into the new elite structure, India offers an interesting example of building democracy from above, in contrast to Western liberal democracies where the democratic structure grew from below.

This resilience of India's democratic political system appears even more astounding because India's main political institutions – the legislature, executive, judiciary and individual rights – have not evolved entirely from within her society and culture. On the contrary, many of these are colonial transplants. And yet their legitimacy is not questioned by India's main political parties, including those that draw their strength from mobilization along the lines of religious cleavages or class conflict. In its attempt to answer these questions, the book has pointed not in the direction of the cultural distinctiveness of India but to its political institutions, process and the political culture that has evolved from the conflict and conflation of tradition and modernity. It has pointed towards cross-culturally comparable factors that account for the Indian success at sustaining a stable political system that combines both democracy and development. In India, norms of democracy are widely shared by all major political parties – including the Communist Party, and right-wing Hindu-nationalist parties like the Shiv Sena, and the Bharatiya Janata Party – although they differ radically in their ideological positions. Even in the lowest political arenas, the right to democratic participation is no longer considered to be an exotic idea. This Indian achievement, puzzling in view of the negative implications of conventional social theory about the survival of democracy in poor, post-colonial, pre-industrial societies, needs to be understood in the larger comparative context.

One sometimes comes across the criticism that the political process of India accepts democracy only as interest aggregation and accommodation but not in terms of liberal values, such as respect for the freedom and dignity of individuals. A further extension of this argument is that vote counting is neither necessary nor sufficient as a guarantee for the long-term survival of a democracy.[16] Scholarly concerns about the rise of *popular* authoritarianism in the wake of competitive and aggressive populism are based on such misgivings. These criticisms reinforce the apprehensions of a possible collapse or, more likely, a surreptitious gnawing away at democratic institutions until the system is reduced to an empty shell.[17] This dark scenario is further reinforced with political insurgency, denial of equal rights to minorities, communal riots, political violence and criminalization of politics.[18] These are not accidental or incidental features of India's political system, but originate from the same process that has given rise to, and sustains, representative political institutions in the first place.[19]

While the danger of a collapse of democracy cannot be ruled out altogether, survey data on legitimacy, efficacy, empowerment of former untouchables, religious minorities and women, and modes of participation and the recruitment of new local elites into mainstream politics show the strength and the potential for a further unfolding of 'pro-democracy' forces in India. This is also supported by statistical data on governance, political order, participation and legitimacy. The results of national surveys are supplemented with evidence of the upward social mobility of underprivileged social groups and the complementarities of institutional as well as radical modes of participation at the local level. The marketplace of politics continues to operate as an efficient arbiter of the contradictory values of the dignity of the individual and the identity of the group, and more recently, of the imperative of integration with the international political economy, and at the same time, the need to maintain India's cultural distinctiveness as well as the interests of the least privileged.

We learn from the Indian case that it is *political* capital (modern political institutions, electoral processes, strategic reform of the social and economic structure and accountability) that leads to democratic transition in postcolonial societies. In its classic form, the main argument of social capital holds that cultural attributes such as trust, social networks and shared norms at the local level trickling up to the top of the political system are what makes democracy work. This is true of the historical evolution of liberal democracy in Western countries where society and institutions have gone through continuous evolution as a result of larger economic and constitutional changes. In the postcolonial context, traditional society (with castes, religions, tribes and linguistic groups which have remained relatively unchanged over centuries) was catapulted suddenly into the modern world under the aegis of modern political institutions. In this case the political system more than the social structure became the main agent of change.[20]

In the final analysis, the universal significance of the Indian experiment lies in showing the democratic potential of politics from below. When it is combined with representative political institutions and tied to political competition and social reform, it can produce unexpected results that support and promote democratic transition and consolidation, despite mass poverty or the exogenous provenance of the concepts of liberty and individual rights. At the same time, it is important to note that local and regional conflicts are a necessary part of India's democratic unfolding. Empowerment of the marginal social groups, while crucial to the functioning of the Indian system, is, in India as everywhere in the world, contested by established social groups. But the commitment of India's key institutions, such as the judiciary, parliament, media and the army, and the national and regional leaders to democracy and secularism remains steadfast. The Indian case shows how her 'million mutinies', ensconced in the context of a responsive state and elites well versed in the art and science of governance, can pave the way of transition to liberal democracy despite predictions to the contrary.[21]

Governance: balancing national unity and regional diversity

The analysis of India's federal arrangements has shown how the state has simultaneously succeeded in the differentiation of the political and administrative landscape through the creation of new units while holding on tightly to the unity and integrity of the state as a whole. The fears of 'Balkanization' that marked the rise of language movements in the 1950s have not been borne out. Instead, thanks to the redrawing of the boundaries of the federal States on the lines of mother tongue, regions have become coherent cultural and political units. Consequently, regions have gained in power just as they have lost their role as economic units. The liberalization of the economy has transformed the whole of India increasingly into one economic unit, producing the kind of economic collaboration across regional frontiers that would not have been possible earlier. Simultaneously, regions have also emerged as a site of governance in their own right, thanks to the transformation of regional movements into parties in power, and the politics of coalitions that has made them partners in national government, or for that matter, the national opposition, giving legitimacy to their regional bases as political units in their own right.

Regional governments, part of the institutional appurtenance of the Indian state analysed in Chapter 5, are crucial cogs in the wheel of national governance.[22] Under the constitution, and by convention, whereas the Union is indestructible, regions are creatures of the national government.[23] The Indian state has devised an ingenious system for enhancing the stability of the political system by rearranging the units below through the creation of new regional and sub-regional governments, substituting representative government with central or even army rule when the regional political system is unable to sustain orderly rule. Such emergency rule at the regional level is usually withdrawn when the need for the suspension of the normal functioning of parliamentary politics is no longer tenable. The legal responsibility for law and order rests primarily with the regional government, but under the watchful eye of the centre. While the State governments control the regional police, the constitution of India provides for them to be superseded by direct rule from Delhi for the failure to maintain lawful governance.

In practical terms, however, following the end of the 'one-dominant-party system' (1947–67) in which the Indian National Congress ruled both at the centre and in the States, States have increasingly acquired autonomy and an authentic political voice. In consequence, the maintenance of law and order has become more of a joint venture between Delhi and the federal States. Still, regional diversity rules at the heart of the legal uniformity of India's regions, as the regions, in view of their social and political evolution, historical context, specific relations with the centre and institutional arrangement, experience the problem of governance in different ways.

Survey findings indicate that the region, along with the nation and the locality, is an important step in the three-tier system of rule built into India's federal design.[24] The rich literature on governance-generating institutions in Indian States provides valuable insights into a comparative analysis of governance in India.[25] The regional government, more than the central authority or the local administration, is the repository of the primary constitutional responsibility for the maintenance of law and order.[26] Regions are important staging posts for upwardly mobile politicians and civil servants. Following the liberalization of India's economy in the 1990s, regional governments have acquired a new international character as entrepreneurs in the fields of fostering technological innovation and initiatives in social and economic policy. Keeping pace with these changes, regional markets have become testing grounds for the service industry and business processing, the cultivation and export of cash crops, agri-business and inter-generational renewal of the political class. The regional arena today is a major conduit for local aspirants eager to move up to the pan-Indian arena and beyond.

General awareness of the region as a critical link in the chain of governance has grown among specialists and ordinary citizens in parallel with the migration of the levers of power from Delhi to the States, reflecting the unfolding logic of India's cooperative federalism. In contrast to the early years after Independence when the Union government, presided over by Jawaharlal Nehru, held all the political cards in its tight grip, regional leaders today have emerged as free-wheeling politicians with independent social bases. They are keen promoters of regional interests, crucial building blocks of government and opposition coalitions in India's national politics. The complexities of coalition building have given considerable leverage to political leaders from the regions, transforming them into statesmen and innovations of the art of governance rather than keeping them as minions of an almighty central government. The threat of the imposition of direct rule from the centre under Article 356 of the constitution on flimsy, partisan grounds to supplant elected governments in the regions has greatly declined under the new dispensation. Instead, State governments have added political muscles to the legislative sinews of their constitutional responsibility for governance. With the region as the empirical backdrop, one can conceptualize the stakeholders in the rules game (Figure 1.1 above) – as Tamil and Bihari politicians, Gujarati rioters or Maratha cooperative bosses, Sikh priests or Bengali *bhadralok* – in their new incarnation as political leaders, and rediscover them as parts of larger political forces, ensconced in the specific historical, social and economic contexts of India's regions.

The scrutiny of the evolutionary path of India's regions provides some insight into the current state of affairs. The narratives show how, under the successive shocks of the Partition of India, the redrawing of boundaries by the States Reorganisation Commission, democratization through reform, political mobilization, and more recently, liberalization of the economy, regional arenas like Gujarat and Karnataka have acquired a dynamism that is a new presence on the Indian political scene. They illustrate the effect of institutional change, social mobilization, legislation and centre–State relations, embodying local history, social structure and political culture on regional governance. Locating the analysis of governance in the regional arena provides a wide spectrum, across time and space, in which to see the combination of factors that help individuals choose between orderly behaviour and criminal self-help. The method has its rewards, for the very diversity of India that makes generalization difficult also becomes an asset in terms of the scale of comparison, giving the observer access to a much richer distribution of the variation in explanatory factors. The thick descriptions thus add local colour to abstract variables such as anxiety induced by insecurity or anger at the denial of an identity that men and women claim legitimately to be theirs. The availability of the material resources that make the political status quo an acceptable basis of organized political and social life, or the apparatus of law and order management that keeps potential law breakers on the narrow and straight path of civic virtue. Despite these significant achievements in democracy and development, or because of these salient achievements that distinguish India from other post-colonial states, the incomplete project of nation-building emerges as one of the core problems of the twenty-first century. Deep underneath the external symbols of democracy and governance, India is haunted by the unresolved issue of national identity.

Ethnicity and territoriality as competing norms of citizenship in India

The serial bomb blasts on 14 September, 2008 which killed 24 people in Delhi form part of a spate of similar attacks all over India. They appear in retrospect to have been a prelude to the terrorist attack on Mumbai in November 2008. By striking at the heart of India's capital city, and subsequently on the financial capital of the country, the terrorists have been able to show to the world, to the government of India, and their own support base that they are able to strike at will. More than the threat to the security of the state, the implication of these attacks for the legitimacy of the state, and the disaffection of sections of the Indian population are issues of crucial importance to our analysis. The presence of local networks, improvised explosives and intelligence demonstrate significant local support for terrorism in India. It has become increasingly clear that a large number of terrorists are Indian nationals – a fact that casts a shade of doubt on the success of India's inclusive democracy and capacity of the state to protect public order.

What might account for alienation on a scale which made this series of terrorist attacks possible and what can the state do about this? Why has the Indian model which has, as we have previously argued, so successfully transformed colonial subjects into citizens, conspicuously failed in the case of a section of the Indian population?[27] Finally, how can one interpret the fact that outside the North-East of India, the bulk of the terrorists, both foreigners and their local accomplices, who have been apprehended, are Muslims (Box 9.1)? What are the implications for citizenship in India? These questions need to be investigated in the backdrop of the broader issue of how India has attempted to turn subjects into citizens and why this project might need to be designed afresh, taking into account the vastly changed circumstances of the twenty-first century. The terrorist threat to India's democracy and the Indian way of politics has become increasingly strident.

The linkage between terrorism and sections of disaffected citizens questions the inclusive nationalism that Jawaharlal Nehru announced in his famous oration 'Freedom at Midnight'.[28] While his intention to find a rightful place for India in the comity of nations was both explicit and firm, a similar clarity was not to be found in his understanding of the actual stakeholders of this new nation. The legal vision of the architects of the new Republic saw citizenship in terms of territoriality, a definition that went back to the Treaty of Westphalia (1648). The hiatus between the moral definition of Indians in terms of their ethnic origin, and the legal definition in terms of territory was first challenged in the language riots of the 1950s that led to the redrawing of India's internal boundaries.[29]

Box 9.1 'Indian Mujahideen terror linked to organized crime', by Praveen Swami

New Delhi: Mumbai investigators have found evidence that organized crime groups could have provided logistics infrastructure for the Indian Mujahideen terror offensive. Based on information provided by the Intelligence Bureau, the Mumbai police have arrested Afzal Usman – a mid-level organized crime figure the investigators believe arranged for the theft of four vehicles used as car bombs in the July 27 serial bombings in Gujarat. Usman has long been known to police as a lieutenant of the jailed ganglord Aftab Ansari, author of the January 2002 Harkat ul-Jihad-e-Islami-supported terrorist attack targeting the United States Information Centre. A one-time resident of Mhow [in Madhya Pradesh, in central India] Usman moved to Mumbai eight years ago. He is thought to have handled several money-laundering and extortion operations for Ansari. Part of the proceeds, police believe, could have funded the Indian Mujahideen's terror offensive. . . . Ansari's links with Islamist terror groups have long been known. His ideological radicalization appears to have taken place while serving a prison sentence in New Delhi's Tihar jail, where he met top Jaish-e-Mohammad operative Syed Omar Sheikh. Sheikh, later released in the December 1999 Indian Airline IC-814 hostages-for-terrorists swap in Kandahar, is now on death row in Pakistan for the murder of US journalist Daniel Pearl.

Source: http://www.thehindu.com/2008/09/21/stories/
2008092160301000.htm.

The legal right to citizenship or, more precisely, nationality is accorded by the state. Identity, and following from it, the moral right to belong, sustains individuals' claims to citizenship. When both converge in the same group, the result is a sense of legitimate citizenship where the individual feels both legally entitled and morally engaged. If not, the consequences are either legal citizenship devoid of a sense of identification with the soil, or a primordial identification with the land but no legal sanction of this. These situations can lead to violent disorder, inter-community riots and civil war. The Indian strategy of turning subjects into citizens is based on an institutional arrangement containing several important parameters. First of these are the legal sources of citizenship as formulated in the Indian constitution (Articles 5–11), the Constituent Assembly debates (which provide insights into the controversy surrounding specific articles), and legislation undertaken by the national parliament to enable and amend, depending on the case, the original provisions of the constitution. 'Judicialization' of citizenship is yet another method of synchronizing the provisions of the law and the new demands emerging from society.[30] The assertion of identity and linkage to India has emerged as a supplementary basis of Indian citizenship, in addition to birth and residence. Property and citizenship have constantly been interwoven: who can own property and how much have had fluid answers. In the case of Kashmir, the laws have always had a slightly different tinge due to the special agreement that Indian acts would not normally be applicable in Kashmir.[31] The typical strategy makes a three-prong attack on conflict issuing out of the hiatus between general legal norms of the state and the assertion of political identity contesting the State. India makes stakeholders out of rebels by adroitly combining reform, repression and selective recruitment of rebels into the privileged circle of new elites (see Figure 9.1 below).

Why has India been more successful than many post-colonial states in turning subjects into citizens? The explanatory model specified in Figure 9.1 is sustained on the basis of five empirical arguments that draw on (a) India's institutional arrangement (the constitution), (b) laws meant to implement the social visions underlying the constitution, (c) the double role of the state – as neutral enforcer and as a partisan supporting vulnerable social groups – in producing a level playing field, (d) the incorporation of elements of bargaining theory into Indian law and political practice,

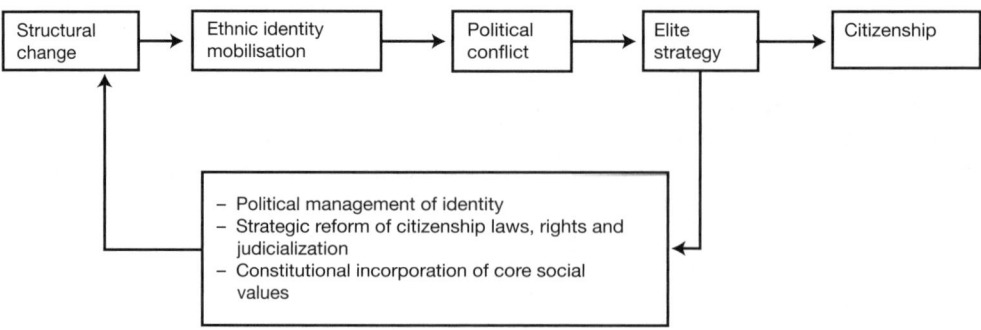

Figure 9.1 Turning subjects into citizens: a dynamic neo-institutional model
Source: Drawn by author.

and, finally, (e) judicialization – evidence of the courts at work in turning subjects into citizens. India's relative success on the issue of citizenship can be attributed to the fact that these tools of citizen-making are used with unusual vigor and imagination by the political decision-makers in India. These are the factors that one has to take into account in order to understand the root cause of disaffection – namely, a sense of legitimacy deficit in some sections of Indian society.

Independence came to India not as a result of a revolutionary war but through protracted negotiation between the colonial ruler and the main actors in the Freedom Movement. The process of negotiation was complex because the discussions between the colonizer and the colonized intersected with conflicts among the colonized themselves. This had one major consequence. The post-Independence regime in India was based on power-sharing among adversaries, who in the process learned to use democratic institutions to constrain the struggle for power. As such, negotiation has become an essential part of India's politics, and indeed, an integral part of everyday life.[32] In fact, the constant presence of conflict in the local arena is also indicative of the growing propensity of people from all walks of life to assert their rights to dignity, basic needs and security.[33]

In changing societies, many of which adopted the norm of territorial citizenship at independence, transnational networks and cultural flows have emerged as challenges to the norm of territorial citizenship, sometimes with violent consequences.[34] In sum, terrorism, new technology of communication, transnational movement of capital and labour, and global norms of human rights have brought the exclusive rights of the territorial state on its citizens into question.

We have seen some of the concrete and specific aspects of the global issue of citizenship in our analysis of India. The Indian constitution accepts and recognizes citizenship by birth, descent and naturalization. The question of 'Who is an Indian?' nevertheless is a complex one. It is further complicated by the rapid internationalization of both territory and individual identity. In consequence, citizenship has evolved from a political right by which a state identifies the people it governs to a benchmark of identity, and in today's global context, one of the many identities the individual seeks to assert for him- or herself. In the political space of India, it is possible today for communities to form and dissolve in order to re-emerge as part of other communities. Seen from a distance and over time, political transaction has taken manifold forms, ranging between voting and lobbying to protest movements and, ultimately, violent conflict. These in turn have produced knowledge of what leads to violence, instilling greater understanding and accommodation of cultural and religious differences. Castes, religious communities and ethnic groups are all impregnated by the spirit of transaction and coalition building. The result is a significant empowerment of minorities.[35]

Violent disaffection of parts of the population, particularly when they belong to minority communities, questions the firm belief in the incremental diffusion of the norms of citizenship that has remained an article of faith on the part of the Indian state. The evidence that one gets from public opinion surveys about systematic difference between the Muslim and Hindu electorate on some critical issues affecting identity in India are indicative of a rift. However, despite a systematic difference on the issues of the Babri mosque, Kashmir, Pakistan and personal law where Hindu opinion tends to be less inclusive than the Muslim opinion (see Diagram 9.1), there is nevertheless an important balancing factor. On each of the three issues of efficacy, legitimacy and trust, Muslim opinion is more ardent than Hindu opinion, indicating

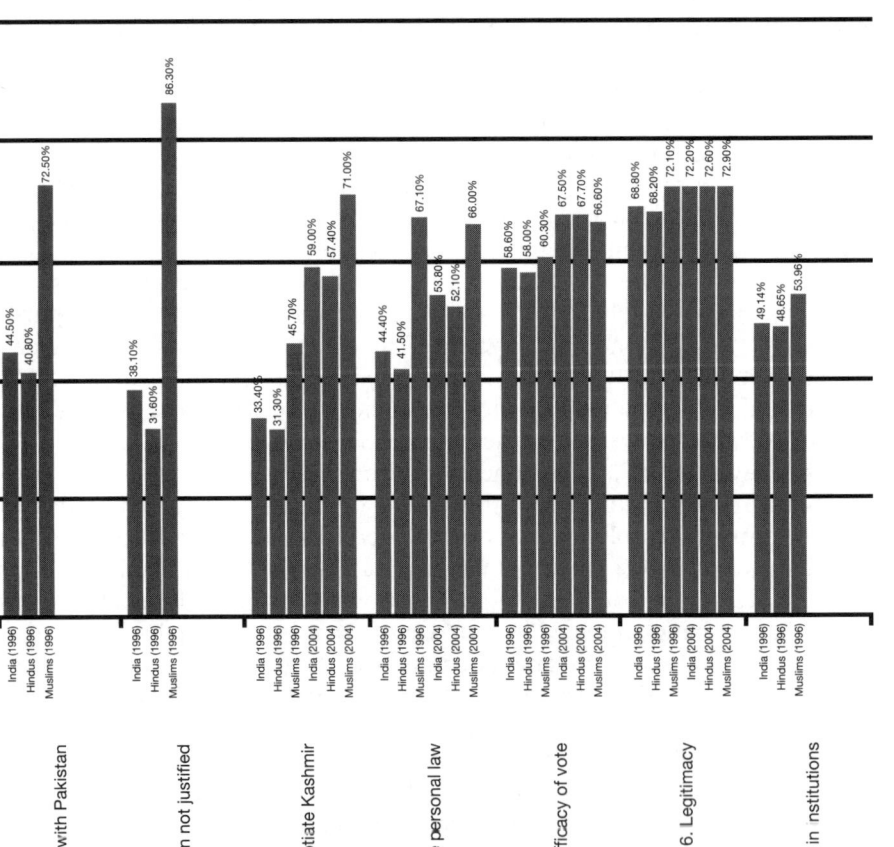

1. 'India should make more efforts to develop friendly relations with Pakistan. Do you agree?' (agree)

2. 'Some people say that the demolition (of Babri Mosque in 1992 by a mob of Hindu fanatics in the northern city of Ayodhya) was justified while others say it was not justified. What would you say – was it justified or not justified?' (not justified)

3. 'People's opinions are divided on the issue of the Kashmir problem. Some people say that Government should suppress the agitation by any means while others say that this problem should be resolved by negotiations/mutual dialogue. What would you say, should the agitation be suppressed or resolved by/ through negotiations?' (solved by negotiations)

4. 'Every community should be allowed to have its own laws to govern marriage and property rights. Do you agree or disagree?' (agree)

5. 'Do you think your vote has an effect on how things are run in this country, or do you think your vote makes no difference?' (vote makes a difference)

6. 'Suppose there were no parties or assemblies and elections were not held – do you think that the government in this country can be run better?' (no)

7. 'How much trust do you have in political institutions?' (overall trust)

1. Friendly relations with Pakistan

India (1996) 44.50%
Hindus (1996) 40.80%
Muslims (1996) 72.50%

2. Mosque destruction not justified

India (1996) 38.10%
Hindus (1996) 31.60%
Muslims (1996) 86.30%

3. Negotiate Kashmir

India (1996) 33.40%
Hindus (1996) 31.30%
Muslims (1996) 45.70%
India (2004) 59.00%
Hindus (2004) 57.40%
Muslims (2004) 71.00%

4. Separate personal law

India (1996) 44.40%
Hindus (1996) 41.50%
Muslims (1996) 67.10%
India (2004) 53.80%
Hindus (2004) 52.10%
Muslims (2004) 66.00%

5. Efficacy of vote

India (1996) 58.60%
Hindus (1996) 58.00%
Muslims (1996) 60.30%
India (2004) 67.50%
Hindus (2004) 67.70%
Muslims (2004) 66.60%

6. Legitimacy

India (1996) 68.80%
Hindus (1996) 68.20%
Muslims (1996) 72.10%
India (2004) 72.20%
Hindus (2004) 72.60%
Muslims (2004) 72.90%

7. Trust in institutions

India (1996) 49.14%
Hindus (1996) 48.65%
Muslims (1996) 53.96%

Diagram 9.1 Contrasting Hindu and Muslim attitudes on issues of identity and empowerment

Source: The data in this table were collected from a national sample representing the Indian electorate. The survey was conducted by the Centre for the Study of Developing Societies, Delhi, in 1996 and 2004.

both the willingness and the ability to use the normal institutional channels of the state to articulate one's political and cultural demands. The existence of this political capital creates the hope that separate and conflicting identities can still share a set of core values common to all the parties, and be open to judicialization.

India has a track-record in transforming identity-based issues into transactional politics by undertaking a reform in the institutional arrangement. The States Reorganisation Commission of 1957 and the recent creation of the three new States of Uttarakhand, Chhattisgarh and Jharkhand are examples of this capacity of the Indian state.[36] The legal–political regime on India's personal law which permits different legal systems in the same State shows how different communities, who consider their laws on marriage, divorce, adoption and succession as essential to and constitutive of their identity, can still share a common territorial space.

Once this is achieved, rather as in the case of many personal laws co-existing within the same constitution, a private sphere, unique to individuals and groups, can gain legitimate acceptance by all concerned. Under the sovereign presence of this core, different communities can negotiate the terms under which they can share the same territorial space (see unshaded area in Figure 9.2 which represents the overlapping values of the three groups), for example, how, in a multi-religious village, the Hindu religious processions will take a specific route so as to avoid disturbing law and order, or for that matter, how much space on public roads can be occupied for Friday prayers.

Finally, in the contemporary world, globalization, which was meant to make national boundaries ever less salient, has in fact revived their importance. The agenda of contemporary international politics is crowded with competing claims of the state

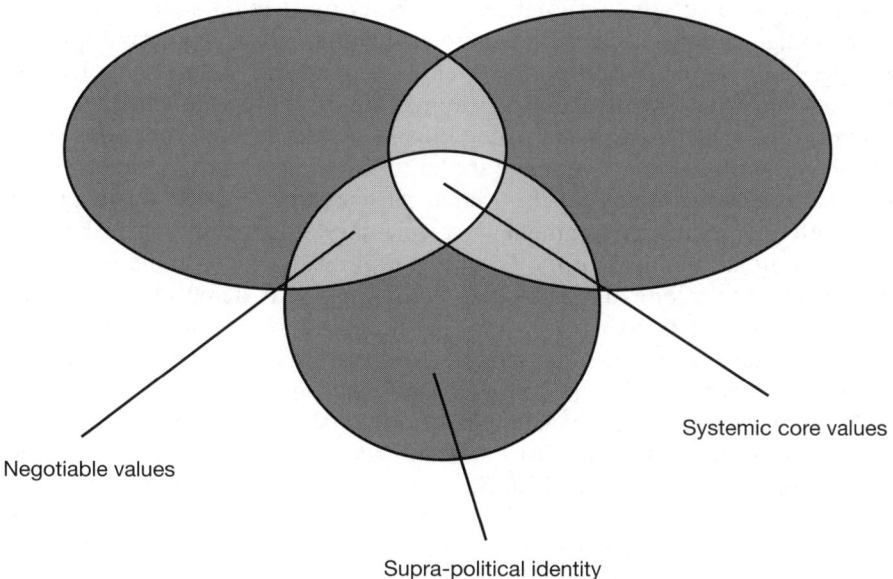

Figure 9.2 Negotiating identity in divided societies: interface of individual values
Source: Mitra (2005), p. 256.

and supra-state agencies on the loyalty of individuals and ethnic groups. In the absence of global governance, States, acting in their capacity as the collective voice of their citizens, remain the most important agents of accountability and enforcement. The complex process through which subjects and immigrants become citizens thus pitches territoriality and ethnicity as competing norms for the entitlement to citizenship.

The Indian case opens up the analytical space for the comparative and general dimensions of the problem of citizenship. One learns from the Indian case that with regard to citizen-making in a post-colonial context, the constitution and law matter, but politics matters too, and most of all history (path dependency) matters enormously. India's relative success at turning subjects into citizens, more successfully at least than neighbouring Pakistan or Sri Lanka, is a function of India's political structure, process and memory, woven together in an institutional arrangement that draws its inspiration from both the modern state and the traditional society. The evidence of disaffection among sections of India's minorities and the linkage between the legitimacy crisis at home and international terror networks suggests that the time for a new round of institutional arrangement and appropriate conceptual rethinking might be ripe.

Conclusion: re-inventing the nation

How to accommodate ethnic separatism within the framework of India's political community, and how to protect the democratic political system from its enemies, both indigenous and external, are issues that call for urgent attention from India's analysts and policy makers. Defining moments in India's post-Independence politics – the destruction of the Babri mosque in 1992, the anti-Muslim pogrom in Gujarat in 2002, the spate of terrorist attacks culminating in the 'siege' of Mumbai in 2008 – all point towards these core questions. What does India's collective identity consist of and how might it be sustained? What responsibility must India's citizens bear in defence of the Indian nation? These issues exercise Indian minds and polarize opinion. But the debate, both scholarly and political, skirts around the main issues, leaving the question of collective identity, vital to any nation, virtually untouched.

A brief perusal of the Indian media in the closing weeks of 2008 provides some evidence to illustrate this point. A tragic parallel to the Indian equivocation in 2001 in reaction to the terrorist attack on the Indian parliament, the 2008 onslaught on Mumbai has left the Indian government in a quandary. Mercifully, there has not been, at this writing, a repetition of the 'coercive diplomacy' when India mobilized a million men at arms along the Pakistani border, only to demobilize after ten months, with nothing specific to show for it. Still, the ambiguous messages emanating from Delhi – simultaneously appearing conciliatory towards the Pakistani state and at the same time accusing the Pakistani government of complicity – are a cause for concern.[37] Prime Minister Manmohan Singh, who has taken an uncharacteristically strong position in his accusation against Pakistan's use of terror as state policy, has stressed that 'inheritance of a great historical experience of a multi-ethnic, multi-religious, multi-caste and multi-lingual society contributed to India's sense of nationhood'.[38] That India has to examine her own record with regard to the disaffection of sections of her minority population has not entered any serious debate. India's opinion makers, reacting mostly to the financial crisis of 2008, aiming no doubt at the Western public and the secondary audience back home, have taken positions that

Box 9.2 India's opinion makers: divergent views

'The Next World Order', by Gurcharan Das
See: http://www.nytimes.com/2009/01/02/opinion/02das.html?ref=opinion

In a much-discussed magazine article last year, Lee Kwan Yew, the former prime minister of Singapore, raised an important question: Why does the rest of the world view China's rise as a threat but India's as a wonderful success story? The answer is that India is a vast, unwieldy, open democracy ruled by a coalition of 20 parties. It is evolving through a daily flow of ideas among the conservative forces of caste and religion, the liberals who dominate intellectual life, and the new forces of global capitalism.

Both the Chinese and the Indians are convinced that their prosperity will only increase in the 21st century. In China it will be induced by the state; in India's case, it may well happen despite the state. Indians expect to continue their relentless march toward a modern, democratic, market-based future. In this, terrorist attacks are a noisy, tragic, but ultimately futile sideshow.

Anand Giridharadas, 'With the spotlight gone, the true India can develop', *International Herald Tribune*, http://www.iht.com/, accessed on January 1, 2009

For romancers of the India Story, the timing couldn't have been crueller. The Story was going down so well. Blue-chip multinationals had been persuaded to outsource any work they could to Indians fresh from college. Companies going on sale had begun to think of Indian buyers first. Tourists from Paris to São Paulo, once fearful of malaria and cobras, had shed old fears to arrive by the planeful.

But 2008 ended badly for this branding [India: Fastest Growing Free Market Democracy] campaign. The world economy entered crisis mode. The outsourcing companies began to collapse. Hedge funds deluging the Bombay Stock Exchange with liquidity began to run dry. And then the savage, 72-hour siege of Mumbai drop-kicked a country already teetering on the cliff's brink.

For now, the India Story is suspended. No more magazine covers with the television celebrity Padma Lakshmi's worshipful hand greeting. No more investors who cannot distinguish Kolkata from Kerala pouring their savings into India nonetheless. No more iPods at Davos. No one is looking for the next big seductively risky thing. What was forgotten during the long boom is that development involves more than earning the praise of that class of globetrotting Westerners who fly among foreign fashion weeks and business meets and bestow blessings on the latest Country-on-the-Make. It is about building a nation, a gruelling task sometimes forgotten when the going is good. The rub with this kind of development is that it concentrates on making countries like India look and smell and sound like a wealthy country on the outside, while ignoring the complex, delicate sequence of events by which currently wealthy countries became so. Indians relish this idea, for it simplifies, even trivializes, their predicament. They love the word 'leapfrogging.' It began as a description of agrarian India's rapid evolution of a services industry, absent a solid manufacturing base. But it now signifies the ambition to jump, in that and every other way, from the back to the front. And so India has not developed as the West did: slowly, systematically; first getting railroads right, then cars, then planes; first bringing drinking water and toilets to people, then figuring out how to bring them Wi-Fi. No: India prefers Last Things First.

range between the complacent and the dismissive, referring to terrorists merely as 'misguided youth' rather than indicating the underlying issues of legitimacy deficit, persistent poverty and disaffection. These debates skirt around a vital issue linked to the project of nation-building in South Asia, one that ties together India and Pakistan, in some sense as still unfolding nations in search of a stable basis.

The violence that marks Hindu–Muslim conflict, aimed particularly at women, and terrorist attacks carry the subliminal message of nations still wrestling to be born.[39] In his excellent review of new Partition literature, Siddhartha Deb links the incomplete project of nation-building in South Asia, religious conflict and terrorist attacks in South Asia to the solicitude of Hindu, Sikh and Muslim elites – the 'educated, middle-class urban milieux of the burgeoning cities' – to cast their new, modern, neo-religious identities onto a national space. The Pakistani 'nation' of 1947 came unstuck on this issue in the Liberation War of 1971 – and remains, still, uncertain. The 'nation' that Nehru stitched together from the fragments of Gandhi's inclusive Hinduism, Fabian socialism, and the colonial legacy of iron rule through judicious accommodation has soldiered on, but has found its limits in Kashmir, the North-East and those parts of India where large Muslim elites and masses remain disaffected and unintegrated with the Indian mainstream.[40]

Taking this scholarly issue further is beyond the remit of this book. India needs to re-invent the fundamental basis of her nationhood, the political consensus that has sustained the state and the expanding civil society that has given it legitimacy, to generate a renewed search for shared norms. This can be best done as part of a political project for the enhancement of social capital and political trust, institution-building, reinforcing India's countervailing forces, and India's indigenous modernity, which consists of taking popular categories seriously. But above all else, there is one thing that is abundantly clear: there is a need to look beyond dangerous expedients such as merely attributing disaffection to 'misguided youth' or to transforming moral outrage into jobs and votes, even through the agency of elections that are free and fair.

These issues that I have raised in the concluding chapter are a difficult challenge as much for the policy maker as for the political scientist. To pretend that the issue of identity, welfare and governance will somehow work themselves out, as Barrington Moore used to remind an earlier generation of students, is the acme of intellectual and moral irresponsibility. Will India be able to meet the challenge successfully, and yet keep her secular and democratic political system intact? The evidence and arguments that I have analysed in this book lead to a cautious optimism. Despite the almost constant presence of turmoil in some parts of the vast country during the past decade, the very fact of successful holding of elections in five Indian States and subsequently in Kashmir in the aftermath of the terrorist attack in Mumbai and Pakistani truculence across the border in 2008 is just one of those hopeful signs.[41] India, in the foreseeable future, will continue to surprise but, perhaps, also to confuse.

Notes

1 Cited by Bernard Williams in Smart and Williams (1973), p. 77.
2 Kay Lawson (2008, p. 524) refers to India as 'the world's most complicated democracy'. 'It is too simple to call [India's] rise a great accomplishment and leave it at that, but also too simple to dismiss the claim as unworthy of a nation in which serious poverty remains so widespread as to make politics all but irrelevant to the daily chore of achieving survival. The truth is multifaceted, and incompletely before us'.

3 The mystical overtones of Kipling's perception of India form part of a long tradition. Forster (1924, p. 92) has remarked in this vein: 'Nothing in India is identifiable, the mere asking of a question causes it to disappear or to merge in something else'.

4 In retrospect, the failure to undertake a similar step began the slow unravelling of the state in Pakistan and continues to be the source of ethnic conflict in Sri Lanka.

5 The creation of Gorkhaland within the State of West Bengal and three new States – Uttaranchal, Jharkhand and Chhattisgarh, testifies to the strategy of containment through the creation of new federal units.

6 Thus, for example, the parliamentary elections of 2009 involve 714 million people, more than twice the population of the United States, who are eligible to vote in an election held in five phases spread over one month (Reuters: New Delhi, 15 April, 2009).

7 Rudolph and Rudolph (1987).

8 Harrison (1960), p. 338.

9 Conservative opinion in Britain was generally opposed to Indian Independence before an acceptable solution to the communal problem between Hindus and Muslims was found. This cautious approach was criticized by some who cited the successful functioning of elected governments in eight out of eleven provinces after the 1937 elections held under the Government of India Act of 1935; see Brailsford (1939).

10 These arguments are stated in detail in Mitra (1999) and Mitra and Singh (2009).

11 Lipset (1959, pp. 69–105) suggests that in order to succeed as a democracy, a society has to attain certain levels of social and economic development.

12 Huntington (1968), p. 55.

13 See Moore (1966).

14 The Indian experience stands in sharp contrast to her South Asian neighbours. Universal adult franchise was introduced in Ceylon in the early 1930s, even before limited franchise was available in some Indian provinces. The Muslim League, which under the leadership of Jinnah, championed the cause of Pakistan, became the ruling party in the new state after Independence. Neither of the two states has been as successful as India in sustaining democracy. See Alavi, pp. 19–71, and Mick Moore, pp. 155–91, in Mitra (1990).

15 There is considerable controversy among scholars regarding the causes and probability of Hindu–Muslim conflict. See Varshney (2002) and Brass (2003) for contrary views. Jaffrelot (2003) gives a graphic account of Hindu–Muslim riots in Gujarat. Wilkinson (2004) suggests a link between electoral competition and ethnic riots in India.

16 See Merkel (2004), pp. 33–58.

17 The Emergency of 1975–77, which is seen as an aberration in the political process in India, is in fact a major landmark in the country's political development. For further information, see 'Images of the Emergency', the theme of a symposium on the subject in *Seminar* (Delhi, March 1977).

18 The rise of lawlessness and the criminalization of politics have been observed by several scholars. See the epilogue in Morris-Jones (1967), pp. 259–72. The mass-circulation *India Today* talks about 'the elevation of violence, defiant indiscipline, and lawlessness to a cult' everywhere in the country, 'not just [among] the armed militants of the Jammu and Kashmir Liberation Front or the Khalistan Commando Force, but ordinary people, lawyers, policemen, shopkeepers, civil servants, students, trade unionists' as well. 'Cult of anarchy', *India Today,* 31 August, 1990, p. 7.

19 India's democratic process continues to be open and inclusive, so much so that sometimes locally influential politicians with criminal records manage to get elected to legislatures, political activists resort to forceful methods of protest leading to the disturbance of public order, and, as one learns from the re-election of Indira Gandhi, the unrepentant author of the Emergency of 1975–77, in 1980, authoritarian political leaders manage to get popular mandates. These practices are tolerated if not condoned by the democratic political process. But the countervailing forces of India's democracy, federalism, and regulatory agencies like the Supreme Court and the Election Commission ensure that they do not spread beyond a point which would choke the vitality of the democratic process and the rule of law altogether.

20 See Mitra (2008a), pp. 557–58.

21 Naipaul (1990), p. 517.

22 In the wake of the terrorist attack on Mumbai, the new Home Minister Mr Chidambaram convened a conference of all Chief Ministers to share the intelligence information gathered by Indian

agencies, and to express solidarity. Despite the fact of the proximity of the next general election, it was significant that the regional leaders rose beyond party politics to express solidarity with the Indian state.

23 The principled position of India as one and indivisible characterizes all the mainstream political parties. An all-party resolution of the Lok Sabha in 1995 declared Kashmir to be an integral and inalienable, part of Indian territory. The initiative and legislative competence for the rearrangement of internal boundaries, creation of new States and renaming of existing units lie very much with the central executive.

24 Mitra and Singh (2009), p. 131.

25 Weiner (1968), Wood (1984), Frankel and Rao (1989/1990).

26 Seventh schedule: Maintaining law and order is a prime responsibility. Failure to do so can invite drastic steps from the Union government under Art. 356.

27 Mitra (2008).

28 See Mitra and Singh (2009).

29 A subsequent revision of the definition came with the demand of Indians living abroad for succession to property in India, leading, eventually, to the Persons of Indian Origin Card (PIO), which explicitly recognizes the rights of citizenship, not as binary, but as incrementally gradual. The ultimate prize of double nationality is in the offing, bringing the discourse full circle, away from the exclusive reliance on territory.

30 Izhar Ahmad Khan vs. Union of India (UOI), AIR 1962, SC 1052. The case dealt in detail with the following questions: the rights to and of citizenship; the issues of Partition-related citizenship; the value of a passport in determining citizenship; and the question of domicile versus citizenship. The issue in this case was the constitutional validity of Section 9(2) of the Citizenship Act, 1955, which dealt with the termination of citizenship. This case exemplified the policies which discouraged multiple or even dual citizenships, and held that upon acquiring in any manner the citizenship of another country, an Indian citizen automatically loses Indian citizenship.

31 See Bachan Lal Kalgotra vs. State of Jammu and Kashmir, AIR 1987, SC 1169. In the last decade, case law has tended towards a more flexible and all-encompassing understanding of Indian stipulations with relation to property and, of course, the onset of economic liberalization has given wings to even further judicial liberalization of these concepts. Similarly, recent laws allowing NRIs (Non-Resident Indians) to own property have already been registered in case law.

32   Negotiation is a basic means of getting what you want from others. It is back-and-forth communication designed to reach an agreement when you and the other side have some interests that are shared and others that are opposed. . . . People negotiate even when they don't think they are doing so. A person negotiates with his spouse about where to go for dinner and with his child about when the lights go out.

Fisher and Ury (1991), p. XIII.

33 The comments of Fisher and Ury are perfectly appropriate for India's everyday life:

Everyone wants to participate in decisions that affect them; fewer and fewer people will accept decisions dictated by someone else. People differ and they use negotiations to handle their differences. Whether in business, government, or in the family, people reach most decisions through negotiations. Even when they go to court, they almost always negotiate a settlement before trial.

Fisher and Ury (1991), p. XIII.

34 The reference here is to the rise of the language movement and the violent separation of Bangladesh from Pakistan, and the civil war in Sri Lanka.

35 When asked 'Suppose there were no parties or assemblies and elections were not held – do you think that the government in this country can be run better?', 69 per cent of Indians argue the opposite. But the number of Muslims, at 72 per cent, making the same argument in favour of retaining the democratic structure, is even higher than the average in 1996. However, by 2004 India's average opinion – at 72.2 per cent – on this issue appears to have converged with that of Muslims.

36 However, the spate of protest movements that greeted the announcement of separate statehood for Telengana in December 2009 indicates the complex and delicate nature of this issue.

37 For a strong criticism of Indian ambiguity, see Siddarth Varadarajan, 'After evidence dossier, direct accusation against Pakistan strikes discordant note', *The Hindu*, 8 January, 2009.

38 The Prime Minister said, in an optimistic tone that 'today, even as Pakistan engages in whipping up war hysteria, we remain steadfastly united and, if anything, the process of national consolidation is becoming stronger.' He did, however, warn the Chief Ministers, and the world at large, of the external dangers that threaten the security and stability of India's political system.

> We must convince the world community that States that use terrorism as an instrument of foreign policy must be isolated and compelled to abandon such tactics. We must engage vigorously in debates to press the point that "soft" support for terrorism cannot any longer be endorsed.' The Prime Minister was pointing towards the structural links between the fragility of the Pakistani political system and its support of terrorism as 'an instrument of state policy.

See Vinay Kumar in *The Hindu*, 7 January, 2009.

39 Khan (2007) corroborates some of the interview data regarding violence against women reported by Sudhir Kakar (see Kakar 1995). Khan writes, 'Women's bodies were marked and branded, with the slogans of freedom, "Pakistan Zindabad" and "Jai Hind", inscribed on their faces and breasts. At least a third of the brutalized bodies recovered later were those of girls under the age of 12.' Cited in Deb (2008), p. 40.

40 Deb (2009) makes this point in his review of two excellent new books on the Partition of India: Khan (2007) and Zamindar (2007). 'Partition was not', he maintains, 'the clean break claimed by national histories.' The violence of the Partition was largely 'willed' by the Indian and Pakistani leadership on both sides of the border, where the new elites in power were redefining their national space (pp. 40–41).

41 Though Assembly elections in the five States – Delhi, Rajasthan, Mizoram, Madhya Pradesh and Chhattisgarh – took place in the shadow of the terrorist attack on Mumbai, the outcome appears to have been affected more by the issues of governance, welfare and incumbency than panic arising out of the televised images of the siege of Mumbai. Even more impressively, the elections in Kashmir which followed drew participation of over 50 per cent – high, considering the conditions of militancy and the boycott call by the Hurriyat, opposed to the election – and produced an outcome that has brought a coalition government of the National Conference and the Congress party into power. See 'Congress Wins 3–2' in *The Statesman Weekly*, 13 December, 2008, p. 1.

10 Further reading

Despite the revolution in information technology and the new global economic linkages that have lifted parts of the Indian population to levels of living and lifestyles comparable to those of the affluent West, vast sections of the population are still mired in poverty and insecurity, struggling with poor infrastructure and adhering to traditional ways. The economic and political institutions of India are often anchored in vernacular categories and local contexts, notwithstanding their modern veneer. To Western students of India's economics and politics, specific features of Indian politics such as the hiatus between modernity and tradition as well as the sporadic outbreak of Maoist violence (long extinct in its homeland) might appear exotic or archaic. For those who wish to delve deeper into the challenge of understanding India, the sources referred to in this section will be a useful guide in their exploration of the darker alleys and crevices of her political system.

General

The general literature on India has grown greatly in volume, keeping pace with the rising prominence of India. The limitations of space make it possible to provide only a glimpse into this vast body of books and articles. I list in this section other books of general interest, history, politics textbooks and travelogues.

Jeannine Auboyer, *Daily Life in Ancient India: From 200 BC to 700 AD* (London: Phoenix; 2007), and Michael Edwardes, *Everyday Life in Early India* (London: B.T. Batsford; 1969), are both excellent introductions to life in ancient India. Those with a taste for fiction might enjoy E.M. Forster's *A Passage to India* and Vikram Seth's *A Suitable Boy* as windows into life under the British Raj and social life in North India in the 1950s. Ramachandra Guha, *India After Gandhi: The History of the World's Largest Democracy* (London: Macmillan; 2007), Shashi Tharoor, *India: From Midnight to the Millennium* (Delhi: Penguin; 1997), Pawan Varma, *Being Indian: The Truth About Why the 21st Century will be India's* (Delhi: Penguin; 2004), and Edward Luce, *In Spite of the Gods: The Strange Rise of India* (London: Little, Brown; 2006), are very good general introductions to the vibrant everyday life of contemporary India. Gurcharan Das, *India Unbound: From Independence to the Global Information Age* (Delhi: Penguin; 2002), and Achin Vanaik, *The Painful Transition: Bourgeois Democracy in India* (London: Verso Books; 1990), offer contrasting views of the problems and potentials of Indian society and the economy. Subrata Mitra, Siegfried Wolf and Jivanta Schoettli, *A Political and Economic Dictionary of South Asia* (London: Routledge; 2006), and Subrata Mitra (ed.), *A Critical Guide to the Modern Politics of South Asia* (London: Routledge; 2008), are both accessible sources on the institutions and politics in India.

Paul Brass, *The Politics of India since Independence.* (revised edition) (Cambridge: CUP; 1992), offers good coverage in terms of issues. Stuart Corbridge and John Harriss, *Reinventing India: Liberalization, Hindu Nationalism and Popular Democracy* (Polity Press; 2000), and Robert L. Hardgrave and Stanley A. Kochanek, *India: Government and Politics in a Developing Nation* (Boston: Thomson Higher Education; 2008), offer a developmental perspective, but from contrasting angles. Ayesha Jalal, *Democracy and Authoritarianism in South Asia* (Cambridge: CUP; 1995), is a highly thematic and comparative overview, principally contrasting India and Pakistan in the immediate wake of Partition. Mushirul Hasan, *Legacy of a Divided Nation: India's Muslims since Independence* (London: Hurst; 1997), and Ian Copland, *India, 1885–1947* (London: Pearson; 2001), are excellent introductions to the historical background of modern India. Ramesh Thakur, *The Government and Politics of India* (London: Macmillan; 1995), and Sumit Ganguly and Neil DeVotta, *Understanding Contemporary India* (Boulder, CO: Lynne Rienner; 2003), are both interesting and useful text books. W.H. Morris-Jones, *Government and Politics of India* [revised edition of original publication in 1967] (Eothen Publishing; 1987) and Rajni Kothari, *Politics in India* (London: Sangam, 1970), though dated, are still very influential. Lloyd I. and Susanne H. Rudolph, *In Pursuit of Lakshmi* (Chicago: University of Chicago Press; 1987), is a fine example of an analysis of India's political economy that remains deeply grounded in India's political culture and history.

Democracy and the modern institutions of India

Granville Austin, *The Indian Constitution: Cornerstone of a Nation* (Mumbai: OUP; 1966), Durga D. Basu, *Introduction to the Constitution of India* (New Delhi: Prentice Hall; 1985), and Richard Park and Bruce Bueno de Mesquita, *India's Political System* (Delhi: Prentice-Hall; 1967), are general introductions to the founding of a modern political system in India. Devesh Kapur and Pratap Bhanu Mehta (eds), *Public Institutions in India: Performance and Design* (Delhi: OUP; 2005), is a very good introduction to the performance of India's modern institutions. Subrata K. Mitra, *The Puzzle of India's Governance: Culture, Context and Comparative Theory* (London: Routledge; 2005), provides a formal analysis of political order and democracy in India.

A clutch of articles in learned journals from the early decades of the twentieth century and in the closing years of colonial rule testify to modern politics as the harbinger of change.[1] Susanne Hoeber Rudolph (1987) brings a method rich with historical and anthropological insights to the field, and rewards the student of politics with an access to the deep, subterranean springs of legitimacy in societies where 'gods have not yet died'.[2] Arendt Lijphart (1996) complements the explanatory power of 'path dependency', which is mainly the role of the past in understanding the present through the effects of institutional arrangement. In his analysis of the 'puzzle' of India's democracy he shows how India reconciles majority rule, with its tendency for the winners to 'take all', with various forms of power-sharing which make it possible for the minority to enjoy office, in proportion to their strength.

The Indian case, something of a model when it comes to transition to democracy, has engaged a number of scholars. The structure and process of the post-colonial state are best explained in two seminal articles by Rajni Kothari, published in 1964 and 1974.[3] They explain the mechanism of intra-party factionalism which introduced a degree of competition to a system where power did not alternate between competing political parties. Further insights into this remarkable phenomenon of democracy striking root on alien soil are provided by Weiner (1964) and Morris-Jones (1967), who show how a pattern of sophisticated, institutionalized power-sharing underpins the first impression of Indian politics as chaotic. Zagoria's analysis (1971) of the social base of India's communist movement provides insight into the process of party formation. Other critical contributions to the study of India's political parties are Franda (1969) on the steady fragmentation of the communist party,[4] and Erdman's (1963–4) depiction of the Swatantra – India's one and only liberal party which has become defunct over the past decades.[5] The steady proliferation of the norms of political competition and the 'routinization of change' are introduced by Michael Brecher (1967).

The unravelling of the state and the recovery of order is taken up by Mitra (1980), the subversion of democratic institutions by the emergency regime of Indira Gandhi by Das Gupta (1978) and, subsequently, the crisis of India's modern institutions by Kaviraj (1984). The mechanisms of the recovery of order have been delineated by several scholars: Subrata K. Mitra, *Power, Protest and Participation: Local Elites and the Politics of Development in India* (London: Routledge; 1992), and Subrata K. Mitra and Alison Lewis (eds), *Subnational Movements in South Asia* (Boulder, CO: Westview; 1996), analyse the coping mechanisms of the Indian state in the face of challenges from below. In a prescient article on the fluidity and flexibility of India's party politics, Brass (1968) showed how the Indian political system made its transition from the charismatic leadership of Jawaharlal Nehru to the collective leadership of the Congress party, and subsequently from the dominant role of the Congress to multi-party coalitions based on competition and collaboration of party, faction and individual leaders in the politics of North India.[6] This structural duality of the Indian political system, which whips up passion and the urge for upward mobility by marginal social groups, threatens to overtake the capacity of the state to meet these new demands, and simultaneously produces new methods of allocation to cope with unrest, reveals an innate, innovative capacity. See Subrata K. Mitra, Mike Enskat and Clemens Spiess, *Political Parties in South Asia* (Westport, CT: Praeger; 2004). Other essays on this theme cover: the role of political parties and the resilience of the system (Chhibber and Petrocik 1989); the role of consociational and federal forms of institutional arrangements (Adeney 2002 and Mawdsley 2002), the role of power-sharing and development (Sinha 2003) and the resilience of India's democracy (Varshney 2000). The same general argument has been reinforced by Sridharan (2005) who has shown that the rise of the Bharatiya Janata Party has come about through the strategy of broad-based coalitions which stymie political excesses as a price of power[7] and Ganguly (1996) who has demonstrated how, even as a deviant case, political insurgency in Kashmir originates more from the decline of modern institutions than from a rejection of modernity by a rival ideology with greater popular support.[8] Mitra (2008) shows how the level of governance goes up when decision-making elites respond to challenges to order through policies that combine sanctions with strategic reform and the accommodation of identity.

Social change: from hierarchy to equality

Freedom from alien rule and the promise of social change constituted the twin threads of the anti-colonial movement. The social agenda that united the various strands of the Freedom Movement resurfaced as the core social policy of the post-colonial state following the Transfer of Power. In his influential 'Caste in Modern India', Srinivas (1957) lays down the main norms of analysis for a social structure in flux. The internal structure of this complex world where social hierarchy found its match in the egalitarian impulse of modernity is the theme of Susanne H. Rudolph (1961), Marc Galanter (1963), Lloyd I. Rudolph (1965) and Richard G. Fox (1969). Two influential articles – Inden (1986) and Madan (1987) – assert the otherness of South Asian societies, which need to be considered in their own terms of the singularity of their discourse, normative structures, the inner conflicts of tradition and the endogenous impulses towards authenticity and change. Judith Brown's 'The Mahatma and Modern India' (1969) rounds off these canonical writings by drawing attention to the ambiguity – at once subjugating and sublimating – of the import of Gandhi's thought with regard to society and modernity and change in India. Subrata K. Mitra and V.B. Singh, *When Rebels become Stakeholders* (Delhi: Sage; 2009), provides an empirical study of social attitudes and mobility in India.

Following Independence, when the logic of universal adult franchise and competitive politics set in (Nandy 1970), subaltern agency, thanks to the impact of institutional changes, modern political communication, and the political connectivity stimulated by vote-hungry politicians and caste associations, found a new voice in the public sphere. The political sociology of state–society interactions in South Asia that resulted from the process has generated a rich array of essays. Mitra (1995), Manor (1996) and Wilkinson (2000) provide a general introduction to the instrumental character of subaltern agency which aims at both material gain and new visions of modernity as their twin objectives. Insightful essays on specific groups such as Baruah (2003) on the Nagas, Calman (1989) on women's movements, Jaffrelot (2000) on Other Backward Classes, Katzenstein (1973) on the Shiv Sena and Wallace (1986) on Sikhs are some of the fascinating essays that illustrate the autonomous character of Indian modernity, that question the canon of social change inspired by the West, even as it implements the policies inspired by it.[9] Ram Prasad on 'Hindutva' (1993) and Amrita Basu on 'Community Conflicts and the State' (1997) on the one hand, and Binder (1958) and Nasr (1995) on the other, indicate the transformative power of competitive politics that has brought about the fusion of imported and indigenous norms of modernity, producing a set of rules and attitudes uniquely South Asian.

The economy

Arvind Panagariya, *India: The Emerging Giant* (New York: OUP; 2008), is a comprehensive account of India's economy. Pranab Bardhan's *The Political Economy of Development in India* (Delhi: OUP; 1984), gives a very good insight into the political economy of pre-liberalization India. The structure of India's model of development and the relevant aspects of general theories of growth are delineated, respectively, in Malenbaum (1958) and Cohen (1955). Ilchman (1967) explains the irony of a model of development that aimed at import substitution but nevertheless required substantial amounts of foreign aid to maintain its pace. Though based on the classic assumption that agricultural surplus would be invested in industry and infrastructure to generate momentum for economic development, the Indian case nevertheless needed to give special attention to the agrarian sector. The Indian peasant, potential victim of industry like peasants in the context of Europe's industrialization, has been able to offer resistance, thanks to the right to vote. Democracy gave a political motivation to the modern state to protect the interests of the peasant through a variety of special programmes, subsidies and reform. The complex consequences for growth, development and democracy are discussed by Francine Frankel (1969) and Barbara Harriss (1972), two leading authors in this field who approach the peasant with great empathy.[10]

The Indian model, eclectic in view of its attempts to combine elements of capitalistic, socialistic and communitarian models of development, did manage to sustain both democracy and a modest rate of growth during the early years after Independence. However, with the acceleration of expectations and relative decline in the capacity of the system to meet them, India's political economy started generating corruption, relative deprivation, problems of governance and negative consequences for the environment. In their insightful essay on the 'Pyraveekar' – the all-purpose fixers of India – Reddy and Hargopal (1985) explain the structural origin of corruption, and what the diverting of resources into non-developmental purposes meant for development. The opposite side of the picture, where the commission-agent also acts as a local leader – *gaon ka neta* – providing agency to people at the lowest levels of the system and functions as the cutting edge of local democracy, is discussed in Mitra (1991). The structural basis of poverty is discussed in Kohli's seminal essay (1983–84) on 'Regime Types and Poverty Reform' where he shows why some regimes strike at the roots of poverty, while others, where political power lies mostly in the hands of the better-off classes, leave mass poverty untouched. Bob Currie (1996) raises the issue of democracy and the problem of economic adjustment. Swain (1996) elaborates on another salient issue pertaining to the intricate relationship between environmental degradation and ethnic conflict, which is likely to remain on the agenda of the economy, environment and ethnic conflict in South Asia in the immediate future.

The radical restructuring of India's economy that started in 1991 has since been known as liberalization. This major overhaul of policy is discussed in detail by Montek S. Ahluwalia (2002). A member of the team of economists which, under the leadership of Manmohan Singh, then the finance minister of India, was responsible for initiating the policy changes that subsequently came to be known as 'liberalization of the economy', Ahluwalia critically evaluated 'gradualism', seen by many as the cornerstone of Indian policy of structural change. The specific implications of liberalization are taken up by several essays in this section. Mukherji (2004), the first of these, discusses the role of independent regulatory commissions in managing competition in India. Lawrence Saez (1999) analyses the implications of the unravelling of the centralized economy, watched over by the central government and the Planning Commission from the 'commanding heights of the economy', and the birth of the federal market economy. He explains how the new political economy has given greater initiative to those responsible for policy making and implementation at the lower levels of the system, and facilitated competition and collaboration among concerned departments of the regional governments. Finally, Devesh Kapur (2002), with a focus on the IT industry, analyses the causes and consequences of the great strides made by the service sector of India's economy.

No discussion of economic change in a post-colonial context would be complete without a special mention of the social sector, because the classic victims of growth – peasants, workers, and those likely to be displaced from their traditional homeland because of the needs of industry and urbanization – are also veto players in the political system, thanks to the media and the countervailing forces of democracy. The need to 'rationalize' the labour component of the process of production and the resistance of unionized labour to such attempts are discussed by Roy Chowdhury (2003) in an essay based on field studies and interviews from several industrial sites in India. Rob Jenkins (2004) continues the discussion with an analysis of the symbiotic relation between liberalization and the labour market. Finally, in his comprehensive analysis of the implications of liberalization and globalization on social stability, Baldev Raj Nayar (2007) provides valuable insights into why the radical restructuring of India's economy has not led to the chaos that one has seen in the former Soviet Union and socialist economies of Eastern Europe in the wake of the break-up of communist rule.

International relations

The peculiar combination of national self-assertion and non-violence that characterized the anti-colonial movement in South Asia distinguished it from the revolutionary fervour and violent politics of similar movements in South-East Asia and Africa. The consequence for the international politics of the successor states are analysed in this volume. The shape of future politics of these states with regard to the international arena – thanks to the long apprenticeship of these states under their colonial master – is analysed by no less a figure than Mahatma Gandhi (1931).[11] However, whereas Gandhi had the vision of British India passing into a confederation of village republics, and an agrarian economy which met local needs through local resources, the steadily unfolding forces of state formation, nation building and economic development found a new focus in the state and the modern politics of South Asia.[12]

Indian foreign policy of the early years after Independence, under the leadership of Jawaharlal Nehru, found an anchor in the concept of non-alignment. *Panchasheela* – the five principles of peaceful co-existence as it came to be known – emerged as the founding principle of the non-alignment movement. The essays in this category delineate the main foundations of Indian foreign policy during the formative decades (Appadorai 1949; Edwardes 1965). The economic dimensions of this policy are discussed by Cohen (1955). Under colonial rule, the government of India had positioned the country as an outpost of the British Empire and had protected the boundaries of the colony through the combination of imperial military power and strategic buffer states. Both these policies were put into question by the new principle of non-alignment and the search for trust and cooperation (as symbolized by *Panchasheela*) rather than force as the basis of politics. Stephen Cohen – *India: Emerging Power* (Washington, DC: Brookings Institution 2001) – offers a strategic study of India as an emerging power. The transition from the one to the other led to problems of uncertainty regarding the status of the former buffer zones, discussed by Leo Rose (1963), and border war with China (Maxwell 1970; Hoffmann 1972; and Cohen 1975).

As already indicated above, the non-aligned foreign policy of independent India sought to achieve a double goal, namely, the transformation of India from British colony to independent state, and from being part of the imperial economy to becoming an independent economy through planning and import substitution. However, the transition was not quite as smooth as the authors of this policy had anticipated. The rise of South Asia's economies was affected by the movement of capital and products internationally.[13] In addition, India's non-aligned policy was vigorously contested by Pakistan which keenly sought alliances as a counterweight to the asymmetry of its size and strength vis-à-vis India. The consequent security dilemma (Dittmer 2001) and the role of China in South Asia's international relations – within the region as well as with powers exogenous to it – have had a deep implication for war and peace in South Asia (Mitra 2001).

The anomalies emerging from a foreign policy based on non-alignment and peaceful co-existence led to its vigorous questioning during Nehru's lifetime but became the staple for foreign policy debates after 1964. India's policies were radically different from the policies of her two immediate rivals, Pakistan and China. These debates came to a peak in the late 1960s, following Nehru's death in 1964, which was, incidentally, also the year of the first Chinese nuclear test. Speculations about India's attempt to go fully nuclear, following the 'Peaceful Nuclear Explosion' of 1974, became a kind of parlour game among foreign policy experts. A series of scholarly articles has recorded the events preceding and following the 1998 tests that established the nuclear status of India and Pakistan in the most unambiguous terms. These developments are reported in Hagerty (1995), Ganguly (1999), Basrur (2001) and Sagan (2001). The final essay in this section by Sreeram S. Chaulia (2002) registers the paradigm shift in India's foreign policy from Nehru's renunciation of force as the basis of foreign policy to the 'realism' of the Bharatiya Janata Party.

Why cooperation among the states of South Asia has had only limited success is the main question raised by Ross Mallick (1993). A variation on this theme is the inability of India and Pakistan to come to an institutional arrangement for the safeguard of their nuclear establishments. The theme is succinctly discussed by Perkovich (1993) in an insightful piece. The article is indicative of the state of play with regard to academic research on the nuclearization of South Asia during these critical years. The article is clairvoyant in view of the fact that it appeared three years *before* India and Pakistan went nuclear publicly. The role of confidence building measures (CBMs), often announced with much fanfare by India and Pakistan locked into a no-war, no-peace situation, is critically analysed by Chari (2005). The same issue is raised in reference to institutional methods of arms control with a view to generating strategic stability by Rodney Jones (2005). The two further essays – Mistry (2004) and Mitra and Schoettli (2007) – focus on India as an emerging power and as a possible fulcrum of South Asia's regional politics, and analyse the ambiguities that this necessarily entails on the part of India's foreign policy.

Notes

1 H. McD. Clokie, 'The New Constitution for India', *The American Political Science Review*, 30 (6), December 1936, pp. 1152–65; Taraknath Das, 'India – Past, Present and the Future', *Political Science Quarterly*, 62 (2), June 1947, pp. 295–304; and Richard Symonds, 'State-Making in Pakistan', *Far Eastern Survey*, 19 (5), 8 March 1950, pp. 45–50.

2 Susanne Hoeber Rudolph has developed the theme further in her presidential address to the American Political Science Association, 2004. See Susanne Hoeber Rudolph, 'The Imperialism of Categories: Situating Knowledge in a Globalizing World', *Perspectives*, 3 (1), March 2005, pp. 5–14.

3 Kothari, Rajni, 'The Congress "System" in India', *Asian Survey*, 4 (12), December 1964, pp. 1161–73; Rajni Kothari, 'The Congress System Revisited: A Decennial Review', *Asian Survey*, 14 (12), December 1974, pp. 1035–54.

4 Marcus F. Franda, 'India's Third Communist Party', *Asian Survey*, 9 (11), November 1969, pp. 797–817.

5 Howard L. Erdman, 'India's Swatantra Party', *Pacific Affairs*, 36 (4), Winter 1963–64, pp. 394–410.

6 Brass (1968).

7 E. Sridharan, 'Coalition Strategies and the BJP's Expansion, 1989–2004', *Commonwealth & Comparative Politics*, 43 (2), July 2005, pp. 194–221.

8 Sumit Ganguly, 'Explaining the Kashmir Insurgency: Political Mobilization and Institutional Decay', *International Security*, 21(2), Autumn 1996, pp. 76–107.

9 For an examination of the struggle over the birthplace of Rama in Ayodhya see Peter Van der Veer, '"God must be Liberated!" A Hindu Liberation Movement in Ayodhya', *Modern Asian Studies*, 21 (2), 1987, pp. 283–301; and on the empowerment of *Dalits* through party agency, see Kanchan Chandra, 'The Transformation of Ethnic Politics in India: The Decline of Congress and the Rise of the Bahujan Samaj Party in Hoshiarpur', *The Journal of Asian Studies*, 59 (1), February 2000, pp. 26–61.

10 Examining how a democratic state deals with crises, Paul Brass's study of the 1966–67 Bihar famine provides valuable insights into the complex forces that lead to a critical situation with regard to the availability of food and the articulation of the situation as one of crisis. See Paul Brass, 'The Political Uses of Crisis: The Bihar Famine of 1966–67', *The Journal of Asian Studies*, 45 (2), February 1986, pp. 245–67.

11 M.K. Gandhi, 'The Future of India', *International Affairs (Royal Institute of International Affairs 1931–1939)*, 10 (6), November 1931, pp. 721–39.

12 See Holden Furber, 'The Unification of India, 1947–51', *Pacific Affairs*, 24 (4), December 1951, pp. 352–71.

13 For a study of the intersection between the compulsions of the world system and regional economies see David Washbrook, 'South Asia, the World System, and World Capitalism', *The Journal of Asian Studies*, 49 (3), August 1990, pp. 479–508.

Bibliography

Adeney, Katharine (2002). 'Constitutional Centring: Nation Formation and Consociational Federalism in India and Pakistan', *Commonwealth and Comparative Politics,* 40 (3), November, pp. 8–33.

Ahluwalia, Montek S. (2002). 'Economic Reforms in India since 1991: Has Gradualism Worked?', *The Journal of Economic Perspectives,* 16 (3), Summer, pp. 67–88.

Akbar, M.J. (1988). *Riot after Riot: Reports on Caste and Communal Violence in India.* New Delhi: Penguin.

Ali, Tariq (1985). *The Nehrus and the Gandhis: An Indian Dynasty.* London: Pan Books.

Allen, Charles (ed.) (1976). *Plain Tales from the Raj: Images of British India in the Twentieth Century.* Newton Abbot: Readers' Union.

Almond, G.A. *et al.* (eds) (2008). *Comparative Politics Today: A World View.* New York: Longman (8th edn).

Ambedkar, B.R. (1945). *What Congress and Gandhi Have Done to the Untouchables.* Bombay: Thacker and Co.

Anon. (2005). *The Penguin Guide to the States and Union Territories of India.* New Delhi: Penguin Books.

Appadorai, Angadipuram (1949). 'India's Foreign Policy', *International Affairs,* 25 (1), January, pp. 37–46.

Appleby, Paul H. (1957). *Public Administration in India: Report of a Survey, 1953.* New Delhi: Cabinet Secretariat, Government of India Press.

Arora, Balveer (ed.) (1995). *Multiple Identities in a Single State: Indian Federalism in Comparative Perspective.* New Delhi: Konark.

Auboyer, Jeannine (2007). *Daily Life in Ancient India: From 200 BC to 700 AD.* London: Phoenix.

Austin, Granville (1966). *The Indian Constitution: Cornerstone of a Nation.* Mumbai: Oxford University Press.

Axelrod, Robert (1984). *The Evolution of Cooperation.* London: Penguin.

Bachrach, Peter and Morton Baratz (1962). 'Two Faces of Power', *American Political Science Review,* 56 (4), December, pp. 947–52.

Bailey, Frederic G. (1970). *Stratagems and Spoils: A Social Anthropology of Politics.* New York: Schocken Books.

Baldwin, Robert (1995). *Rules and Government.* Oxford: Clarendon Press.

Bardhan, Pranab (1984). *The Political Economy of Development in India.* New Delhi: Oxford University Press.

Barnett, Marguerite R. (1976). *The Politics of Cultural Nationalism in South India.* Princeton, NJ: Princeton University Press.

Baruah, Sanjib (2003). 'Confronting Constructionism: Ending India's Naga War', *Journal of Peace Research,* 40 (3), May, pp. 321–38.

Basrur, Rajesh M. (2001). 'Nuclear Weapons and Indian Strategic Culture', *Journal of Peace Research,* 38 (2), March, pp. 181–98.

Basu, Ajit N. (1997). 'Reflection on Community Conflicts and the State in India', *The Journal of Asian Studies,* 56 (2), May, pp. 391–97.

Basu, Durga Das (1985). *Introduction to the Constitution of India.* New Delhi: Prentice-Hall.

Bates, Robert H., Avner Greif, Magaret Levi, Jean-Laurent Rosenthal and Barry R. Weingast (1998). *Analytic Narratives.* Princeton, NJ: Princeton University Press.

Bayley, David (1983). 'The Police and Political Order in India', *Asian Survey*, 23 (4), April, pp. 486–96.

Bayly, Chris A. (1983). *Rulers, Townsmen and Bazaars: North Indian Society in the Age of British Expansion, 1770–1870.* Cambridge: Cambridge University Press.

—— (1988). *Indian Society and the Making of the British Empire.* Cambridge: Cambridge University Press.

—— (1996). *Empire and Information: Intelligence Gathering and Social Communication in India; 1780–1870.* Cambridge: Cambridge University Press.

Beals, Alan R. (1963). *Gopalpur: A South Indian Village.* New York: Holt, Rinehart and Winston.

Bendix, Reinhard (1960). *Max Weber: An Intellectual Portrait.* New York: Anchor Books.

Bendix, Reinhard (1962). *Max Weber: An Intellectual Portrait.* Garden City, NY: Doubleday, p. 196.

Berger, Peter and Thomas Luckmann (1966). *The Social Construction of Reality: A Treatise in the Sociology of Knowledge.* Garden City, NY: Doubleday.

Berger, Peter, Brigitte Berger and Hansfried Kellner (1973). *The Homeless Mind: Modernization and Consciousness.* New York: Random House.

Bertsch, Gary K., Seema Gahlaut and Anupam Srivastava (eds). (1999) *Engaging India: U.S. Strategic Relations with the World's Largest Democracy.* New York: Routledge.

Bhalla, A.S. (2002). 'Sino-Indian Growth and Liberalisation: A Survey', *Asian Survey*, 42 (3), May–June, pp. 419–39.

Bhattacharyya, Harihar (1998). *Micro Foundations of Bengal Communism.* New Delhi: Ajanta.

—— (2001). *India as a Mulicultural Federation: Asian Values, Democracy and Decentralisation (in Comparison with Swiss Federalism).* Basle, Geneva, Munich: Helbing & Lichtenhahn.

Binder, Leonhard (1958). 'Problems of Islamic Political Thought in the Light of Recent Developments in Pakistan', *The Journal of Politics*, 20 (4), November, pp. 655–75.

Blank, Stephen (2007). 'The Geostrategic Implications of the Indo-American Strategic Partnership', *India Review*, 6 (1), January–March, pp. 1–24.

Bolingbroke, Henry, J. (1975). 'A Dissertation upon Parties (1733–34)', in: George H. Sabine (ed.) *A History of Political Theory.* New Delhi: Oxford University Press/IBH.

Bose, Pradip K. (1985). 'Social Mobility and Caste Violence: A Study of the Gujarat Riots', in: I.P. Deasi, Shah, Ghanshyam *et al. Caste, Caste-conflict and Reservation.* New Delhi: Ajanta.

Brailsford, Henry Noel (1939). *Democracy for India.* London: The Fabian Society.

Braithwaite, Valerie and Margaret Levi (eds) (1998). *Trust and Governance.* New York: Russell Sage Foundation.

Brass, Paul (1968). 'Coalition Politics in North India', *American Political Science Review*, 62 (4), December, pp. 1174–91.

—— (1986). 'The Political Uses of Crisis, the Bihar Famine of 1966–67', *The Journal of Asian Studies*, 45 (2), February, pp. 245–67.

—— (1992). *The Politics of India since Independence* (revised edn). Cambridge: Cambridge University Press.

—— (1997). *Theft of an Idol: Text and Context in the Representation of Collective Violence.* Princeton, NJ: Princeton University Press.

—— (2003). *The Production of Hindu–Muslim Violence in Contemporary India.* Seattle: University of Washington Press.

—— (2003a). *Ethnicity and Nationalism.* New Delhi: Sage Publications.

Brecher, Michael (1967). 'Succession in India 1967: The Routinization of Political Change', *Asian Survey*, 7 (7), July, pp. 423–43.

Brown, Judith (1969). 'The Mahatma and Modern India', *Modern Asian Studies*, 3 (4), Gandhi Centenary Number, pp. 321–42.

—— (1985). *Modern India: The Origins of an Asian Democracy.* New Delhi: Oxford University Press.

Burghart, Richard (1984). 'The Formation of the Concept of Nation-State in Nepal', *The Journal of Asian Studies*, 44 (1), November, pp. 101–25.

Butler, David, Ashok Lahiri and Prannoy Roy (1995). *India Decides: Elections 1952–1995*. New Delhi: Books and Things.

Calman, Leslie J. (1989). 'Women and Movement Politics in India', *Asian Survey*, 29 (10), October, pp. 940–58.

Canetti, Elias (1973). *Crowds and Power* (Translation by Carol Stewart). Harmondsworth: Penguin.

Casey, D. and D. Lury (1987). *Data Collection in Developing Countries*. Oxford: Clarendon.

Chakma, Bhumitra (2002). 'Road to Chagai: Pakistan's Nuclear Programme, Its Sources and Motivations', *Modern Asian Studies*, 36 (4), pp. 871–921.

Chakrabarty, Bidyut (2007). *Indian Politics and Society since Independence: Events, Processes and Ideology*. London and New York: Routledge.

Chakrabarty, Dipesh, Rochona Majumdar and Andrew Sartori (eds). (2007). *From the Colonial to the Postcolonial: India and Pakistan in Transition*. New Delhi: Oxford University Press.

Chandra, Bipan, Mridula Mukherjee and Aditya Mukherjeee (2000). *India after Independence, 1947–2000*. New Delhi: Penguin.

Chandra, Kanchan (2000). 'The Transformation of Ethnic Politics in India: The Decline of Congress and the Rise of the Bahujan Samaj Party in Hoshiarpur', *The Journal of Asian Studies*, 59 (1), February, pp. 26–61.

Chari, P.R. (2005). 'Strategic Stability in South Asia: The Role of Confidence-building and Threat Reduction Measures', *Contemporary South Asia*, 14 (2), June, pp. 211–17.

Chaulia, Sreeram S. (2002). 'BJP, India's Foreign Policy and the "Realist Alternative" to the Nehruvian Tradition', *International Politics*, 39 (2), June, pp. 215–34.

Chellaney, Brahma (1991). 'South Asia's Passage to Nuclear Power', *International Security*, 16 (1), Summer, pp. 43–72.

Chhibber, Pradeep K. and John R. Petrocik (1989). 'The Puzzle of Indian Politics: Social Cleavages and the Indian Party System', *British Journal of Political Science*, 19 (2), April, pp. 191–210.

Chhibber, Pradeep K. (1999). *Democracy without Associations: Transformation of the Party System and Social Cleavage in India*. New Delhi: Vistaar.

Chowdhury, Supriya R. (2003). 'Public Sector Restructuring and Democracy: The State Labor and Trade Unions in India', *The Journal of Development Studies*, 39 (3), February, pp. 29–50.

Churchman, C. West (1961). *Prediction and Optimal Decision: Philosophical Issues of a Science of Value*. Englewood Cliffs, NJ: Prentice-Hall.

Clokie, H. McD. (1936). 'The New Constitution for India', *The American Political Science Review*, 30 (6), December, pp. 1152–64.

Cohen, Jerome B. (1955). 'India's Foreign Economic Policies', *World Politics*, 7 (4), July, pp. 546–71.

Cohen, Stephen P. (1975). 'Security Issues in South Asia', *Asian Survey*, 15 (3), March, pp. 202–14.

—— (1988). 'The Military and Indian Democracy', in: Atul Kohli (ed.), *India's Democracy: An Analysis of State-Society Relations*. Princeton, NJ: Princeton University Press.

—— (2001). *India: Emerging Power*. Washington, DC: Brookings Institutions.

Copland, Ian (2001). *India: 1885–1947*. London: Pearson.

Corbridge, S. and J. Harriss (2000). *Reinventing India: Liberalization, Hindu Nationalism and Popular Democracy*. Malden: Polity Press.

Currie, Bob (1996). 'Governance, Democracy and Economic Adjustment in India: Conceptual and Empirical Problems', *Third World Quarterly*, 17 (4), December, pp. 787–808.

—— (2001). 'Political Authority, Public Deliberation and the Politics of Poverty Reduction', in: Niraja G. Jayal and Sudha Pai (eds). *Democratic Governance in India: Challenges of Poverty, Development and Identity*. New Delhi: Sage.

Cybert, R. and J. March (1963). *A Behavioral Theory of the Firm*. Englewood Cliffs, NJ: Prentice-Hall.

Dandekar, V.M. and Nilakantha Rath (1971). 'Poverty in India', *Economic and Political Weekly* VI (1 and 2).

Das, Arvind (1992). *The Republic of Bihar.* New Delhi: Penguin.

Das, Gurcharan (2002). *India Unbound: From Independence to the Global Information Age.* New Delhi: Penguin.

Das, Suranjan (1993). *Communal Riots in Bengal 1905–1947.* New Delhi: Oxford University Press.

Das, Taraknath (1947). 'India – Past, Present and the Future', *Political Science Quarterly*, 62 (2), June, pp. 295–304.

Das, Veena (ed.) (1990). *Communities, Riots and Survivors in South Asia.* New Delhi: Oxford University Press.

Das Gupta, Jyotirindra (1970). *Language Conflict and National Development: Group Politics and National Language Policy in India.* Mumbai: Oxford University Press.

—— (1978). 'A Season of Caesars: Emergency Regimes and Developmental Politics in Asia', *Asian Survey*, 18 (4), April, pp. 315–49.

—— (1989). 'India: Democratic Becoming and Combined Development', in: Larry Diamond, Juan Linz, and Seymour Martin Lipset (eds), *Democracy in Developing Countries.* Boulder, CO: Lynne Rienner.

Dash, Kishore C. (1996). 'The Political Economy of Regional Cooperation in South Asia', *Pacific Affairs*, 69 (2), September, pp. 185–209.

Deb, Bimal J., Keya Sengupta and B. Datta-Ray (2008). *Globalization and North-East India.* New Delhi: Concept.

Deb, Siddharta (2009). 'Enemy Citizens', *London Review of Books*, 31 (1) (January), pp. 40–41.

De Long, J.B. (2003). 'India since Independence: An Analytical Growth Narrative', in: D. Rodrik (ed.), *In Search of Prosperity: Analytical Narratives on Economic Growth.* Princeton, NJ: Princeton University Press.

Dhar, P.N. (2000). *Indira Gandhi, the 'Emergency', and Indian Democracy.* New Delhi: Oxford University Press.

Dhavan, Rajeev (1980). *Justice on Trial: The Supreme Court Today.* Allahabad: Wheeler.

Diamond, Larry, Juan J. Linz and Seymour M. Lipset (eds) (1989). *Democracy in Developing Countries.* Boulder, CO: Lynne Rienner.

Dirks, Nicholas (1987). *The Hollow Crown: The Ethno-history of an Indian Kingdom.* Cambridge: Cambridge University Press.

Dittmer, Lowell (2001). 'South Asia's Security Dilemma', *Asian Survey*, 41 (6), November–December, pp. 897–906.

Drèze, Jean and Amartya Sen (2007). *India: Economic Development and Social Opportunity* (4th edn). New Delhi: Oxford University Press.

Dumont, Louis (1970). *Homo Hierarchicus: The Caste System and its Implications* (Complete revised English edn). Chicago and London: University of Chicago Press.

Dynes, R. (1970). *Organized Behavior in Disaster.* Lexington, MA: Heath Lexington.

Edwardes, Michael (1965). 'Illusion and Reality in India's Foreign Policy', *International Affairs*, 41 (1), January, pp. 48–58.

—— (1969). *Everyday Life in Early India.* London: Batsford.

Elias, Norbert (1994). *The Civilizing Process.* Oxford: Blackwell.

Elster, Jon (1989). *The Cement of Society.* Cambridge: Cambridge University Press.

Embree, Ainslee (ed.) (1991). *Sources of Indian Tradition, Vol. I: From the Beginning to 1800.* London: Penguin.

Emerson, R. (1954). 'Paradoxes of Asian Nationalism', *The Far Eastern Quarterly*, 13 (2), February, pp. 131–42.

Enskat, Mike, Subrata K. Mitra and V.B. Singh (2001). 'India', in: Dieter Nohlen, Florian Grotz and Christoph Hartmann (eds), *Elections in Asia and the Pacific: A Data Handbook. Vol. I: The Middle East, Central Asia and South Asia.* Oxford: Oxford University Press.

Erdman, Howard L. (1963–64). 'India's Swatantra Party', *Pacific Affairs*, 36 (4), Winter, pp. 394–410.

Finan, Bill (2005). 'Nuclear Diplomacy Up Close: Strobe Talbott on the Clinton Administration and India', *India Review* 4 (1), pp. 84–97.

Findlay, Roland (1991). 'The New Political Economy: Its Explanatory Power for LDS's', in M. Meier (ed.), *Politics and Policy Making in Developing Countries*. San Francisco: International Center for Economic Growth.

Fisher, Roger and William Ury (1991) *Getting to Yes: Negotiating an Agreement without Giving In* (2nd edn). London: Business Books.

Fishlow, Albert, Catherine Gwin, Stephan Harrard, Dani Rodrik and Robert Wade (1994). *Miracle or Design: Lessons from the East Asian Experience*. Washington, DC: Overseas Development Council.

Forster, Edward Morgan (1924). *A Passage to India*. Harmondsworth: Penguin.

Foucault, Michel (1991). *Discipline and Punish: The Birth of the Prison*. London: Penguin.

Fox, Richard G. (1969). 'Varna Schemes and Ideological Integration in Indian Society', *Comparative Studies in Society and History*, 11 (1), January, pp. 27–45.

—— (1971). *Kin, Clan, Raja and Rule: State–Hinterland Relations in Preindustrial India*. Berkeley, Los Angeles, London: University of California Press.

Franda, Marcus F. (1969). 'India's Third Communist Party', *Asian Survey*, 9 (11), November, pp. 797–817.

Frankel, Francine R. (1969). 'India's New Strategy of Agricultural Development: Political Costs of Agrarian Modernization', *The Journal of Asian Studies*, 28 (4), August, pp. 693–710.

—— (1971). *India's Green Revolution. Economic Gains and Political Costs*. Princeton, NJ: Princeton University Press.

—— (1978). *India's Political Economy: 1947–1977. The Gradual Revolution*. Princeton, NJ: Princeton University Press.

Frankel, Francine R. and M.S.A. Rao (eds) (1989). *Dominance and State Power in Modern India: vol. 1: Decline of a Social Order*. New Delhi: Oxford University Press.

Freeman, Edward R. (1984). *Strategic Management: A Stakeholder Approach*. London: Pitman Books.

Freeman, James M. (1979). *Untouchable: An Indian Life Story*. London: George Allen & Unwin.

Fuller, Lon L. (1971). *The Morality of Law*. New Haven, CT: Yale University Press.

Furber, Holden (1951). 'The Unification of India, 1947–51', *Pacific Affairs*, 24 (4), December, pp. 352–71.

Galanter, Marc (1963). 'Law and Caste in Modern India', *Asian Survey*, 3 (11), November, pp. 544–59.

—— (1972). 'The Aborted Restoration of Indigenious Law in India', *Comparative Studies in Society and History*, 14 (1), January, pp. 53–70.

—— (ed.) (1989). *Law and Society in Modern India*. New Delhi: Oxford University Press.

Gandhi, Mohandas K. (1931). 'The Future of India', *International Affairs (Royal Institute of International Affairs 1931–1939)*, 10 (6), November, pp. 721–39.

Ganguly, Sumit (1996). 'Explaining the Kashmir Insurgency: Political Mobilization and Institutional Decay', *International Security*, 21 (2), Autumn, pp. 76–107.

—— (1999). 'India's Pathway to Pokharan II: The Prospects and Sources of New Delhi's Nuclear Weapons Program', *International Security*, Spring, pp. 148–77.

—— (2001). *Conflict Unending: India-Pakistan Tensions since 1947*. New York: Columbia University: Woodrow Wilson Center Press.

Ganguly, Sumit and Neil DeVotta (2003). *Understanding Contemporary India*. Boulder, CO: Lynne Rienner Publishers.

Geertz, Clifford (1973). *An Interpretaion of Cultures*. New York: Basic Books.

Gilmour, Ian (1992). *Riots, Risings and Revolutions: Governance and Violence in Eighteenth-Century England*. London: Hutchinson.

Gopal, Sarvepalli (ed.) (1991). *Anatomy of a Confrontation: The Babri Masjid-Ram Janambhoomi Issue*. New Delhi: Penguin.

Government of India. *The Constitution of India, 1950* [2009].

Government of India, Ministry of Home Affairs (1951–96). *Crime in India*. New Delhi: Government Press.

Graham, Hugh D. and Ted R. Gurr (eds) (1969). *Violence in America: Historical and Comparative Perspectives. A Report Submitted to the National Commission on the Causes and Prevention of Violence.* New York: Bantam Books.

Gray, John (2004). *Al Qaeda and What it Means to be Modern.* London: Faber and Faber.

Greenough, Paul (1982). *Prosperity and Misery in Modern Bengal: The Famine of 1943–1944.* New York: Oxford University Press.

Griffiths, (Sir) Percival (1971). *To Guard My People: The History of the Indian Police.* London: Ernest Benn.

Grindle, Merilee (ed.) (1997). *Getting Good Government: Capacity Building in the Public Sectors of Developing Countries.* Cambridge, MA: Harvard Institute for International Development, Harvard University Press.

Guha, Ramachandra (2007). *India After Gandhi: The History of the World's Largest Democracy.* Basingstoke: Macmillan.

Gupta, Dipak (1990). *The Economics of Political Violence: The Effect of Political Instability on Economic Growth.* New York: Praeger.

Gurcharan, Das (2001). *India Unbound.* New York: Knopf.

Gurr, Ted R. (1970). *Why Men Rebel.* Princeton, NJ: Princeton University Press.

Hagerty, Devin T. (1995). 'Nuclear Deterrence in South Asia: The 1990 Indo-Pakistani Crisis', *International Security*, 20 (3), Winter, pp. 79–114.

Hansen, Thomas B. (2001). *The Wages of Violence: Naming and Identity in Post-colonial Bombay.* Princeton, NJ: Princeton University Press.

Hardgrave, Robert L. (1965). *The Dravidian Movement.* Mumbay: Popular Prakashan.

—— (1968). 'The Breast-Cloth Controversy: Caste Consciousness and Social Change in Southern Travancore', *The Indian Economic and Social History Review*, 5 (2), June, pp. 171–87.

—— (1979). *Essays in the Political Sociology of South Asia.* New Delhi: Manohar.

Hardgrave, Robert L. and Stanley A. Kochanek (1993). *India: Government and Politics in a Developing Nation* (5th edn). Fort Worth, TX: Harcourt Brace Jovanovich.

—— (2008). *India: Government and Politics in a Developing Nation* (7th edn). Boston: Thomson Higher Education.

Harris, John, Janet Hunter and Colin Lewis (eds) (1991). *The New Institutional Economics and Third World Development.* London: Routledge.

Harrison, Selig (1960). *India: The Most Dangerous Decades.* New Delhi: Oxford University Press.

Harriss-White, Barbara (1972). 'Innovation Adoption in Indian Agriculture – the High Yielding Varieties Programme', *Modern Asian Studies*, 6 (1), pp. 71–98.

Hasan, Mushirul (1997). *Legacy of a Divided Nation: India's Muslims since Independence.* London: Hurst.

Hause, E. Malcolm (1960). 'India: Noncommitted and Nonaligned', *The Western Political Quarterly*, 13 (1), March, pp. 70–82.

Hay, Stephen (ed.) (1991). *Sources of Indian Tradition, Vol. II: Modern India and Pakistan.* London: Penguin.

Heesterman, J.C. (1985). *The Inner Conflict of Tradition: Essays in Indian Ritual, Kingship, and Society.* New Delhi: Oxford University Press.

Hegewald, Julia and Subrata K. Mitra (2008). 'Jaganath Compared: The Politics of Appropriation, Re-use and Regional Traditions in India', *Heidelberg Papers in South Asian and Comparative Politics* (26) January.

—— (eds) (forthcoming). *Re-use: The Art and Politics of Integration and Anxiety.* New Delhi: Sage.

Herring, R.J. (1989). 'Dilemmas of Agrarian Communism: Peasent Differentiation, Sectoral and Village Politics', *Third World Quarterly*, 11 (1), January, pp. 89–115.

Hibbs, Douglas (1973). *Mass Political Violence: A Cross-National Causal Analysis.* New York: Wiley.

Hobsbawm, Eric J. (1993). *Customs in Common.* London: Penguin.

Hoffmann, Steven A. (1972). 'Anticipation, Disaster, and Victory: India 1962–71', *Asian Survey*, 12 (11), November, pp. 960–79.

Hollis, Martin (1987). *The Cunning of Reasons*. Cambridge: Cambridge University Press.

Hossain, Akhtar (2000). 'Anatomy of Hartal Politics in Bangladesh', *Asian Survey*, 40 (3), May–June, pp. 508–29.

Howarth, David, Aletta J. Norval and Yannis Stavrakakis (eds) (2000). *Discourse Theory and Political Analysis: Identities, Hegemonies and Social Change*. Manchester, Manchester University Press.

Huntington, Samuel P. (1968). *Political Order in Changing Societies*. New Haven, CT: Yale University Press.

Ilchman, Warren F. (1967). 'A Political Economy of Foreign Aid: The Case of India', *Asian Survey*, 7 (10), October, pp. 667–88.

Inden, Ronald (1986). 'Orientalist Constructions of India', *Modern Asian Studies*, 20 (3), pp. 401–46.

—— (1990). *Imagining India*. Oxford: Blackwell.

International Institute for Strategic Studies (2004–5). *Strategic Survey 2004/05*. Oxford: Oxford University Press.

Jaffrelot, Christophe (2000). 'The Rise of the Other Backward Classes in the Hindi Belt', *The Journal of Asian Studies*, 59 (1), Februrary, pp. 86–108.

—— (2003). *A History of Pakistan and its Origins* (revised edn, 2004). Anthem Press.

—— (2003a). 'Communal Riots in Gujarat: The State at Risk?' *Heidelberg Papers in South Asian and Comparative Politics*, (17), July.

Jalal, Ayesha (1995). *Democracy and Authoritarianism in South Asia: A Comparative and Historical Perspective*. Cambridge: Cambridge University Press.

Jayal, Niraja G. and Sudha Pai (eds) (2001). *Democratic Governance in India: Challenges of Poverty, Development and Identity*. New Delhi: Sage.

Jeffrey, Robin (1986). *What's Happening to India? Punjab, Ethnic Conflict, Mrs Gandhi's Death and Test for Federalism*. Basingstoke: Macmillan.

Jenkins, Rob (1999). *Democratic Politics and Economic Reform in India*. Cambridge: Cambridge University Press.

—— (2004). 'Labor Policy and the Second Generation of Economic Reform in India', *India Review*, 3 (4), October, pp. 333–63.

Jennings, I. (1954). 'Politics in Ceylon since 1952', *Pacific Affairs*, 27 (4), December, pp. 338–52.

Jetly, Rajshree (2003). 'Conflict Management Strategies in ASEAN: Perspectives for SAARC', *The Pacific Review*, 16 (1), pp. 53–76.

Johnson, Chalmers A. (1983). *MITI and the Japanese Miracle: The Growth of Industrial Policy, 1925–1975*. Stanford, CA: Stanford University Press.

Jones, Bryan D. (2001). *Politics and Architecture of Choice: Bounded Rationality and Governance*. Chicago and London: University of Chicago Press.

Jones, Rodney W. (2005). 'Prospects for Arms and Strategic Stability in South Asia', *Contemporary South Asia*, 14 (2), June, pp. 191–209.

Joshi, Vijay and I.M. Little (1996). *India's Economic Reforms, 1991–2001*. Oxford: Oxford University Press.

Kakar, Sudhir (1995). *The Colours of Violence. Cultural Identities, Religion, and Conflict*. New Delhi: Viking.

Kane, A.E. (1944). 'The Development of Indian Politics', *Political Science Quarterly*, 59 (1), March, pp. 49–82.

Kapur, Devesh (2002). 'The Causes and Consequences of India's IT Boom', *India Review*, 1 (2), April, pp. 91–110.

Kapur, Devesh and Pratap B. Mehta (eds) (2005). *Public Institutions in India: Performance and Design*. New Delhi: Oxford University Press.

Kashyap, Subhash C. (1989). *Our Parliament: An Introduction to the Parliament of India*. New Delhi: National Book Trust.

Katzenstein, Mary F. (1973). 'Origins of Nativism: The Emergence of Shiv Sena in Bombay', *Asian Survey*, 13 (4), April, pp. 386–99.

Kautilya (1987). *The Arthashastra* (1992, edited, rearranged, translated and introduced by L.N. Rangarajan). New Delhi: Penguin.

Kaviraj, Sudipta (1984). 'On the Crisis of Political Institutions in India', *Contributions to Indian Sociology*, 18 (2), pp. 223–43.

Khan, T.A. (2000). 'Economy, Society and the State in Pakistan', *Contemporary South Asia*, 9 (2), July, pp. 181–95.

Khan, Yasmin (2008). *The Great Partition: The Making of India and Pakistan*. New Haven, CT: Yale University Press.

Khilnani, Sunil (1997). *The Idea of India*. London: Hamish Hamilton.

—— (2005). 'India as Bridging Power', in: P.K. Basu and P. Khanna (eds), *India as New Global Leader*, London: The Foreign Policy Centre, pp. 1–15.

King, Gary, Robert O. Keohane and Sidney Verba (1994). *Designing Social Inquiry: Scientific Inferences in Qualitative Research*. Princeton, NJ: Princeton University Press.

King, Robert D. (1998). *Nehru and the Language Politics of India*. New Delhi: Oxford University Press.

Kipling, Rudyard [1895] (1995). *The Jungle Book II*. New York: Tom Doherty Associates.

Kochanek, Stanley A. (1968). *The Congress Party of India: The Dynamics of One Party Democracy*. Princeton, NJ: Princeton University Press.

Kohli, Atul (1983–84). 'Regime Types and Poverty Reform in India', *Paciffic Affairs*, 56 (4), Winter, pp. 649–72.

—— (1987). *The State and Poverty in India: Politics of Reform*. Cambridge: Cambridge University Press.

—— (1990). *Democracy and Discontent: India's Growing Crisis of Governability*. Cambridge: Cambridge University Press.

—— (ed.) (2001). *The Success of India's Democracy*. Cambridge: Cambridge University Press.

Kooinman, Jan (2003). *Governing as Governance*. London: Sage.

Kothari, Rajni (1964). 'The Congress "System" in India', *Asian Survey*, 4 (12), December, pp. 1161–73.

—— (1970). *Politics in India*. Boston: Little, Brown.

—— (1974). 'The Congress System Revisited: A Decennial Review', *Asian Survey*, 14 (12), December, pp. 1035–54.

—— (1988). *The State Against Democracy: In Search of Humane Governance*. New Delhi: Ajanta.

—— (1994). *Politics in India*. London: Sangam.

Krishna, Anirudh (2002). *Active Social Capital: Tracing the Roots of Development and Democracy*. New York: Columbia University Press.

Krishna, B. (1995). *Sardar Vallabhbhai Patel: India's Iron Man*. New Delhi: Harper Collins.

Kulke, Hermann (ed.) (1995). *The State in India, 1000–1700*. New Delhi: Oxford University Press.

Kumar, V. (2009). 'Manmohan Points the Finger at Pakistan', *The Hindu*, 14 January, retrieved 14 January.

Laclau, Ernesto and Chantal Mouffe (1985). *Hegemony and Socialist Strategy: Towards a Radical Democratic Politics*. London: Verso.

Lawson, Kay (ed.) (1994). *How Parties Work: Perspectives from Within*. London: Praeger.

—— (2008). 'In this Issue', *International Political Science Review*, 29 (5), November, pp. 523–24.

Leaf, Murray J. (1980/1981). 'The Green Revolution in a Punjab Village, 1965–1978', *Pacific Affairs*, Winter, pp. 617–25.

Lerner, Daniel (1958). *The Passing of Traditional Society: Modernizing the Middle East*. New York: Free Press.

Lijphart, Arendt (1996). 'The Puzzle of Indian Democracy: A Consociational Interpretation', *The American Political Science Review*, 90 (2), pp. 258–68.

Lipset, Seymour Martin (1959). *Political Man: The Social Bases of Politics*. Garden City, NJ: Doubleday.

Little, D. (1991). 'Rational Choice Models and Asian Studies', *Journal of Asian Studies*, 50 (1), February, pp. 35–52.

Luce, E. (2006). *In Spite of the Gods: The Strange Rise of Modern India*. London: Little, Brown.

Lukes, S. (1974). *Power: A Radical View*. London: Macmillan.

Madan, T.N. (1987). 'Secularism in Its Place', *The Journal of Asian Studies*, 46 (4), November, pp. 747–59.

Maddison, Angus (2003): *The World Economy: Historical Statistics*. Paris: OECD.

Mahmood, Cynthia Kepley (1997). *Fighting for Faith and Nation: Dialogues with Sikh Militants*. Philadelphia: University of Pennsylvania Press.

Malenbaum, W. (1958). 'Some Political Aspects of Economic Development in India', *World Politics*, 10 (3), April, pp. 378–86.

Malik, Iftikhar H. (1996). 'The State and Civil Society in Pakistan: From Crisis to Crisis', *Asian Survey*, 36 (7), July, pp. 673–90.

Malik, Yogendra and V.B. Singh (1992). 'Bharatiya Janata Party: An Alternitive to Congress (I)?', *Asian Survey*, 32 (4), April, pp. 318–36.

Mallick, Ross (1993). *Development Policy of a Communist Government: West Bengal since 1977*. New York: Cambridge University Press.

Manor, James (1983). 'Anomie in Indian Politics: Origins and Potential Wider Impact', *Economic and Political Weekly*, 18 (19/21), May, pp. 725–34.

—— (1996). ' "Ethnicity" and Politics in India', *International Affairs*, 72 (3), July, pp. 459–75.

—— (ed.) (1994). *Nehru to the Nineties: The Changing Office of Prime Minister in India*. London: Hurst.

Mansingh, Surjit (1984). *India's Search for Power: Indira Gandhi's Foreign Policy; 1966–1982*. New Delhi: Sage.

March, James G. (1988). *Decision and Organizations*. Oxford: Basil Blackwell.

—— (1989). *Rediscovering Institutions: The Organizational Basis of Politics*. New York and London: The Free Press/Collier Macmillan.

March, James G. and Johan P. Olsen (1995). *Democratic Governance*. New York.

—— (1996). 'Institutional Perspectives on Political Institutions'. *Governance*, 9 (July), pp. 247–64.

Mawdsley, Emma (2002). 'Redrawing the Body Politic: Federalism, Regionalism and the Creation of New States in India', *Commonwealth & Comparative Politics*, November 40 (3), pp. 34–54.

Maxwell, Neville (1970). *India's China War*. London: Jonathan Cape.

McGarry, John and Brendan O'Leary (eds) (1993). *The Politics of Ethnic Conflict Regulation*. London: Routledge.

Mehta, Pratap Bhanu (2006). 'India's Judiciary: The Promise of Uncertainty', in: Davesh Kapur and Pratap Metha (eds), *Public Institutions in India: Performance and Design*. New Delhi: Oxford University Press.

Meier, M. (ed.) (1991). *Politics and Policy Making in Developing Countries*. San Francisco: International Center for Economic Growth.

Menski, Werner (2003). *Hindu Law: Beyond Tradition and Modernity*. New Delhi: Oxford University Press.

Merkel, Wolfgang (ed.) (2000). *Systemwechsel 5: Zivilgesellschaft und Transformation*. Opladen: Leske + Budrich.

—— (2004). 'Embedded and "Defective Democracies"', *Democratization*, 11 (5), pp. 33–58.

Metcalf, Thomas (1998). 'Past and Present: Towards an Aesthetics of Colonialism', in: G. Tillotson (ed.), *Paradigms of Indian Architecture: Space and Time in Representation and Design*. Richmond, Surrey: Curzon.

Migdal, Joel S. (1988). *Strong Societies and Weak States: State–Society Relations and State Capabilities in the Third World*. Princeton, NJ: Princeton University Press.

Misra, Bankey Bihari (1961). *The Indian Middle Classes: Their Growth in Modern Times*. London: Oxford University Press.

Mistry, Dinshaw (2004). 'A Theoretical and Empirical Assessment of India as an Emerging World Power', *India Review*, 3 (1), January, pp. 64–87.

Mitra, Subrata K. (1978). *Governmental Instability in Indian States: West Bengal, Bihar, Uttar Pradesh and Punjab*. New Delhi: Ajanta.

—— (1980). 'A Theory of Governmental Instability in Parliamentary Systems', *Comparative Political Studies*, 13 (2), July, pp. 235–63.

—— (1987). 'The Perils of Promoting Equality', *Journal of Commonwealth and Comparative Politics*, 25 (3), pp. 292–312.

—— (1988). 'The Paradox of Power: Political Science as Morality Play', *Commonwealth and Comparative Politics*, 26 (3), November, pp. 318–37.

—— (1988a). 'Succession in India: Dynastic Rule or Democratization of Power?', *Third World Quarterly*, 10 (1), pp. 129–59.

—— (ed.) (1990). *The Post-Colonial State in Asia: Dialectics of Politics and Culture*. London: Harvester.

—— (1991). 'Desecularising the State: Religion and Politics in India after Independence', *Comparative Studies in Society and History*, 33 (4), October, pp. 755–77.

—— (1991a). 'Room to Maneuver in the Middle: Local Elites, Political Action, and the State in India', *World Politics*, 43 (3), April, pp. 390–413.

—— (1992). *Power, Protest and Participation: Local Elites and the Politics of Development in India*. London: Routledge.

—— (1994). 'Religion, Region and Identity: Sacred Beliefs and Secular Power in a Regional State Tradition of India', in: Noel O. Sullivan (ed.), *Aspects of India: Essays on Indian Politics and Culture* (pp. 46–68). Hull: University of Hull.

—— (1994a). 'Caste, Democracy and the Politics of Community Formation in India', in: M. Searle-Chatterjee and U. Sharma (eds), *Contextualising Caste: Post-Dumantian Approaches* (pp. 49–72). Chicago: Chicago University Press.

—— (1994b). 'Party Organization and Policy Making in a Changing Environment: The Indian National Congress', in: Kay Lawson (ed.), *How Political Parties Work: Perspectives from Within* (pp. 153–177). Westport, CT: Praeger.

—— (1995). 'The Rational Politics of Cultural Nationalism: Subnational Movements of South Asia in Comparative Perspective', *British Journal of Political Science*, 25 (1), January, pp. 57–77.

—— (1997). 'Nehru's Policy towards Kashmir: Bringing the State Back in Again', *Commonwealth and Comparative Politics*, 35 (2), pp. 55–74.

—— (1999). *Culture and Rationality: The Politics of Social Change in Post-Colonial India*. New Delhi: Sage Publications.

—— (2001). 'Language and Federalism: The Multi-ethnic Challenge', *International Social Science Journal*, March, pp. 51–60.

—— (2001a). 'War and Peace in South Asia: A Revisionist View of India–Pakistan Relations', *Conemporary South Asia*, 10 (3), pp. 361–79.

—— (2005). *The Puzzle of India's Governance: Culture, Context and Comparative Theory*. London: Routledge.

—— (2005a). 'The NDA and the Politics of "Minorities" in India', in: Katherine Adeney and Laurence Sáez (eds), *Coalition Politics and Hindu Nationalism* (pp. 77–96). London: Routledge.

—— (2008). *A Critical Guide to the Modern Politics of South Asia*. London: Routledge.

—— (2008a). 'Level Playing Fields: The Post-colonial State, Democracy, Courts and Citizenship in India', *German Law Journal*, 9 (3), March 1, pp. 343–66.

—— (2008b). 'Politics in India', in: Gabriel A. Almond *et al.* (eds), *Comparative Politics Today: A World View*. New York: Longman (8th edn).

—— (2009). 'Nuclear, Engaged and Non-aligned: Contradiction and Coherence in India's Foreign Policy', *Indian Quarterly* LXV (I), January–March, pp. 15–35.

—— (2010). 'Citizenship in India: Some preliminary results of a national survey', *Economic and Political Weekly of India*, 45 (9), pp. 46–54.

Mitra, Subrata K. and Alison Lewis (eds) (1996). *Subnational Movements in South Asia*. Boulder, CO: Westview.

Mitra, Subrata K. and Jivanta Schoettli (2007). 'The New Dynamics of Indian Foreign Policy and its Ambiguities', *Irish Studies in International Affairs* (18), pp. 19–34.

Mitra, Subrata K. and V.B. Singh (1999). *Democracy and Social Change in India: A Cross-sectional Analysis of the National Electorate*. New Delhi: Sage Publications.

—— (2009). *When Rebels become Stakeholders: Democracy, Agency and Social Change in India.* New Delhi and Thousand Oaks, CA: Sage Publications.

Mitra, Subrata K., Mike Enskat and Clemens Spiess (eds) (2004). *Political Parties in South Asia.* Westport, CT: Praeger.

Mitra, Subrata K., Siegfried O. Wolf and Jivanta Schoettli (2006). *A Political and Economic Dictionary of South Asia.* London: Routledge.

Moon, Penderel (1947). *Warren Hastings and British India.* New York: Macmillan, Collier (repr. 1962).

Moore, Barrington (1966). *Social Origins of Dictatorship and Democracy: Lord and Peasant in the Making of the Modern World.* Boston: Beacon.

Moore, Mick (1990). 'Economic Liberalization versus Political Pluralism in Sri Lanka', *Modern Asian Studies*, 24 (2), pp. 593–642.

—— (1993). 'Thoroughly Modern Revolutionaries: The JVP in Sri Lanka', *Modern Asian Studies*, 27 (3), July, pp. 593–642.

Moore, Wilbert (1968). 'Social Change', *International Encyclopedia of the Social Sciences*, 14, p. 366.

Morris-Jones, W.H. (1966). 'Dominance and Dissent', *Government and Opposition*, 1 (4), August, p. 455.

—— (1967). 'The Indian Congress Party: A Dilemma of Dominance', *Modern Asian Studies*, 1 (2), pp. 109–32.

—— (1977). 'Creeping but Uneasy Authoritarianism in India', *Government and Opposition*, 12 (1), pp. 39–47.

—— (1987). *The Government and Politics of India.* London: Hutchinson University Library (revised edition of original publication in 1967, Eothen Publishing).

Mouffe, Chantal (1993). *The Return of the Political.* London: Verso.

Mukherjee, Radhakamal (1937). 'Caste and Social Change in India', *The American Journal of Sociology*, 43 (3), November, pp. 377–90.

Mukherji, Rahul (2004). 'Managing Competition: Politics and the Building of Independent Regulatory Institutions', *India Review*, 3 (4), October, pp. 278–305.

Myrdal, Gunnar (1968). *Asian Drama: An Inquiry into the Poverty of Nations.* New York: Pantheon.

Naipaul, V.S. (1990). *India: A Million Mutinies Now.* London: Heinemann.

Nandy, Ashis (1970). 'The Culture of Indian Politics: A Stock Taking', *The Journal of Asian Studies*, 30 (1), pp. 57–79.

—— (1980). *At the Edge of Psychology: Essays in Politics and Culture.* New Delhi: Oxford University Press.

—— (1983). *The Intimate Enemy: Loss and Recovery of Self under Colonialism.* New Delhi: Oxford University Press.

Nasr, S.V.R. (1995). 'Democracy and Islamic Revivalism', *Political Science Quarterly*, 110 (2), Summer, pp. 261–85.

Nasr, Vali R. (2000). 'International Politics, Domestic Imperatives, and Identity Mobilization: Sectarianism in Pakistan', *Comparative Politics*, 32 (2), January, pp. 171–90.

National Crime Records Bureau, Ministry of Home Affairs (2004). *Crime in India, 2002.* New Delhi: Government of India Press.

Nayar, Baldev Raj (2007). *Globalization and Politics in India.* New Delhi: Oxford University Press.

Nehru, Jawaharlal (1985). *Letters to Chief Ministers, 1947–1964.* New Delhi: Oxford University Press.

—— (1989). *Letters to Chief Ministers* (5 volumes). New Delhi: Jawaharlal Nehru Memorial Fund.

North, Douglas C. (1991). *Institutions, Institutional Change and Economic Performance.* Cambridge: Cambridge University Press.

Nossiter, T.J. (1988). *Marxist State Governments in India.* London and New York: Barnes & Noble.

Nugent, Nicholas (1990). *Rajiv Gandhi: Son of a Dynasty.* London: BBC Books.

Oldenburg, P. (1985). '"A Place Insufficiently Imagined": Language, Belief and the Pakistan Crisis of 1971', *The Journal of Asian Studies*, 44 (4), August, pp. 711–33.

Omvedt, Gail (1993). *Reinventing Revolution: New Social Movements and the Socialist Tradition in India*. London: East Gate.

Panagariya, Arvind (2008). *India: The Emerging Giant*. New York: Oxford University Press.

Pandian, M.S.S. (1987). *Caste, Nationality and Ethnicity: An Interpretation of Tamil Culture, History and Social Order*. Mumbai: Popular Prakashan.

Pant, A.D. and S.K. Gupta (1990). *Bureaucracy, Development, and Change: Contemporary Perspectives*. New Delhi: Segment Books Distributors.

Pape, Robert (2003). 'The Strategic Logic of Siucide Terrorism', *American Political Science Review*, 97 (3).

Parekh, Bhikhu (1989). *Colonialism, Tradition and Reform: An Analysis of Gandhi's Political Discourse*. New Delhi: Sage.

Park, Richard L. and Bruce Bueno de Mesquita (1979). *India's Political System*. Englewood Cliffs, NJ: Prentice-Hall.

Perkovich, George (1993). 'A Nuclear Third Way in South Asia', *Foreign Policy*, 91, Summer, pp. 85–104.

—— (1999). *India's Nuclear Bomb: The Impact on Global Proliferation*. Berkeley: University of California Press.

Potter, David (1986). *India's Political Administrators. 1978–83*. Oxford: Oxford University Press.

Prasad, C. Ram (1993). 'Hindutva Ideology: Extracting the Fundamentals', *Contemporary South Asia*, 2 (3), pp. 285–309.

Pressler, Franklin (1987). *Religion under Bureaucracy: Policy and Administration of Hindu Temples in South India*. Cambridge: Cambridge University Press.

Przeworski, Adam and Henry Teune (1970). *The Logic of Comparative Social Inquiry*. New York: Wiley & Sons.

Pushpendra and B.K. Sinha (2000). *Land Reforms in India: An Unfinished Agenda* (Vol. 5). New Delhi: Sage.

Putnam, Robert D., Robert Leonardi and Raffaella Y. Nanetti (1993). *Making Democracy Work: Civic Traditions in Modern Italy*. Princeton, NJ: Princeton University Press.

Quarantelli, E.L. and R.R. Dynes (1977). 'Responses to Social Crisis and Disaster', *Annual Review of Sociology*, 3, pp. 23–49.

Quigley, Declan (1993). *The Interpretation of Caste*. Oxford: Clarendon Press.

Rajgolpal, P.R. (1987). *Communal Violence in India*. New Delhi: Uppal Publishing House.

Rao, M. Govinda and Nirvikar Singh (2004). Asymmetric federalism in India. Paper 567, Department of Economics, University of California, Santa Cruz. Available online at http://escholarship.org/uc/item/0v59942g#page-3.

—— (2005). *The Political Economy of Federalism in India*. New Delhi: Oxford University Press.

Ram, Neevalar Vasudevarao Raghu (1978). *Games Bureaucrats Play*. New Delhi: Vikas.

Ratanlal and Dhirajlal (1992). *The Indian Penal Code* (27th edn). Nagpur: Wadhwa and Company.

Reddy, G. Ram and G. Haragopal (1985). 'The Pyraveekar: "The Fixer" in Rural India', *Asian Survey*, 25 (11), pp. 1148–62.

Remmer, K.L. (1997). 'Theoretical Decay and Theoretical Development: The Resurgence of Institutional Analysis', *World Politics*, 50, pp. 34–61.

Reserve Bank of India (2006). *Handbook of Statistics on Indian Economy*. New Delhi.

Rhodes, Rod A.W. (2001). *Understanding Governance: Policy Networks, Governance, Reflexivity and Accountability*. Buckingham: Open University Press.

Riker, William and Peter Ordeshook (1973). *An Intraduction to Positive Political Theory*. Englewood Cliffs, NJ: Prentice Hall.

Roberts, Michael (1978). 'Ethnic Conflict in Sri Lanka and Sinhalese Perspectives: Barriers to Accommodation', *Modern Asian Studies*, 12 (3), pp. 353–76.

Roberts, W.H. (1923). 'A Review of the Gandhi Movement in India', *Political Science Quarterly*, 38 (2), June, pp. 227–48.

Rose, Leo (1963). 'The Himalayan Border States: "Buffers" in Transition', *Asian Survey*, 3 (2), pp. 116–22.

Rosen, George (1966). *Democracy and Economic Change in India*. Mumbai: Vora.

Rosenthal, Jean-Laurent (1992). *The Fruits of Revolution*. Cambridge: Cambridge University Press.

Rothermund, Dietmar (1988, repr. in 1993). *An Economic History of India: From Pre-colonial Times to 1991*. London: Routledge.

Roy-Chaudhury, Rahul (1998). 'India', in: Sam Bateman and Stephen Bates (eds), *Regional Maritime Management and Security (Canberra Papers on Strategic Defence No. 124)* (pp. 19–27). Canberra: Australian National University/Strategic and Defence Studies Centre.

Rudolph, Lloyd I. (1965). 'The Modernity of Tradition: The Democratic Incarnation of Caste in India', *The American Political Science Review*, 59 (4), December, pp. 975–89.

Rudolph, Lloyd I. and Susanne Hoeber Rudolph (1967). *The Modernity of Tradition: Political Development in India*. Chicago: The University of Chicago Press.

—— (1982). 'Cultural Policy, the Text Book Controversy and Indian Identity', in: A.J. Wilson and D. Dalton (eds), *The States of South Asia: Problem of a National Integration* (pp. 131–54). London: Hurst.

—— (1987). *In Pursuit of Lakshmi: The Political Economy of the Indian State*. Chicago: The University of Chicago Press.

Rudolph, Susanne Hoeber (1961). 'Consensus and Conflict in Indian Politics', *World Politics*, 13 (3), April, pp. 385–99.

—— (1987). 'Presidential Address: State Formation in Asia – Prolegomenon to a Comparative Study', *The Journal of Asian Studies*, 46 (4), November, pp. 731–46.

—— (2005). 'The Imperialism of Categories: Situating Knowledge in a Globalizing World', *Perspectives*, 3 (1), March, pp. 5–14.

Rupesinghe, Kumar (1988). 'Ethnic Conflicts in South Asia: The Case of Sri Lanka and the Indian Peace Keeping Force (IPKF)', *Journal of Peace Research*, 25 (4), December, pp. 337–50.

Rushdie, Salman and Elizabeth West (eds) (1997). *The Vintage Book of Indian Writing, 1947–1997*. London: Vintage.

Ruud, Arild Engelsen (2003). *Poetics of Village Politics: The Making of West Bengal's Rural Communism*. New Delhi: Oxford University Press.

Saberwal, Satish (1986). *India: The Roots of Crisis*. New Delhi: Oxford University Press.

Sabine, George Holland (1966). *A History of Political Theory*. London: Harrap.

Saez, Lawrence (1999). 'India's Economic Liberalization, Interjurisdictional Competition and Development', *Contemporary South Asia*, 8 (3), pp. 323–45.

—— (2002). *Federalism Without a Center: The Impact of Political and Economic Reform on India's Federal System*. New Delhi: Sage.

Sagan, Scott D. (2001). 'The Perils of Proliferation in South Asia', *Asian Survey*, 41 (6), November–December, pp. 1064–86.

Said, Edward (1978). *Orientalism*. New York: Vintage Books.

—— (1993). *Culture and Imperialism*. London: Vintage.

Samarasinghe, S.W.R. de A. (1990). 'The Bhutanese Economy in Transition', *Asian Survey*, 30 (6), June, pp. 560–75.

Sanghavi, Nagindas (1996). *Gujarat: A Political History*. Surat: Centre for Social Studies.

Sankaran, S.R. (2002). *Committee of Concerned Citizens, Third Report, 1997–2002*. Hyderabad: Committee of Concerned Citizens.

Sarkar, Sumit (1984). *Modern India: 1885–1947*. Madras: Macmillan.

Sartre, Jean-Paul (1963). *Search for a Method* (Translated from the French and with an Introduction by Hazel E. Barnes). New York: Vintage Books.

Schama, Simon (1989). *Citizens: A Chronicle of the French Revolution*. Harmondsworth: Penguin.

Schulman, David Dean (1985). *The King and the Clown in South Indian Myth and Poetry*. Princeton, NJ: Princeton University Press.

Scott, James C. (1976). *The Moral Economy of the Peasant: Rebellion and Subsistence in South East Asia.* New Haven, CT: Yale University Press.

Seabright, Paul (2004). *The Company of Strangers: A Natural History of Economic Life.* Princeton, NJ: Princeton University Press.

Segal, Ronald (1965). *The Anguish of India.* New York: The New American Library.

Sen, Kunal (2009). 'What a Long, Strange Trip It's Been: Reflections on India's Economic Growth in the Twentieth Century', *Heidelberg Papers in South Asian and Comparative Politics* (47), April.

Sen Gupta, Bhabani (1996). *India: Problems of Governance.* New Delhi: Konark.

Seth, Vikram (1994). *A Suitable Boy.* London: Phoenix.

Shah, Ghanshyam (1977). *Protest Movements in Two Indian States: A Study of the Gujarat and Bihar Movements.* New Delhi: Ajanta.

Shankardass, Rani Dhavan (1988). *Vallabhbhai Patel: Power and Organization in Indian Politics.* London: Sangam Books.

Sharma, Jyotirmaya (2003). *Hindutva: Exploring the Idea of Hindu Nationalism.* New Delhi: Penguin.

Shastri, Amita (1997). 'Constitution-making as a Political Resource: Crisis of Legitimacy in Sri Lanka', in: Subrata Mitra and Dietmar Rothermund (eds), *Legitimacy and Conflict in South Asia.* New Delhi: Manohar.

—— (2005). 'Channelling Ethnicity through Electoral Reforms in Sri Lanka', *Commonwealth & Comparative Politics*, 43 (1), pp. 34–60.

Shiva, Vandana (1991). *The Violence of the Green Revolution.* London: Zed Books.

Singh, Anita Inder (1987). *The Origin of Partition in India: 1936–1947.* New Delhi: Oxford University Press.

Singh, Gurharpal (1993). 'Ethnic Conflict in India: A Case-study of Punjab', in: John McGarry and Brendan O'Leary (eds), *The Politics f Ethnic Conflict Regulation* (pp. 84–105). London: Routledge.

Singh, Jaswant (1999). *Defending India.* Basingstoke: Macmillan.

Singh, N. (1996). *The Plain Truth: Memoirs of a CBI Officer.* New Delhi: Konark.

Sinha, Aseema (2000). 'Divided Leviathan: Comparing Subnational Developmental States in India'. Cornell University: Unpublished Doctoral Dissertation.

—— (2003). 'Rethinking the Developmental State Model: Divided Leviathan and Subnational Comparison in India', *Comparative Politics*, 35 (4), pp. 459–76.

Sirsikar, V.M. (1995). *Politics of Modern Maharashtra.* London: Sangam Books.

Skocpol, Theda and Charles Tilly (1985). 'War Making and State Making as Organized Crime', in: Peter B. Evans, Dietrich Rueschenmeyer and Theda Skocpol (eds), *Bringing the State Back In.* Cambridge: Cambridge University Press.

Smart, John J.C. and Bernard Williams (1973). *Utilitarianism: For and Against.* Cambridge: Cambridge University Press.

Smith, Donald Eugene (1963). *India as a Secular State.* Princeton, NJ: Princeton University Press.

Sobhan, Rehman (1962). 'The Problem of Regional Imbalance in the Economic Development of Pakistan', *Asian Survey*, 2 (5), July, pp. 31–7.

Sontheimer, Guenther-Dietz and Hermann Kulke (eds) (1989). *Hinduism Reconsidered.* New Delhi: Manohar.

Spear, Percival (1958). 'From Colonial to Sovereign Status: Some Problems of Transition with Special Reference to India', *The Journal of Asian Studies*, 17 (4), August, pp. 567–77.

Spencer, Jonathan (1990). 'Collective Violence and Everyday Practice in Sri Lanka', *Modern Asian Studies*, 24 (3), July, pp. 603–23.

Sridharan, E. (2005). 'Coalition Strategies and the BJP's Expansion, 1989–2004', *Commonwealth & Comparative Politics*, 43 (2), July, pp. 194–221.

Srinivas, M.N. (1957). 'Caste in Modern India', *The Journal of Asian Studies*, 16 (4), August, pp. 529–48.

Srinivas, M.N., A.M. Shah and E.A. Ramaswamy (1979). *The Fieldworker and the Field: Problems and Challenges in Sociological Investigation.* New Delhi: Oxford University Press.

Srivastava, Chandrika Prasad (1995). *Lal Bahadur Shastri: Prime Minister of India, 9 June 1964–11 January 1966: A Life of Truth in Politics.* New Delhi: Oxford University Press.

Stavrakakis, Yannis (1999). *Lacan and the Political.* London: Routledge.

Stein, Burton (1982). 'South India. Some General Considerations of the Region and its Early History', in: T. Raychaudhuri and D. Kumar (eds), *The Cambridge Economic History of India* (Vol. 1). Cambridge: Cambridge University Press.

Stokes, Eric (1959). *The English Utilitarians and India.* Oxford: The Clarendon Press.

Swain, Ashok (1996). 'Displacing the Conflict: Environmental Destruction in Bangladesh and Ethnic Conflict in India', *Journal of Peace Research*, 33 (2), May, pp. 189–204.

Swamy, Arun (1996). 'Sense, Sentiment and Populist Coalitions: The Strange Career of Cultural Nationalism in Tamil Nadu', in: Subrata K. Mitra and R. Alison Lewis (eds), *Subnational Movements in South Asia.* Boulder, CO: Westview Press.

Swtompka, Piotr (1999). *Trust: A Sociological Theory.* Cambridge: Cambridge University Press.

Symonds, Richard (1950). 'State-Making in Pakistan', *Far Eastern Survey*, 19 (5), 8 March, pp. 45–50.

Tambiah, Stanley J. (1990). 'Presidential Address: Reflections on Communal Violence in South Asia', *The Journal of Asian Studies*, 49 (4), November, pp. 741–60.

Tarrow, Sidney (1998). *Power in Movement: Social Movements and Contentious Politics.* Cambridge: Cambridge University Press.

Tata Services Limited, Department of Economics and Statistics (2006). *Statistical Outline of India 2005–06.* Mumbai: Tata Services Limited.

Tellis, Ashley (2001). *India's Emerging Nuclear Posture: Between Recessed Deterrent and Ready Arsenal.* Santa Monica, CA: Rand.

Thakur, Ramesh C. (1995). *The Government and Politics of India.* Basingstoke: Macmillan.

Tharoor, Shashi (1997). *India: From Midnight to the Millennium.* New Delhi: Penguin Books.

The International Institute for Strategic Studies. (2004). *Military Balance 2004–2005.* London: Routledge.

Thompson, E.P. (1963). *The Making of the English Working Class.* London: Victor Gollancz.

—— (1971). 'The Moral Economy of the English Crowd in the Eighteenth Century', *Past and Present*, 50, February, pp. 76–136.

Tilly, Charles (ed.) (1975). *The Formation of Nation States in Western Europe.* Princeton, NJ: Princeton University Press.

—— (1985). 'War Making and State Making as Organized Crime', in: Peter Evans, Dietrich Rueschemeyer and Theda Skocpol (eds), *Bringing the State Back In*, pp. 169–91. Cambridge: Cambridge University Press.

Trivedi, Lisa N. (2003). 'Visually Mapping the "Nation": Swadeshi Politics in Nationalist India, 1920–30', *The Journal of Asian Studies*, 62 (1), February, pp. 11–41.

Upendra, Baxi (1980). *The Supreme Court and Politics.* Lucknow: Eastern Book.

Van der Veer, Peter (1987). '"God must be Liberated!" A Hindu Liberation Movement in Ayodhya', *Modern Asian Studies*, 21 (2), pp. 283–301.

Vanaik, Achin (1990). *The Painful Transition: Bourgeois Democracy in India.* London: Verso Books.

Vanderbok, William G. (1990). 'The Tiger Triumphant: The Mobilization and Alignment of the Indian Electorate', *British Journal of Political Science*, 20 (2), April, pp. 237–61.

Varma, Pawan K. (2004). *Being Indian: The Truth about Why the Twenty-First Century Will be India's.* New Delhi: Penguin Books.

Varshney, Ashutosh (2000). 'Is India Becoming More Democratic?', *The Journal of Asian Studies*, 59 (1), pp. 3–25.

—— (2002). *Ethnic Conflict and Civic Life: Hindus and Muslims in India.* New Haven, CT: Yale University Press.

Verma, Shivendra Kishore and S.K. Kusum (eds) (2000). *Fifty Years of the Supreme Court of India: Its Grasp and Reach.* Delhi: Oxford University Press.

Wall, John (1978). 'Foodgrain Management: Pricing, Procurement, Distribution, Import and Storage Policy in India', *Occasional Papers*, World Bank Staff Working paper No. 279. Washington, DC: World Bank, pp. 88–9.

Wallace, Paul (1986). 'The Sikhs as a "Minority" in a Sikh Majority State in India', *Asian Survey*, 26 (3), March, pp. 363–77.

Wariavwala, Bharat (1992). 'Security Issues in Domestic Politics', in: Subrata K. Mitra and James Chiriyankandath (eds), *A Changing Landscape: Electoral Politics in India.* New Delhi: Segment.

Washbrook, David A. (1989). 'Caste, Class and Dominance in Modern Tamil Nadu: Non-Brahmanism, Dravidianism and Tamil Nationalism', in: Francine Frankel and M.S.A. Rao (eds), *Dominance and State Power in Modern India: Decline of a Social Order* (Vol. I). New Delhi: Oxford University Press.

—— (1990). 'South Asia, the World System, and World Capitalism', *The Journal of Asian Studies*, 49 (3), August, pp. 479–508.

Watts, Ronald L. (1998). 'Federalism, Federal Political Systems and Federations', *Annual Review of Political Science,*1, pp. 117–37.

—— (1999). *Comparing Federal Systems.* Montreal and Kingston: Mc Gill-Queen's University Press.

Weiner, Myron (1964). 'Traditional Role Performance and the Development of Modern Political Parties: The Indian Case', *The Journal of Politics*, 26 (4), November, pp. 830–49.

—— (1968). *Party Building in a New Nation: The Indian National Congress.* Chicago: Chicago University Press.

—— (ed.) (1968a). *State Politics in India.* Princeton, NJ: Princeton University Press.

Wendt, Alexander (1999). *Social Theory of International Politics.* Cambridge: Cambridge University Press.

Wheare, Kenneth C. (1964). *Federal Government* (4th edn). New York: Oxford University Press.

Widlung, Ingrid (2000). *Paths to Power and Patterns of Influence: The Dravidian Parties in South Asia.* Uppsala: Uppsala University Press.

Wilkinson, Steven Ian (2000). 'India, Consociational Theory, and Ethnic Violence', *Asian Survey*, 40 (5), pp. 776–91.

—— (2004). *Votes and Violence: Electoral Competition and Ethnic Riots in India.* Cambridge: Cambridge University Press.

Windrem, Robert and Tammy Kupperman (2001). 'Pakistan Nukes Outstrip India's, Officials Say', *MSNBC International News*, 6 June, 2000. Available at http://www.msnbc.com/news/417106.asp.

Wirsing, Robert G. (2003). *Kashmir in the Shadow of War: Regional Rivalries in a Nuclear Age.* Armonk, NY: Sharpe.

Wood, John R. (1984). *State Politics in Contemporary India: Crisis or Continuity?* Boulder, CO: Westview.

Woodruff, Philip (1953/1954). *The Men Who Ruled India* (Vols I and II). New York: Schocken Books.

World Bank (1993). *The East Asian Miracle.* New York: Oxford University Press.

Zagoria, Donald S. (1971). 'The Ecology of Peasant Communism in India', *The American Science Review*, 65 (1), March, pp. 144–60.

Zamindar, Vazira Fazila-Yacoobali (2007). *The Long Partition and the Making of Modern South Asia: Refugees, Boundaries, Histories.* New York: Columbia University Press.

Ziring, Lawrence (1988). 'Public Policy Dilemmas and Pakistan's Nationality Problem: The Legacy of Zia ul-Haq', *Asian Survey*, 28 (8), August, pp. 795–812.

Zizek, Slavoj (1989). *The Sublime Object of Ideology.* London: Verso.

Index

Page numbers in **bold** refer to figures and diagrams, page numbers in *italic* refer to tables, page numbers in ***bold italic*** refer to boxes.